Polity and Society in Contemporary North Africa

STATE, CULTURE, AND SOCIETY IN ARAB NORTH AFRICA

Series Editors

John P. Entelis, Professor of Political Science and Co-Director, Middle East Studies Program, Fordham University

Michael Suleiman, Professor of Political Science, Kansas State University

Advisory Board

Dale Eickelman, Professor of Anthropology, Dartmouth College
Elbaki Hermassi, Professor of Sociology, University of Tunis
Jean Leca, Professor of Political Science, Institut d'Etudes Politiques, Paris
Afaf Lutfi Al-Sayyid Marsot, Professor of History, University of California–Los Angeles
Elias Tuma, Professor of Economics, University of California–Davis
John Waterbury, William Stewart Tod Professor of Politics and International Affairs, Princeton University
El Sayed Yassin, Director, Center for Political and Strategic Studies, *Al-Ahram,* Cairo

The states and societies of Arab North Africa have long been neglected in the scholarly literature dealing with the Arab world, the Middle East, and Islam, except in the context of dramatic international events. Yet this region has a rich historical and cultural tradition that offers important insights into the evolution of society, the complexity of cultural life, forms of social interaction, strategies of economic development, and patterns of state formation throughout the developing world. In addition, as the region has assumed more importance in geopolitical terms, both the United States and Europe have become more directly involved in its economics and politics. Few books of a scholarly or policy nature, however, analyze and interpret recent trends and changes in the constellation of relations between regional and global powers. This new series—the first in English to focus exclusively on Arab North Africa—addresses important conceptual and policy issues from an interdisciplinary perspective, giving special emphasis to questions of political culture and political economy.

Books in This Series

Development and Disenchantment in Rural Tunisia: The Bourguiba Years, Mira Zussman

State and Society in Algeria, edited by John P. Entelis and Phillip C. Naylor

Port Sudan, Kenneth J. Perkins

Polity and Society in Contemporary North Africa, edited by I. William Zartman and William Mark Habeeb

Polity and Society in Contemporary North Africa

edited by
*I. William Zartman
and William Mark Habeeb*

Westview Press
Boulder • San Francisco • Oxford

To Leon Carl Brown

*for opening the surest path
to North African studies*

State, Culture, and Society in Arab North Africa

All rights reserved. No part of this publication may be reproduced or transmitted in any form or by any means, electronic or mechanical, including photocopy, recording, or any information storage and retrieval system, without permission in writing from the publisher.

Copyright © 1993 by Westview Press, Inc.

Published in 1993 in the United States of America by Westview Press, Inc., 5500 Central Avenue, Boulder, Colorado 80301-2877, and in the United Kingdom by Westview Press, 36 Lonsdale Road, Summertown, Oxford OX2 7EW

Library of Congress Cataloging-in-Publication Data
Polity and society in contemporary North Africa / edited by I. William Zartman and William Mark Habeeb.
    p. cm. — (State, culture, and society in Arab North Africa)
Includes bibliographical references and index.
ISBN 0-8133-7669-6
  1. Africa, North. I. Zartman, I. William. II. Habeeb, William Mark, 1955– . III. Series.
DT204.P65 1993
961—dc20
                                                           92-31912
                                                                 CIP

Printed and bound in the United States of America

∞ The paper used in this publication meets the requirements of the American National Standard for Permanence of Paper for Printed Library Materials Z39.48-1984.

10   9   8   7   6   5   4   3   2   1

Contents

Preface ... ix

PART ONE: History and Politics

1. The Historical Context, *Michel Le Gall* ... 3

2. The Second Stage of State Building, *Elbaki Hermassi and Dirk Vandewalle* ... 19

3. Political Parties, *Clement Henry Moore* ... 42

PART TWO: Society and Economics

4. Alienation of Urban Youth, *Mark Tessler* ... 71

5. Islam and the State, *Mohammed Tozy* ... 102

6. Demographic Pressures and Agrarian Dynamics, *Hamid Ait Amara* ... 123

7. Economic Crisis and Policy Reform in the 1980s, *Rhys Payne* ... 139

8. Local Societies, *Nicholas S. Hopkins* ... 168

PART THREE: Foreign Relations

9. The Arab Maghribi Union and the Prospects for North African Unity, *Mary-Jane Deeb* ... 189

10	The Maghribi States and the European Community, *William Mark Habeeb*	204
11	The United States and North Africa, *John Damis*	221
12	15/21: The Maghrib into the Future, *I. William Zartman*	241

Appendix A: Political Parties in North Africa	251
Appendix B: Economic and Demographic Tables	255
References	261
About the Book	277
About the Editors and Contributors	279
Index	281

Preface

In 1966 L. Carl Brown edited one of the first comprehensive volumes in English on the newly independent nations of North Africa. *State and Society in Independent North Africa*, the product of a conference sponsored by the Middle East Institute, initiated a new generation of scholars and policy analysts to a region of the world that despite its long-standing ties with the United States had lived in the shadow of colonial powers throughout most of the twentieth century. Organized on the tenth anniversaries of two Maghribi states (Morocco and Tunisia; Libya gained independence in 1951 and Algeria not until 1962), Brown's book addressed the political, economic, and social questions about a region that had been largely outside the scope of U.S. scholarly concern. It served as both the catalyst and the cornerstone of much subsequent scholarship on North Africa and has remained one of the best introductions to the issues confronting the Maghrib at the hour of independence.

The inspiration for this current volume arose at the twenty-fifth anniversary of the publication of *State and Society in Independent North Africa* and after over three decades of North African independence. The idea was to revisit many of the same issues that were addressed in the original volume in the light of a quarter century of North African political independence, not to mention profound economic and social change. It is hoped that this volume, like Brown's, will spark a new interest in the Maghribi states and propel scholars to focus on the region's future.

The attractiveness of North Africa is that it is a truly developing region, not an underdeveloping region like much of the Third World. Twenty-five years have brought about remarkable progress, the implications of which we asked the contributors to investigate in this volume. Because much of what has transpired in the Maghrib since independence has deep roots, Michel Le Gall begins the book by providing a historical overview as a referent for the ensuing chapters. Chapter 1 introduces such themes as the growth of separate national societies in North Africa; the consolidation of their monarchial states; the articulation of state-society relations, particularly through the nationalist movements of the twentieth century; and the increasing influence of the outside world. These themes form the framework for the rest of the book, divided into sections on history and politics, society and economics, and foreign relations.

The state-building leaders who won independence for North Africa have all now left the scene, and in Chapter 2 Elbaki Hermassi and Dirk Vandewalle discuss the "second stage" of state building in North Africa. The political structures and dynamics of the Maghrib have been transformed. In Morocco the political rhythm is characterized by a changing mixture of cooperation and confrontation between the monarchy and the other political forces. In Algeria and Tunisia, the 1980s witnessed movement toward multiparty democracy and greater political openness, with some backtracking in the early 1990s. In Libya the issue of succession is key to all other political changes. Clement Henry Moore, in Chapter 3, surveys the development of political parties in the Maghrib. In recent years, however, the confrontation between secularism and Islamism has dominated the political process in Algeria and Tunisia and to a certain extent has put on hold these states' political evolutions; many of the same characteristics, with currently different results, appear in Morocco and Libya. In Chapter 5 Mohammed Tozy addresses the tension between political Islam and the secular state.

The successors to the independence-era leaders also face the challenges of economic systems in need of revitalization and social unrest caused by rapidly rising populations, especially youth and the marginalized sectors of society. In Chapter 7 Rhys Payne describes both the internal and external motivations for economic policy reform and the strategies the Maghribi states have pursued to reform their economies. Mark Tessler (Chapter 4) looks at the problems of urban youth and the ways in which they have vented their frustration at unfulfilled aspirations. Hamid Ait Amara (Chapter 6) and Nicholas S. Hopkins (Chapter 8) focus on land tenure and social structure, respectively, in rural North Africa, as it too has undergone demographic, political, and social changes.

Foreign relations of the Maghribi states over the past twenty-five years have concentrated largely on the regional (Maghribi), Mediterranean (European), and Atlantic (U.S.) arenas. The siren call of Maghribi unity, which predates independence, has helped to mitigate, but not resolve, conflict among the North African states and with the neighboring Mashriq. In Chapter 9 Mary-Jane Deeb surveys the history of the unity movement and analyzes its future prospects. The most recent institutional effort at regional integration—the Arab Maghribi Union—sees the European Community as both a model and a challenge. William Mark Habeeb (Chapter 10) investigates how the Maghribi states might best cope in their relations with the giant across the Mediterranean. Across the Atlantic, the United States once saw the Maghrib as a region of cold war importance and commercial attractiveness, but only the latter interest remains, as discussed by John Damis in Chapter 11.

I. William Zartman sums up the volume by projecting these themes into the next century. He examines the implications of a doubling of population, the effects of democratization on the consolidating state, the tensions between Islamicist popular movements and modernizing elites, and the impetus toward self-reliance in a region forced into cooperation and conflict with Europe. These are the questions and issues on which the next volume, twenty-five years from now, will focus.

* * *

The editors wish to thank first of all the contributors, who patiently waited for the volume to come together and willingly made revisions and updates throughout the process. Barbara Ellington and Martha Robbins of Westview Press also deserve applause for their ever greater patience, encouragement, and fine editorial suggestions. Houria Bouatba, Sharon Dulaney, and Lynn Wagner assisted with tables, the bibliography, and the index. Theresa Taylor Simmons kept track of the manuscript through its extraordinary evolution. Wendy Mills offered support and encouragement.

I. William Zartman
William Mark Habeeb

PART ONE

History and Politics

1

The Historical Context

Michel Le Gall

As a region bordering on the Mediterranean, North Africa has been shaped in some measure by the geography, climate, and cultural values of that great inland sea. Yet despite some common denominators that North Africa shares with its neighbors on the shoreline—those elements that contribute to the category of historical factors Fernand Braudel labeled *"la longue durée"*—its history is a unique mix of political and cultural forces (see Hess 1978). Some are indigenous. Others originate from the three surrounding directions: from the east, Islam; from the north, first Christian then colonial Europe; and to a lesser extent from the south, mercantile West Africa.

For much of its early Islamic history, the Maghrib ("the place of the sunset"), as it became known to its inhabitants, was a frontier. By the sixteenth century, as a result of internal economic, social, and political dynamics coupled with Europe's drive to explore Asia, Africa, and the Americas, North Africa's isolation ceded to greater integration into both the Islamic world of the Ottoman Empire and the turbulent politics of Western Europe. In that same century, the seeds of the current political organization of North Africa took root, and it is there that we can uncover the political origins of those regions that were to become the modern states of Morocco, Algeria, Tunisia, and Libya.

By and large, the notion of broad political participation has been foreign to the Maghrib. Instead, a history of renewed political mobilization has unfolded; in most cases, the mobilization and co-optation of small groups of military or religious elites who gave legitimacy and power to the regime and the state it created. In those few cases where the political mobilization drew in a wider segment of society, the process never gave way to one of wide-scale participation. It is only in the twentieth century that, as a result of popular mobilization on behalf of independence, there has been growing pressure for broad political participation at all levels of society. Yet the political agendas of the current regimes in the Maghrib are so diverse that the very notion and mechanics of participation are highly problematic.

The Influence of the East

The first four centuries of Islamic rule, from the first conquests in the late seventh century until the mid-eleventh century, witnessed the reproduction in the Maghrib of the political and religious controversies that gripped the eastern Islamic world (Mashriq). At the heart of the dispute was the very nature of the political order of the Islamic *umma* (community), and with that the fundamental question of political legitimacy: Who was a fit successor (*khalifa*, or caliph) to the prophet Mohammed? In the east, the problem manifested itself in many forms, including disputes between the more radical, purist dissidents named Kharijites and those elements loyal to the existing order first embodied by the Umayyad dynasty based in Damascus (661–750), and then by the Abbasids in Baghdad (750–1258).

In the Maghrib, these debates were carried on by the small minority of Arab tribespeople who had participated in the conquests. The indigenous popuation, a complex conglomerate of ethnic groups, including Romanized urbanites and Berber tribespeople, and a reflection of a host of cultural and religious influences, the latest of which was Christianity, was in the first century or so largely proscribed from the political process. Kharijite elements did seek to forge a small following for themselves among some Berber tribespeople who resisted the idea of an exclusive imperial state, but their dynasties were short-lived and geographically restricted and isolated. The creation of these independent dynasties reflected not only the political fragmentation of the Maghribi frontier but also two other important realities: first, that the line of the Islamic conquests was neither straight nor unbroken and hence was inconsistent and incomplete; second, that the piecemeal nature of the conquests meant that the process of conversion, Arabization, and Islamization was, as in the east, slow, incomplete, and frequently divisive.

The Aghlabid dynasty (800–909) is regarded by many historians of North Africa as a turning point in the course of the Islamic conquests. Its existence was at once testimony that the Arab military elite was well entrenched in North Africa; yet the very independence of the dynasty, despite its oath of fealty to the Abbasid caliph, belied the immutability of the ties between the Arab conquerors and their kin in the east. Finally, its restricted sovereignty (in Tunisia and eastern Algeria) marked the western limit of the advance of the Abbasid-sponsored Hanafi school of Sunni Islam in the Maghrib. At odds with the state-sponsored, rational Hanafi Sunnism was Maliki Sunnism, which, with its narrower and more rigorous notions of legal authorities and sources, was to make its way among the mixed ethnic world of the urban traders and ulama (religious authorities).

The Fatimid conquest of Tunisia (909) and the subsequent elimination of the Aghlabid dynasty reaffirmed at one level that Maghribi politics was still powerfully influenced by the east. The victory of the Ismaili Shiʿite Fatimid dynasty, whose original strongholds were in remote villages of Syria and Yemen, was predicated upon co-opting a powerful Berber tribe—the Kutama—a process that earlier Kharijite dynasties had followed with only limited success. The Fatimids' innovation lay in their ability to foster a powerful tribal symbiosis between the army, caliph, and ulama that would allow them to wrest Egypt from Abbasid authority in 969. Their power waned quickly: The Fatimid state collapsed in Tunisia in 972 and was followed by two successor states, the Zirids (972–1148) in Tunisia and the Hammadids (1015–1152) in Algeria; the Fatimids remained in Egypt until 1178. But the Fatimid recipe was to be repeated soon after, with one significant variation. In addition to combining a Berber army and select loyal ulama, subsequent states would also assign authority to a Berber dynasty.

Berber Dynasties and Maliki Reformism

The first dynasty to build a state of a significant scale on this premise was that of the Almoravids (1073–1276), whose capital was in Marrakesh. Their state apparatus rested on a consensus between a righteous Berber "commander of the faithful" (the traditional caliphal title); a reformist version of Maliki Sunnism, which first developed among the religious scholars in Qayrawan; and a military and administrative elite recruited among the Sanhaja Berbers of the middle Atlas and Western Sahara. Maliki Islam at once allowed the Almoravids to portray their defense of Islam as one that combined a strict and rigorous implementation of *shariʿa* (Islamic law) at the level of state administration with a zealous propagation of the faith that rewarded its Berber military through a struggle to gain control of the lucrative trans-Saharan trade to West Africa or through the *jihad* (holy war) mounted against the Andalusian Christian states. At its height in about 1100, the Almoravid state stretched from southern Morocco east to Algiers and north into Spain to embrace Saragossa.

A number of unexpected military reversals at the hands of the Castilians and Aragonese, notably at Toledo in 1109 and Saragossa in 1118, respectively, undermined earlier triumphs in Andalusia. More importantly, Andalusian influences began to make themselves felt in the more populist and personal version of Islam that was embodied in Sufism, a mystical way (*tariq*) systematized by the great thinker al-Ghazali and imported to the Maghrib by such scholars as Abu Madyan al-Andalusi (d. 1197), who integrated personal asceticism with legal studies. In contrast to the narrow rigors of a sometimes faceless Islam interpreted for the state by the ulama, Sufism challenged the individual to encounter God on a personal level. In time Sufism, and with it a populist Islamic civic culture, spread not only within cities and towns but also into West Africa and to the remoter *ribats* (forts) manned by Muslim warriors. The function of Sufism as vehicle for popular and political discontent was to appear time and again in Maghribi history.

The Almohad movement led by the Berber religious reformer Ibn Tumart (1080–1130) challenged the Almoravid state on the very ground upon which it had been built: a reassertion of a vigorous, strict, and orthodox Islam. The Almohads (1130–1276) conquered the Almoravid capital of Marrakesh in 1147. In addition, they reasserted Islamic rule in a number of Spanish cities that had turned against the Almoravids, notably Seville and Córdoba, in 1149. At its height, the Almohad state embraced in one empire all of North Africa from Tripoli in Libya to Tinmallal in Morocco.

Despite Almohad military prowess, in the following two centuries the Andalusian states and the Italian city-states launched a counterattack, both military and economic, that led to the eventual expulsion of Islam from Spain (1492), the creation of small Christian political and trading enclaves in North Africa, and the division of the Almohad state among three competing dynasties: the Marinids (1244–1420), who ruled principally in Morocco; the Zayinids (1236–1318) in Algeria; and the Hafsids (1228–1574) in Tunisia and Tripolitania (western Libya).

The *reconquista,* as the Christian "reconquest" was called, changed not only the political but also the commercial balance in North and West Africa. Prior to the fifteenth century, various northern African dynasties had struggled with West African kingdoms—notably in Ghana and Mali—over the division of the profits of the trade. By pushing the Islamic-Christian frontier across the straits to North Africa, the Portuguese and Spanish challenged one of the economic pillars of North Africa: control of the northern termini of the trans-Saharan trade. The struggle for the numerous northern routes of the trans-Saharan trade would continue through the nineteenth century. Nevertheless, one of the immediate effects of the European naval attack on North African commerce was the development of the counter-*jihad* of piracy that drew the Ottomans into the western Mediterranean.

The Maghrib from 1500 to the Eve of Colonialism

What remained of the Almoravid and Almohad state legacy by the turn of the sixteenth century was the emergence of the Maghrib as a distinct political and cultural entity, separate from Andalusia and the Mashriq. In a more ideological vein, these two regimes had advanced the concept of a just Islamic state linked to a reformist Maliki doctrine, thereby fostering the ideal that Islam was the main force for legitimizing any supratribal authority. Furthermore, through the combination of Maliki legalism and Sufism, these political suppositions indirectly spawned the basis for popular mobilization against—

though far short of popular participation in—governments, especially those that failed to uphold the tenets of Islam.

With the demise of Islamic Spain by 1492 and the advent of Ottoman naval forces into the western Mediterranean, Islamic North Africa slowly abandoned the classical Arab models of government predicated on the person of a righteous caliph and entered a new period in which government would be increasingly influenced by Turkic, Mamluk, and Mongol political models and practices (see Fleischer 1986). These governments revolved around a small patrimonial bureaucracy supported by an army of slaves or mercenaries rather than the tribal armies common before. Similarly, the growing influence of Sufism in both rural and urban communities obliged post-Almohad states to forge new understandings between the patrimonial state, the urban political and commercial elite, and the religious community. Although only some of the rulers ceded their roles as exclusive guardians of Islam, they all recognized, albeit sometimes begrudgingly, that the Sufis and ulama would act as intermediaries between the ruler (*al-hakim*) and the ruled (*al-mahkum*).

The imposition of the Ottoman Turkic patrimonial state nevertheless mitigated the full impact of a politically active Sufism. In this model of government, both ulama and Sufi organizations in the urban areas became increasingly dependent upon the munificence of the ruler and in turn became a pillar in legitimizing the regime. In Tunisia, first under direct Ottoman rule (1574–1591) and thereafter under the Muradids (1591–1705) and Husaynids (1705–1957), the state, under the aegis of a government and army dominated by the janissaries (elite Ottoman slave troops), for a while recovered some of the civic functions and political prerogatives that had progressively been assumed by Sufi brotherhoods. In Algeria and Tripolitania a comparable phenomenon also emerged. In Algeria as of 1689, the chief of the janissaries (*agha*) assumed the title of "dey" and with the janissaries and their offspring (*kulughli*) from marriages to local Arab women formed a dominant political caste. In Tripolitania after the demise of direct Ottoman authority, the Qaramanlis (1711–1835) shaped a dynasty with similar foundations.

The reproduction in Algeria, Tunisia, and Tripolitania of a modified Ottoman-style administration, which did not always clearly distinguish between civil and military functions, prompted numerous abuses of power and influence and tended to restrict effective state power to a small dynastic circle and its military retainers. As a result, over two centuries the effective political control of the states shrank to the coastal areas, tribal and Sufi leaders in the interior reasserting their authority in all aspects of everyday life. In order to compensate for the consequent diminishing of the internal tax base, these states relied ever more heavily on piracy and trade with Europe.

The fate of Morocco was very different. In the wake of Marinid decline and the onslaught of Portuguese traders and troops who occupied Ceuta (1415) and Tangier (1471), the political order that emerged rested in good part on what one might call, in modified Weberian terms, underinstitutionalized charismatic dynasties that were based more on the Arab caliphate model than on an Ottoman patrimonial bureaucracy. These dynasties forged on the anvil of an unprecedented Sufi authority—derived from the brotherhoods' resistance to the Christian invaders—a claimed descendance from the Prophet Mohammed (the descendant was a *sharif*, pl. *shurafa'*) and a pretense to enforcing a purer form of Islam. The first to establish a viable state along these lines were the Sa‘diyans (1554–1659), a family that hailed from southern Morocco. On the level of state building, Sa‘diyan rule rested on tribal alliances that were reinforced by membership in Sufi brotherhoods. The failure of the Sa‘diyans to establish a satisfactory procedure for succession led to infighting, the alienation of prominent Sufi leaders, and the dynasty's ultimate demise in the mid-seventeenth century. The new Alawi dynasty (1664–present) preserved much of the Sa‘diyan raison d'être and *raison d'état*, but attempts were made to define a new military and political order in the reign of Mawlay Ismail (1672–1727): He decreed the construction of more outposts on the coasts and deserts and tried to raise a black slave army from the existing slave population. The absolutist tendencies of Ismail met with opposition in commercial, bureaucratic, and religious circles alike. The progressive erosion of relations between the Moroccan state and the Sufi brotherhoods resulted in the resurgent power of Sufi orders in the countryside and mountains and, in the eighteenth and early nineteenth centuries, in the proliferation of Sufi shaykhs and the political predominance of new Sufi orders such as the Sherqawiya, Tayibiya, and Darqawiya (O'Fahey 1990).

The Precolonial and Early Colonial Period, 1800–1918

By the early nineteenth century, the regimes and lands of the Maghrib had begun to distinguish themselves more and more from one another. The continuation of this trend was to result from both their precolonial reactions to European imperialism and then to their colonial experiences—French for Algeria, Tunisia, and Morocco, and Italian for Libya.

Algeria was thrust directly into the fires of colonialism virtually unaware of what awaited it, and the French colonial experience proved to be long, brutal, and thorough. Libya and Tunisia, in contrast, enjoyed an extended precolonial period during which their respective regimes introduced Ottoman-style reforms before the imposition of colonial rule. Finally, Morocco had the longest, but relatively most uneventful, precolonial stretch disturbed very little by reforms. Morocco's subsequent colonial experience, following World War I, was much milder than that of its neighbors, which may explain why much of its political tradition remained intact, albeit in a "modernized" form.

The French invasion of Algeria in 1830 swept away the Ottomanized elite and the bey, leaving in its wake a hinterland society dominated by Sufi and tribal traditions and organizations. From the interior, the Sufi shaykh ʿAbd al-Qadir al-Jilani mounted a populist *jihad* against the French *kuffar* (infidels). The sustained struggle from 1832 to 1841, which expressed itself largely in religious terms, was a formative event for the Algerian political and national consciousness, for the revolt was unprecedented in its scope and unparalleled in its organization. The memory of this brave but unsuccessful struggle would reverberate for subsequent generations of Algerians as an example of political commitment on behalf of a nation in search of itself and its past.

The defeat and exile of ʿAbd al-Qadir cleared the way for the beginning of systematic French settlement and transformation of Algeria over a forty-year period (1841–1881) that was punctuated by periodic Sufi and tribal revolts in the countryside. French authorities ruthlessly replaced tribal and Sufi leaders with a new generation that was perfunctorily French-trained; large tracts of land were seized from the tribes and religious organizations and turned over to French settlers (colons). Roads and communication networks were built and staffed by troops. Islamic schools and culture were overshadowed by French schools drawn up according to the lay curriculum first systematized by Napoleon, but few Muslims graduated from them. Instead, the new schools serviced the growing French settler population. The effect of these policies was to produce an Algeria with an infrastructure that allowed a central administration to enjoy for the first time unrivaled means of coercion. By the 1870s, the colons, whose number exceeded a quarter of a million, began pressing for—and by the turn of the century won—the integration of Algeria into the French metropole. In practice, nevertheless, French Algeria reflected the spirit and even the law of apartheid under which the colons enjoyed exclusive privileges to the detriment of the indigenous Algerians.

In Tunisia the Husaynids launched their own version of the Tanzimat (the nineteenth-century Ottoman reform movement) in an effort to refurbish the central authority of the state and forge a new bureaucratic elite loyal to the bey. In the reign of Ahmed (1837–1855) and Mohammed (1855–1859), military and fiscal reforms were introduced along rationalized European lines, and in 1861 a constitution was enacted that promised just taxation for all subjects, security of property from illegal appropriation, and freedom of religion (Brown 1974). The endeavor was extremely costly, and few qualified Tunisian personnel were trained, especially as the government chose to exclude the ulama from a prominent role in the new order. Consequently, the reforms enjoyed limited Tunisian support and instead attracted European capital and advisors, both of which came at a heavy price. The reforms did allow Tunisia to emerge in the late nineteenth century as an integrated state with a renewed and modernized tradition of centralized administration. Yet the inordinate presence of France, by dint of its investments, and Italy, by virtue of its immigrants, prompted the bey in 1871 to reaffirm Tunisia's status as a "distinguished province" (*vilayet-i mumtaze*) within the Ottoman Empire.

Following the Congress of Berlin (1878) France made good on its economic and political investments in Tunisia, and in 1881 French forces conquered the country and imposed a protectorate. Although in theory the Husaynid dynasty continued to rule, in fact French officials had the upper hand. By comparison with Algeria, however, the regime was relatively mild. Because Tunisia was not a settler colony on the scale of Algeria (by 1900 there were fewer than 30,000 French settlers), Tunisia was never integrated politically and economically into the metropole, with the result that French policies were less devastating on the traditional religious and political elites. Their offspring graduated from modernized Muslim schools (like the recast Zeitouna mosque, a center of Muslim learning in the Maghrib) and French-endowed institutions. And just as the Husaynids had earlier sought political inspiration in the Mashriq, the new generation cultivated ideas drawn from the protonationalist and Islamic reformist trends that sprouted in Egypt after the British occupation of 1882. The message of modernist, reformist Muslims and Pan-Islamists, such as Jamal al-Din al-Afghani and his student, Mohammed ʿAbduh, appealed to a group known as the Young Tunisians (Kerr 1966). The agenda of the Young Tunisians (who modeled themselves after the Young Turks) called for the updating of the Islamic legal system rather than its replacement by civil codes of either French or Swiss inspiration. With this they pushed Arabic language reform and a consequent renewal of Arabic culture, along with the introduction of the new Western education. In the wake of World War I and developments in Europe and the Middle East, they would advance a more narrowly defined political program.

In Libya economic failure and dynastic disputes crippled the Qaramanli dynasty in the second decade of the nineteenth century. As a result of the French invasion of Algeria and renewed French support for the separatist policies of Mohammed Ali Pasha of Egypt (1805–1848), the Ottoman government seized the opportunity of political turmoil in Tripoli to reassert direct Ottoman rule over the twin provinces of Tripolitania and Cyrenaica in 1835. The tribal populations of the hinterland resented the efforts of the new coastal authority to tax and control them, and revolts persisted until 1858. Thereafter, Ottoman authority slowly made its way into the Fezzan, but always with hesitation and setbacks. In the 1860s and 1870s, the Ottoman government initiated Tanzimat-style reforms, primarily road building, communications, and primary education, but their implementation foundered for lack of revenue to pay for them. It was only after the French and British occupations of Tunisia and Egypt, respectively, that Ottoman reform in Tripolitania received new impetus under Governor Ahmed Rasim Pasha (1881–1896). The indigenous elites, notably the *kulughli*, opposed many of his reforms because they aimed at undermining their fiscal and political independence by instituting policies that allowed the Ottoman state direct control over the agricultural and mercantile revenues of the province. In addition, the Ottoman administration sought to create a military capable of defending the provinces. These reforms were important, for they prepared Tripolitania and its population to resist the Italian invasion of 1911. Indeed, the measure of their success was the effectiveness of indigenous and Ottoman resistance to the Italian troops throughout the winter of 1911–1912 until the Balkan wars obliged the Ottomans to abandon Libya the following summer.

By contrast, Cyrenaica remained relatively unaffected by the nineteenth-century Ottoman reforms. As a result, Libya, unlike Algeria or Tunisia, was not a politically integrated whole but rather two provinces run in tandem. In Cyrenaica, a powerful revivalist Sufi order, the Sanusiya, emerged in the 1840s—much in the spirit of the Sufi movements of eighteenth-century Morocco—and won the adherence of many of the bedouin tribes. Although relations with the Ottoman government were sometimes tense, over the decades a modus vivendi was worked out between the Ottomans and the Sanusiya that allowed the order great leeway in the interior as long as it agreed to pay taxes; this, however, it did not always do, and Ottoman soldiers were occasionally sent to the interior to extract tax arrears.

In the coastal towns of Libya, the ideas of Islamic modernism or more secular Western ideologies (especially those related to protonationalism, which made some headway in Tunisia) were very slow to take hold, largely because the indigenous Libyans did not view the Ottomans as foreigners or imperialists and hence had little need for or attraction to these ideas.

Nineteenth-century Moroccan history lies very much in the shadow of events in Algeria. Confronted with French expansionism in the western Mediterranean and the decline of piracy in the first half of the century, the Alawi sultans embarked on a complex game to neutralize the great European powers by carefully stitching together various commercial treaties and creating government monopolies on certain exports (leather, wool, and olive oil) and certain imports (sugar, tea, gunpowder, and the like). These policies benefited a small urban mercantile elite that became the civil backbone of the Alawi dynasty's support.

In 1856 a treaty with Great Britain—very much in the style of the trade agreements the Ottoman Empire signed with European nations beginning in the seventeenth century and known as the Capitulations—lifted some of the barriers to free trade. It also helped Great Britain secure the Straits of Gibraltar and in turn offered the sultan an important counterweight to French ambitions.

Not to be outdone, the Spanish government joined the mercantile fray and annexed the Zafarin Islands (1848), which it added to its already existent outposts at Sabta (Ceuta), Malila, Peñon de Velez, and Al-Husayma (Alhucemas). In a war in 1860, the Spanish also occupied Tetouan before exacting concessions. The sultans paid heavy domestic costs for their economic policies and their concessions to the British, Spaniards, and the French.

As Tangier and other cities opened to the foreigners, resentment in the Moroccan Rif exploded into rebellion. It appeared that the Alawi sultans had sacrificed the very premises of their state—a righteous *sharifa*n leadership bent on resisting the infidel. A beleaguered Sultan Mawlay Hassan (1873–1894) introduced administrative and military reforms in an attempt to reassert control over the interior. They failed. By the turn of the century, there was little that the Alawi sultans could do to slow the pace of French, British, and Spanish economic control in Morocco and with that the signing of agreements on their respective spheres of influence. By 1904 France and Spain had all but divided Morocco, whereas Britain had ceded its interests to France in exchange for surrender of French rights in Egypt.

On the eve of World War I, the political development of the Maghrib was very uneven, and inequities in political culture and state formation remained. After eighty-four years of settler colonialism, Algeria was thoroughly rooted in the political and administrative psyche of France and, like India for Great Britain, it was the pride of French overseas possessions. In contrast, Tunisia retained many of its Maghribi-Ottoman traditions and elites; political awareness took traditional and newer Islamic forms as well as Western ones. Libya had just been conquered by Italy, and the remnants of the old Ottoman classes were on the verge of being uprooted, though the political organizational skills of the Sanusiya were yet to be honed. In Morocco, two unequal zones existed: a large French one and a small Spanish one in the north across from Gibraltar. The authority of the Alawi sultan, which had retreated to the major cities by the eighteenth century, was now entirely at the mercy of French and Spanish protectorate authorities. In the countryside and mountains, traditional Sufi orders and tribal shaykhs still reigned supreme.

The Struggle for Independence

World War I aroused aspirations to independence in North Africa and the Middle East largely because of the military and economic assistance and sacrifices rendered by the colonies. Most of these hopes were disappointed in the postwar peace that instead provided for the prolongation, though also the liberalization, of the mechanisms of colonialism. The reformist Islamic movement (Salafiya) of Egypt furnished one of the first contexts for articulating the nationalist aspirations of many Maghribi Muslims, both the traditionalists and those more marked by French culture and values.

Yet the path to independence would be difficult, marked as it was with contradictions: Both the colonizer and colonized felt at once respect and contempt for each other; each had been changed by the other yet was reluctant to recognize the degree and range of these influences—cultural, political, and economic. The most painful and violent divorce was between Algeria and France; French departure from Tunisia and Morocco was more amicable largely because French commitment there had been weaker. In Libya the defeat of Italy in World War II was transformed into Libyan independence.

The independence movement in Algeria had not only practical political implications but also important consequences in terms of state and cultural integration: Originating among diversely educated elites, the movement eventually made nationalism, and thereby national unity, a popular program and for the first time in Algeria's history initiated systematic, articulate, popular political mobilization. At the same time, it obliged culturally divided elites to compromise, cooperate, and eventually coordinate a revolutionary movement.

The elites were organized into numerous committees and groups that, like living organisms, merged, separated, died, or reemerged. Understanding the history of the Algerian independence movement, which owed much of its organizational talents and shortcomings to the labor movements of the French Third Republic, requires the mastery of a plethora of acronyms and abbreviations. To simplify, the Algerian opposition to French rule consisted of three broad and diverse groupings: First, the Islamic group that included conservatives, known to the French as the *vieux turbans* (old turbans), as well as Islamic reformist ulama inspired by the Salafiya; second, a small but articulate French-educated professional elite of lawyers and the like, who at first demanded equality for Algerians within a French Algeria and later embraced the idea of Algerian independence; third, a more radical nationalist camp, in part fostered by French Communists, that appeared in the late 1920s and consisted of Algerians who had worked and lived extensively in France.

ʿAbd al-Hamid Ben Badis was the leading spokesman for the reformist wing of the Islamic groups that emphasized independence as a prerequisite to the creation of a Muslim Algeria rooted in Islamic social, economic, and educational values. Ben Badis and his associates drew their support from the disenfranchised urban masses, many of whom made their way to the cities following the war, and from the small bourgeoisie of the coastal cities. More conservative elements, notably the Sufis, who had progressively lost their grip on the countryside, resented the reformists, especially because they emerged in 1936 at the forefront of a coalition that included the French-educated liberal professionals.

The liberal professionals (known in French as the *évolués*), headed by Mohammed Salah Ben Jallul and Ferhat Abbas, were for all intents and purposes assimilationists who held out the hope of becoming full-fledged French citizens in a thoroughly French, progressive, Muslim Algeria. Their initial denial of Algerian nationhood and their occasional open disdain of Islam meant their ideas never enjoyed mass appeal.

The radicals acquired their organizational skills in France among Algerian workers' groups. Their principal political organ, L'Étoile Nord-Africaine (ENA) was revived by the hybrid Communist-nationalist Massali al-Hajj, who in the 1930s forged the ENA into an effective political tool to attract mass support with the use of Islamic symbolism.

A final and critical ingredient in Algeria's struggle were the French colons, who were leery of any changes by the metropole in the existing order that might undermine their political and economic privileges.

Following World War II and the full independence of the French mandates in the Middle East, the Algerian nationalists proposed an Algerian republic as part of a special North African Union bound to France. The idea was rejected by Paris in favor of increased autonomy under the aegis of French rule. In 1954 the Front de Libération Nationale (FLN), an offshoot of Massali al-Hajj's groups, launched a well-planned revolution led by Ahmed Ben Bella and Houari Boumedienne, who took his name from the medieval Sufi saint Abu Madyan al-Andalusi. The FLN combined elements of Massali's radicalism with strong Islamic strains and a modernist bent that appealed to the *évolués*. Although the coalition framed by the FLN was fragile, its urban guerrilla warfare was so effective that it drove the angry French colons to topple the government of Algeria and with it the Fourth Republic in May 1958. The new president of the Fifth Republic, Charles de Gaulle, tried in vain to bridge the gap between the aims of the FLN and the demands of the colons; in 1962 he granted Algerian independence.

In Tunisia the independence movement had an easier time; the French protectorate had not swept away the traditional elites; society was less polarized than in Algeria; the bey, who officially continued to rule, provided a fatherly foil for the nationalists; finally, the French residents in Tunisia did not carry the weight or suffer from the same narrowness of political vision that the colons did in Algeria.

Building on the reformist agenda of the Young Tunisians, the first nationalists were politicians of the old Ottoman stock who demanded greater opportunity in the administration of their own country and the reinstatement of the 1861 constitution (*dustur*), hence the name of their group, the Destour. It was only in the 1930s that a generation born in the twentieth century, of small entrepreneurial classes and educated in France, challenged the older generation. In 1934 these newcomers, led by Habib Bourguiba, captured control of the Destour, renamed it the Neo-Destour, and fashioned from it a political party driven by an ideology of secular nationalism but organized at the grassroots level through labor and student organizations, womens' groups, and party-mosque affiliations. Bourguiba won the support both of the people and of Munsif Bey, who continued to advance the agenda of Tunisian independence despite Bourguiba's exile by French authorities for most of the period from 1938 to 1955.

In 1949 the Neo-Destourians and followers of the deposed bey—removed in 1943 after trying to form a new government over the objections of the French resident general—demanded self-determination for Tunisia. The government of Pierre Mendès-France wanted to jettison French colonies and so began negotiations with the Neo-Destour in 1954. Although the Mendès-France government collapsed in February 1955, the rising tide of urban and Algerian violence persuaded French authorities to grant Tunisia autonomy in June 1955 and independence in March 1956.

In Morocco the independence movement did not entail the emergence of decidedly new activist elites nor the creation of a coalition of conflicting ideologies as in Algeria. In contrast to that of its eastern neighbors, the Moroccan independence movement in some sense marked the recovery of old but transformed elites that had been politically disenfranchised under French rule and the greater integration of the Berber population into the social and political mainstream.

As of 1912, the French protectorate began subduing the countryside, forcing tribes to become sedentary, and co-opting the Sufi orders, which in time were displaced in their role as mediators and facilitators by French officials. Education was made available only to a small elite of court and religious functionaries. Finally, French officials cultivated the Berbers in the hope that by upgrading the political and social standing of that ethnic community, France would create a grateful and strong ally to the detriment of the political interests of the Arab majority. French policies had the contrary effect. Administrative changes at the expense of Sufis and the ulama, the confiscation of tribal lands, and the manipulation of the Berbers only helped to coalesce opposition to France.

Spanish Morocco was the first to witness a revolt against European colonialism in the person of ʿAbd al-Karim al-Khattabi, a *sharif* who declared an independent republic in the Rif. Animated at once by nationalist fervor and by Salafiya tendencies, ʿAbd al-Karim was deemed dangerous by the French, who helped their Spanish neighbors stamp out this movement in 1926.

In the decades that followed, the Salafiya tradition of Mohammed ʿAbduh found fertile ground in Morocco, where traditionally purity and uprightness were important qualities in religious observance and political practice. In the 1930s, in reaction to French laws aimed at fostering Berber national identity (the *zahir,* or proclamation, of May 1930), the National Action Bloc (originally separate nationalist groups from Fez and Rabat, they adopted the code name Zawiya, the Arabic word for a Sufi lodge) was created and efforts were made, as in Tunisia, to involve the ruler in the nationalist cause. In 1934 the bloc presented Sultan Mohammed V and French officials with a reform plan that called for greater Moroccan autonomy and an end to laws designed to encourage formation of a distinct Berber nationality.

French protectorate authorities ignored the plan and went about their business, confiscating land and displacing tribes and peasants alike. By the late 1930s they were saddled with an increasingly discontented rural and urban proletariat. Following World War II, the nationalist movement passed the reins from those inspired by the Salafiya to the Istiqlal (independence) movement, a broad coalition of ulama, French-educated urbanites, government officials, and the sultan. The principal task of the movement, primarily an organizational machine, was to arrange demonstrations in support of Sultan Mohammed V, who advocated an independent Moroccan state. In an effort to decapitate the Moroccan independence movement, French authorities in 1953 exiled Mohammed V to Madagascar. The charismatic figure of the sultan, in traditional Alawi fashion, served as a rallying point for the Moroccan people, who were determined to secure his return and restoration. For two years French authorities were confronted with unending demonstrations and acts of civil disobedience. In fall 1955 the sultan returned, and in the new year he proclaimed Morocco a constitutional monarchy. He negotiated Morocco's independence in March 1956.

Libyan independence was the result of a combination of indigenous resistance, British assistance, and United Nations action. After the Ottoman surrender to Italy in 1912 and in the course of World War I, the Sanusiya learned to mobilize and organize their *jihad* against the Italians. Moved primarily by a sense of religious commitment, the Sanusiya led the Libyan tribal resistance to Italian rule until the early 1930s, by which time the Italian authorities had executed Omar al-Mukhtar (principal lieutenant of the head of the Sanusiya, Shaykh Idris) and had exiled most of the activist Sanusi leaders. Fascist Italian rule intended to revive in Libya the ancient Roman presence in North Africa. However, plans were delayed in the 1930s because of Italian efforts in Ethiopia and events in Europe. The result was that Italy could invest only limited time, capital, or human resources in Libya. Finally, in the decade before the outbreak of the war, some 100,000 Italian colonists hastily made their way to Libya.

During World War II Great Britain occupied Cyrenaica and Tripolitania; France seized Fezzan. In 1949 the United Nations decided not to recognize the interests of any foreign power in Libya, and in 1951 it declared Libya an independent country. King Idris, the exiled Sanusi chief, returned from Cairo to assume the throne of the new kingdom. The task of developing a sense of national identity was yet to be addressed. That King Idris administered his country by flying back and forth in a single-engine plane between Tripoli and Benghazi was ample proof that the new state had yet to reach any level of political integration.

The Maghrib Since Independence

In the four decades since independence, the countries of the Maghrib have struggled both to define and execute a postindependence agenda. Whatever the differences among the four countries in terms of social, economic, and political development, one problem and one accomplishment are common: All share a search for the means to bring about effective political participation; all benefit from the existence of a strong state apparatus inherited from the colonial administrations but transformed and appropriated by the indigenous leadership during the struggle for independence.

Algeria has been subject to the greatest political upheavals since independence largely because of the divided Algerian society that emerged under French rule. At the expense of other groups involved in the drive to liberation, the FLN leadership has dominated the postindependence period; Ben Bella governed from 1962 to 1965; Boumedienne from 1965 to 1978; Chadli Benjedid was president until 1991. Ben Bella launched a not entirely popular program for the radical socialization of Algeria's economy and society that Boumedienne continued, albeit with a much stronger Islamic flavor and with the benefit of a military dictatorship. Although such a dictatorship may be detrimental to political participation, it has contributed to the consolidation of the new state's power and the institutionalization of party and political machinery. Still, despite its significant oil revenues, Algeria has been plagued with severe troubles such as inflation, high unemployment, and failed agricultural reform. Until his 1991 ouster by the military in response to a challenge by Islamic groups, Benjedid pursued a more conservative vision of socialism. But Algeria faces identity problems similar to those of contemporary Turkey. The French cultural brand burned deep into the Algerian identity. Today the debate continues over which cultural and political orientation Algeria should pursue: one more closely connected to Europe through French language and culture, or one allied more with the Arab world to the east? In the past several years, powerful Islamic groups have also emerged to challenge the status quo and to lay claim to Algeria's Muslim legacy, one they argue has been lost in the secular political shuffle.

After Bourguiba eliminated the Husaynid dynasty in 1957, he ruled virtually unchallenged for thirty years in Tunisia. He relied on his image as father of the nation, à la Kemal Atatürk, and on his ability to promote a moderate secularism—his modified socialist experiment failed—through the apparatus of his party and regime. Although Bourguiba's charisma waned in his later years, since his removal from the political scene in 1987 it has become clear that he nevertheless left behind a strong state apparatus that the current regime has been able to appropriate effectively. Still, Tunisia, like Algeria, faces growing unrest among activist Islamic groups who question the prevailing secular state structure.

In Morocco the Alawi dynasty rules autocratically, and the reign of King Hassan II (1961–present) has reflected a traditional reliance on the Islamic, charismatic nature of Moroccan kingship. The viability of the Moroccan state is not in doubt, but the level of state and political institutionalization is less than in Algeria and Tunisia. Rather, the royal touch pervades all aspects of government. Supported by a loyal military, however, the king has been able to play off various technocratic, bureaucratic, and religious elites, all the while preserving good economic and political relations with France and the West.

Libya, since Muᶜammar Qadhafi's 1969 coup, has developed a growing sense of nationhood and national identity based on a special blend of state socialism and Qadhafi's personal understanding of Islam, which he mixes with a strong sense of bedouin pride. Notwithstanding some of his foreign policy antics, it is undeniable that Qadhafi has improved the economic lot of the average Libyan, thanks in large part to increased oil revenues and a small population (about 4 million). National integration has gone ahead by means of both education and political indoctrination.

It is not the prerogative of historians to venture any prediction on the political future of the Maghrib. This caveat notwithstanding, it is clear that the Maghrib will continue to be marked by the effects of colonialism. The legacy of colonialism has been beneficial in terms of modernization and state building. Still, Maghribi society retains the wounds of colonialism: a widening income and cultural gap between the new urban postindependence technocratic elites and the rural and urban proletariat; and governmental failure to transform the political mobilization of popular sentiment into effective public participation in politics. It is perhaps for this reason that Islamic fundamentalism, with its appeal to Islamic political authenticity over foreign systems, has made such headway among the urban proletariat in the past decade.

2

The Second Stage of State Building

Elbaki Hermassi
Dirk Vandewalle

Throughout the Maghrib, the Arab region, and the world at large, the 1980s will be remembered as the beginning of a period of difficult adjustments to a number of new and powerful realities that are profoundly reshaping the role of the state in economic and political decisionmaking. If much of our attention was captured by the dramatic causes and effects of *perestroika* and *glasnost* in Eastern Europe and the Soviet Union, developments in the Middle East and North Africa proved equally rewarding to investigate. In all countries of the region, the state—defined here as the institutional mechanism by which the extraction and distribution of resources and law and order is maintained—has become omnipresent through its institutions and agencies.

But pervasiveness has not always meant strength or capability: Throughout the decade the state's representatives were forced to conclude that the state no longer can act as the only hand on the tiller but must now deal openly with countervailing tendencies in society at large and must recognize that the state's dominating role has often made it the focus rather than the mediator of conflict. Indeed, what is at stake in North Africa in the 1990s is a reshaping of the role of the state—and by implication the accommodation of different groups within each country. It is certainly not surprising that each Maghribi country is coming to terms with this new reality—which pits powerful changes in the international economic environment against local political concerns—in slightly different ways. Each country has historically been indelibly marked by certain notions about economic and political development and has constructed various levels of institutional strength to handle possible readjustments a generation after independence.

Despite their differing responses, no single government from Rabat to Tripoli has been able to avoid certain powerful exigencies: the necessity of greater economic efficiency, the challenge of intergenerational political renewal, the need for a new consensus, and the call for the creation of greater public liberties. Neither Habib Bourguiba nor Houari Boumedienne would have admitted the existence of such needs and difficulties a generation ago, guided as they were by the notion that the state, through its institutions and centralized organization, could overpower each country's society.

Two developments effectively symbolize the disarray and the retreat of the state during the last decade. One is the emergence in all Maghribi countries of *infitah* strategies (here defined as the permanent transfer of the production of goods and services from public bureaucracies and enterprises to private companies and other nonpublic organizations) to overcome the bottlenecks of earlier economic management. The other is the gathering strength of political contestation and the limited liberalization to which most rulers in the region now at least pay lip service. More than a generation after independence, the North African countries have, often willy-nilly, recognized that the political configurations and the economic strategies that previously sustained their development can no longer meet current challenges in a dramatically changed world economy and amid state-society relations that were fundamentally altered during the past four decades.

A few examples point out this change. Normally immune from economic or internal political desiderata, the Qadhafi government in 1987 and 1988 felt obliged to relax its injunctions on private trade—once one of the cornerstones of the regime's "revolution"—and initiate some political liberalization that ultimately resulted in the publication of a document that in the Libyan context can only be termed highly unusual: the Great Green Charter of Human Rights (Libya 1988). If in Algeria, Tunisia, and Libya some of the old rhetoric, with its hackneyed references to the struggle for independence and the imperative to preserve *dirigisme* (state-controlled economic and political development) persists, a number of new words have crept into public discourse these last years. References to "austerity," "efficiency," and "productivity" linked to "personal responsibility" and "human rights" now punctuate the political vocabulary of each of the North African leaders.

In Algeria, after almost three decades of monolithic one-party rule, the government suddenly called upon "civil society" to behave responsibly during the June 1990 local and municipal elections. A few months earlier Algeria's new constitution had pointedly dropped any reference to socialism and, after castigating multinational companies for years in several international forums, allowed direct foreign investment. Tunisia's new president, Zine al-Abidine Ben Ali, in November 1988 proposed a national pact that would give all organized groups in the country a chance to help elaborate its future, this after a period of personal rule under Bourguiba that had seen the virtual evisceration of any form of opposition (Anderson 1991).

In Morocco a certain amount of political pluralism, a more market-oriented economy, and the extraordinary religious and charismatic link between ruler and ruled has seemingly muted the growing bifurcation between state and society found in the other Maghribi countries. Political difficulties in the kingdom have been less the result of friction between the population and its ruler and more the outcome of conflict between monarchy and political elites over how the state should be managed. Even so, the 1981 and 1984 upheavals in the kingdom's major cities showed to some extent how fragile this carefully calibrated system remains. The king's answer to the lingering difficulties has been to introduce a number of economic measures—including fiscal reform with higher taxes, particularly for the middle class; reform and privatization of public enterprises; and greater attention to exports—but no meaningful political concessions.

The State After Independence

The legitimacy of the state during the first period of state building in Morocco, Tunisia, and Algeria originated and was sustained by the dual roles it assumed after independence. The state became both the guardian of a strong and carefully nurtured symbolic bond to its subjects and the arbiter and broker for economic patronage. The symbolic link was particularly important in Algeria and Tunisia (and after 1969 in Libya), where the state emerged as the embodiment of the nationalist struggle and as the only force capable of creating an internal *thawra* (revolution) that would modernize the political community. In Tunisia and Algeria this fusion of symbolic and real (economic) power was institutionalized in one-party systems: the Front de Libération Nationale and the Destour dispensed patronage and were the symbols of independence, even if in the latter case the confusion between charismatic ruler and party was part and parcel of the political game. As opposed to Morocco, where the constitution expressly forbids a one-party system, all other political parties in Algeria, Tunisia, and Libya were outlawed or simply eviscerated. The state controlled most forms of social and political expression. In Algeria and Tunisia (and in Libya after 1969) leaders talked of the creation of a seemingly irreversible social order that would transform even the attitudes and identities of individuals. So convinced of the success of their mission was the first generation of reformers in Tunisia that many observers claimed that Bourguiba had created the "new state." And so thorough was the state's apparent political and ideological hegemony that at least one observer writing on the country's labor union—his prediction turned out to be completely erroneous but was certainly believable at the time—wondered whether it could ever reemerge as an autonomous social force in the country (Ahmed 1967).

By 1980 the claim that the state could create—or recreate—national societies was heard less often and its role as a catalyst in transforming society no longer taken as self-evident. By that time both aspects of the earlier state-society relationship had been substantially altered throughout the Maghrib: Rapid population growth and overall economic stagnation made the task of keeping the social contract intact virtually impossible in all countries except Libya. The initial rationale for extending or maintaining state power in order to survive challenges posed by the former colonial power had dissipated, and the nationalist myth of the state as modernizer in Algeria and Tunisia lost its former coherence as the ruler or party that had embodied it lost appeal. The continued existence of what Ahmed Ben Salah once called an "inevitable tutelage" was questioned (Camau 1987:31). Indeed, the Islamicist movements that emerged full-blown in the 1980s in all North African countries after a little-noticed or ignored gestation period that dates back to the 1960s brought to the fore a number of groups who challenged the lingering symbolic pretensions of the government and who denigrated its performance as economic allocation agent (Burgat 1988b). The rapid emergence of private voluntary associations and parallel markets in each country—Algeria's *trabendo,* Tunisia's *marché noir,* Libya's *suk tunisi*—were only one expression of the shortcomings of the state in economic matters.

Perhaps no country has better demonstrated the erosion of the two pillars of the state's legitimacy than Algeria, where the Marxist-Leninist development strategy designed after independence had once been attractive because it combined the promise of a modern society with a barely disguised hostility toward the West, the latter a powerful element in the establishment of a symbolic bond that ensured consensus within Algerian society during the first postindependence generation. By the early 1980s, that promise and the dissociative economic strategy that accompanied it looked tarnished and outdated: Algeria's nationalist and diplomatic credentials were beyond reproach and hardly retained the mobilizational value they once possessed. Despite occasional setbacks, the country had engaged upon productive state-to-state negotiations with its former metropole. Above all, as a new generation emerged, the myth of the war of independence as an element of legitimacy had started to lose its former centrality, and the FLN, which had stood at the interface between the Algerian state and its society, proved corrupt and unable to mobilize the population any further.

In Tunisia, Morocco, and the then kingdom of Libya (1951–1969), the mixture of ideology and economic orientation proved less troublesome. By the end of 1969, Tunisia had abandoned the socialist strategy of Ahmed Ben Salah and turned toward a form of etatism and economic *dirigisme* guided by the country's charismatic supreme commander, Bourguiba. As did Algeria, Tunisia adopted a one-party system where the myth of nationalism—as personalized by Bourguiba—was key to the creation of a powerful link between state and society.

The two monarchies, Morocco and Libya, were at diametrically opposite ends. Since independence, their respective leaders (Mohammed V and Hassan II in Morocco, King Idris and Muʿammar Qadhafi in Libya) have reigned rather than ruled, and both countries shared a laissez-faire economic approach (in the Moroccan case a virtual extension of colonial economic policy, in Libya a literal doling out of growing oil revenues by King Idris). Yet the link between ruler and subjects differed radically. In Morocco the centuries-old bond, brokered by the *makhzen* and kept intact in part by the highly symbolic role and presence of the monarch, had created a much more varied—even though still closely controlled—political community. The Moroccan king has never been tied directly to the fate of a single political party, even though different political parties have skillfully promoted his interests at differing times.

Of all four Maghribi countries, the link between institutions and the state remained weakest in Libya. Much of this was the heavy legacy of the country's colonial past (Anderson 1986). Its independence was brokered by the United Nations. The concept of statehood was virtually unknown among the population of the three disparate provinces that would not become truly unitary until 1963, when the federal system was abolished for essentially economic reasons. Neither *dirigisme* nor etatism took place in Libya, a phenomenon exacerbated even further when oil was discovered, allowing King Idris (and later Qadhafi) to dole out money in lieu of granting real political participation (Davis 1987). Thus a party through which a neopatrimonial system could be maintained directly (as in Tunisia or Algeria) or indirectly (as in Morocco) did not emerge in Libya. The king voided the results of the only elections held in 1954, and Qadhafi introduced his system of "direct democracy." The economic and political experiments of the Qadhafi government since the 1969 coup are not surprising in light of this history. Aided by revenues that remained virtually unlimited until the mid-1980s, Qadhafi's policies have combined in virulent form a symbolically important dissociative economic stance with an attempt to perpetuate this statelessness by projecting nationalism on a regional basis. Only in the Libyan *jamahiriya* (a state governed directly by the people, without governmental institutions) are yesteryear's slogans about Arab unity still heard, and only there does the unrestrained spending to some extent continue. In Algeria and Tunisia, the single political party was deliberately used as an active instrument for the further institutionalization and subsequent strengthening of the state; on at least two important occasions—the succession to Boumedienne after 1978 and the takeover by Ben Ali on November 7, 1987—the strength and the importance of this institutionalization became apparent. In Qadhafi's Libya, however, the abolishment of parties and the attempt to abolish the bureaucracy was meant to reinforce the statelessness inherent in the leader's notion of a *jamahiriya*.

The Politics of Economic Stagnation and Adjustment

The *infitah* strategies in Morocco, Tunisia, and Algeria emerged at roughly the same time in the early 1980s, even though in the Tunisian case it is perhaps more accurate to speak of a restructuring or reprivatization after the lackluster attempt at market economics that followed Ben Salah's dismissal. In Libya the reversal was postponed until 1987, partly because the enormous revenues the government continued to enjoy allowed it to ignore economic imperatives. By the end of 1986, Morocco and Tunisia had revised their investment codes to allow for greater private-sector participation. Each government had either rescheduled part of its debt or had accepted standby arrangements or restructuring plans suggested by the World Bank or the International Monetary Fund (IMF). Despite a self-imposed austerity plan after 1983, Algeria finally entered an agreement with the IMF in July 1989. By that time its investment code (1986) had dramatically extended facilities for the private sector in the country.

In Libya the March 1987 introduction of *tasharukiya* allowed for private trading and for enterprises in which individuals could contribute capital, violating one of the regime's cornerstones of its previous "partners, not wage earners" policy that had been encoded in the three-volume collection of Qadhafi's thoughts, the Green Book. And though in Libya this limited form of *infitah* was imposed from above (not the result of pressures from below, as in the other countries), the unexpected change hinted at the economic hardships under which the *jamahiriya* labored.

In each case the redefinition of the role of the state in economic development has been fostered not only by an emerging reconceptualization of the state's part in economic development but also by a rapidly changing international economic environment and a global logic that has progressively narrowed the scope of intervention left to the local governments. In Latin America and sub-Saharan Africa, the inquiry into the relationships among international capital, local capital, and weak or strong structures has led to the formulation of a number of competing explanations; so far this has not been the case in studies of North Africa. In lieu of a systematic review, at this point we want to make only a few preliminary remarks on what the interaction between changing local and international economic conditions has been.

It is important first of all to put the *infitah* that each North African country has adopted into a wider context. As in most other areas of the world, the new economic sensibility in North Africa is both part of a global phenomenon and a reflection of objective conditions inside each country and within the region. The rethinking of what is now considered the development orthodoxy of the 1950s and 1960s has been a powerful reality since the 1970s, stimulated in part by international financial institutions such as the World Bank and the IMF. The ambitious efforts made at independence to prove that the state could be the initiator, regulator, and enforcer of irreversible social and economic reforms—the state as Leviathan—were scaled back.

It was in this sense that President Benjedid noted in 1981 that "the kind of management which regulated [national enterprises] during the 1960s and the beginning of the 1970s . . . no longer fits with the present exigencies of national development . . . [nor] . . . with the necessities of management for the decade of the 1980s." And it was also this realization that prompted the director of Tunisia's Central Bank, Ismail Khelil, to call for a renewed commitment to private-sector initiative (Khelil 1988a).

In all Maghribi countries, but most importantly in Algeria and Tunisia, the story of development since independence had been one of active state intervention in all sectors of the economy. With the exception of Libya until the 1969 coup, each country's legal system, its fiscal and monetary policy instruments, and a tangle of regulatory mechanisms were meant to protect internal markets from undue interference. Particularly in Algeria until 1980 and Tunisia until 1969, the adoption of a command system was seen as a promising road toward impressive economic growth and social restructuring—a strategy that demanded the creation of an intricate structure of multiple layers of bureaucracy and control mechanisms derived either from the Soviet model or from the experience with economic controls and extensive central planning left by the French. Thus the state not only occupied the traditional commanding heights of the respective economies but had penetrated the lowest levels of economic interaction as well. The most extreme form of state intrusion in the economic lives of its citizens, however, was found in Libya. After 1975 a private sector was not only discouraged in Libya but became outright illegal, sparking the growth of a black market that eventually contributed to the recall of some of the regime's earlier economic measures.

If in Libya this disappearance of the private sector had taken place for ideological reasons, in the other Maghribi countries strong state intervention was seen as a pragmatic necessity. It would allow planners to circumvent a number of potentially troublesome realities that could offset economic progress: the persistence of factions and regional differences, the existence of weak institutions for implementing economic policy, the presence of underdeveloped markets or trade structures oriented toward the former metropole, and, finally, the private sector's suspect ability or willingness to shoulder part of the burden of development. Running through much of Algeria's and Tunisia's economic literature of that early period was the strong conviction that markets could bring only incremental change, not the wholesale restructuring necessary to effect the desired strategy. Second, planners judged that markets were incapable of fine-tuning the country's economy in the absence of administrative fiat—a fiat that would allow the country to forgo the chaos of the market economy by intervening early and consistently.

To varying degrees, then, the state in Morocco, Tunisia, and Algeria had been called upon to take charge of the transfer of resources and authority in the wake of France's withdrawal. In Morocco this takeover resembled more an extension of colonial economic policy than a radical departure: One observer noted the remarkable sense of policy continuity in the country's agricultural sector since independence (Swearingen 1987). Other sectors of Morocco's economy as well were marked by this continuity, which was modified only temporarily by the so-called Moroccanization campaign that took hold in March 1973 and was rendered largely impotent by the 1983 investment code. Neither Mohammed V nor Hassan II has shown a determination to dramatically alter the benign laissez-faire approach that traditionally marked economic relations between ruler and ruled. From the end of the 1950s on, Moroccan laws continued to favor private local and foreign investment, and the *zahirs* published at the time of the Moroccanization measures carefully skirted any notion of outright expropriation. The government's economic role was largely restricted to large-scale projects shunned by the private sector. As opposed to its neighbors, Morocco did not try to create or recreate a new class to guide its development strategy. On the contrary, the king attempted to preserve the power of the urban bourgeoisie and the old ruler elites: Because of its social role and historical emergence, the Moroccan bourgeoisie in part legitimates both the political and the economic system.

Until the marketing of oil in 1961, the Libyan kingdom remained highly dependent on the rents Great Britain and the United States paid for military bases in the country. Because the population had but a weak sense of statehood, King Idris felt little inclination to attempt the creation of a political community or state institutions. Until the king's removal in 1969, only a few trusted advisers were needed to run a typical rentier economic system that showed more interest in simple disbursement of funds than in actual economic planning or policy. Despite its claims to a radically different political vision—mobilizational rather than passive; popular rather than exclusionary—the Qadhafi government after 1969 intensified even further the *dirigiste* nature of the country's economy, excluding at one point all private economic actors entirely. In contrast to Algeria or Tunisia, however, in Libya it was unclear whether this added to the capabilities of the state. Indeed, one of Qadhafi's assertions was that the country's political and economic system was run by "people power" rather than the institutions of a state. Because the extraction of resources from the population has at any rate never been a necessity in light of the country's oil riches, the claims of Libya's leader have not yet been put to the test. If ever they are, they will perhaps be found severely lacking.

In Tunisia and Algeria, the transfer of authority at independence led to an important rupture with the political and economic legacy of the colonial past. Both countries opted for one-party systems and some form of socialism (rescinded in Tunisia in 1969) that replaced a large part of the old economic and cultural elite and produced a consensus for intensive reform and for an extension of the state's administrative capacities. Although both countries managed impressive economic growth during most of the two decades following their independence, by the end of the 1970s much of the early optimism about the ability of the state to manage and direct economic development had dissipated. The questioning of economic paradigms and their appropriateness spurred the awareness that despite economic growth, a number of severe structural problems characterized each country's economy. The difficulties were further exacerbated by growing political contestation and a decade of uncertainty and crisis beginning in the mid-1970s (Chatelus 1987).

At least three major objective economic conditions seemed to make the *dirigiste* strategy of the first period less desirable. The most important factor was unquestionably economic performance. Despite the differing approaches in each country, a number of standard economic indicators reveal structural similarities among them. Each country's public sector was characterized by low productivity and bureaucratic redundancy. Investment codes (particularly in Algeria, Tunisia, and Libya) presented formidable legal hurdles to the development of a private sector, much of whose energy was channeled toward economic activities at the margins of the inefficient public sector or that contributed little to improving the productive capacity of the country. Agricultural production lagged substantially behind the needs of a rapidly growing population, placing not only greater pressures on tightly controlled markets but also making growing imports of food unavoidable. Most of those imports were paid for in hard currency, a scarce commodity throughout the Maghrib. At the same time, the pressure on official markets was compounded by a rapid monetary expansion, especially in Algeria and Libya, that led to excess liquidity and the growth of parallel markets where the real value of the country's currency was a fraction of its official price. The growing shortage of food and consumer goods, inflation (and, by the mid-1980s, stagflation), and the overall inefficient use of capital led to burgeoning debt burdens for all countries except Libya. These debts had mounted in part because of a banking system that until its reforms in the 1980s had often functioned simply as a conveyor of capital and subsidies to public companies as part of overall economic planning.

The second factor that caused the abandonment of earlier economic strategies was closely linked to the first but concerned specifically the appropriateness in the 1980s of an approach that had been adopted in the aftermath of independence. With varying degrees of success, the first stage of economic development, in which the creation of a basic industrial structure had figured prominently, had been completed in all countries. In the second stage the objectives for development subtly changed. Although the industrial infrastructure and industrial production remained important, the new exigencies that appeared in each country's multiyear development plans in the late 1970s concerned agricultural production and the production of consumer goods. These seemed less likely to be addressed in a satisfactory fashion by the closely coordinated processes that had fueled production in the first stage. Creating an industrial infrastructure may necessitate economic *dirigisme,* but neither the production of agricultural goods nor the creation and marketing of consumer items that now emerged as the real challenge for each government lends itself very well to command-style economics. As the dismal record in each country demonstrated, *dirigisme* is unlikely to produce the amount of information needed to generate such goods; only direct communication, channeled through the market, conveys the necessary information efficiently.

The crisis of the agricultural sector and the need for improved consumer goods, however, was indicative of a broader reality that has marked each country since its independence: the rapid growth of an urban population. Throughout the Maghrib, this was caused not only by a rural exodus of the poor but also by the need for a highly educated managerial and bureaucratic class and the necessary physical concentration of decisionmaking authority in the coastal cities, an unavoidable aspect of the *dirigisme* adopted after independence. By 1980 each government would attempt, without much success, to decentralize its economy in an effort to relieve the unrelenting pressure on the cities. The urban population explosion not only added to the growing burden of maintaining the social contract (primarily by subsidizing food and other necessities) but also led to the creation of a more vocal population with increasingly divergent views on what constituted the public interest.

The final factor in the reassessment of *dirigisme* linked economic and political concerns. The dismal performance of the local economies had an important and unintended political side effect. In all Maghribi countries, part of the earlier rhetoric—outspoken in Algeria and Libya, somewhat muted in Tunisia and Morocco—had been the state's insistence that it took an active interest in pursuing equity and economic justice for its citizens. As economic performance faltered, so did state representatives' claims to be the sole actors capable of promoting development, a pretense further tarnished by charges of mismanagement and corruption that had overwhelmingly benefited public-sector managers, the party apparatchiks, or the economic elites. In all cases—although somewhat subdued in Morocco and controlled in Libya—this close identification of the state or party with economic progress and subsequent stagnation inevitably produced a spillover effect that led to a number of sustained political crises in systems where contestation was closely circumscribed or impossible. The contestation or urge to reform has come in essence from two groups: those who argue that the state's institutions can be reformed and act as new catalysts for development, and those who insist that they have lost their ability and credibility to do so.

The Politics of Institutional Decline and Renewal

In every type of regime found in the Maghrib by the late 1970s—monarchist, military, semidemocratic—the questioning of the role of the state in economic development was matched (and sometimes partly caused) by the emergence of increasingly vocal and diverse groups. Discussion about the crisis of the state and the institutions that represented it and about possible alternatives to it emerged first within underground publications and speeches among an opposition that was often deliberately left atomized. After a number of subterfuges that still continue, the debate was taken up by the representatives of the state, then filtered into official forums.

Sometimes this shift toward official recognition of a fundamental realignment of forces between state and society took years to accomplish—and most often occurred only as a result of impending political or economic chaos. Morocco's first stage of state building had been characterized by conflictual relations between the monarchy and the political parties. It pitted the monarchy, with its insistence on preserving the structures of the colonial system, against the modernizing vision of the country's political parties, who wanted to construct a modern state with its own economic, political, and social institutions. It resulted in the creation of a mixed authoritarian and populist system in which the king carefully distanced himself from those who claimed to represent popular opinion. The outcome, as in Tunisia, was a personalized system in which political power was highly concentrated, corruption became endemic, and any institutional possibility for criticism almost completely disappeared. Indeed, such was the hegemonic nature of power in both countries that whatever tolerated opposition appeared in the 1970s played safely within the rules of the game. In Morocco this consensual nature was reinforced by the dual roles of the king as secular ruler and as commander of the faithful: The secular opposition may contest the decisions of the head of the state but has overwhelmingly refused to attack those that carry a religious imprimatur. Similarly, the Moroccan military may attack the king as the head of the *makhzen* but (as happened at Skhirat) lays down its arms to pray alongside him when he recites the *fatiha* (the quranic verses used to start prayers). Despite its extraordinary ability to circumscribe contestation, the monarchy was not immune from extralegal or extrainstitutional dissent: Morocco witnessed military coup attempts in July 1971 and August 1972 and an army uprising in March 1973. Although all were contained, they led to the realization that closer attention to the nurturing of political institutions and to some limits on the king's virtually absolute power was necessary.

In Tunisia the political system never recovered from the 1969 crisis—the demise of the socialist experiment—and the falsified parliamentary elections of 1981. The entire population, in particular the peasants, carries the bitter memory of the adoption of socialism, of the depossessions and the abuses committed in the name of a cooperative system that at one time remained beyond criticism and suddenly was recognized as a fraud. As a result of that defeat, the implicit social contract between the state and civil society was ruptured. Nothing, not even the period of rapid economic growth under Hedi Nouira, could put an end to the disappointment and the suspicion. And it would take the removal of Bourguiba before the country's political parties reluctantly returned to the political arena.

After 1969 the Destour party started to lose its support, and in the 1970s a number of its elites started to form opposition parties: the Mouvement des Démocrates Socialistes (MDS) and the Mouvement d'Unité Populaire (MUP). In reality the retreat was from the regime as a whole. As in Algeria, part of the elite as well as the new generation took up their grievances in a number of long-suppressed organizations, particularly the unions, or at places that fell substantially outside the traditional forms of institutional control by the Neo-Destour or the FLN: the universities and the mosques. In all Maghribi countries, including the *jamahiriya,* these new (or renewed) forms of opposition became arenas for political substitution throughout the 1970s and the 1980s. All opposition, political, syndicalist, and Islamicist, thus originated in the failure of the political system that is indicative of a broader weakening of the state. In Tunisia and Algeria, meaningful political discourse was suspended for almost three decades while this gradual decline took place. Under Bourguiba the discourse was sidetracked by the succession issue; it took almost twenty years before it eventually transpired. During that time the growing bifurcation between the paternalistic pretensions of the party-state and the deepening social and economic malaise not only led to the demoralization of the state's cadres but brought the country to the brink of civil war.

In Algeria the dramatic reversal of economic policy after Benjedid's assumption of power gave way to a lingering crisis that was even more profound than in neighboring Tunisia. The commitment to socialism under Boumedienne had been an indelible part of the country's political discourse. Unable to isolate the opponents to the new economic strategy, as Bourguiba had quickly and effectively done with regard to Ben Salah's public supporters, Benjedid was faced with a crisis that festered into a barely concealed struggle inside the FLN, infighting that slowed down the *infitah* perceptibly and fanned the flames of the struggle between the party and the growing outside opposition. The pro- and anti-*infitah* factions within the Central Committee, the Politburo, and the National Assembly remained unified on only one issue: prevention of the dispersal of power beyond the party. For that purpose, intimidation or outright violence (during the 1988 riots) had become acceptable. But for a long time the FLN's fortunes had mirrored those of the Neo-Destour: It had slowly become valued for what it could deliver rather than what it stood for. The symbolic place it had shared with the Armée de Libération Nationale (ALN) as the guarantor of national independence and egalitarianism had all but vanished. Then the adverse economic conditions in the early 1980s and the government's subsequent austerity policies after 1983 proved that the party could no longer provide the patronage either. What once looked like a strong state almost collapsed when the riots broke out. The symbolic role of the FLN and the ALN was irrevocably shattered when the "people's army" started shooting at the young protesters who had systematically singled out for destruction the FLN offices and state organizations in Algiers and other major cities. A regime whose legitimacy had for so long been based on what amounted to nothing more than its citizens' shared perception of its invincibility quickly lost its power once that perception changed: President Benjedid's panicked speeches in the weeks leading up to the riots, his vacillation on what strategy to adopt during the first few days, and the divisiveness among the top leaders produced a momentary sense of impotence that was quickly seized upon by the young demonstrators and then by the Islamicists (Vandewalle 1988a).

In the aftermath of the riots, Algerian leaders referred to them as the catalyst of the country's "second revolution" that would lead to democracy and greater personal freedom. But the historical analogy is perhaps wrong. More than any other event in the country's recent history, the few days in October 1988 resembled December 11, 1961, when for the first time Algerians took massively to the streets, pouring from the housing projects of Diar al-Mahsoul and Diar al-Saada into a unified manifestation against the French. It was an act of defiance that most French historians now agree stimulated the European's psychological turnaround, the understanding that things could never be as they had been before. Those were precisely the words Benjedid repeated in his first public speech after the disturbances.

Faced with growing and sustained opposition and with acute crises of legitimacy, Maghribi rulers have attempted partly to reconstruct some of the institutions and agencies that represent the state. Perhaps not surprising in light of each country's political history, the initial effort in both Algeria and Tunisia has focused on reforming the FLN and the Rassemblement Constitutionnel Démocratique (RCD, formerly the Neo-Destour) and on creating some form of political pluralism. Although the rejuvenation of the party in each country had been announced and timidly attempted on several occasions since the late 1970s, it took the removal of Bourguiba and the October 1988 riots in Algeria to make real reform possible. In each country the party has been the victim of the abuse of personal power and the object of infighting between clans, one of the reasons Qadhafi decided to avoid political parties, based on his notion that "parties abort democracy." The party stopped being a force of progress and produced among its members a feeling of detachment, indifference, and cynicism; such was the sclerotic nature of the FLN, for example, that on the eve of the first free local and municipal elections in June 1990, a sizable minority of the party's apparatchiks defected when the party's fortune was clearly declining.

In attempting party reform, Ben Ali and Benjedid's alternatives were threefold: to institute a radical restructuring to make the party more compatible with the new challenges it faced, to move toward a multiparty system, and to disengage the party from the state. To some extent all three alternatives have been attempted with varying success. Much was done in each country to restructure the party in terms of new people, new ideas, and a new organization. Both the FLN and the RCD structures, from the local cells on up, were renewed. At the national congress of each party, new delegates replaced old stalwarts, and a certain amount of generational change took place.

In both countries the political leaders hoped that the National Pact of 1988 and the preliminary reforms in the wake of the Algerian riots would usher in the start of an interim period that could be used to settle the remaining interparty disputes. This has obviously not happened. On the surface it seemed both countries had made remarkable progress in setting the parameters for a renewed debate on the role of the state. They allowed the creation of a myriad of political associations or parties that included human rights organizations and, in Algeria, the Front Islamique du Salut (FIS). Libya, with its commitment to people's committees and people's congresses rather than parties, remains the only Maghribi country where multiparty politics did not exist at the end of 1991—but even Qadhafi had announced some sort of *perestroika*, highlighted by the publication of the Great Green Charter of Human Rights and the release of hundreds of political prisoners (Vandewalle 1990a, 1990b).

By mid-1992 events already demonstrated how tenuous those earlier developments had been. In hindsight it is easy to discern what little promise the attempt to redefine the role of the state and its guiding elites held in both Tunisia and Algeria. Tunisia until now and Algeria before the June 1990 local and municipal elections could only be described as "hegemonic party systems" in which some opposition parties are legal but in reality have little or no chance to compete for power against the party that dominates politics. The April 1989 legislative elections in Tunisia, for example, in which no opposition party managed to win a single seat to Parliament, provided the first clear indication of the difficulties involved in moving away from a single-party system.

In this regard Morocco presents a slight variation. The local and municipal reforms of 1976 did delegate real authority over local administration—backed by budgetary power—to elected officials. Elections, although certainly not free from interference, are periodically contested at the local and national levels (Eickelman 1986, 1987). The June 1990 elections in Algeria were a significant exception to the trend noted above, but the disastrous consequences for the FLN and the threat these results constituted were not lost on either

Hassan II, Ben Ali, or the Algerian ruling elite. Indeed, the military coup in January 1992 spotlighted the self-preservation instincts among the country's leaders.

But such outright intervention is not always necessary. In Tunisia the RCD has systematically preempted politics by incorporating opposition programs (and even its leaders) into governmental platforms, in effect reducing the political arena to one that pits the dominant party against a still unrecognized Islamic party. The hoped-for unity among political contenders after the signing of the National Pact in November 1988 did not materialize. It represented Ben Ali's attempt to reach some form of national consensus on a more formal basis but through limited consultation, as he put it, "to define a common denominator and a minimum of principles on which all Tunisians can agree and that can be adopted as a basis for political action and development " (Ben Ali 1988b). As one former labor leader who had led several of the country's syndicalist battles with the government shrewdly remarked, the National Pact represented an agreement "no one would have signed a few months ago, and no one will sign a few months from now" (Achour 1989).

Events in both Algeria and Tunisia suggest that each country's attempt at its own *perestroika* remained fragile and uncoordinated. The most worrisome development was that virtually all secular opposition had been incapacitated, leaving Benjedid and Ben Ali in a precarious struggle against an Islamicist movement that was growing rapidly and that was at the same time imbued with a symbolic value both the FLN and the RCD have lost. As the Algerian coup indicates, it also left both leaders dependent on political elites who often perceived security as more important than any real reform—a development that had sparked considerable earlier speculation about the retention or potential for military influence in the politics of each country (Zartman 1987b; Ware 1985). Only in Morocco has the social and economic elite shown a sustained ability successfully to merge both security and reform concerns.

The difficulties in revitalizing the FLN in the wake of the June 1990 elections and the RCD in Tunisia reopened the question of their usefulness in helping to reconstruct the state. In each country suggestions were made to create an alternate "presidential party" that would limit a further polarization between the FLN and the Front Islamique du Salut or the RCD and the Mouvement de la Tendance Islamique (MTI). In Tunisia, Serge Adda (1989) has suggested, this new party could fall "within the dynamics of the presidential program and . . . with the alliance of the Destour but independent, will be the guarantor of the values held by civil society and by the defenders of public liberties and human rights." Only in Morocco, where extreme polarization has not taken place, has the king skillfully managed to stay above this kind of fray.

In stepping back from its traditional etatism, the state in the Maghrib has been offered two choices: to hand down authority to lower levels or to hand decisionmaking over to nonofficial actors. It is clear that in all countries some form of subterfuge—outright subversion in Algeria—has taken place: In its own way each government has tried the former option and ignored the latter, except for economic purposes. It is hard to avoid the perception that in the Maghrib an attempt has been made to reshape economic policies that would allow each country to meet some of the expectations of the new international economic context without upsetting local political arrangements. There has been a growing concern with economic rationality, stimulated by international economic considerations, and a simultaneous attempt to ignore local political rationality—or at least an attempt to disconnect the two. It is this Machiavellian strategy of fusing authoritarian liberalism and the attempt to reap the rewards of a new wave of development without any of its unpleasant side effects that Clifford Geertz (1989:238) has called "the rise of a combination of a Smithean idea of how to get rich with a Hobbesian idea of how to govern."

It is not surprising, then, that a heavy dose of *dirigisme* remains and that every move toward economic and political liberalization has been difficult and has more often than not been matched by a retrenchment of liberties in other areas or by an increase in bureaucratic control. Indeed, during the phase of Algeria's *infitah* that lasted until the October 1988 riots, it remained unclear whether its slow pace and restrictive scope concerning reform of the public sector was not simply an attempt by the state to postpone meaningful reform but an attempt to impose a new division of economic tasks that shifted the burden of efficiency toward nonstate actors yet left the state ultimately in charge. To that extent, it resembled what C. H. Moore (1986:637) has noted elsewhere:

> Changing patterns of allocation rather than ownership may produce the kind of political economies that will give an exhausted statist regime a new lease on life. Instead of managing economic exchanges directly, such a regime may manage them indirectly, while still continuing in principle to own the means of production. Supporting client groups then becomes less exensive because some of the costs are farmed out.

Similarly, the political liberalization the Maghribi rulers now routinely refer to has also been matched by a substantial recentralization of power. In Tunisia, Bourguiba had always been an ardent supporter of centralization but because of his deteriorating health had been forced to give up part of his prerogatives. If Tunisians had not been quite accustomed to this diffuse character of power, they had long observed its dilution in practice. The new government, led by a strong and motivated leader, almost spontaneously started to halt this dispersal. In Algeria, too, the creation of a strong presidency, with close and personal links to Politburo and Security Council members, had centralized power to a high degree. In each country ministers implement what has been decided elsewhere. In light of Tunisia's political culture and recent political history, this development risks compounding the difficulty in separating centralization from personal power, as amply demonstrated by the increasingly expressed charge that "Ben Alisme" has replaced "Bourguibisme."

In all Maghribi countries this recentralization of power has paradoxically also been linked in part to greater reliance on international capital needed for local development. Relatively small groups of decisionmakers become allocative agents, using the power of the purse to pursue certain economic and political goals. As a rentier economy, the Libyan *jamahiriya* represents the most extreme example of this recentralization (or, perhaps more accurately, continued centralization). In Morocco the impact of foreign capital has been more subtle but perhaps as far-reaching. Particularly after the 1981 and 1984 riots, the maintenance of political order has become more dependent on international capital, which can buy food, than upon the traditional power of the rural notables. In all cases this new power has been justified by the wish to reconstruct a state needed to confront the socioeconomic challenges ahead, a barely veiled restating of the earlier strategy that has been shown to be severely flawed.

It is obvious, however, that neither the *infitah* strategy nor the institutional restructuring nor the timid attempt at political pluralism will suffice to allow the state to recapture the loss of energy and confidence it has suffered. Political reforms, at least initially and often for long periods of time, remain an elite occupation; the needed economic reforms, in contrast, are popular preoccupations. And here the states in the Maghrib face a paradox: Each is able, if perhaps not always willing, to move forward much more rapidly with political reforms than with the improvement of the living conditions of most of its people. It is at this precise point that the economist's lag between the implementation and tangible results of economic policy becomes the politician's nightmare. For no state in North Africa seems likely to succeed in reconstructing itself without rebuilding one of the two pillars that once sustained its fortunes: providing patronage and maintaining at least part of its social contract.

In the Maghrib this will undoubtedly prove very difficult, partly for the economic reasons specified above. Furthermore, in the past tensions over the maintenance of the social contract were tempered by the implicit consensus provided by the other pillar: the strong symbolic bond between the state and its subjects. In Tunisia and Algeria and to a lesser extent in Morocco and Libya, this link has been irrevocably altered. The state in the years ahead will have less room to maneuver, with fewer resources at its disposal and with a greater degree of cynicism or outright contestation than it has ever encountered since independence.

Symbolic Politics and Cultural Renewal

Writing about the importance of myths in the maintenance of a political community, William McNeill (1982:1) has noted that "A people without a full quiver of relevant agreed-upon statements, accepted in advance through education or less formalized acculturation, soon finds itself in deep trouble, for, in the absence of believable myths, coherent public action becomes very difficult to improvise or sustain." The contestation in the Maghrib in recent years has amply demonstrated the difficulties the state currently faces in maintaining its claim to be the sole legitimate representative of each country's political community. There has always been a strong symbolic aspect to politics in North Africa: The struggle for independence in Algeria and Tunisia and the "revolution" in Libya after 1969 laid the cornerstone of a legitimacy that was heightened by the presence of charismatic leaders like Bourguiba and Qadhafi or channeled toward the more impersonal mechanism of the single party in Algeria. The reason for the persistence of the one-party system in Algeria and Tunisia (and of Qadhafi's politically unique configuration of popular committees and popular congresses) was that they could solve problems—deliver the goods—and were simultaneously charged with the highly symbolic value of nationalism, often expressed in a virulently anti-West language in the case of the *jamahiriya*. All countries have used some sort of symbolic management—myths, ceremonies, and special language—to maintain, renew, or reinforce the legitimacy of the state. Even today this subtle management continues: The Parti Socialiste Destourien in Tunisia was renamed the Rassemblement Constitutionnel Démocratique shortly after Bourguiba's removal—"assembly" rather than a single party in an attempt to project the RCD as a broad-based political organization, and "democratic" to bolster Ben Ali's claims of pluralism.

Only in Morocco, where the legitimacy of the Alawi dynasty was fostered for four centuries, has the symbolism surrounding the king transcended this link to independence or to a specific Moroccan nationalism; it explains in part why the monarchy has been able to avoid some of the contestation engendered in other countries by the loss of confidence in those individuals or parties who claimed to symbolize the link to independence. Jean-François Clément (1989) aptly summarized the multidimensional mixture of symbolic and pragmatic politics of the Moroccan monarchy:

> The king today is at the center . . . of a [number of] concentric [circles]. He is the chief of the small clan of Alawites. He directs those families [the *makhzen*] that have longstanding ties with the reigning family. . . . Then, dressed in white with a red fez he is the "shadow of God" on earth. But if he appears in suit and tie, he is the head . . . of the modern State bequeathed to Morocco by Napoleon via Lyautey. It is often said that this modern state, composed of technocrats,

runs the matters [of the kingdom] while the Makhzen manages its people through the controls of matrimonial exchanges . . . and through the distribution of wealth.

But in the other Maghribi countries, too, the manipulation of the symbolic link between ruler and ruled has been at issue, and the state's representatives as well as those contesting the state now brandish the powerful symbols of national identity and legitimacy. The concept of a cultural renewal and of the extension of public liberties has invaded or, perhaps more accurately, been readopted into the political vocabulary by each side after a hiatus of almost three decades. Although some of the calls for this renewal have been expressed in secular terms—former Algerian president Ben Bella's offer to return to Algeria and profoundly reshape Algeria because he is "a revolutionary"; Hocine Ait Ahmed's call for Kabyle cultural rejuvenation; Qadhafi's call, at the twentieth anniversary celebration of his coming to power (September 1, 1989), for *tawsi^c al-thawra* (broadening of the revolution); Ben Ali's concept of a New Era after November 7, 1987—all clearly carry a religious undertone.

If a single, common element marked the 1989 and 1990 elections in Algeria and Tunisia, it was the claim by virtually all parties that they represented the protectors of Islam in their societies. Tunisia's Ben Ali pointedly visited a number of Arab countries and went on the *umrah* (the lesser pilgrimage to Mecca) before embarking on a tour of Western countries after he came to power. The June 1990 local and municipal elections in Algeria, however, indicated that voters were not persuaded by the FLN's religious pretensions: The Islamicists won overwhelmingly.

These claims to a certain religious status are certainly not new, but a number of factors have made their reappearance important at this time. It was significant that in their pursuit of national development, several Maghribi leaders (particularly Bourguiba, who publicly drank orange juice during the fast of Ramadan and closed the Zeitouna theological school) were more aggressive toward their country's cultural symbols than even the colonial power had been, a point often stressed by the Islamicists. Islamicism in the Maghrib, as elsewhere, represents an enduring opposition to the form, and content, of the type of nationalism earlier used by the state. But the symbols now invoked by Abdessalem Yacine in Morocco, Rashid Ghannouchi in Tunisia, Abassi al-Madani in Algeria, and underground Islamicists in Libya—solidarity, equity, Arabization—are those a first generation of Maghribi rulers skillfully manipulated in their own search for legitimacy and national unity.

There is, however, a substantial difference in modus operandi between the governments in power and the Islamicists: In Morocco, Algeria, and Tunisia the state continues at least to pay lip service to the Western notion of popular sovereignty as a guarantee for responsible government, whereas the Islamicists, with their insistence on the immutability of religious law and the notion of divine right, do not.

It is obvious that the link to independence invoked by the governments in power—a unique occurrence whose symbolic value may never again be matched—has now lost much of its appeal. Significantly, most of the recent attacks against the state and those who claimed to represent it in North Africa were initiated by a younger generation who do not share the historical memories or the ideological references that had been at the heart of the bond between their elders and the state. In every country the decline of the state's fortunes has been felt most acutely among the young, particularly among university students. The infighting at the educational institutions has often been described as an ideological struggle between Islamicists and leftists. Indeed, all Maghribi governments have at one point deliberately fostered that image and have attempted to use one group against the other. The real struggle at the universities, however, is ultimately over a volatile mixture of symbolic and real power: In each country the educational system has emerged as the primary system of social stratification.

Throughout the Maghrib there is the potential for an important intergenerational change and for a new *dawla* in the sense Ibn Khaldun assigned to the word: the emergence of a new state no longer based on the values that provided political cohesion until now but marked by the search—still largely inchoate and hotly disputed—for a new consensus on what its precise role should be. But in trying to create this new consensus, promote a younger generation, and develop a new role for its institutions, the state in the Maghrib now faces formidable obstacles and opponents. Beside the subterfuges noted above, in essence the use of state institutions and the manipulation of electoral rules to postpone meaningful political reform, it now also inherits the legacy of its earlier strategies: the growth of an Islamic movement that has in part proliferated because of the growing bifurcation between impotent opposition parties and state-controlled political parties.

In Morocco the king has skillfully manipulated the issue of the Western Sahara to maintain legitimacy; in the countryside the three words that symbolize the unity of the country and the legitimacy of the regime—God, king, country—remain omnipresent and continue to represent a strong symbolic link. In Libya the confrontation with the West has provided the Qadhafi regime with an indispensable source of legitimacy that is constantly renewed by successive waves of popular mobilization. But the charismatic qualities of the leader are slowly being downgraded as routine and bureaucratization take their inevitable toll, and the lack of institutionalization of the political system does not augur well for rebuilding consensus once Qadhafi leaves the political arena. In Algeria and Tunisia, the declining fortunes of the FLN and the RCD have laid bare the apparent inability of the single party that for so long defended the status quo to adapt to a changing environment without losing its identity and coherence. The 1988 October riots in Algeria starkly brought into view the problems of the FLN and contributed even further to a stretching of the symbolic bond that was severed completely with the 1992 coup.

Finally, it is perhaps not surprising that with the relative loss of the state's legitimacy and the diffusion of its symbolism, the focus of both those in power and those in opposition has fractionalized at the substate level, raising questions of ethnicity, and at the supranational level, where Islam and the call for a Greater Maghribi union are meant to reassert each country's position within a larger Maghribi cultural and religious community.

Conclusion

Thirty years after independence, North African societies have been irrevocably altered. High urbanization rates, limited educational opportunities, the decline of local political systems, and disillusionment with local economies all have contributed to this profound change. In each country the contours of society have been transformed—but they have not been redrawn as political leaders originally envisioned. In the progress the changing structure of each society has also altered the capabilities each state possessed at independence. Decline and reconstruction of the state in North Africa have gone hand in hand: They are two sides of the same coin.

The retreat from its earlier social and economic management and the attempt to reduce the costs of government have led to a number of paradoxes with which the state must now deal. Economic reconstruction can only be achieved if the logic of the social contract each country subscribed to (an admittedly often minimalist cradle-to-grave welfare system) is abandoned. To break this logic, however, will involve drastic measures that will unavoidably lead to difficulties among all levels of a society that—for an entire generation at least—has known the state as a provider. Only Libya until now has been cushioned, though not immune, from this clash between the previous generation's dreams and economic expectations and the current reality. But when that inevitable moment arrives in the *jamahiriya*, the results will undoubtedly be traumatic: a political system with a low level of institutionalization, little sense of statehood and of the rights and duties of ruler and ruled, and little legitimacy beyond the charismatic leader will almost certainly be subject to long-term contestation.

In the other Maghribi countries, this turning around of the old logic also involves a paradox: If less will be demanded of the state, it will have no choice in the short run but to assume greater power to guarantee that this process can take place in a nonconfrontational fashion. The dilemma is well summed up in the words of one observer:

> If you accept the idea of less government, you are talking neither about less discipline nor less power. It probably takes greater discipline and greater power for government to step out of the market than to become more intimately involved. . . . to allow the market to function is something that governments do not want to do. If they try to do it, their own constituents will stop them, so it is not a matter of giving up power. It is a matter of taking on more power in a way, but with the object of ultimately giving it up. (Roemer 1989:88)

Except in Algeria, it is not certain whether the state in the Maghrib can amass greater power to bring about change under the current climate of lingering contestation or whether each country's political elites would not simply solidify their positions if the state is successful in doing so. Only a clear spelling out of the rules of the game could prevent this. In Algeria and Tunisia on at least two crucial occasions—the succession after Boumedienne and the takeover from Bourguiba—the rules were both sufficiently clear and precisely followed. Yet they broke down in Algeria in January 1992.

If Algeria is a harbinger of things to come, in the end it may well be the political imperative of stability, often stability for stability's sake, that will determine which way Maghribi elites will move. And the side-by-side appearance of repression and concessions in Tunisia, Morocco, and Libya may well be matched by an attempt to contain the politically disturbing consequences of development while emphasizing its welfare-creating effects. No one can deny that following the disenchantment that has manifested itself since the mid-1970s with regard to the political direction and the economic realities, the Maghribi states tried to redefine the rules of power and to create new links with societies that have become (in part because of earlier state intervention) more differentiated, more complex, and more demanding. In the 1980s the Maghribi states have tried somewhat to enlarge the basis of popular consultation and to allow a more equitable representation of social forces in each country—thus the themes of decentralization, responsible democracy, and greater self-reliance at the local level, all concepts that are now part of the political landscape.

Despite the richly varied contests and different speeds in which political adjustment to the ensuing crises took place or was postponed across the region in the 1980s, a single basic economic question surrounding the role of the state now sustains both the ongoing debate and the contestation it engenders as liberalization and privatization proceed: Who should pay for the state's extraction of resources in the dramatically different economic context and how should these resources now be distributed? Any number of different groups of course strongly disagree on these issues and have politicized the struggle for social control.

Maghribi governments are now scrambling to at least suggest new political arrangements to meet the challenge. First among the reasons for this move are the objective conditions that have saddled each country with a high potential for popular unrest against the state: growing social inequalities; large groups of unemployed urban poor who often have no prospects but mounting poverty and lifelong unemployment; restive and increasingly vocal labor unions and Islamicist movements; regional economic and cultural disparities; and continuing high migration toward the cities. In addition, reslicing a shrinking pie is difficult; in essence the government has to renegotiate part of its social contract with the local population. Moreover, the political reforms accompanying the economic reforms remain in essence an elite preoccupation.

The structural reforms each country except Libya has now embarked upon will not have a real impact on the people for some time. The economic reforms, however, have a much more immediate effect. The rapid increase in the numbers of those who have no stake in their country's growth or future—a group Adda (1987:404) has called "the second country," marginalized by each nation's *développement à deux vitesses* (two-track economic development)—poses a severe threat to whatever political and economic experiments are attempted. This growing group has little to gain or lose by what is decided between the state and the opposing forces in society. If, as David Marquand (1981: 2) observes, "the undistorted market automatically rewards those who have the wit and the will to adjust, while punishing those who lack them," then a substantial part of the North African poor will at least in the short run remain dependent on the shrinking provisions of the social contract. Events in Algeria have given ample evidence that this group of *mustadhafin* (disinherited) forms a ready source of recruitment for what is now a powerful group inside Maghribi society: the Islamicists. Although their solutions may not necessarily provide a better alternative, they offer, to use Sayyid Qutb's (1964) term, signposts to those bewildered by the world around them.

3

Political Parties

Clement Henry Moore

A party is a durable, differentiated organization seeking popular support for the conquest or direct exercise of power (Charlot 1985:432). Because the party may already be in power, it need not be autonomous. It may simply mobilize support for the incumbent rulers. On this reading the Algerian Front of National Liberation qualifies as a party, as does Tunisia's ruling Rassemblement Démocratique Constitutionnel, the eventual successor of the Neo-Destour. Apart from these and some Moroccan entities, however, few North African parties have had time to develop durable, differentiated structures, much less to empower people. Thirteen of them were founded in Tunisia after 1987, and some fifty-eight have legally surfaced in Algeria since 1989, but their very novelty makes it difficult to determine how many really qualify as parties rather than as transient groups of personalities.

However numerous the entities that may meet formal definitions of a political party, the old ones seem to have lost much of their credibility throughout North Africa, whereas the new ones have yet to be tested. Authoritarian barriers to entry have certainly not yet broken down in Morocco, where the industry of manufacturing political parties is the most mature. Tunisia remains a dominant one-party system: Unable to form joint electoral lists to protect sympathetic minority parties, the RCD submerged the opposition in the parliamentary elections of April 1989. In Algeria, by contrast, the FLN was obliged to relinquish its theoretical monopoly over political life in the wake of massive rioting in October 1988, and then this official governing party was deflated, perhaps beyond repair, in the municipal and provincial elections of June 12, 1990. It ran a miserable third place in the first round of the parliamentary elections on December 26, 1991. The military then halted the elections.

The poles of "state" and "society" were too twisted together for political parties to acquire any autonomy or real staying power as intermediaries between state and society anywhere in the region. Of course there were differences: in Algeria and Tunisia, postcolonial bureaucracies encapsulated their respective societies, whereas the king privatized the state and retraditionalized society in Morocco (Camau 1979:405–406). But whether the state assimilated society or a few families took over the state, the parties could neither aggregate nor represent the interests of various segments of any of these societies. Although differentiated on paper and more or less durably organized, they lost credibility. For lack of autonomy, they could not meet a limited functional definition of recruiting political leaders and mobilizing support from distinctive segments of society. Instead, they occupied imaginary political spaces, the fusion of state and society preventing any real political activity. The real intermediaries operating in North Africa's constricted interstices between state and society seemed to be patron-client networks.

Clientelism took different shapes, however, depending upon whether society was being socialized or the state privatized. Deep and durable vertical networks of patrons, clients, and clients of clients were perfectly compatible with the Moroccan *makhzen*'s project of privatization, whereas egalitarian Algeria and modernizing Tunisia rejected such assymetrical relationships but could not eliminate shallow, fragile combines of dyads held together by patronage. Deep and durable networks, in turn, buttressed multipartism, whereas shallow and fragile ones kept one-party systems unitary. Today, though, North Africa is in the midst of an economic crisis that is changing the parameters of patronage in all three political economies in ways that may separate state and society, opening up new political spaces. Consequently, political parties again merit study, more than a generation since they concluded their respective struggles for independence.

In this chapter I focus on relationships of political parties to changing patterns of patronage. I reexamine the hypothesis raised in the conclusion of the chapter on political parties in *State and Society in Independent North Africa* (Moore 1966:39):

> The Moroccan political arena, displaying diversity as well as unity, may provide the stage for a new Maghrebi political culture to develop. Given the realities of power and participation in all three executive-dominated systems, politics remains a spectacle for most North Africans. But if parties become one-way transmission belts for those in power, they will lose touch with the people and thus lose their political relevance. New attitudes toward power and new styles of participation are needed that a multi-party system may be better able to provide, if parties are to remain a significant factor in North Africa.

The first question concerns the impact of Morocco's multiparty system: Did its underlying royal patronage networks encourage new styles of participation? Second, how may the readjustment of Morocco's political economy affect patronage and party competition? Third, how relevant to emergent multipartism in Tunisia is the Moroccan experience, and, can Algeria, beset with greater economic pressures for change, selectively assimilate its neighbors' political experimentation?

Morocco

In the short run, royal patronage certainly reinforced multipartism in Morocco. By reestablishing the French protectorate's ties with rural notables (Leveau 1985), the monarchy gained counterweights to their Istiqlal party rivals. In 1958 the Popular Movement (MP) was already undermining the Istiqlal's claim to single-party hegemony, and the split within the party the following year effectively confirmed a multiparty system. For the following two decades, however, the *makhzen* and the National Bloc (Al-Kutla al-Watani), consisting of the Istiqlal and its derivative parties, articulated conflicting definitions of legitimate authority. Beholden to the parties he had dismissed in 1965, once his military support turned against him in 1971 and again in 1972, King Hassan finally weaned the Istiqlal away from the *kutla* into power on his terms in 1977. He consummated his victory in 1979 by obliging the legal parliamentary opposition—the most significant remnants of the *kutla*—to wear the traditional *djalaba* (Claisse 1987:44), in other words to join the political arena on his terms. It was then just another little step in 1984 for the Socialist Union of Popular Forces (USFP) to become a party like the others at election time, partaking of a ritual quota system (Sehimi 1985: 27, 39). Has royal patronage thus in the end corrupted the multiparty system beyond redemption?

Over the years, beginning in 1958, the monarchy decimated the parties by playing one off against the other and by co-opting individuals within key parties, enticing them to break with party discipline. Patronage networks usually cut across and blurred distinctions between the government and the opposition parties. Thus defection from a party could also be viewed as the party's promoting of its leaders, individually, to power. The major casualties of the system were principled leaders like Mehdi Ben Barka and Omar Benjelloun, who rejected royal patronage, and some of the hundreds of repressed opposition party, trade union, or student militants who did not survive to reap the benefits of royal amnesties and return to the royal stables in the late 1970s. But note that political imprisonment was also a form of empowerment: It rendered tame, "complementary" oppositions (Zartman 1988a) credible to their constituents—for a time (Moore 1970:190).

A look at electoral returns, however, suggests that time may be running out for the parties. Table 3.1 presents the results of the parliamentary elections of 1963, 1977, and 1984, the three relatively free competitive national elections. Less interesting than the partisan totals, which were subject to administrative

TABLE 3.1 Moroccan Parliamentary Elections

	1963			1977			1984		
	Votes	Seats	% Votes/ % Seats	Votes	Seats	% Votes/ % Seats	Votes	Seats	% Votes/ % Seats
Governmental									
FDIC	1,132,595	69	0.70						
RNI				2,254,297	141	0.84	763,396	61	0.86
PND							396,371	24	1.14
UC							1,101,502	83	0.91
National Opposition									
Istiqlal	998,478	41	1.04	1,091,000	49	1.17	681,083	43	1.09
USFP	753,800	28	1.15	738,541	16	2.42	550,291	39	0.97
PPS				116,470	1	6.09	102,314	2	3.52
MP				625,786	44	0.74	695,021	47	1.02
MPDC				102,358	3	1.79	69,862		
OADP							32,766	1	2.26
Other	485,910	6	3.46	116,951	10	0.61	50,398	6	
Null ballots	123,846			324,068			556,642		
Totals	3,494,629	144	1.00	5,369,471	264	1.00	4,999,646	306	1.00
Estimated population	12,700,000			18,000,000			21,400,000		
Potential electorate	5,588,000			7,920,000			9,416,000		
Registered voters	4,784,949			6,519,301			7,416,846		
Voting as % registered	73.0			82.4			67.4		
Valid as % registered	70.4			77.4			59.9		
Valid as % eligible	60.3			63.7			47.2		

Sources: Octave Marais, "L'Election de la chambre des représentants au Maroc," *Annuaire de l'Afrique du Nord, 1963* (Paris: CNRS, 1965), p. 104; Mustapha Sehimi, "Les Elections legislatives au Maroc," *Maghreb-Machrek* 107 (1985):27.

manipulation, are the proportions of the total potential electorate that actually voted in each election. Participation sharply declined, reaching U.S. norms—quite low by the standards of most competitive democracies—in 1984. If the electoral campaign of 1984, postponed after massive food riots in January, was timed to pass quietly around a lengthy religious holiday, it is still surprising that the USFP could mobilize no more than 2,000 to attend a political rally of its leader in his hometown, the Istiqlal leader faring even worse in his (Sehimi 1985:32). One seasoned observer wondered whether the USFP would be able to contain Islamicist tides, were the king to submit to genuine constitutional government (Leveau 1985:273).

By 1984 the regime was deliberately supporting the parties by barring independent candidates, thereby reversing its classic strategy of encouraging independent local notables to compete with parties. The king insisted that it would henceforth be "anticonstitutional" (on a creative reading of Article 3 of the constitution of 1972) for a candidate without a party label to run for Parliament (Sehimi 1986:63). The new constitutional interpretation seemed designed to "prevent Islamist candidates, to avoid the camouflaging of 'progressive' candidates behind 'neutral' labels, to prevent a scission in the Popular Movement, and, finally, to oblige tens of cadres . . . to rejoin the Constitutional Union," the principal government party (Sehimi 1985:33). It enabled royal clients better to control the selection of government party candidates, perhaps thereby reinforcing the cohesion of the parliamentary majority.

Majority voting in single-member constituencies—often gerrymandered so as to inject supervised rural populaces into urban districts—ensured comfortable majorities for the government parties in the 1977 and 1984 elections. As a further precaution, one-third of Parliament was indirectly elected. In 1984 the results of these elections, coming three weeks after the direct ones, "modulated" the outcomes not so much to favor the government parties as to restore a sort of balance between the Istiqlal and the USFP. Excluded from the informal cartel that had organized the direct elections, the Istiqlal had fared poorly, winning only 11.6 percent of the seats for 14.4 percent of the vote, compared to the USFP's 17 percent of the seats for only 12.5 percent of the vote (Sehimi 1986:80). But "in a manner unhoped for" the Istiqlal gained nineteen seats to the USFP's four in the indirect elections (Sehimi 1986:116). Table 3.1 (final column) indicates that the USFP still had needed fewer votes for its ultimate allotment of seats than the Istiqlal, but the differences had been evened out. Only the Mouvement Populaire, Démocratique, et Constitutionnel (MPDC), a breakaway from the Popular Movement, the Communist Parti du Progrès et du Socialisme (PPS), and the Organisation d'Action Démocratique et Populaire (OADP) seemed seriously underrepresented in Parliament, if the share of seats was supposed to reflect the share of votes. In Morocco's three parliamentary elections, the allocations had generally tended to favor the government parties (columns 4, 7, 10), but no more so in 1984 than in previous years.

Morocco's advanced electoral technology—offered for export to Iran before the shah's downfall (Eickelman 1987:93)—elicited so much cynicism and apathy among Moroccan political elites and masses, however, that it is not so clear in the long run that King Hassan really was, as Paul Balta put it, the principal victor in 1984 (Sehimi 1985:47). If even the opposition candidates were "mal élu" (badly elected), did not the election simply discredit the democratic process the king was trying use (Leveau 1985:253)? Elections had become virtually meaningless once "the number of seats allotted to each party [was] established confidentially in accordance with a 'quota' system" (Claisse 1987:45) or an "implicit political pact" (Leveau 1985:252) rigged with alternating opposition parties—the Istiqlal in 1977, the USFP in 1984. A semblance of competition occurred in only 51 of Morocco's 199 constituencies in 1984 (Sehimi 1985:39).

The opposition parties were aging, perhaps more than the government (Zartman 1982:25), in their thinking as well as their leadership. One sign of the Istiqlal's debility was its response to defeat in the Taza by-elections of 1978: "The citizens who chased away the colonialists and fought the feudalists cannot vote for any other than the Istiqlal candidate" (Rousset 1979: 210). Thirty years after independence, few voters can remember the anticolonial epic. The USFP has perhaps stayed more closely in touch with younger generations, but the regime has also encouraged new formations in order to counter party corrosion. Thus a splinter of Frontists, unconditional Marxist-Leninist opponents of the monarchy in the 1960s, was recognized as a political party, the OADP, in 1983 and awarded a seat in 1984 for rallying to the regime's Sahara policy (Sehimi 1986:106). But the regime's major efforts have focused on building governmental parties.

Although the Rassemblement National des Indépendants (RNI) originated in 1978 as an assemblage of deputies elected as independents, it gradually acquired a partisan identity. Headed by the prime minister, the king's brother-in-law, former classmate, and close friend, it first served merely to mobilize majorities in Parliament. Once the prime minister was changed, it suffered a split in 1981 as agricultural interests broke away to get seats in a new government. As his majesty's loyal opposition, the RNI formed a shadow government and projected a centrist liberal image. Though little more than a political club, it fared respectably in the 1984 elections. With sixty-one deputies (a net loss of twenty-two), it did much better than its offshoot, Parti Nationale Démocrate (PND), which won only twenty-four, for a net loss of thirty-three. But the big government winner was an even newer party, the Union Constitutionnelle (UC).

Also organized from above, by an incumbent prime minister, the UC was intended to be a real party of cadres with an independent organization capable of competing in the cities with the Istiqlal and the USFP, with which its founder had been associated. "A new cadre is to be created and organized," declared the founder at the UC's inaugural congress in 1983 (Sehimi 1986: 102). Indeed, he assembled some 10,000 higher civil servants, professionals, teachers, and private-sector managers—roughly one-fifth of these "middle" strata by one count (Saaf 1987:140–141). Preparations for the big event had been under way since 1980. Class alumni lists had been collected for mailing the invitations. As if by magic, the UC became Morocco's leading vote-getter, polling a plurality in communal elections only two months after its founding. Like the RNI, it then went into an opposition of sorts when a new prime minister relieved its founder for the 1984 elections. Making an "appeal for renewal," the UC again won the most votes, polling over one-fourth of the total. It has made itself the principal advocate of economic deregulation, privatization, and regional decentralization. Its middle-class constituents, like the opposition parties', presumably resent the royal patronage networks that had facilitated multiparty politics in the first place and now opened the way for the UC. The party might indeed become the cutting edge of a new system.

For behind the scenes significant economic changes may be affecting the patronage networks. The problem may be not so much the multiplicity of new generations of potential actors whom clients of clients cannot quite absorb (Leveau 1985:266–267) as the diminishing resources needed to fuel the networks (Leveau 1987). Deep and durable networks require alienable riches as well as intimidation to keep clients in line. Patronage indeed is perfected: A veritable treasure of crown jewels, it runs deepest and is most centralized in Morocco because the monarchy shepherded the resources left by departing colonists more strategically than the Algerians or Tunisians. Two-thirds of the colonial lands, for instance, were distributed surreptitiously to the king and his followers rather than politically wasted in state farms or sales on the open market (Leveau 1985:247). French commerce and industry was barely touched until 1973, when Moroccanization could serve a useful political purpose. Senior administrators could then be shuffled off to the private sector, opening the way to government promotions for a new generation of king's men (Leveau 1985:255). But once production is in native hands, there is little left to redistribute. Dramatic rises in world phosphate prices kept the party going a while longer, but their collapse, coupled with unsupportable increases in international debt, broke it up in 1978.

Either cheaper forms of patronage had to be discovered or the system changed. The king has tried a bit of both. Support for small and medium enterprises, for instance, satisfies foreign lenders insisting upon export-oriented growth yet rebuilding clienteles to offset "legitimacy deficits" (Doumou 1987:212). The UC favors political restructuring as well as economic liberalism—to consolidate "democracy." Meanwhile, since 1983 Morocco has undertaken a series of economic workouts with the IMF that diminish the government's margin for economic maneuver. Freezes on government employment, tariff reductions and freer trade, the elimination of most price controls and some state trading monopolies, and various other measures of economic liberalization required by either the IMF or the World Bank have tended to undercut traditional sources of patronage that rely on selective implementations of government regulations. The international agencies have in effect devalued the treasure of crown jewels.

As much on the supply as on the demand side, then, the royal patronage networks may be in trouble. Yet the king, an astute political actor, acts as if he wishes to give some of his jewels away. His official application to join the European Community, for instance, opens up Moroccan economic decisionmaking to European as well as international pressures for deregulation (Leveau 1987). Some speculation about royal intentions may be in order because patronage and selective co-optations have always driven the party system.

The *makhzen*'s purchase in 1980 of Omnium Nord-Africain (ONA) may have signaled a major change of political strategy. This holding company is Morocco's most powerful conglomerate and the one best positioned to compete in liberated internal markets. With gross revenues amounting to 4.7 percent of Morocco's gross domestic product (GDP), new potentials for patronage seemed enormous. In 1987 ONA added Morocco's top performing bank to the portfolio of banks under its direct control or influence, which now totaled some 15 percent of the commercial banks' total assets, including at least one-third of the private sector's. Significantly, too, the first thrust of "privatization" was the sale of a government sugar refinery to ONA. Perhaps the *makhzen* is now in position to repeat the political achievements of the 1973 Moroccanization campaign.

If privatization becomes a political strategy, the *makhzen* will have elegantly adapted to the new international pressures placed on the Moroccan economy. The trouble is that the political arm and beneficiary of such a strategy, the UC, seems even less capable than the hard-pressed USFP to contain the resulting pressures from the Left and from the Islamic radicals. Yet it is already at work: The new party is using Islam to motivate young, educated cadres (Eickelman 1987:94). King Hassan, politically much better equipped to neutralize Islamic appeals than Anwar Sadat had been (Leveau 1981a), may escape the latter's fate. And by disengaging the state from the economy, he may not only develop new clienteles but lighten their political burdens. In fact a more genuine practice of constitutionalism could be in keeping with the new strategy. The electoral law, which promotes bipartism under normal conditions (Charlot 1985:501, 511), might then even give rise to alternating UC and USFP/Istiqlal governments.

Tunisia

The fine art of royal patronage could not be exercised in Tunisia. It was viewed not only as corrupt but archaic and, most conclusively, as superfluous for a triumphant Tunisian nationalist elite that already controlled a well-honed party of cadres at independence and easily eliminated the traditional Tunisian monarchy sixteen months thereafter. Demystified in a world of petty cadres and bureaucrats, patron-client networks were consequently fragile, shallow, and furtive. They posed little resistance to an increasingly monolithic single-party system revolving around Bourguiba. The president's lieutenants, to be sure, controlled administrative satrapies, but Bourguiba was skilled in shifting people from their power bases and encouraging their divisions so as to sustain his personal power. In this respect presidential rule resembled that of the Moroccan monarchy, but with one important difference: Patronage networks depended more heavily upon volatile second-order resources of influence and power than upon tangible assets. Volatile "clans" (cf. Roberts 1983) within the party-state could not be functional equivalents of parties.

In fact personal alliances, the stuff of Moroccan politics, were constantly manipulated in Tunisia so as to neutralize political infrastructure. The tone was set as early as 1956, when a presidential courtier engineered a scission within the labor movement. For the rest of his career, the complaisant labor ally would face similar challenges from other clans, cutting across union lines, sapping the autonomy of Tunisia's potential second party (Achour 1989). Despite a more eminent anticolonial legacy, indeed, the Union Générale Tunisienne du Travail (UGTT) fell into greater disarray by the late 1980s than did its Moroccan counterpart, the Union Marocaine du Travail, which since 1963 had been restricted to purely trade union activities contested by other unions backed by rival political parties.

Once Bourguiba broke with a state socialist model of development in 1969, the one-party system faced a crucial transition. Development no longer justified the party monolith, and forces within the party favored institutionalizing political competition within it. Instead of bowing to possible constraints on his personal power, however, Bourguiba eliminated the liberals and reinforced the party's fusion of state and society. The logic of personal power, now legitimated by appeal to tradition rather than by an instrumental socialist discourse, continued to decimate potential countervailing centers of power. Whereas Hassan had checked parties by building up competitors, Bourguiba manipulated clans so as to prevent factions from organizing. As few as two or three allies among his top lieutenants could constitute a threat; typically half of them would then have to be disgraced, removed to less strategic offices, or set at odds with one another. Thus Hedi Baccouche, for instance, was promoted from the directorship of the party in 1987 to a technical ministry, but it was already too late to destroy the power center he shared with Interior Minister Ben Ali. They seized power on November 7, 1987, shortly after Bourguiba had designated Ben Ali to be his prime minister and heir apparent.

Having exercised a minimum of coercion in removing Tunisia's president-for-life, the new leaders claimed to act within the framework of the constitution and stood for continuity as well as for democratic reforms. But how credible could the reforms be if political continuity was to be preserved? The major problem was the party system. Could the Destourian Socialist party (PSD) be reformed, or should it be scrapped in favor of November 7 clubs, which surfaced in support of Ben Ali just after his coup? What would be the role of opposition parties?

Bourguiba had just barely tolerated certain opposition parties toward the end of his career. The first one he recognized, in 1981, was the Tunisian Communist party (PCT) rather than a more popular, mainstream party that had broken away from his own Destourian Socialist party: the Mouvement des Démocrates Socialistes (MDS). Constituted from a nucleus of the ruling party's leaders who had advocated institutionalized intraparty competition in the early 1970s, the MDS seemed to be the most credible competitor. In 1983 Prime Minister Mohammed Mzali finally gained Bourguiba's official, if grudging, seal of approval for this party, founded in 1978. The Parti de l'Unité Populaire (PUP), a party of state socialists, was also recognized, but the MUP, which enjoyed better credentials to represent this current, was not. Thus until Bourguiba's enforced retirement, there were three official opposition parties, together with a Tunisian League of Human Rights (founded in 1977) that also advocated institutionalized restraints on the regime's increasingly arbitrary power.

These parties, especially the MDS, were thoroughly tamed. When their newspapers were not being seized or censored, they faced financial difficulties. For instance, state enterprises were prevented from advertising in the opposition press, and private businesses, too, preferred not to risk administrative harassment. The MDS leader regretted that the Moroccan system of newspaper subsidies, liberal public advertising, and various other subventions to political formations was not practiced in Tunisia. But worst of all were the electoral practices.

The authorities prevented the parties from doing any serious organization outside major towns, but the MDS enjoyed substantial support in Tunis at the very least. Though not then legally recognized, it was permitted to compete in the 1981 elections. Bourguiba, however, countermanded the political opening he had initiated only months earlier by ordering a total government party victory; the rigging was pursued so energetically that the MDS list received only 1,700 votes in Tunis (Mzali 1987:28). In 1986 the MDS boycotted the parliamentary elections when the authorities excluded its popular general secretary, Ahmed Mestiri, from running. It was still necessary to stuff the ballot boxes to make it appear that Tunisians had turned out massively to perform their civic duty.

Once Ben Ali effected his constitutional coup, he promised further political reform. Though most of the opposition parties, including the MDS, boycotted partial elections held in early 1988, they supported the new president and awaited reforms that would ensure proper guarantees for future partisan competition. In April Bourguiba's old Parliament passed a law on political parties that guaranteed a multiparty system and met most of the specifications of the MDS. It did not altogether satisfy the opposition, however, because the provision interdicting parties based on "religion, language, race, or region" apparently excluded the Mouvement de la Tendance Islamique (MTI) from any hopes of official recognition. MTI leaders remained in contact with President Ben Ali, however, and one of its representatives was included in the consultations leading, on the first anniversary of Ben Ali's presidency, to his promulgation of a national pact. On this date Ben Ali stole the opposition's thunder by announcing general elections for April 1989, in which a total of seven recognized parties would compete. Eventually reconstituted as the Nahda, the Islamicists were not recognized as a party, but they were allowed to compete in the elections on lists of independents. The major problem facing Tunisia's new leaders, however, was not the relatively docile opposition but rather what to do with what had once been the ruling Destourian Socialist party. Housed since the early 1980s in huge central offices that symbolically overlooked the government's headquarters in the Casbah, would the party retain its trappings of power?

To signify rupture with past practices, the Central Committee changed the name of the venerable party to the Rassemblement Constitutionnel Démocratique (RCD). As if to minimize its role in decisionmaking, Ben Ali reshuffled his government before rather than after the extraordinary congress held in July 1988. During the transition, however, the party remained as top-heavy as in Bourguiba's vintage years of personal power. The extraordinary congress did not materially affect the president's power to name the Central Committee, an innovation Bourguiba had established in 1986 to subdue clans and potential factions. Ben Ali appointed 122 of its 200 members, and the elections were so well organized that a delegate claimed "they should have allotted at least twenty places to delegates to raise interest in the debates" (Mezoughi 1988:6).

Evidently the complexities of transfusing new blood into the party's leadership had required tactics hardly in keeping with internal party democracy. Preparations for the party congress had included free elections throughout the party's vast apparatus, resulted in a 62 percent turnover at the local level and 70 to 80 percent at higher levels. The local cells, in turn, had elected some

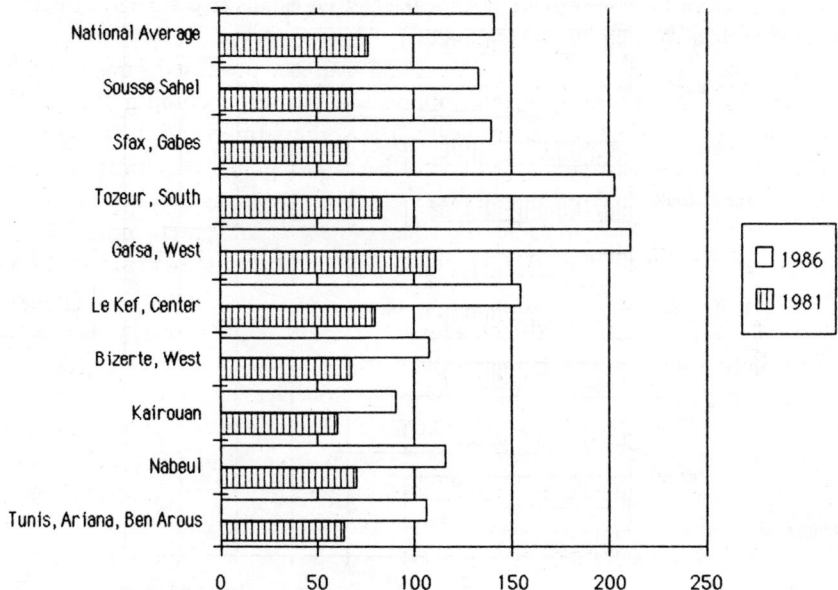

FIGURE 3.1 Tunisia: PSD members per thousand inhabitants (*Source:* Clement Henry Moore, "La Tunisie après vingt ans de crise de succession," *Maghreb-Machrek* 120 [April 1988]:17–18, using data provided by the PSD)

new blood to serve as their delegates to the party congress. But balancing the new with the old on the Central Committee could not be left to the party congress.

If press reports were correct, this already massive apparatus—1,025,084 strong at the end of 1986 (Moore 1988:17)—had increased its membership by 50 percent to total 1,502,291 "militants" by July 1988 (Mezoughi 1988). In other words half the adult population, and in all likelihood a majority of adult males, belonged. Professionals and intellectuals, university professors, and even students had flocked to the RCD after years of political apathy and isolation outside the tradition-bound PSD. The densities of party cells and membership by governorate presented in Figures 3.1 and 3.2 are consequently understated. Tunis probably continued to have fewer members and cells per capita than most other governorates, but the movement to the party after November 7 may have affected the capital more than the provinces. The important point to note, however, is that the number of party cells was not keeping up with the flood of new members. Totaling 5,248 across the country and overseas in 1988, the cells had increased by only 19 percent since 1986. Rapid growth obviously compounded the party's problem of defining itself.

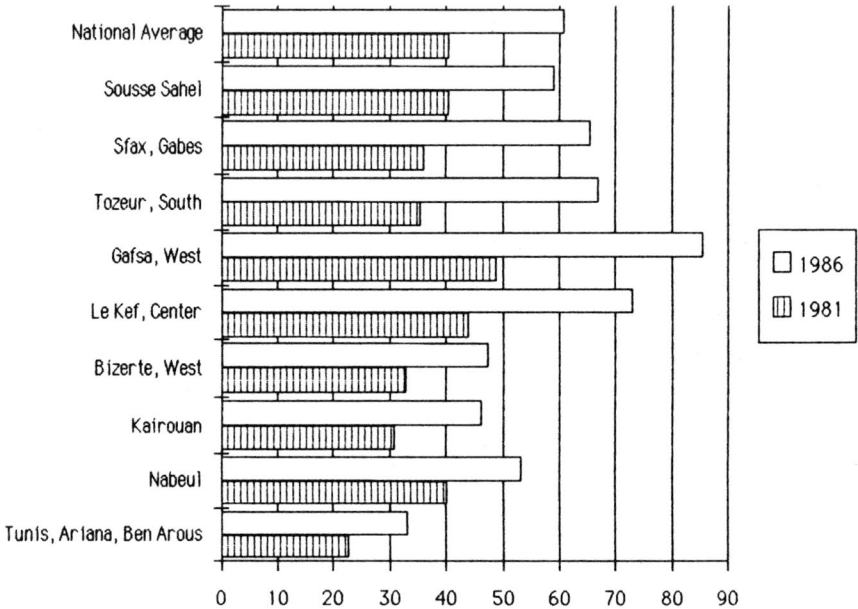

FIGURE 3.2 Tunisia: PSD cells per hundred thousand inhabitants (*Source:* Clement Henry Moore, "La Tunisie après vingt ans de crise de succession," *Maghreb-Machrek* 120 [April 1988]:17–18, using data provided by the PSD)

By including everybody, the party represented nothing in particular—even the name, Destour, connoting its historical memories, only barely survived (as an Arabic adjective meaning "constitutional").

The parliamentary elections of April 2, 1989, underlined both the strengths and weaknesses of the refurbished party. Under the controversial electoral law, the RCD demonstrated its strength by taking all the seats, but the party rank and file did not necessarily support the party-government's candidates. Symptomatically, when Mestiri, leader of the opposition MDS, toured the region of Nabeul in early 1989, many party cell leaders cheered him on. Like that in Tunis, Nabeul's party apparatus had shown relative weakness before 1987 (see Figures 3.1 and 3.2). Not only Mestiri but virtually all the opposition party leaders had once been members of the PSD, and the new members of the RCD could gravitate at least as easily to those politicians who had broken with Bourguiba's cult as to those who had stayed on, often compromising themselves. The party in the end swept the polls, winning absolute majorities in all of the governorates, and took all the seats—with some help from a zealous administration, which would prompt Mestiri, for instance, to quit politics altogether. But the legally recognized opposition parties were weakly organized. Voting participation, the percentage of valid votes to the eligible electorate, sank to a nationwide average of 51 percent, almost as low as the depths reached by Morocco in the 1984 elections. Table 3.2, comparing voting participation in the three North African countries, reveals steady Tunisian declines after 1979. Voting registration was substantially lower than in Morocco, suggesting that Tunisia's vaunted party-administration might still (as Mestiri and others complained) be discriminating against potential opposition voters.

Figure 3.3 reveals the geographic contours of the strongest opposition force, the lists of independent Islamicist candidates who ran in all but four governorates (Jendouba, Mahdia, Siliana, and Zaghouan) and won up to 29 percent of the vote in Tunis and its environs and in the south. In total, the opposition parties gained 37 percent of the vote in Tunis and 41 percent in the southern governorate of Tozeur, whereas the governing party fared best in the periphery, mobilizing up to 67 percent of the theoretically eligible electorate (and 95 percent of the actual vote) in Jendouba. In fact the percentages of those voting for the RCD in each governorate, virtually the mirror image of the Islamicist vote, are inversely correlated with the governorate's degree of urbanization ($r=-.80$, $p<.0001$), defined as the percentage of the population living in legally defined "urban communes" (Guen 1988:235), and with regional location, a dummy variable distinguishing the governorates of Gabes, Gafsa, Kebili, Mednine, Tataouine, and Tozeur from the rest ($r=-.37$, $p<.08$). The linear regression of the RCD vote on urbanization and southern location, shown in Table 3.3, explain 68 percent of the variation in RCD voting. Both independent variables are significant at the .03 level or better, and, as indicated by the beta coefficient, a 1 percent increase in a governorate's urbanization would decrease a governorate's vote for the RCD by $-.395$ percent according to the model.

Of course this model of voting behavior is incompletely specified; it leaves out politics, notably Mestiri's allegation that voting registration discriminated against the government's opponents. From demographic data, however, it was possible to devise the variable *Registration* indicating the percentage of people of voting age who were registered to vote in each governorate. It bore only a very weak relationship to the RCD vote ($r=-.16$, $p<.46$), albeit in the direction that Mestiri would have expected. Voter turnout, measuring the percentage of registered voters actually voting, could also be construed as a "political" variable, possibly indicating some administrative mobilization of the registered voters, and it was in fact quite strongly correlated with RCD voting ($r=.80$, $p<.0001$). But would these relationships hold up when analyzed in conjunction with the effects of geography?

A linear regression of the RCD vote on urbanization, southern location, voter turnout, and voter registration, shown in Table 3.4, indeed presents a better explanation of the vote for the RCD than does Table 3.3. All of the in-

TABLE 3.2 Participation in North African Legislative Elections

	1963	1977	1979	1981	1982	1984	1986	1987	1989
Morocco									
Estimated population	12,700,000	18,000,000				21,400,000			
Potential electorate	5,588,000	7,920,000				9,416,000			
Registered voters	4,784,949	6,519,301				7,416,846			
Total voters	3,494,629	5,369,471				4,999,646			
Null ballots	123,846	324,068				556,642			
Registered as % eligible	85.6	82.3				78.8			
Voting as % registered	73.0	82.4				67.4			
Valid as % registered	70.4	77.4				59.9			
Valid as % eligible	60.3	63.7				47.2			
Algeria									
Estimated population		18,200,000			19,954,000			22,972,000	
Population over 19, 17 years[a]		7,826,000			8,966,000			9,939,880	
Registered voters		7,709,000			8,990,800			11,155,000	
Total voters		6,037,500			6,054,700			9,889,100	
Registered as % eligible		98.5			100.3			101.5	
Voting as % registered		78.3			67.3			87.3	
Voting as % eligible		77.1			67.5			88.7	
Tunisia									
Estimated population			5,930,000	6,554,000			7,465,000		7,805,000
Population over 19 years			3,042,090	3,362,202			3,829,545		4,004,000
Registered voters			2,008,628	2,311,031			2,622,488		2,711,925
Total voters			1,621,975	1,962,127			2,175,093		2,073,719
Null ballots			61,322	20,269			10,036		31,836
Registered as % eligible			66.0	68.7			68.5		67.7
Voting as % registered			80.8	84.9			82.9		76.5
Valid as % registered			77.7	84.0			82.6		75.3
Valid as % eligible			51.3	57.8			56.5		51.0

[a] Assuming that the minimum voting age was reduced after 1982 from 20 to 18.

Sources: Michel Camau et al., *Contrôle politique et régulations électorales en Tunisie* (Aix-en-Provence: CRESM, 1981), pp. 213, 251; *Le Renouveau* (Tunis), April 4, 1989.

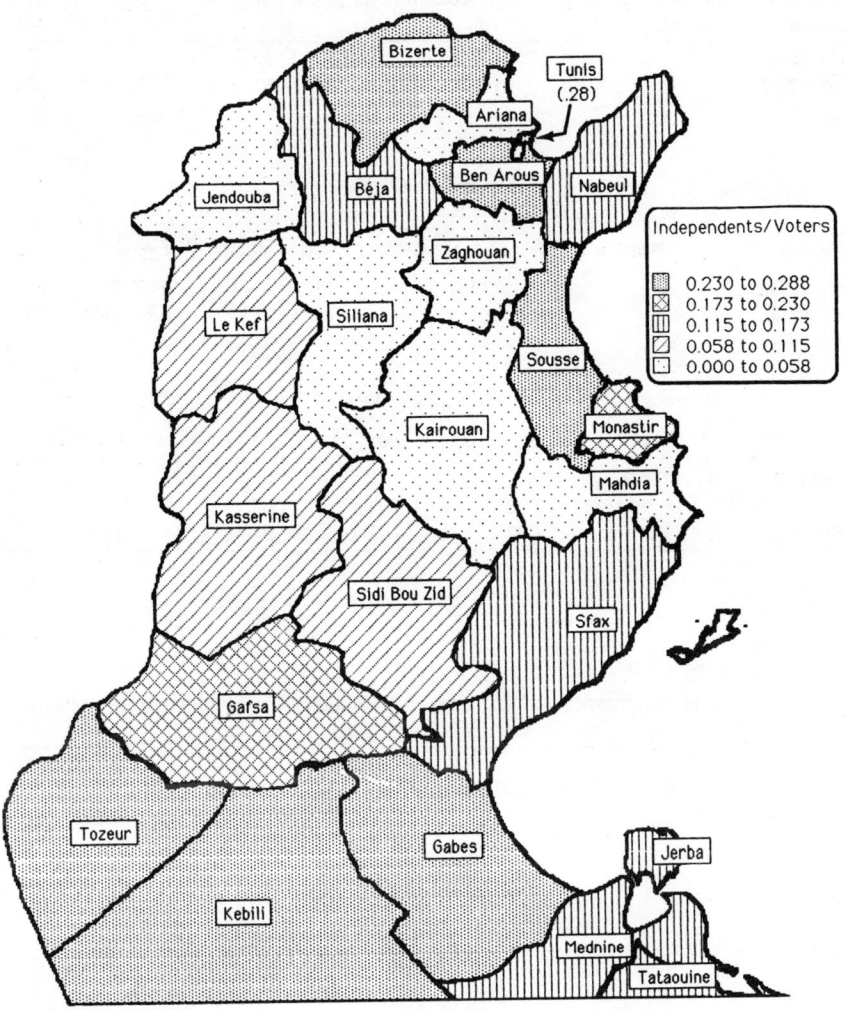

FIGURE 3.3 Tunisia: Independent (Islamicist) voters by governorate, 1989 (*Source:* Tunisian Interior Ministry)

dependent variables are significant at the .07 level or better, and turnout is shown to have been crucial for the RCD: an increased turnout of 1 percent of the registered voters gave rise in this model to an additional .667 percent of the vote for the RCD. In this more completely specified model, moreover, Mestiri's theory of voter registration gains real credence. In cutting back the registration of eligible voters by 1 percent, the party-government apparatus could increase its share of the vote by .294 percent. The fewer the people of

TABLE 3.3 Linear Regression of RCD Vote in 1989 Legislative Elections on Urbanization and Southern Location

Degrees of Freedom	R	R-squared	Adj. R-squared	Std. Error
22	.844	.712	.683	.068

Analysis of Variance

Source	Degrees of Freedom	Sum Squares	Mean Square	F-test
Regression	2	.232	.116	24.742
Residual	20	.094	.005	p = .0001
Total	22	.326		

Beta Coefficients

Parameter	Value	Std. Error	Std. Value	t-Value	Probability
Intercept	.993				
Urbanization	−.395	.063	−.762	6.31	.0001
South	−.077	.033	−.284	2.348	.0293

TABLE 3.4 Linear Regression of RCD Vote in 1989 Legislative Elections on Urbanization, Southern Location, Voter Turnout, and Voter Registration

Degrees of Freedom	R	R-squared	Adj. R-squared	Std. Error
22	.894	.799	.754	.06

Analysis of Variance

Source	Degrees of Freedom	Sum Squares	Mean Square	F-test
Regression	4	.26	.065	17.837
Residual	18	.066	.004	p = .0001
Total	22	.326		

Beta Coefficients

Parameter	Value	Std. Error	Std. Value	t-Value	Probability
Intercept	.586				
Urbanization	−.204	.1	−.393	2.049	.0554
South	−.072	.029	−.264	2.458	.0244
Turnout	.667	.291	.444	2.289	.0344
Registration	−.294	.15	−.212	1.964	.0651

TABLE 3.5 Linear Regression of Voter Turnout on Urbanization and PSD General and Professional Membership Density

Degrees of Freedom	R	R-squared	Adj. R-squared	Std. Error
22	.884	.781	.746	.041

Analysis of Variance

Source	Degrees of Freedom	Sum Squares	Mean Square	F-test
Regression	3	.113	.038	22.566
Residual	19	.032	.002	p = .0001
Total	22	.144		

Beta Coefficients

Parameter	Value	Std. Error	Std. Value	t-Value	Probability
Intercept	1.005				
PSD members	−.654	.244	−.331	2.681	.0148
Prof members	−2.157	1.275	−.296	1.691	.1072
Urbanization	−.256	.058	−.74	4.393	.0003

voting age who were registered, the better the governing party did, when the effects of the other variables, notably urbanization, are taken into account. A comparison of the beta coefficients in Tables 3.3 and 3.4 shows that the political variables diminished the adverse effects of urbanization (but not of southern location) upon the party's vote.

The turnout of the registered voters appears to have been the key to RCD success. Turnout was significantly lower in Tunisia's more urbanized governorates than in the more rural ones ($r=-.83$, $p<.0001$). Presumably the more critical, urbane Tunisians were less likely to bother to vote—or the government could more efficiently herd the rural folk to the polls. Because data on the old PSD apparatus are available, it is interesting to see whether its legacy helped or hindered the successor party to mobilize the vote in 1989. Despite the flood of new members, the RCD inherited the PSD's administrative infrastructure. It had developed a substantial cadre of general members, grouped into cells by their place of residence, and also a cadre of professional members organized in cells at their place of work. During the final Bourguiba years, Baccouche had placed special stress on the professional cells to confront the rising challenges to party hegemony in urban Tunisia. To see whether these efforts had paid off, voting turnout was regressed on urbanization together with the proportions of general PSD members and professional cell members in each governorate. The results, shown in Table 3.5, suggest that the efforts had been counterproductive. PSD general membership significantly ($p<.02$) diminished turnout after the adverse effects of urbanization were taken into account, and professional cell membership, though displaying less statistically significant effects ($p<.11$), also pulled in the "wrong" direction. A 1 percent increase in professional cell membership decreased voter turnout by over 2 percent, according to the model. In short, the RCD seems to have inherited a party apparatus that is most effective in mobilizing the country's uncontested backwaters. In the cities and in the south, it may already have lost the political initiative to the Islamicist opposition.

In the long run, however, Tunisia's direction of political change would depend as much upon the government's economic policies and strategies as on its electoral tactics and treatment of the various opposition groups. During the political transition, the parties were so preoccupied with issues of national identity and new rules of the political game that the economic policies decided in 1986 remained in force. Ben Ali implicitly confirmed them by including their architect, who had already been named governor of the Tunisian Central Bank, just before Bourguiba's retirement, on the seven-man Political Bureau of the RCD. As in Morocco, these policies of economic and financial liberalization are likely to have an impact, through patronage, upon the emerging multiparty system.

In Tunisia clientele networks have remained shallow and fragile, reflecting the primacy of fluid political influence, but policies favoring the development of the private sector may give them new roots. Unlike Morocco's, Tunisia's networks will be decentralized, for the monarchy's private sector cannot be emulated. A multiplicity of parties may benefit by representing new business interests. The RCD has already pointed the way, raising money for its special congress and subsequently for its electoral campaign chest from businesspeople and bankers. Were the party fully to separate itself from the state administration, as its reformers advocate, it would need an annual 3 million dinars ($3.75 million) to make up for the transfer from the presidency's state budget, plus salaries, presumably, for an army of bureaucrats detached from state service. If, as some participants in the party's economic commissions suspect, the RCD is unable to meet the minimal policy needs of a new generation of Tunisian businesspeople, they may secede and found a new party or support one of the existing opposition parties. However, the law on political parties does not address the issue of political funding. Market forces are likely to threaten political as well as economic oligopolies. The result could be a real two-party (RCD versus business) or multiparty system, the contours of which have yet to be outlined. Or, following the Algerian example, the RCD could break up and the Nahda could become a leading element in a multiparty system. In May and again in September 1991, however, the Tunisian authorities claimed to discover a plot to overthrow the government and assassinate senior officials, including the president. They arrested thousands of Nahda activists in the course of the year, and "there were increased numbers of credible reports of torture and brutal treatment of detainees, particularly Islamists"

(U.S. Department of State 1992:1616). The Islamicist party remained illegal, and the military and police supports of Ben Ali's regime became more visible, tarnishing the image of the Arab world's last civilian republic.

Algeria

The Algerian one-party system also underwent a metamorphosis in 1988: The October riots would cost the ruling National Liberation Front (FLN) its official monopoly, so that by 1991 some fifty-eight parties were officially recognized. Theoretically a vanguard socialist party, the FLN had become a rearguard in disarray, decisively defeated in municipal and provincial elections in June 1990 yet trying to stave off urgently needed economic reforms.

Unlike the inclusive Tunisian Destour, the FLN had consisted until 1988 of some 200,000 "militants," no more than 1 percent of the population. To become a member, one had to be "competent," a person of "integrity," and "committed" to the party's ideology, but because the ideology of Algerian socialism admitted a variety of Islamic, Marxian, and other interpretations, the principal condition for membership was sponsorship by other members. Sociologically, the FLN resembled a political club more than a Leninist party; politically, however, it was supposed to exercise a Leninist hegemony over state and society. Deprived of the substance of power, it achieved its full trappings in 1984 by occupying the government "palace" dominating downtown Algiers. This huge modern structure had once housed the top French colonial authorities and then sheltered independent Algeria's central government. Ernest Gellner (1981:149–173) once compared the party bureaucrats to medieval religious scholars, the ulama, whose political task had been to legitimate the janissaries, or military and administrative elites, in precolonial times. Manipulated by the power holders, the FLN rarely enjoyed any autonomy in independent Algeria.

The paradox of a theoretically omnipotent yet "phantom" party had plagued Algerian politics from the start (Écrement 1986:293, n. 53; Bennoune 1988:303). Unlike the Neo-Destour before independence, the FLN never developed autonomous structures. Finally, in 1978, Boumedienne achieved a vanguard of sorts to institutionalize his revolution, but he fell ill and died before a party congress could consecrate its autonomy. It was not the party but the army that determined his succession, and President Benjedid then decimated the FLN leadership in efforts to consolidate himself (Zartman 1984; Roberts 1984).

Still, in the early 1980s there was some truth to the observation that "Algeria today is governed by a complex network of interactive structures that provide institutional stability, direction, and predictability to the political system" (Entelis 1986:168). The FLN bureaucracy had nominated candidates for elections to communal, state (*vilayet*), and national legislative bodies with impressive regularity since 1967. It also elected a president in 1976, 1979, and 1984. The FLN provided more spice to Algerian elections than had the PSD to Tunisian elections. In 1977 the Algerian party nominated three candidates for each position in the Popular National Assembly. The Tunisians then emulated the Algerians by offering two candidates for each seat in their parliamentary elections of 1979. In 1982 the Algerians went a step further, permitting some independent candidates to run for office; as a result, the FLN elected only 197 out of 281 deputies, and the experience was not repeated in the 1987 elections.

Table 3.2 demonstrates the party's efficiency in managing Algeria's voting rites. Turnouts as a proportion of eligible voting age populations are compared with Moroccan and Tunisian voting participation. Except for slightly hard times in 1982, the FLN regularly mobilized from 15 percent to 40 percent more of its potential electorate to vote in elections to their national legislature than the Tunisians or Moroccans could do for theirs. The party in Algeria made sure (more reliably than the census?) that virtually everyone was registered, whereas a quarter or more of the eligible Moroccans and Tunisians stayed or were kept away. Table 3.2 shows that Algerian registration never fell below 98 percent of the potential electorate. By contrast, registration gently but consistently diminished in Morocco, and Tunisian rates were at least 10 percent lower.

Vanguard or rearguard, the Algerian party commanded a certain political edge by virtue of its exclusive character. It was not ideologically homogeneous; indeed, ideology was displaced in Algeria by concrete achievements like ironworks and steelworks (El Kenz 1987:28, 53) and other "industrializing industries," the failure of which would signify a legitimacy crisis. The FLN nevertheless articulated vested interests more explicitly than its more broadly based Tunisian counterpart dared. Confronted with Benjedid's reforms, the FLN fought back, whereas the Tunisian party had opened up as if to envelop Ben Ali.

By 1988 the Algerian party was barely holding onto its monopoly with the support of a narrow and shrinking base. It was still strong enough to have significant influence over economic policy, but the influence really pointed more to its weakness than any strength, because it was exercised through informal personal alliances with high state officials, including military officers, whose prebends were being threatened by efforts to restructure the public sector (Soudan 1988a:38). After years of state socialism, the party was perceived as little more than a blanket for covering the mistakes of government officials (Soudan 1988b:30), and being a member no more than carrying a party card (El Kenz 1987:358)—even though rank-and-file membership carried few privileges (Leca and Vatin 1979:77).

Until the mid-1980s, the one-party system had circumvented opposition by doling out jobs and services—special development programs to disinherited regions and the like—because the *état providence* (welfare state) enjoyed reasonable oil revenues and good international credit ratings. Algeria would therefore be politically as well as economically more vulnerable to the oil recession of the mid-1980s than were its neighbors, yet it preferred to cut food and other consumer imports rather than to reschedule crushing debt-reservicing payments. The party militants also distrusted foreign private investment, and their delegates to the People's National Assembly waged rearguard campaigns against government efforts to encourage it. There was one semiofficial opposition party, the Parti de l'Avant-Garde Socialiste (PAGS), an offshoot of the Algerian Communist party (PCA), which had been officially dissolved in 1966. Former PAGS militants allied with others in the FLN and the Union Générale des Travailleurs Algériens (UGTA) to oppose Benjedid's restructuring of the public sector. Other potential political oppositions were not permitted to organize and consequently turned to violence, emulating the patriots who had launched Algeria's war of independence. Radical Islamic reformers were the most recent example. Though weaker and less articulate than their Tunisian counterparts, some of them had been incorporated into the FLN, but others were pushed almost by accident, victims of their fragmentation, into armed struggle that ended with the gunning down of their leader in 1987 (Burgat 1988a). Some "Berberists" had earlier met a similar fate for aspiring to cultural (not political) autonomy.

Apparently, elements of the FLN, encouraged by PAGS, were preparing in 1988 to withdraw support for Benjedid in the coming presidential elections. When the president lashed back in his speech of September 17, 1988, the party counterattacked, but mass rioting on October 4 preempted the general strike called by its trade union ally for October 5. The resulting slaughter of hundreds of people enabled Benjedid, ironically, to purge the party and keep the support of the army. Supplemented by unusually large army reinforcements—one-third rather than the usual one-fifth of the delegates—an emergency FLN congress ratified Benjedid's leadership but still prevaricated on some of the proposed reforms. Finally, on February 23, 1989, the Algerian constitution was decisively amended: References to socialism and to the traditional principle of single-party hegemony were eliminated, and a law permitting alternative political parties was duly promulgated on July 5 (Djeghloul 1990:200–205). The FLN was even removed from its palatial headquarters, to which some of the central government returned.

Within a few months, more than twenty "parties" materialized. A few of them, like PAGS and the FFS, had a real history inside Algeria, but most of them were brand new, creating an alphabet soup of acronyms. Most did not have the advantage of association with prominent personalities, yet before they could organize nationally, they were faced with provincial and municipal elections on June 12, 1990.

The Front Islamique de Salut (FIS) astonished most Algerians as well as the rest of the world by capturing 54:3 percent of the vote and 853 (55.4 percent) of Algeria's 1,541 townships. The FLN ran a lackluster campaign and came in a poor second, with 28.1 percent of the vote and 31.6 percent of the townships; like the Tunisian government party, it did best in the peripheries. The other principal victors of the elections were various independents; the other parties fared poorly. Only the Kabyle-based RCD received enough support to gain a significant number of townships—eighty-seven, with 2.1 percent of the vote—whereas the Parti National pour la Solidarité et le Développement (PNSD), the PSD, and the Parti du Renouveau Algérien (PRA) each picked up two townships with from 0.8 to 1.6 percent of the vote. The Front des Forces Socialistes (FFS) and the Mouvement pour la Démocratie en Algérie (MDA) kept the prestige of their respective leaders intact by boycotting the elections, whereas Benyoussef Benkhedda's Umma party had not yet taken shape. The other parties sufficiently organized to field some lists of candidates fared miserably at the polls.

It was by no means evident, however, that Algeria was evolving into a two-party system. FIS had been quick to benefit from the genuinely neutral administration of the elections, from the other parties' greater degree of disorganization, from relatively low voter turnout, and from widespread resentment against FLN corruption—reflected in the way public opinion took at face value a former prime minister's speculation that government officials had pocketed $26 billion—the entire foreign debt—in commissions from foreign contractors over the previous decade (*Middle East Economic Digest* [*MEED*] 34, 14 [April 13, 1990]: 19). But FIS was not well organized. Only two years earlier, France's closest academic observer of Islamicist movements in North Africa had quite correctly written that the Algerian movement was "one of the least developed and structured [and hence among] the least known" (Burgat 1988b:143). His book barely mentioned the new FIS leader, Abassi al-Madani, an obscure Algiers University lecturer who had spent over a decade in London to obtain a Ph.D. in education. Al-Madani emerged in 1982 to co-author a petition calling for more Arabization, the banning of alcohol, and a conservative personal-status law in response to student rioting and police repression. A jail sentence increased his status, and he was swept into the political leadership vacuum in October 1988. Together with a younger, more radical high school teacher and imam, Ali Belhadj, he founded FIS on March 10, 1989. FIS then benefited from access to most of Algeria's mosques and financial support from small merchants as well as from Saudi Arabia. No other party could command such resources, but the front's advantages were modest: There had not been sufficient time to develop as strong an organization as the Tunisian Nahda's, even if the Algerian Islamicists *appeared* stronger at elections.

Though the front's call for a general strike in June 1991 failed, it persuaded President Benjedid to postpone the legislative elections and redress inequities in the electoral law, which overrepresented rural and southern regions of the country thought to be more supportive of the FLN. When the elections were finally held on December 26, FIS won 188 seats outright and threatened on the second round of the elections to win a two-thirds majority in the 430-seat Popular National Assembly—enough to impose constitutional amendments. Fearing the specter of an Islamic republic of Algeria, the army moved on Algiers, inducing Benjedid to resign on January 11, 1992, before the second round could be held. The senior officers then called Mohammed Boudiaf out of exile to head a five-man Higher Council of State. They hoped that Boudiaf, who had founded the FLN in 1954, could legitimate the new regime. A state of emergency was proclaimed, and the Ministry of Interior admitted to arresting 6,786 people in January and February (*MEED* 36, 14 [April 10, 1992]: 10).

Algeria's strongest party was now banned. In the elections it had won twice as many votes as the next most powerful party, the FLN, and more than six times as many as Ait Ahmed's FFS, which had broken out of its Kabyle strongholds to get some support throughout the country. FIS had clearly outmaneuvered the other parties. Its suppression further discredited the FLN, so that it may still be "only a matter of time before the FLN dissolves or breaks up into smaller parties" (Kapil 1990:35). The FLN timidly echoed Ait Ahmed's strong protest against interrupting electoral processes. Algeria's emerging party system was in a state of shock.

Algeria's political economy was also undergoing change. As in Tunisia, patronage networks remain shallow and fragile, decentralized in the hands of a fragmented political-economic-military elite. But Algerian networks differed from Tunisian ones in at least two respects. Regional cleavages, also a factor in Tunisian politics, seemed more pronounced in Algeria, and they could help stabilize clans and networks. Private property, which also helps to stabilize relations between patrons and clients, was less developed in Algeria than in Tunisia, where state socialism was stopped in 1969. But the small private sector that survived the Boumedienne era achieved greater recognition and legitimacy under Benjedid (Leca and Grimaud 1986) and could begin to play a public political role in the immediate future. Article 25 of the 1989 law on political associations permits personal donations of up to 200,000 dinars ($25,000 at the official exchange rate, or $7,000 at the market rate), though they are not to exceed 20 percent of the revenues coming from membership dues (Djeghloul 1990:203). Private resources are becoming available. A massive privatization of Algerian agriculture has been under way since 1986, generating further potential political bases and resources. Foreign direct investment, encouraged as part of the reform process toward a more market-oriented economy, is already resulting in significant joint ventures, including one with an Islamic bank. The FIS economic program supported the market-oriented reforms as well as Islamic banking.

Conclusion

The political party systems of North Africa are undergoing major changes in at least two of the three countries. And even in Morocco, where the continuity since the early years of independence seems greatest, economic restructuring may exercise a profound impact upon the party system.

Pressured by their international debt obligations, the states are disengaging from direct administrative supervision of large parts of their respective economies. New economic policies are in turn altering the parameters of patronage. The centralized Moroccan system of patronage is under pressure. Market discipline may reinforce the monarchy by favoring the royal holding company, but patronage is apt to become less centralized when exercised through market power than directly through the state administration. More economic competition, foisted on Morocco by international authorities and donors as well as by indigenous capitalists, may also reinvigorate political parties and make them less dependent on royal governmental largesse.

The same economic dynamic is also at work in Tunisia, with greater potential to restructure politics. Whether in banking or other strategic economic sectors, the Tunisian private sector is less developed but more competitive than, by definition, are Morocco's established oligopolies. Patronage networks are much more decentralized—indeed fragmented and illegitimate—because not even Bourguiba, much less Ben Ali, could play the "great patron" role of the Moroccan commander of the faithful. Tunisia's legal parties are skeletons awaiting a living flesh of economic interests—as Tunisia's only real historical potential opposition party, the UGTT, had anticipated in the 1960s when it acquired hotels, cooperatives, and even a bank. Currently, the skeleton parties all seem to favor proportional representation and guaranteed state subsidies, but they have avoided raising economic issues. Privately financed business and labor parties might yet emerge to articulate basic Tunisian cleavages in a multiparty system still dominated outside the major cities by a strong RCD.

As of mid-1992, however, Tunisia remained basically a single-party system, structurally little changed since Bourguiba's retirement. Unlike the FLN, the RCD still occupied its sumptuous party headquarters rather than handing it over to the government. In a curious burst of energy Algeria had outraced Tunisia toward an effective multiparty politics. The irony is only too evident when it is recalled that the director of the FLN, who lost his job because of the October riots, had as late as July 1988 been urging Tunisians to slow down their progress toward multipartism, for fear it would infect Algerian politics and "lead us all to catastrophe" (Mahroug 1988). Yet Algeria energetically pressed both political and economic reform, the government being tacitly supported, in effect, by the market-oriented Islamicist forces. But then Algeria's crackdown on its Islamicist movement in 1992 relieved Tunisian fears of too much democracy next door and gave a seal of neighborly approval to Tunisia's crackdown the previous year. Each regime still eventually had to reach compromises with its respective oppositions or else retreat into its bunkers and give up any pretence of democratic legitimacy.

The hypothesis raised two decades ago still awaits confirmation. Morocco's experience to date has demonstrated that multiparty systems are no less prone to losing their constituencies than one-party systems. Moreover, it is still not clear whether either Algeria or Tunisia, were they to develop more credible multiparty systems, would be able to facilitate political intermediation any more effectively than their respective one-party systems had. Emerging interest groups in both countries—autonomous enterprises, private-sector businesspeople, private farmers, and certain categories of workers—might prefer to develop alternative parties, but they are untested. The RCD could conceivably retain its de facto monopoly in Tunisia, just as in Algeria, too, a new consolidation of power could eliminate contending parties. Any fair test of the hypothesis about the adaptability to economic changes of one-party versus multiparty systems must await further political experimentation. If the experiments are allowed to continue, the parties may recover some of the political relevance lost after the early years of independence.

PART TWO

Society and Economics

4

Alienation of Urban Youth

Mark Tessler

A generation ago, in the years immediately following independence, the young people of North Africa were seen as the solution to many of the region's most pressing problems; now there does not appear to be any solution on the horizon, and young people are often regarded as a major source of the difficulties confronting the Maghribi countries.

The Unrest of the 1980s

Morocco, Algeria, Tunisia, and Libya have all experienced serious unrest in recent years, and young people in all four countries have been at the center of these disturbances. In June 1981, for example, tensions associated with economic and political grievances exploded in the form of violent riots in Casablanca. The immediate cause of the disturbances was a reduction in food subsidies, which the government enacted in response to pressure from foreign creditors, but the scope and intensity of the rioting revealed the depth of public anger, and Casablanca's youth played a leading role in giving this anger violent expression. Thousands of young men from the city's sprawling slums poured into the streets and fought police and military support units for control in some areas, as roaming mobs attacked banks, auto dealerships, and other businesses as well as public buildings identified with elite privilege or government authority. In subduing the rioters, police sometimes fired into the crowd, and in the end at least 200 youthful protesters were killed. Some estimates place the number much higher.

Making it clear that the Casablanca disturbances were not an aberration was the rioting that broke out in Tunisia and Morocco in early 1984. The unrest in both countries reflected discontent among many sectors of society and involved adults as well as young people. Nevertheless, as in Casablanca in 1981, young people played a leading role in articulating generalized complaints and translating them into violent protest. Rioting took place in many parts of Tunisia and Morocco in January 1984, and disturbances lasted for a week or more, leaving each country badly shaken when order was finally restored.

Rioting in Tunisia actually began at the end of 1983, with the government's December 29 announcement of a rise in the price of semolina serving as catalyst. Pent-up frustration, the result of intensifying economic and social problems, initially triggered protests and demonstrations in the oases of the south, some of the nation's poorest and most neglected communities. On New Year's Day, the announcement of a rise in the price of bread brought a new wave of rioting. Disturbances broke out in major towns of the south, including Kasserine, Gafsa, Mitlaoui, and Gabes. By January 3 there was rioting in Sfax, the country's second largest city, and in Tunis, as well as in other urban centers. In the capital, thousands of students, workers, and unemployed young men from the city's slums roamed the streets, shouting antigovernment slogans and attacking symbols of authority and wealth. Order was not restored until January 5, by which time security forces had killed over 150 people and wounded hundreds more (Paul 1984; Tessler 1987).

Knowledgeable Tunisians described the mood of demonstrators in the capital as one of rage or even hatred. This mood was most apparent in the attacks on shops selling luxury goods and the incursions into fashionable elite neighborhoods. Anger appeared to be directed not only at the government but also at the consumption-oriented middle and upper classes, population categories perceived to be prospering at a time when the economic circumstances of the masses were steadily deteriorating and the regime was asking the poor to tighten their belts even more.

January 1984 was also a time of violence in Morocco, and both the immediate catalyst and the underlying popular grievances were strikingly similar to those observed in Tunisia. A rise in prices on basic commodities subsidized by the government was announced at the beginning of the year, and again the burden fell most heavily on the working class and the poor. The first disturbances to occur at this time were relatively limited. They involved high school students in Marrakesh, whose immediate concern was a spreading rumor that school registration fees would be increased substantially. The youthful protesters were soon joined by university students, however, and adults and unemployed youth from poorer neighborhoods also took part in some instances. Marches and demonstrations occurred frequently until the middle of January; property damage was extensive in some areas. Moreover, the disturbances soon spread beyond Marrakesh, with student-based demonstrations also flaring up in Agadir, Safi and Casbah-Tala in the south and in Rabat and Meknes in the central part of the country.

By mid-January the disturbances had spread north to the most neglected and underdeveloped region of Morocco. Here students were joined by adults in what became riots of much greater intensity. The worst violence was in Nador, but there were also serious disturbances in Al-Husayma, Tetouan, Oujda, and Berkane. In Nador attacks on banks and the agency of the national airline, Royal Air Maroc, demonstrated anger at the government and special bitterness at institutions symbolizing elite privilege. The sentiments heard were similar to those recorded in Tunisia and in Casablanca in 1981, with many protesters linking their plight to the waste, corruption, and indulgence of the privileged classes and their accomplices within the government. Some protesters carried pink parasols to express their disdain for royal pomp and their indignation at the excesses of the king and the elite. Moroccan security forces used considerable violence in quelling the riots. The government's official report stated that 29 demonstrators were killed and 114 wounded, but most observers placed the numbers far higher. Press reports from Spain spoke of 150 to 200 deaths—in some cases even more—as well as hundreds of injured.

Although the situation in Libya was very different, that country, too, experienced unrest in 1984. Blessed with substantial revenues from petroleum exports, Libya has had ample resources with which to meet the needs of its small population. Moreover, the Qadhafi regime has spent heavily on projects designed to promote national development and enhance the welfare of the common citizen. Thus, in contrast to Tunisia and Morocco, grievances related to poverty and relative deprivation have not been a major source of conflict in Libya. It is rather the repressive and sometimes brutal political climate that has spawned most of the tension, and in this connection high school and university students have been among the most active of Qadhafi's domestic opponents.

Although it had for a time been regarded as more politically stable than its neighbors to the east and west, Algeria has also experienced serious unrest. In April 1985, for example, following rumors that homes being built for the poor would be allocated instead to government bureaucrats, there were riots in the Algiers Casbah that brought police units into the streets. Fall 1986 brought additional and more serious disturbances in Algeria, with the most intense of these sparked by student demonstrations in Constantine. In November a protest over poor campus conditions and a change in examination requirements ignited three days of rioting, which resulted in four dead and many wounded, as well as considerable property damage. The Constantine riots were followed almost immediately by disturbances in other cities, including Setif, Batna, Annaba, Skikda, and Oran.

In October 1988 Algeria was shaken by the most intense rioting since its independence in 1962, experiencing its own equivalent of the January rioting in Tunisia and Morocco (Vandewalle 1988a). In Algeria, Oran, Constantine, and several other cities, thousands of young people came into the streets to vent their anger over worsening economic and social conditions, and their protests touched off three days of rioting. There was considerable property damage, with rioters setting fire to government buildings in several parts of Algiers. There were also lethal clashes between the protesters and security forces charged with putting an end to the disturbances. Estimates of the number of casualties varied widely, but it is generally agreed that at least several hundred of the protesters were killed and many more wounded. After order was restored, the government imposed a state of emergency on the capital and nearby areas.

The unrest of the 1980s in Morocco, Tunisia, Libya, and Algeria was by no means limited to the young people of each country. Adults took part in some of the rioting and in other forms of protest. Nor did the grievances that produced disturbances involve issues of concern to young people alone. Problems related to poverty, social injustice, and political uncertainty affect many sectors of society and many age groups. Nevertheless, the Maghrib's youth have for the most part been more dispirited, alienated, and volatile than other categories of the population. Concerned about the future that awaits them as they reach adulthood and enter the mainstream of society, and less constrained than adults by a stake in the established social and political order, young people (particularly though by no means exclusively young men) have played a leading role in the violent disturbances that have in recent years rocked all four North African countries.

The Promise of Youth at Independence

This bleak and troubling picture of unrest in the Maghrib contrasts sharply with the hopes and expectations held for the region's youth in the years immediately following independence. The young men and women of Tunisia, Morocco, Algeria, and Libya were at the time regarded as members of a new political generation, the first to be raised in an environment free from the distorting influences of colonial domination and to be educated in postindependence school systems dedicated to producing a new class of forward-looking citizens. In short, young people were the future; they constituted a critical mass that would reach adulthood within a few years and then, by virtue of its demographic, intellectual, and political weight, provide a new center of gravity and a foundation for progressive social engineering.

The logic of this positive vision was based partly on the high proportion of young people in the population (see Table 4.1). With high rates of population growth in all four countries, the age distribution was strongly skewed in favor of the young. Roughly 40 to 50 percent of the Maghrib's population was under the age of fifteen, and 50 to 55 percent was under the age of twenty. There would come a time, a decade or two later, when rapid population growth would be seen as a serious obstacle to development, with economic gains being consumed by the needs of a rapidly expanding population and

TABLE 4.1 Population Distribution by Age

	Total Population	Cumulative Percent			
		Under 15	Under 20	Under 25	Under 30
Algeria					
1960	9,745,480	45	52	59	66
1966	12,096,347	47	56	63	69
1989	24,450,000	44	55	62	67
Morocco					
1960	11,626,232	44	50	58	67
1971	15,153,806	46	56	63	69
1989	24,570,000	42	51	61	68
Tunisia					
1956	3,943,260	41	50	58	66
1966	5,137,000	46	56	63	69
1989	7,990,000	40	51	61	69
Libya					
1954	1,088,873	38	46	55	63
1973	2,249,237	49	57	64	71
1989	4,390,000	46	–	–	–

Source: United Nations Demographic Yearbook (New York: United Nations, 1990).

with young people's demands for jobs growing faster than the economy's ability to create them. This was not a major concern when Tunisia and Morocco became independent in 1956, however, or when Algeria gained its freedom in 1962 after an eight-year war in which 1 million Algerians died. And it certainly was not regarded as a problem when Libya became independent in 1951. A large country whose population was very small in absolute as well as relative terms, Libya even today is required to import much of its labor force. In the late 1950s and early 1960s, therefore, the high proportion of young people in the population was seen as offering an opportunity to bring about rapid social and cultural change. When this new generation reached adulthood in a decade or two, its massive size would allow it to impose its values and life-style on the whole of society. Within a few years, in other words, patterns of society, culture, and politics would be determined in significant measure by the attitudes and behavior of those who had grown up after independence and who would then constitute the largest and most important segment of the Maghrib's adult population.

These assumptions about the social and political contribution to be made by the nation's youth were most explicitly articulated in Tunisia, which almost immediately began to invest heavily in policies designed to translate its vision into reality. To prepare young people for their apparent destiny, the government in Tunis made education its top priority. At the time of independence,

TABLE 4.2 School Enrollment Ratios[a]

Level/Age	1965	1967	1971	1974	1977	1980	1983	1989
Algeria								
Primary/6–11	68	68	79	87	95	95	94	94
Secondary/12–18	7	8	13	17	27	33	43	61
University/20–24	0.8	–	2	–	4.3	4.9	–	11
Morocco								
Primary/7–11[b]	60	55	53	56	69	78	86	68
Secondary/12–18[b]	10	12	13	15	19	25	29	36
University	–	–	1.5	–	4.2	6.0	6.7	11
Tunisia								
Primary/6–11	91	106	99	92	100	103	114	115
Secondary/12–18	16	19	23	20	23	27	34	44
University	–	–	2.8	–	5.0	5.5	5.3	8

[a]Number of students enrolled divided by total school-age population.
[b]Prior to 1970, Moroccan ratios use ages 6–10 and 11–17 as bases for computing primary and secondary school enrollment ratios.

Sources: *UNESCO Statistical Yearbook,* 1976, 1983, 1986, 1988 (New York: United Nations, 1976, 1983, 1986, 1988); *World Development Report, 1992* (Washington, D.C.: World Bank, 1992).

the literacy rate was about 15 percent, only a quarter of the nation's children were attending primary school, and only about one child in thirty had completed high school. As long as the country's youth was characterized by these low levels of education, it was unlikely that the new generation would be a force for progressive change upon reaching adulthood. But the Tunisian government addressed this problem squarely. It invested 20 to 25 percent of the national budget in education on a sustained basis (Toumi 1975:38), and within a decade dramatic results were apparent.

By 1966 the percentage of Tunisian pupils attending primary school had more than tripled (see Table 4.2). Gains were initially most pronounced in the cities, but there was rapid progress in the rural areas as well, with estimates of school enrollment among six- and seven-year-olds, children who should be beginning their studies, ranging between 80 and 90 percent by the mid-1960s. It is notable, too, as the latter figures indicate, that education was becoming a mass phenomenon among girls as well as boys. Postprimary education also expanded during these years. Between 1956 and 1960, the number of students in intermediate and secondary schools quadrupled. Between 1960 and 1970, responding to pressure from the vast number of primary school graduates, the size of the secondary school population tripled again, bringing the proportion of high school–age children attending class to 20 to 25 percent. Finally, the number of Tunisians attending universities at home and abroad increased from slightly over 2,000 in 1956 to almost 10,000 a decade later (Gallagher 1966:80; Government of Tunisia 1972:107).

Changes in education were qualitative as well as quantitative, and this was part of a broader program of social and cultural engineering designed to prepare young people (and others) to contribute to the nation's future. Under the leadership of the country's dynamic president, Habib Bourguiba, the decade following Tunisian independence witnessed a vigorous and calculated attempt to persuade the populace to abandon what the president described as "outmoded beliefs" and to achieve what he called a "psychological revolution" (Bourguiba 1961 and 1963). Education was a major part of this effort at mobilization and directed socialization. Extensive reforms in 1958 laid the basis for an educational system that sought to decolonize learning by giving increased attention to the Arabic language and Arab culture at the same time that it encouraged modernist interpretations of Islam and its teachings related to work, women, family, and other social concerns (Brown 1973:371ff). In 1965 Bourguiba explicitly stated that Tunisia's school system was designed to "disengage the physiognomy of our national culture" (Bourguiba 1965:18). That culture, he went on to say, respects permanent moral and spiritual values but is also capable of evolving on an intellectual and scientific plane and is open to a constructive dialogue among civilizations and cultures.

In addition to education, Tunisia pursued its psychological and cultural revolution by other means as well. These included legal reforms, most notably the promulgation of a new personal-status code shortly after independence; a public information campaign carried out in the press and, especially, through the broadcast of special programs on the state-run radio network; rallies and meetings organized by the country's single political party, the Destourian Socialist party, which used its 1,250 local cells to bring its message to the masses; and similar efforts at mobilization and socialization undertaken by the party's auxiliary institutions, such as the General Union of Tunisian Students (UGET), the National Union of Tunisian Women, and the General Union of Tunisian Workers (Tessler 1973:220–255; Micaud 1964:131–186). As with work in the field of education, these policies and programs sought to inculcate among the populace attitudes and values deemed appropriate for an Arab state in the second half of the twentieth century and thereby to shape the future of culture in Tunisia. Youth were not the only targets of these efforts. But it was understood and expected that young men and women would be particularly likely to adopt new ideas about social, cultural, and political life.

Young people were also considered important for the future in Morocco, Algeria, and Libya. Even though efforts undertaken to mobilize and educate them were not as well developed in these countries as they were in Tunisia, and even though there were additional problems that limited what was accomplished, significant progress was nonetheless made. In Morocco, for example, the proportion of school-age children attending primary school increased from 18 percent in 1955–1956, the year in which independence was achieved, to 43 percent in 1962–1963. To instruct this influx of pupils, the number of teachers graduated by Moroccan normal schools increased from 300 in 1958 to almost 2,000 in 1963. In addition, 1,000 or more schools were constructed annually during this period. Although gains were slower in coming at the secondary level, with only 11 percent of the eligible age group attending high school as late as 1966 (*Moroccan Report* 1968:12–14), this growth in Moroccan primary school education does not fare badly in comparison with that of Tunisia, which experienced an increase from 26 percent to 55 percent during the eight academic years between 1955–1956 and 1962–1963 (Gallagher 1963:188ff; Gallagher 1966:83; Ashford 1967:251–257). Moreover, Morocco's accomplishments during these early years are all the more notable in view of the difficulties it encountered as a result of a decision at independence to offer all instruction in Arabic. Enrollments declined alarmingly because of an inadequate supply of instructors capable of teaching in the Arabic language. Two years later, the government in Rabat determined that attempts to Arabize education should proceed more slowly, and school enrollments once again began to increase (Gordon 1962:65ff).

Important educational gains also followed independence in Algeria. Although primary school enrollments increased in the 1950s as a result of belated French efforts to justify colonial rule, as late as 1961, the year before independence, only about one Algerian child in six between the ages of six and thirteen was attending school. Five years after independence, by contrast, during the 1966–1967 academic year, the proportion of children enrolled in primary schools stood at 57 percent (*Algerian Report* 1968:14) or even higher, according to some sources (see Table 4.2). The distribution of enrollments was still uneven; school enrollments, like patterns of literacy more generally, were much higher among boys than girls and in the cities than in the rural areas. Nevertheless, the contrast with the pre-independence period was striking, even among categories of the population that remained relatively disadvantaged. For example, whereas fewer than 20 percent of the children attending school in 1961 were girls, 38 percent of pupils were girls in 1966–1967. As the number of primary school graduates grew, the number of Algerian children attending middle school and high school soon began to increase as well, from about 50,000 in 1962–1963 to roughly 100,000 in 1964–1965, almost 165,000 in 1966–1967, and nearly 235,000 in 1969–1970. The latter figure represented about 12 percent of the secondary school–age population. Gains continued through the 1970s, moreover, with almost 30 percent of the national budget devoted to general education and vocational training during this period (Dufour 1978; Bennoune 1988: 219ff; Entelis 1986:91ff).

The situation in Libya was somewhat different in that educational advances during the colonial period were even more limited than elsewhere in North Africa and because the country's meager resources, until the discovery of oil in the early 1960s, prevented any significant investment in education. Thus, almost a decade after independence, "more than 90 percent of the population was illiterate and only a handful of Libyans had been given an opportunity to study at a university or to qualify for a recognized profession" (Fathaly et al. 1977:13). Important gains were registered in the 1960s, however, with total school enrollment rising from 150,000 in 1962 to about 360,000 in 1969 and the proportion of suitably aged children enrolled in primary school reaching about 50 percent in the latter year. Gains became even more dramatic following the revolution that brought Qadhafi to power in 1969. With a fourfold increase in government spending for education during the first five years of Qadhafi's rule, school enrollments reached 600,000 by 1974, and 1.2 million a decade later. This included major gains at the secondary as well as the primary school level; whereas the ratio between primary and postprimary students had been 7:1 in 1962 and was still more than 6:1 in 1969, it was approaching 3:1 in 1974 and was less than 2:1 in 1986 (Metz 1989:296). This progress benefited girls as well as boys, moreover. By 1976, girls made up 43 percent of all students and 46 percent of primary school pupils in Libya, figures that compare favorably with those in the rest of North Africa.

Despite these impressive accomplishments, problems associated with the educational advances occurred throughout the Maghrib. Teachers, especially experienced ones and those able to teach modern subjects in Arabic, were in short supply. So, too, were classrooms, as well as texts and other teaching materials in the Arabic language. Thus, with facilities strained and instructors of dubious ability often pressed into service, the quality of the education offered to the pupils of the Maghrib frequently left much to be desired, particularly in poorer urban neighborhoods and rural areas. Educational planners and other governmental officials were aware of these problems and took what steps they could to reduce their intensity. As noted, all four countries spent heavily on education, working diligently to train teachers, build schools, and do whatever else they could to preserve educational quality at a time of rapidly expanding enrollments. Beyond this, recognizing that many problems were not amenable to short-term solutions, they affirmed that democratizing educational opportunity was more important than offering high-quality instruction to a small number of children, and they proclaimed their faith that investments in education would bring a diminution of problems in the years ahead.

The decade or so following independence in North Africa was thus a period of high expectations for young people. The generation of young men and women growing up at this time was distinguished by its size, by its relatively high level of education, and by the fact that it was passing through its formative years during a period when, for the first time, the Maghrib was in control of its own political and cultural destiny. In all three respects, the generation of young Maghribis heading for adulthood was, at least potentially, radically different from the one that preceded it, and its entry into the mainstream of adult society accordingly held out the possibility of a far-reaching transformation of social, cultural, and political life. Writing in 1971, a U.S. student of North Africa described this emergent, postindependence political generation as the Maghrib's "critical mass." Noting its potential political and cultural impact, he articulated both the hope for the future that was routinely expressed in North Africa at the time and the challenges associated with the absorption of the new generation that have in recent years become more evident:

> The young Arabs approaching adulthood, that critical mass of the 1970's, will increasingly determine the outcome of competing trends. In addition to employment, the new generation will be seeking social status and a meaningful identity as Arabs. As they take their place in [North African] society, there may well be eruptions and conflicts, and new political movements could arrive, based on this class of young adults. Perhaps they will offer an original kind of neo-nationalism, or perphaps neo-Arabism, or, conceivably, why not, of neo-traditionalism. Whether they will eventually turn out to be bridge or blockbuster in the national culture, cement or tinder in the fabric of the nation, their impact on the Arab world, its development and future will be critical. (Mattson 1971:13)

The Limits to Social Mobility

A U.S. scholar conducting research in Morocco in the immediate postindependence period offered a series of observations about the attitudes of the country's youth, reporting that young men and women for the most part shared the view that Morocco stood on the brink of an important social and political transformation. Some young people, he noted, remained aloof from politics or confined their political activities to discussions with small groups of friends. Some were also said to be unsure about what their political role should be. More generally, however, young Moroccans appeared to be politically conscious and concerned. According to this assessment, the nation's youth were "almost universally intensely patriotic, scornful of any vestige of the Protectorate . . . [and held] high expectations of the changes that independence can produce in their country" (Ashford 1961:389). Furthermore, at least among those benefiting from recent gains in education, young Moroccans were judged to be more interested in national and international affairs than comparably educated young people in more developed countries. With their hopes and expectations heightened during the late 1950s, "all young Moroccans realize that their new opportunities were made possible as a result of independence and that their futures rest with the nation's progress" (Ashford 1961:390). In addition, consistent with this forward-looking, achievement-oriented point of view, Moroccan youth appeared to be "less tolerant of inefficiency, procrastination and rationalization" than were members of the older, pre-independence generation (Ashford 1961:389).

Yet disenchantment and doubt about the future were visible to the same observer only a few years later (Ashford 1963; see also Ashford 1967:256ff), with two interrelated problems increasingly in evidence so far as young people were concerned. First, the government was proving incapable of creating jobs on the scale needed to accommodate the country's expanding population. With a population growth rate of roughly 3 percent per year, the number of young people entering the labor market each year was climbing more rapidly than the number of new jobs. Urban unemployment, which had risen rather than fallen since independence, was estimated at 14 to 15 percent in 1962, and the seasonal nature of agricultural labor meant that as many as half of the nation's rural workers were underemployed. Unemployment rates were even higher a few years later, with the greatest burden falling upon the young.

Second, the expansion of the educational system at the primary school level was not matched by comparable growth at higher levels, requiring most young Moroccans who began their studies after independence to drop out after five or six years. As late as 1977, for example, only 19 percent of the children between the ages of twelve and eighteen were attending secondary school. This was all the more troublesome because primary schooling alone did not enable Moroccans to compete effectively for those jobs that were available, especially in a society moving rapidly toward mass literacy, and young men with little or no secondary education were accordingly having an especially difficult time finding regular employment. Moreover, it was clear by the mid-1960s that these problems were not the result of temporary bottlenecks; they were becoming more rather than less intense. Writing in 1965, a decade after independence, Ashford stated that "had the secondary [school] system, or other aspects of Moroccan life, begun to make more preparation for the impact of increased lower-level education, more optimism could be expressed" (Ashford 1967:257). Unfortunately, however, this was not the case.

As a result, many young Moroccans were beginning to express concern both about the course of the nation's development and about the diminishing prospects that their own aspirations would be realized. With respect to government development efforts, young people and others increasingly complained of political confusion and opportunism at the national level and of inefficiency and apathy at the local level. These were not abstract grievances, however; they were related not only to the uncertain future of the country as a whole but also, and perhaps even more immediately, to the fading hopes of many young individuals for an improvement in their personal and professional circumstances. Many of these sentiments were reported in a study carried out among rural Moroccan youth in 1969, which found particular concern about the lack of jobs for young people who acquired some schooling and then entered the labor market (Pascon and Bentahar 1972). According to the authors, "a formidable desire for change has been overtaken by a profound dissatisfaction, a deep disappointment." As expressed by one young respondent, "We put children in school for five years and then reject them as if they had never gone?" (Pascon and Bentahar 1972:166–169).

The situation has become worse in the two decades since this study was undertaken. As the rioting of 1981 and 1984 makes clear, hundreds of thousands of young Moroccans have lost any hope that the promise held out by independence will be realized so far as their own lives are concerned. The circumstances of these individuals are reflected not only in the violent outbursts that periodically shake the Moroccan political landscape but also, and even more, in mundane statistics that tell of the difficulties of daily living. According to a household survey carried out in December 1984 by the semiofficial *Le Matin du Sahara* (Sahara morning), urban unemployment in Morocco stood at 18.4 percent, with 44.9 percent of those having jobs employed as unskilled or semiskilled laborers. In addition, 79.3 percent of the active urban population was either illiterate or had received only a primary school education. These figures were also cited by an economic report published in 1987, which stated that they underline the severity of the urban employment problem, particularly among the young, and then concluded that "it is unlikely that these proportions have altered much since 1984" (*Quarterly Economic Review of Morocco* 1, 1987:19).

The same obstacles to advancement confronted young people in Tunisia. These were not particularly serious during the years immediately following independence, when the number of high school and university graduates remained small and when many jobs were created by the departure of European settlers and indigenous Maghribi Jews. By the mid- to late 1960s, however, many who had entered school in the years after independence were finding their opportunities for advancement severely constrained. An interesting study, which sheds light on both the educational and the professional dimensions of this phenomenon, was carried out in three representative Tunisian communities in 1965–1966 and 1968–1969. Among the findings was evidence that the country had indeed made significant strides in the democratization of education. On the one hand, the vast majority of the young men surveyed had not only received at least some primary schooling but were the sons of fathers with no modern education, leading the author to conclude that "the broadening of access to educational institutions has been dramatic indeed in these and most Tunisian communities" (Allman 1976:317). On the other hand, revealing clearly the limits of the educational opportunities that had been created, only 60 percent of these sons of fathers with no modern education had completed even five years before leaving school, and only 10 percent had gone on to secondary school. Aggregate statistics, summarized in

Table 4.2, show that these figures are not unrepresentative; and a decade later, in 1977, the proportion of high school–age children enrolled in the nation's postprimary education institutions was still only 23 percent.

The Tunisian study also examined employment patterns and reached a similar conclusion. With the nation's population increasing at a rate of at least 2.5 percent per year, and probably more, the demand for jobs was growing more rapidly than the supply, and education, at least for the young, was accordingly no guarantee of personal and professional mobility. Comparing the occupations of fathers and sons, the study found as much downward as upward movement in intergenerational mobility, and much more of the former among younger individuals. Among men between the ages of sixteen and nineteen who had grown up and received their primary schooling after independence, 41 percent held a job with lower status than that of their fathers, whereas only 16 percent held a better job. This is all the more significant considering that most of the fathers had received no modern education. It might be argued that the young men surveyed were at the beginning of their occupational lives and would eventually move into better positions, superior to those held by their fathers. The author of the study concluded that this was unlikely, however, reporting that "since the Tunisian economy has not expanded rapidly in the last ten years and the jobs left vacant by Europeans were largely filled in the early sixties, there are insufficient jobs available for the masses of young Tunisians who attempt to enter the labor market each year." He also added, correctly as it turned out, that "the situation is likely to worsen in the future" (Allman 1976:318).

Comparable findings were produced by another research project carried out in Tunisia in the late 1960s. Literate and regularly employed men and women from Tunis and three representative small towns were interviewed about their personal and professional circumstances, and in the analysis of these data, young people who had grown up and received their education after independence were compared to members of the older generation. Among the findings: job satisfaction was much lower among younger than among comparably educated older Tunisians, and job satisfaction increased as a function of education among older respondents but not among members of the postindependence generation (Tessler 1976).

Although the need for cadres was initially somewhat greater in Algeria, the situation was in most respects quite similar to that observed in Tunisia and Morocco. A need to replace departing French settlers and Jews and to rebuild the country following an eight-year war of national liberation created professional openings in the immediate postindependence period. Further, revenues from petroleum exports provided resources for economic development that were absent in Morocco, and to a considerable extent in Tunisia as well. Nevertheless, social mobility, both in general and as a function of education, was severely limited for the vast majority of Algeria's young men and women.

A decade or so after independence, many and probably most of the young Algerians who entered school as the country expanded its educational system at the primary level were encountering serious obstacles in their quests for continued schooling and satisfying jobs. With population increasing at a rate estimated to be in excess of 3 percent a year, in Algeria, as in Morocco and Tunisia, supply was consistently falling behind demand with respect to both jobs and places in postprimary educational institutions. As a result, a steadily rising number of young people were finding it impossible to fulfill their aspirations for social mobility and a better life.

An Algerian scholar accordingly reports in this connection that "in spite of democratization, the new educational system turned out to be highly selective" (Bennoune 1988:227), and he presents statistics from the late 1970s that graphically illustrate this conclusion. Using the 1978–1979 academic year as an example, he notes that of 100 pupils enrolled in primary schools, twenty would drop out before the end and forty would fail to pass the examination for the certificate of primary education, which meant that they would not be allowed to stay at school. Of the remaining forty pupils, only about eighteen would be admitted to high schools, of whom sixteen would subsequently be candidates for the *baccalauréat* examination. The pass rate was 25 percent for 1978–1979, however, which meant that only four pupils out of the original 100 would have a chance to go to the university. A decade later, the situation had not improved; it had in fact become somewhat worse, at least at the upper level. In 1989 only 20 percent of those taking the *baccalauréat* exam were successful. This high failure rate, coupled with the inability of the labor market to absorb those leaving school and seeking employment, created a situation that could fairly be described as explosive (Digne 1989).

The Libyan case was different in important respects. With a relatively small population (reaching only 3.6 million as late as 1984), the country was plagued not by a shortage of jobs but by the small size of its domestic labor force. This problem became particularly acute in the 1970s, by which time economic growth and development funded by oil revenues had assumed significant proportions. Even with a high birthrate, expanded education, and migration to the cities by villagers seeking better jobs, the number of Libyan workers still fell considerably short of the country's needs. As a result, in contrast to the situation in Morocco, Algeria, and Tunisia, educated Libyans had no trouble finding jobs and, as a matter of fact, the country was required to import a substantial number of foreign workers to meet its manpower needs. By 1975, expatriate workers, most from neighboring countries, numbered 225,000 and made up 33 percent of the total labor force. By 1983 the number had climbed to 560,000, with foreign workers constituting roughly 18 percent of Libya's total population. These figures declined in the mid-1980s. As a result of a sharp drop in the price of oil, the government was unable to finance some of its development programs and this, along with political factors, led to the expulsion of many foreign workers in 1985. Nevertheless, non-Libyans still made up a significant proportion of the labor force, with little appreciable change either in the country's dependence on foreign workers or in the broad availability of employment opportunities for educated Libyans.

Although finding a job has not been a serious problem for well-educated young Libyans, the situation in Libya is similar to that of Morocco, Algeria, and Tunisia with respect to educational attrition. The problem is less acute than it was in the years before the revolution, but it remains the case that a high proportion of the students who complete primary school do not continue with their education. As late as 1974, fewer than 11 percent of the primary school graduates went on to intermediate school, and only 2.4 percent continued through high school (Fathaly 1977:14). As noted earlier, the ratio between primary and postprimary school enrollments declined substantially in the late 1970s and in the 1980s. Nevertheless, with half or more of those beginning school leaving the system after five or six years, and with a significant proportion of those who do continue completing only three or four additional years, there are hundreds of thousands of young Libyans who have not received an education that prepares them for professional advancement.

A major survey of adults in Libya's Zawia province in 1973 sheds light on the implications of this situation for purposes of employment and indicates that despite the country's relative affluence, many were dissatisfied with the job opportunities available to them. Among the 570 respondents in the sample, 47 percent disagreed or disagreed strongly with the proposition that a job is available to any Libyan who needs one (Fathaly and Palmer 1980:91). According to an even larger survey conducted in 1978, Libyans with fewer educational and occupational skills were both less satisfied with their past and present situation and more pessimistic in their expectations about the future (Attir and Peterson 1979).

Both differences and similarities between Libya and the other countries of North Africa should be noted in this regard. On the one hand, for understandable economic and demographic reasons, it is probable that levels of personal and professional satisfaction are significantly higher in Libya than in Tunisia, Algeria, and Morocco. Although comparative data are not available, both of the studies mentioned above reveal high levels of individual satisfaction in absolute terms. The Zawia province survey, for example, reported that 75 percent agree or strongly agree that "our economic system is fair and just," and 76 percent rate their income as either adequate, satisfactory, or very satisfactory. At the time of this study, and more recently as well, it was extremely unlikely that anything approaching such high levels of satisfaction would be found elsewhere in the Maghrib. On the other hand, although economic grievances may be less acute in Libya than elsewhere in North Africa, a very large number of young Libyans have had no more than a basic education, and there is no shortage of complaints about the conditions of education. For example, 51 percent of the Zawia respondents judged the overall quality of the educational system to be poor or bad, and this figure jumped to 62 percent among a subsample of politically active individuals (Fathaly and Palmer 1980:94). Even more important, as noted, almost half of these respondents were dissatisfied with the employment opportunities available to them. These latter findings indicate that despite their country's relative wealth, the limits to social mobility so pronounced in other North African states are familiar to many Libyans as well.

In sum, in all four countries of the Maghrib, and especially in Morocco, Algeria, and Tunisia, the government has been unable for two decades or more to create new jobs or broaden opportunities for secondary and postsecondary education at a rate that keeps pace with the demand generated by population growth and the expansion of education at the primary school level. As a result, unemployment rates of 20 to 25 percent have become common (see Parker 1984:17), and among urban young men under the age of thirty, particularly those with only primary schooling or less, estimates of the proportion without regular employment range as high as 40 percent. Unable to compete for available positions, often because their education is limited, these unemployed young men while away their days on street corners or in coffee houses, becoming ever more disillusioned and embittered. A 1986 Paris colloquium on cities and social movements in the Maghrib and the Middle East thus concluded that the urban areas of North Africa are "accumulating a mass whose transition is blocked" and that increasingly lives at a level "below that of normal city life" ("State, City and Social Movements," 58). And three years later, according to a Moroccan economist, "the population/job problem," which has already exploded on several occasions, remains "a time bomb that is ticking away" (Moffett 1989:6).

Compounding the problem of limited mobility and unfulfilled aspirations has been the uneven distribution of opportunities for post-primary education and professional advancement. In both areas, those who obtain the desirable positions that are available are drawn disproportionately from the more privileged sectors of society, and this, understandably, adds to the frustration of those who are less favored. An investigation of Tunisian professionals in the early and mid-1960s offers confirmation of this assessment, revealing that administrative and economic cadres were recruited overwhelmingly either from the urban environments of Tunis, Sfax, or Sousse or from other traditional sources of elite incumbents, such as the Sahel and Djerba. They were also drawn to a disproportionate degree from families that already belonged to the middle class or the elite (Ben Salem 1969b). Further, a subsequent study carried out by the same investigator in the early 1970s revealed that the characteristics of middle-level and upper-level professionals remained about the same (Ben Salim 1976). Favoritism in allocating good jobs and other opportunities for advancement appears to have been even more pronounced in Morocco. Family connections were probably more important there than in any other North African country, prompting a scholar writing in 1970 to report that "student and other surveys point to considerable political frustration with the closed [Moroccan] system" (Moore 1970:289, 291).

Focusing on university students in the mid-1960s, a study based on data from both Tunisia and Morocco reported similar findings. As with young professionals, a disproportionate number who had reached the upper echelons of the educational system came from major urban centers, or the Sahel in Tunisia, and from professional and middle-class family backgrounds (Stone 1973; Moore 1970:283ff; Moore and Hochschild 1968; see also Ben Salem 1969a). Further, these characteristics were overrepresented to an even greater degree among student leaders. At the time of the survey, in 1966, a majority of the students expressed confidence about the future. Most expected significant professional mobility and entry into their country's elite, whereas young people with less schooling were increasingly disillusioned about the opportunities available to them. This was true of students in both Tunisia and Morocco, although, especially in the latter country, there was less optimism about the future among those without good family connections. Moroccan students were also more likely to state that their family situation would be more important than hard work in enabling them to get ahead (Moore 1970: 289–291).

In the case of both Tunisia and Morocco in the 1960s, it was plausible to assert that it would be another decade before young people of modest origin would make their way in significant numbers to one of their nation's universities and, upon graduation, join the middle class or even the elite. Unfortunately, however, education would fulfill its assigned role as a vehicle for social mobility among the poorer and more traditional social classes in only a very small number of cases. Although the democratization of education after independence did result in a more socially heterogeneous university student population by the 1970s—and was helped in Tunisia by free tuition and grants for living expenses to qualified needy students—men and women from rural areas and low socioeconomic backgrounds continued to be significantly underrepresented on university campuses in both Tunisia and Morocco. Thus the more important observation would seem to be not that there were more students of modest origin at institutions of higher learning but rather that those who managed to achieve this impressive degree of social mobility constituted only a tiny proportion of the boys and girls whose families had enrolled them in primary school with such high hopes ten or fifteen years earlier. Summarizing the situation in Tunisia in the early 1980s and focusing on patterns of both educational and professional advancement, an observer accordingly reported that "university students and skilled cadres [still] come predominantly from middle- and upper-middle-class social strata" (Stone 1982:164).

Algeria's experience has been similar to that of Morocco and Tunisia. In the period just after independence, recruitment to important government positions may have been less exclusive than in the other two countries, in the sense that there was less favoritism shown to people from a particular region or caste at the expense of technical competence (Moore 1970:290). Nevertheless, an analysis of educational data reveals not only the limited magnitude but also the uneven distribution of opportunities for postprimary schooling, with the low quality of primary schools in poor neighborhoods and rural areas contributing to the difficulty that pupils from these environments have had in pursuing their studies beyond the primary level (Bennoune 1988:227–228). As a result, the secondary school population is unrepresentative in relative if not in absolute terms, meaning that although a majority of high school students are of modest origin, the children of well-to-do families have a much better chance than others of gaining admission.

At the university level, the offspring of the elite prevail in both relative and absolute terms. A study conducted in the mid-1970s, for example, reported that the son of an agricultural manager was 30 times more likely to enter university than the son of a farm laborer, and the son of a technocrat or businessman was 285 times more likely (Dufour 1978). Noting that students at Algerian universities thus constitute a select group drawn from the most favored sectors of society, one observer described them as "the 1 to 3 percent of Algerians who are destined, because of their family and personal connections, acquired wealth and influence, type and level of education, multilingual fluency, and technical-scientific accreditation, to assume the top- and secondary-level positions in each of the principal institutional components of the technocratic system: government, party, military, bureaucracy" (Entelis 1986:92).

Intensifying the problem of uneven access to opportunities for advancement is the establishment at Algerian universities of parallel Francophone and Arabophone programs of study. Although the former prepare students for the most desirable jobs, men and women of modest and rural backgrounds are often slotted into the latter track. Indeed, giving expression to their uncertainty and resentment, those in the latter track have frequently protested on issues of academic status, job opportunities, and cultural orientation. Some of these demonstrations have turned violent, moreover, as at the University of Constantine in 1974, 1975, and 1976 and at the University of Algiers during the 1979–1980 academic year. In the latter instance, Arabic-language students, who constitute 25 percent of the student body and tend to come from the lower socioeconomic classes, went on a two-month strike to protest discrimination and a lack of employment opportunities in government and business (Entelis 1986:93; see also Entelis 1982:119–120).

The situation in Libya is somewhat but not completely different from that prevailing in the other countries of North Africa. The opportunity gap between Libyans from advantaged and disadvantaged backgrounds (the latter defined in terms of rural residence, low socioeconomic status or both) was substantial until the revolution that brought Qadhafi to power in 1969 but has diminished appreciably since that time, especially in the late 1970s and throughout the 1980s. For example, with respect to the availability of education in the rural areas, whereas approximately one-half of the country's primary, intermediate, and secondary schools were in either Tripoli or Benghazi in the early and mid-1970s, a recent study notes that "by the late 1980's schools were well distributed around the country, and boarding facilities for students from remote areas were available at some schools at all academic levels" (Metz 1989:113). With respect to social mobility more generally, including entry into the ranks of the political elite, another study reports that wealth and tribal or family status have declined in importance as usable resources for mobility to elite status, and that the Qadhafi regime "has expanded and more equally distributed the social resources needed for political recruitment and it has opened up more and better channels leading to greater upward mobility than hitherto obtained" (Hinnebusch 1982:216–217).

Still, even though Qadhafi's policies have emphasized egalitarianism in the distribution of educational opportunity and other social benefits, and though this aspect of the Libyan revolution appears to be recognized and appreciated by much of the populace, evidence suggests that important inequities remain. So far as the uneven distribution in opportunities for personal and professional mobility is concerned, one of the studies cited above points out that national leaders are still disproportionately likely to come from middle-class backgrounds. According to this assessment, civilian and military officials and senior bureaucrats "are for the most part said to be well-educated, and it seems to be assumed that they are recruited essentially from the urban upper-middle and middle classes. In particular, many carry-overs from the old regime are sons of Tripolitanian bourgeois families educated in the West" (Hinnebusch 1982:186–187). Focusing on the other end of the socioeconomic status continuum, a few studies have shown, not surprisingly, that the quality of education is lower in schools in poor areas. For example, a survey of 224 primary and intermediate school teachers and principals, carried out in Benghazi in 1980, found that the educational climate was more open and supportive of learning at schools serving pupils from families of high socioeconomic status. Again according to the perceptions of teachers and principals, there was more openness and less rigidity in girls' schools than in boys' schools (Alarafi 1980).

Finally, beyond the problem of unequal access, the future is uncertain even for those who do manage to obtain a university education in Tunisia, Algeria, and Morocco. By the mid-1970s, university graduates in all three countries were no longer guaranteed social and professional mobility, with the result that some of the anxiety and frustration characteristic of less-educated young people was beginning to manifest itself on college campuses as well. Competition for jobs in desirable occupations, and especially for work in the middle and upper echelons of the government administration, had by this time become much more intense. On the one hand, the supply of educated job candidates had grown steadily in response to both general population growth and the expansion of education. On the other, there were few vacancies created by retirement, many jobs being held by young people who had secured them only a few years earlier, and the rate at which new positions were being created was limited. Thus even university students, who a decade earlier had had relatively few doubts about their personal and professional futures, were increasingly restive and uncertain by the 1970s.

The situation in Tunisia was summarized by one scholar, who wrote that "supply has caught up with and overtaken demand for elite incumbents and cadres. Mobility channels to elite positions have become blocked. A university degree or a certified technical skill no longer warrants anticipated mobility to elite status, as previous studies had assumed" (Stone 1982:165). And the expected result, that university students had become apprehensive and anxious about the future, was documented in the Tunisian case as early as 1972 by another investigator (Entelis 1974). Similar conclusions emerged from research in Morocco as well, where a major study reported as early as 1970 that an "absorption crisis" loomed on the horizon and that most who aspired to join the elite were destined to have their ambitions unfulfilled (Waterbury 1970). An inquiry into the situation in Morocco in the late 1970s produced the same conclusion: "Many and probably most would-be elites will not obtain the kind of prestigious and influential position on which they have set their sights . . . [and accordingly most have] little hope of realizing their ambitions" (Tessler 1982:81). An absorption crisis was also visible in Algeria by the mid- to late-1970s, especially for university students in the Arabophone academic track but increasingly for other students as well. Only in Libya were these trends not clearly visible, and even there, despite a continuing shortage of well-educated workers, a 1973–1974 study among students at the University of Tripoli found a discrepancy between expectation and reality in occupational prospects (Al-Nouri 1975).

Political Alienation

Political alienation has been widespread among the youth of the Maghrib for some time and is the result of two distinct sets of factors that young people usually judge to be strongly interrelated. First, as the preceding analysis makes clear, frustrations associated with limited social mobility have fostered discontent and anxiety about the future among many of North Africa's young men and women. Understandably, those who believe their personal aspirations are destined to be unfulfilled are restive and disillusioned, and these sentiments often give way to bitterness and anger, especially if it appears that others have privileged access to those opportunities for advancement that do exist.

Second, many young people are extremely critical of the government and voice grievances that are by no means limited to their own desires for greater social mobility. In Morocco, Algeria, and Tunisia, there are widespread complaints about inefficiency and, more generally, about a failure to identify policies that will reduce poverty and promote reasonable levels of growth and development. Perhaps even more widespread is discontent about the large and growing gap between rich and poor, which is said to be encouraged by favoritism, corruption, and the absence of a desire to distribute equitably those burdens of underdevelopment that are unavoidable. Finally, in Libya as well as the other countries of the Maghrib, there are complaints about a lack of meaningful democracy, defined in terms of citizen influence and government accountability, and about the repressive measures often employed to stifle dissent. Although there are differences in the nature and timing of the process by which these grievances have come to be articulated in Morocco, Tunisia, Algeria, and Libya, they have been regularly and widely expressed by the youth of all four countries for some time.

Government officials in North Africa often contend that these complaints about regime performance are unreasonable and exaggerated. They frequently assert, not necessarily without reason, that young people make unrealistic demands and fail to appreciate that development goals can be achieved only over the long haul, especially in view of rapid population growth and the economic backwardness that characterized the Maghrib when it finally put an end to years of colonial domination. These officials also insist that much has been accomplished and sometimes add that young people's complaints are the result not of government failures but rather of aspirations fostered by successful development efforts, most notably in the field of education. So far as political life is concerned, Maghribi leaders frequently state that meaningful progress toward the construction of democratic political systems is being made, even though here, too, patience is needed if there is to be change without instability. Finally, many officials acknowledge that mistakes have been made in the past but insist that these do not reflect actions taken in bad faith and that the Maghrib is therefore capable of learning from experience and doing better in the future.

Whatever the degree of accuracy in these official rebuttals, they rarely strike a responsive chord among the disillusioned and alienated youth of North Africa, perhaps because so many young people find confirmation in their lives of the charge that something fundamental is amiss in the state of the nation as a whole. As noted, young people see a strong connection between their personal grievances and their complaints about broader patterns of political economy. They reason, logically enough, although perhaps somewhat simplistically, that if the government were allocating resources wisely, in accordance with the true interests of the citizens of North Africa, they, their families, and so many of their friends would not be confronted with stagnation or even a decline in their modest standards of living and with little prospect of finding the jobs that would permit them to improve their life circumstances. But the leaders of the government are not wise and do not give highest priority to the welfare of the masses, these youthful critics continue. They instead preside over a political and economic system that is dedicated to the preservation of elite privilege and that accordingly distributes resources and opportunities on the basis of family and personal relationships.

Illustrative of the thinking of young and not-so-young critics of the government, and of the perceived relationship between personal and political grievances, is a conversation that took place during the riots in Tunisia in January 1984. A Tunisian professional, who was about forty years old, told me of a discussion with several young men who worked in menial and low-paying jobs at the institution where he held a senior position. Although they did not condone the damage caused by the riots, the young workers claimed to understand the motivation of the rioters and expressed their own belief that the majority of Tunisia's elite prospered because of personal and political connections, gaining preferential access to, and then spending frivolously, resources that should be devoted to national development. Moreover, most of these privileged individuals were said to offer the country little in return, preferring to spend their wealth on imported luxury goods and only rarely investing in ventures that either created employment or increased economic productivity. According to the Tunisian professional, this conversation vividly revealed to him the basis of the popular rage that had led to violence against the established political and economic order (Tessler 1991:13–14).

The anger visible during the 1984 riots in Tunisia had not come into existence only recently. As mentioned earlier, discontent and political alienation have been prevalent among young people in North Africa for some time. These orientations probably emerged first in Morocco. Studies focusing on high school and university students indicated widespread criticism of the government by the early 1960s. Not only were students educated after independence more politically radical than those who preceded them, they were also, according to several contemporary observers, strongly attracted by radical ideologies, with as many as half supporting parties of the leftist opposition. Although some young people were apathetic or simply intimidated, one observer wrote, "others are alienated and many are repelled. Very clearly, little has been done to give youth an image of government as an instrument for change within which each person can individually seek his role and make his contribution" (Ashford 1963:52ff). As a result, surveys taken during the mid-1960s found that many Moroccan students felt intense hostility toward the government. Indeed, according to another observer who carried out research in Morocco during this period, "no survey can do justice to the resentment the average Moroccan student feels toward the regime" (Moore 1970: 291).

The years between 1965 and 1973 were a period of serious student unrest in Morocco (Tessler 1982:78–79). In 1965, high school and university students were joined by unemployed young men and others in the streets of Casablanca, and hundreds were killed in the rioting that followed. Order was restored by the army and numerous student leaders arrested. In late 1971 and early 1972, high school and university students went on strike, prompting another round of arrests and the closure of most branches of Mohammed V University. Additional disturbances and more student arrests followed as 1972 drew to a close, and this pattern continued during much of the 1972–1973 school year. Public agitation diminished during the mid-1970s but research conducted during this period indicates that students were still strongly opposed to the government and the established political system. For example, even though there had been a relaxation of political controls and competitive elections in 1976 and 1977, a survey carried out during the 1978–1979 academic year reported that most university students were high in political alienation and judged the government to be unresponsive to the nation's needs. Most also held the country's political institutions in low regard, condemning political officials for favoritism and stating that attempts to achieve political goals by democratic means were almost hopeless (Nedelcovych and Palmer 1980).

Although a pattern of disturbances going back to the Casablanca riots of 1965 makes it clear that political alienation is by no means confined to students and young people who are better educated, it is among the latter categories of Moroccan youth that antiregime attitudes have been most systematically documented. Summarizing the lessons to be drawn from several major studies carried out in Morocco, including his own 1980 survey of pupils and students in Rabat, Casablanca, and Marrakesh, Micheal Suleiman, writing in 1987, offered several general conclusions about the political orientations of Moroccan youth (Suleiman 1987:115; see also Suleiman 1985). Young people tend to be well-informed and highly attentive to politics but unlikely to participate in political life. Further, among those who are well educated, low participation is the result of a clear recognition that the political system is not responsive to their needs and demands. These disgruntled young men and women have antiregime attitudes, and their lack of participation in Morocco's quasi democracy is thus a condemnation of the system and an indication of their alienation. As an alternative, they identify with antiregime movements, either parties of the left or militant Islamic groups, and await an opportunity to tear the regime down violently. They constitute an "anomic interest group" and participate in the major riots and demonstrations that have punctuated the recent history of Morocco. All of Suleiman's conclusions appear to remain accurate in the early 1990s.

Although the situation in Tunisia has been similar since the early or mid-1970s, most university students and well-educated young Tunisians were not politically alienated during the 1960s. Writing in 1963, one analyst described this category of the country's youth as "relatively moderate" and explained the origins of this moderation with the reference to the policies of Tunisian government at the time. "Growing up in a society where some major advances toward modernization have been made and where the goals of the modernized youth have been widely accepted, they do not feel driven to more extremist solutions." Communists and other agitators, he added, "would, therefore, unquestionably have more difficulty generating acts of violence among Tunisians than among Moroccans" (Ashford 1963:55). A survey conducted at the University of Tunis in spring 1966 also revealed political moderation and generally positive attitudes toward the government (Moore and Hochschild 1968). So, too, did a broader survey carried out in Tunis and several smaller towns in 1966–1967, which found younger, university-educated Tunisians to be politically confident and ascending (Tessler 1976:82–86). Though educated primarily after independence and only at the beginning of their professional careers, these young men and women stood out as the most politically active and efficacious members of the postindependence generation. They were also as positively oriented toward political life as were comparably educated members of the pre-independence generation, most of whom were already professionally established.

Less-educated young Tunisians, by contrast, did display significant levels of political alienation in the 1960s. According to the 1966–1967 study mentioned above, "alienation is the central fact of political life" among younger intermediate school graduates, those between the ages of seventeen and twenty-seven who had received only eight or nine years of schooling (Tessler 1976:85). The study also found political discontent among members of the postindependence generation who had completed high school, although the pattern was not as striking as among those with only an intermediate school education. In seeking to explain the negative political attitudes of these categories of the population, the study placed greatest emphasis on unfulfilled expectations. "Too young to remember very well the successful struggle for independence, they probably judge the government by the success or failure of its development programs. And despite some objective gains, it is doubtful that these young Tunisians have had a fair share of the benefits of independence" (Tessler 1976:85). This interpretation is reinforced by another analysis of the same data, which revealed that increased education did not, by itself, produce positive political attitudes. In the context of Tunisia at this time, political alienation declined as a function of education only to the extent that the latter variable was correlated with professional and economic status. Alternatively, increased professional and economic status was associated with positive political attitudes even when education was held constant (Tessler 1979).

Political alienation increased in the 1970s, probably at least partly in response to a change in the leadership and orientation of the Tunisian government (see Tessler and Freeman 1981); and though the change in mass political attitudes was pronounced among all sectors of society, it was particularly clear among the young. For example, a replication of the 1966–1967 study in 1972–1973 revealed a drop from 64 to 39 percent in the proportion of respondents expressing the view that "the government cares about people like me," and among members of the postindependence generation, those under the age of twenty-seven, the fall was from 62 to 30 percent. Similarly, the proportion agreeing that "it is possible for people like me to have political influence" dropped from 51 to 35 percent for all respondents and from 51 to 30 percent among younger respondents.

Moreover, both this study and others revealed that political discontent was no longer pronounced only among less-educated members of the younger generation. By the early or mid-1970s, widespread political alienation was evident among young Tunisians who were receiving or had recently completed a university education. In the 1972–1973 replication of the 1966–1967 survey, for example, the proportion of young Tunisians with a university education who expressed the view that the government cares about them declined from 69 to 18 percent, in other words from a level higher to a level lower than that of other respondents. A study of Tunisians attending university about this time also revealed that political alienation had become pronounced. It reported that a counterculture at variance with both the theory and practice of Tunisia's guided democracy was emerging among university students, and that this counterculture was characterized by political disaffection and open opposition to the philosophical assumptions, institutional arrangements, political processes, and elitist behavior of the government and its leaders (Entelis 1974). The study also reported that students perceived inequality of opportunity for social mobility and access to jobs, believing that the system favored people of higher social status.

These antisystem political attitudes persisted through the 1970s and 1980s. According to one journalistic investigation, for example, there was growing agitation and tension on university campuses in Tunisia and other North African countries, and this tension and agitation were rooted in socioeconomic circumstances. Indeed, the unhappy mood of the students, "on campuses which are being steadily transformed into ghettos, symbolizes a malaise that is increasingly taking hold in the entire country" (Bourgi 1989: 38). Typical of the militant denunciations of the government articulated in student circles are the views expressed in *North African News,* a bimonthly newsletter published in the United States by an organization calling itself North African Students for Freedom. Writing of the current Tunisian regime, which came to power in 1987 and proclaimed its top priority to be movement toward democracy, the newsletter recently charged that although the regime in Tunis advocates democracy it in fact delivers oppression: The government "speaks about human rights yet hundreds are being tortured in its jails, [it] preaches pluralism yet the ruling party monopolizes everything" ("Special Report on Tunisia" 1990:1).

By the late 1970s and early 1980s, these complaints had led many young Tunisians, including an unknown but apparently significant proportion of university students, to turn toward Islamic movements as a vehicle for expressing their political discontent. The growth of Islamic tendency movements during the 1970s has been documented by a number of investigations (see Tessler 1980; see also Waltz 1986), and a Tunisian scholar who conducted empirical research on this phenomenon in the early 1980s reported that "the Islamic movement is first and foremost a movement of educated youth, it being principally high school and university circles that serve as centers of propagation and bases of support" (Hermassi 1984:41). Further, this trend has continued and, if anything, become even more pronounced during the early 1990s. For example, students oriented toward Islam formed the General Tunisian Union of Students (UGTE), which was legalized in 1988 after several years of operation without formal recognition and which, according to one account, has been responsible for as much as 80 percent of the protest activities on Tunisian campuses (Soudan 1989b). UGTE, described as an extension of the Islamicist Nahda party, is not only opposed to the orientation of the regime in general but is particularly hostile to its educational policies, which the union views as too secular and pro-French. Thus overall, with many observers agreeing that increased support for militant Islamic groups is largely a symptom of the deeper political and economic crises confronting Tunisia (see Vandewalle 1988b:617), the growth of young people's interest in Islamic movements is yet another important indication of the political alienation of the country's youth.

Although there has been less empirical research concerning the situation in Algeria, it appears that political alienation among the country's young people, and especially among better-educated members of the postindependence generation, did not assume significant proportions until relatively recently. Thus, although currents of militant Islam were beginning to make inroads among some university and high school students during the 1970s, leading to occasional clashes on university campuses and elsewhere, a U.S. scholar describing the situation at the end of the decade could characterize most university students as "relatively politically docile" (Entelis 1986:121).

Political alienation was much more evident among well-educated young Algerians during the 1980s, however, expressing itself both in terms of leftist ideologies and, as in Tunisia and Morocco, through the vehicle of Islamic militancy. Indeed, opposition movements with an Islamic focus grew rapidly in

Algeria during this period, and the activities of these movements were highly visible in high schools and on university campuses, particularly but not exclusively among students in the Arabophone sections. Islamic groups demand greater attention to Muslim social codes, as well as political and economic reform, and in this context they have frequently clashed with leftist students. Some of these clashes have been violent, moreover, as when protests by militant Islamic students at the University of Algiers in November 1982 led to confrontations in which one leftist student was killed and a number of others injured. Four hundred Muslim activists were subsequently arrested. The scholar who noted relative docility in the late 1970s thus found a different situation five or six years later: "Many of the secondary school graduates are unemployed, and university students represent a radical faction that the current government fears as an automatic threat, a genie that cannot return to its bottle" (Entelis 1986:108).

It is probably among less-educated young people that political alienation in Algeria is most intense. Antiregime sentiments appear to have been present during the 1970s, as many who enrolled in primary school after independence found their opportunities for advancement blocked, and these sentiments increased in both scope and intensity during the 1980s, producing a number of disturbances over the course of the decade and finally exploding in the riots of October 1988. Prior to these riots, the most violent confrontations had occurred in November 1986, when students in Constantine and the eastern region demonstrated against poor living conditions and spawned a wider youth protest that degenerated into rioting.

Poorly educated young men and women are no longer impressed by tales of their leaders' accomplishment in securing independence. "Young people no longer ask their elders what they did during the war," writes one analyst. "To them the war is a two hour weekly history lesson. They want to know, as one student bitterly stated . . . why more than half of them are jobless 'while we earn billions per year from natural gas, and [the former head of the ruling party] lives like a king'" (Vandewalle 1988a:2). Another account makes the same point, stating that the revolt of the students is actually the revolt of the future unemployed. Discussing the riots in Constantine in 1986, for example, the author notes that the overwhelming majority participating were born after independence and then states that although they were exposed to a generation of socialist ideology, they were also exposed to "state corruption, social problems and political abuse." The overall cause of political alienation among students and others is defined by this scholar as the problem of the "three p's," a characterization that is apt for other North African countries as well: "The core of the problem is the system of power, patronage and privilege that entrenched interests in the party, government and the economy are unwilling to sacrifice in the name of some larger good" (Entelis 1988:52–53).

Under these circumstances, young Algerians, like their counterparts elsewhere in the Maghrib, are turning to opposition movements that proclaim Islam to be the solution, most notably (in the Algerian case) to the Islamic Salvation Front (Belhassen 1989). Evidence of the magnitude of this trend is provided by the municipal and provincial council elections of June 1990, in which the FIS received almost two-thirds of the votes and won control of 32 out of 48 provinces and 853 out of 1,535 municipal councils. It is impossible to determine the extent to which those who voted for the FIS did so merely to express discontent with the regime, rather than because they genuinely believe that Islam can provide answers to the country's political and economic problems. Yet many—perhaps most—young Algerians are probably not concerned with a distinction of this sort. As one young Algerian seeking to explain his support for the FIS said, "In this country, if you are a young man . . . you have only four choices: you can remain unemployed and celibate because there are no jobs and no apartments to live in; you can work in the black market and risk being arrested; you can try to emigrate to France to sweep the streets of Paris or Marseilles; or you can join the FIS and vote for Islam" (Ibrahim 1990:1)

In Libya as well there are indications of widespread political alienation among university students and other young people. In contrast to the situation in the rest of the Maghrib, however, grievances derive primarily from the regime's political and ideological rigidity and only secondarily from general economic uncertainty. In addition, unlike the case elsewhere in North Africa, students appear to be divided, with both a fair number of supporters and opponents of the government (Metz 1989:200).

One set of complaints centers on government interference in student affairs. Following the revolution, the regime altered the university curriculum to bring it in line with the official ideology. It also dismissed professors and administrators and, on occasion, intervened in student elections. Opposition to such behavior was reflected not only in demonstrations organized by students but in a survey carried out among university students, faculty members, and civil servants in the mid-1970s, which found broad agreement that regime policies toward the university were inappropriate and ineffective (Bubtana 1976). Furthermore, confrontations over the issue of government interference in university life were actually part of a larger struggle that pitted the ideological vision of the regime against the desire of many students, particularly those from middle-class backgrounds, for greater personal freedom. This was an especially important source of student discontent in the 1970s, before Islamic movements came to prominence on the campuses of North Africa. As summarized by Raymond Hinnebusch, "Qadhafi's radical policies led to open clashes with students in the streets. . . . [His] puritanical, nativistic cultural policies seemed [to the students] an effort to repress personal freedom; the prohibitions on imported Western music and alcohol, on holding hands between the sexes, the forcible cutting of long hair, were all seen as encroachments by the state on legitimately private concerns." The regime, for its part, considered the students "a conduit of Western cultural contagion which had to be cut" (Hinnebusch 1982:209). The agitation and conflict to which this test of wills gave rise was most intense in the 1970s but was by no means unknown in the 1980s. In spring 1986, for example, students in the faculties of English and French at al-Fatah University organized protests in response to Qadhafi's continuing campaign to increase Arabization and eliminate Western influence, which in this instance included an attempt to close these faculties and destroy their libraries (Metz 1989:115).

The cultural issues underlying these confrontations should not be permitted to give the impression that protests by students and other young Libyans are devoid of explicitly political content. The authoritarian character of the regime is also a major focus of student complaint, in some instances giving rise to clashes between students and police. Among these were confrontations organized by the Muslim Brotherhood in 1984 and 1985, which led to the arrest of a number of students and the hanging of two of them. Also indicative of opposition to the regime, though not an operation in which students were directly involved, was a May 1984 attack on the Bab al-Azziziya barracks. The attack was planned and carried out by a coalition of dissident groups, including the National Front for the Salvation of Libya and the Muslim Brotherhood. During the late 1970s and early 1980s, there were also demonstrations and even attacks organized by Libyan students residing outside the country, including politically damaging invasions of Libyan diplomatic missions abroad (Hinnebusch 1982:212); and this in turn led the government in Tripoli to recall the 4,000 to 5,000 young Libyans attending universities in Western countries. In 1985 the study grants and travel permits of most of these students were terminated, obliging them to return home in order to continue their education.

Less information is available about the attitudes of nonelites toward the regime, although, as noted, there appears to be considerable appreciation of the government's willingness to invest in programs aimed at promoting development and enhancing the welfare of the average citizen. Further, in that these policies have required an assault on established social hierarchies and traditional patterns of leadership, at least one major study suggests that attitudes toward such efforts have tended to split along generational lines, with opposition being most intense among older Libyans and with young people more supportive of the government's approach to development. For example—although based on empirical work carried out in the mid-1970s and thus not necessarily indicative of popular attitudes in the 1990s—this study found a strong correlation between youth and support for many of the modernist values championed by the regime (Fathaly and Palmer 1980:108–109). To the extent that these conclusions are generalizable and currently valid, Libya emerges as something of a deviant case in the North African arena. As citizens of a country with a small population and considerable financial resources at its disposal, Libyan nonelites benefit from official programs and policies in a way that is unmatched in Tunisia, Algeria, and Morocco, and hence they apparently do not share the intense political alienation common elsewhere in the Maghrib.

There was hope at the end of the 1980s and the beginning of the 1990s that the political alienation of young people in the Maghrib would diminish in the years ahead. In Morocco there had been a modest but not insignificant opening up of political life following the disturbances of 1984, and economic growth in the late 1980s had been another encouraging sign. In Tunisia a change of regime in November 1987 had brought meaningful progress toward democracy, including new press freedoms and the holding of competitive parliamentary elections in April 1989. Finally, in Algeria major economic and political reforms were called for and to a considerable extent implemented by government leaders in the wake of the October 1988 riots, with genuinely competitive municipal and provincial council elections taking place in June 1990. Thus, although to varying degrees, developments under way in the Maghrib had the potential to address many of the grievances of young people and to create patterns of political economy that would reduce the alienation of North Africa's youth.

Unfortunately, movement toward more democratic patterns of governance quickly came to a halt in Tunisia and Algeria, the two countries where progress had been most pronounced. In Tunisia, because of electoral laws favoring the ruling party and also because the government refused to grant legal status to the most important opposition movement, the Nahda, opposition parties did not capture a single seat in Parliament in the April 1989 balloting. Further, beginning in fall 1990 and continuing through 1991, the government took forceful and sometimes violent action to suppress the Nahda party and silence its Islamicist message. Hundreds of party members were arrested, a dozen opposition publications were shut down or suspended, and the pro-Islamicist UGTE was banned. These actions produced several violent confrontations and brought widespread unrest to virtually all of the country's university campuses.

In Algeria the municipal and provincial elections of June 1990 resulted in broad gains for the major opposition movement, the Islamic Salvation Front, leading some to conclude that Algerian citizens would be given meaningful choices and a political opening whose outcome was not predetermined. But the government changed course with the approach of national parliamentary elections, scheduled for June 1991. It first proposed a change in electoral laws to enhance the position of the ruling party and then postponed the elections when the FIS responded by calling a general strike. Shortly thereafter, the government declared a state of emergency, sent soldiers into the streets of Algiers and other cities, and arrested opposition leaders. Finally, when the FIS scored a decisive victory in the first round of the postponed parliamentary elections, which were permitted to take place in December 1991, the military intervened and Algeria's experiment in democratization came to an end, at least for the time being. Accompanying the army's intervention and cancellation of the second round of balloting were the dissolution of the existing parliament and the resignation of the country's president.

As a result of these developments, the political situation in North Africa has drifted back toward the unrest and confrontation that characterized most of the 1980s. Many North Africans, especially the young, appear to be concluding that their leaders remain committed to preserving the status quo and with it their own power and privilege, and that they are hence unwilling to see genuine progress toward democratization and government accountability. The anger and alienation to which these judgments contribute were visible in North Africa during the 1991–1992 crisis in the Persian Gulf. In Tunisia, Algeria, and Morocco, opposition to the status quo was reflected in public demonstrations in favor of Iraq and in expressions of militant opposition to the action of the U.S.-led coalition (Tessler 1991:7–9).

Democratization and increased government accountability will not, by themselves, bring about a wholesale transformation in the political attitudes of young people. The most important source of frustration and discontent is the unmet demand for more goods and services, increased access to higher education, and above all jobs. Moreover, no matter what course the government pursues, these problems will remain intense in the immediate future, and, as in the past, they will fall most heavily on the young in general and the poorly educated young in particular.

Nevertheless, if the unrest of the 1980s is to be avoided in the 1990s, and if young people and others are to give their leaders time in which to address problems that can only be solved in the long run, they will have to be convinced that the government is struggling honestly and with dedication on behalf of all citizens, and that it is distributing as equitably as possible those burdens of underdevelopment that cannot be avoided. Governments can do this only by holding themselves genuinely accountable to the people and by working to eliminate privilege and corruption in the midst of widespread poverty. This is a lot to ask, and recent developments do little to inspire confidence that governments will undertake the necessary political reforms. Yet the degree of movement in this direction will surely determine whether the uncertainty of young people will be tempered by patience and hope or whether anger and alienation will continue or even deepen, leading to more unrest in the 1990s.

5

Islam and the State

Mohammed Tozy

For an understanding of Islam, the Maghrib of Morocco, Algeria, and Tunisia is a natural unit, not just as a geographic entity but also in the similarity of its countries' historical itineraries after independence; Libya followed a similar pattern but is treated here more briefly. Beyond the social programs set up by the three regimes, the same historical experiences mark their relations with Islam: an acceleration of secularization and state control in the early years of independence; an adjustment of Islam and its integration into the language of legitimacy, leading to a government monopoly of the interpretation of religious precepts; the birth of a more or less powerful Islamicist movement; and total state control of the means of expression and diffusion of the Muslim religion.

Emancipation and Secularist Temptations

Independence put an end to the formal domination of the European powers, but everywhere in the Maghrib, especially in Tunisia, the elites that came afterward went further in their desire to break with the precolonial legacy than the colonial authorities who preceded them. The programs of the "Westernized" elites (Yacine 1980) were consistent with the ones carried out by the vilified colonial authorities and were marked by the precipitation that characterizes the action of an elite convinced that it is the vanguard of progress. With varying intensity, depending on the relative weight of the different factions of the national movement, a conception of the future of society was forged that reduced the role of religion to a symbol. The speed with which a set of secularist measures was enacted—a family code in Tunisia, nationaliza-

---

This chapter has been updated and material on Libya added by the editors.

tion of the *habous* (religious property) land in Algeria, neutralization of the Qarawiyin mosque university in Morocco—was restrained only by the degree of resistance from religious figures and by the crises of growth of the different regimes. As a result of these factors, a balance was established that allowed the state to make Islam the official religion on the condition that it restrict its activities to civil society. Only under the Sanusi monarchy in Libya was the pressure for secularization weaker and the religious resistance more entrenched.

Tribulations of the Istiqlali Left

It took Morocco only four years (1956–1960) to find a stable balance between a Salafi interpretation of religion preached by all the nationalist factions and a *makhzen*ian interpretation giving the king the role of guardian of all actors in the religious arena, even those who collaborated with the protectorate. The drive of the Istiqlal (Independence) party to promote a single interpretation of Islam carried it into a witch-hunt against the brotherhoods and marabouts (local saints). Two crises gave the king the opportunity to impose himself as the referee and to start the process of taking over the religious discourse: the Qarawiyin crisis and the Bahai trials.

Often overlooked, the Qarawiyin crisis marked a turning point in Moroccan religious life and set the stage for the organization of the League of the Ulama. The battle with state power took place in two acts: First, when the celebration of the millennium of the Qarawiyin University was organized by a part of the modernist elite, the ulama felt deprived of their turf and resented it. They boycotted the festivities and delayed them for six months; it took the personal intervention of Mohammed V to gather an audience, and then only to attend his speech and leave (Daoud and Tozy 1987). Three years later, the Ministry of National Education planned to unify the education system by integrating the primary cycle of rural religious education and the first years of the secondary cycle to the general curriculum, and attaching the Qarawiyin to the Mohammed V University under a new director who was not an *alim*. The response by the religious community was swift and effective.

> Our reaction was to organize a congress in Rabat which was attended by 400 ulama representing all the different regions of Morocco for two days [September 18–19, 1960]. They studied the problems and the threats facing religious education. They also announced their rejection of a director of the Qarawiyin who did not graduate from it. . . . The protest led by the recently [1961] created Rabita of the Ulama induced the King to intervene and one of the first texts that Hassan II promulgated was a decree establishing the Qarawiyin [as an independent] University. (Hassani 1970:112, 115)

The issue of the Bahais, a sect that grew away from Islam, occurred in a different environment. As a result of a trial of Bahais for apostasy in Nador, a rather strong secular faction provoked the crystallization of a religious front around *alim* and Istiqlal leader Allal al-Fassi (minister of religious affairs at the time) and obliged the king, despite his sympathy for the secularist faction led by royal counselor Ahmed Redha Guedira, to support the condemnation of the Bahais in his role as religious head of the Moroccan Muslim community.

A Failed Secularization in Algeria

The victory of Ahmed Ben Bella and his followers at the time of Algerian independence brought to light the hidden structures and Islamic conception of state power. The perception of the revolutionary concepts through the prism of Islam informed the process of evicting the factions of Ferhat Abbas and later of Mohammed Harbi and replacing them with a power machine based on collective leadership. It produced a reinterpretation of representation as attached to the tradition of *shura* (consultation). Nevertheless, it was a time of "Islamic secularism" (Sanson 1983); indeed, revolutionary legitimacy, strengthened by a war of national liberation, could afford to overlook religious attachment. Moreover, from the beginning the state was called to rid itself of a troublesome ally, the Association of the Reformist Ulama.

Between 1956 and 1962, relations with Islam on the part of most of the components of the nationalist movement fluctuated between nonaggression (statutes of the FLN in 1958) and obvious hostility. The Federation in France of the FLN (FFFLN) advocated the separation of state and religion, and the Communist party (PCA) favored the elimination of religion from any future political project. The pressures exercised by the ulama (declaration of August 22, 1962) were successful in bending this secularist faction toward the status quo. It was not until 1964 that the state launched an offensive aimed at weakening the independent religious actors (brotherhoods, minor marabouts, Ibadite minority), whereas the Salafi imams who belonged to the Association of the Reformist Ulama were recruited as civil servants. The integration of private and public *habous* holdings into the property of the state on September 1, 1962, was the climax of this operation that led the Algerian authorities to adopt a single version of Islam adapted to a Jacobin conception of the state.

The Hunt for Zeitounians

Tunisia went further than any other Maghribi state toward marginalizing religion, although less as a system of beliefs than as a principle of social organization. From its inception, Bourguiba's regime made systematic attack against Islam a proof of modernity and efficiency. A series of daring measures were announced as of 1956: abolition of the *habous* (decrees of May 13, 1956, and July 18, 1957), reform of personal-status laws (decree of August 13, 1956), suspension of the *shari*ʿa courts (decrees of March 29, 1956, and October 1, 1958), and contesting the obligation to fast during the month of Ramadan.

The affair of the renegade Salah Ben Youssef (Debbasch 1962:143; Ben Achour 1979:69) and the support he received from a majority of the religious figures partly account for the passion with which the new regime attacked the Zeitouna mosque university system, symbol of an "outmoded" society and locus of reproduction of a small, competing elite of a few important families (Ben Achour, Djait, and others). The decrees of March 29, 1958, and October 1, 1958, put a definitive end to the Zeitouna by reducing it to a simple affiliate of the University of Tunis, consecrating the unification of the education system.

The relationship between Bourguibism and Islam, however, was not as simple as is usually presented. At stake was more the control of religious initiative than religion itself, even though history will only remember the verbal excesses of the Tunisian president. Before and after independence, the opportunistic Bourguiba did not hesitate to manipulate Islam without giving it the major role in the legitimacy of the regime. His tactics were evident in, for example, his speech of December 8, 1958, when he criticized the inhabitants of Ghomrassen for not having a mosque; his use of a *fetwa* of a few ulama to endorse the republic; his official celebration of the Friday prayer; and the conversion of his first wife after more than twenty years of marriage (Debbasch 1962:146f). After the Kairouan riots on June 17, 1961, the regime avoided direct attacks on religion in deference to public opinion (Debbasch 1962:144).

A Sufi Monarchy in Libya

The absence of a modern nationalist movement and the small size of the urban population produced little pressure for secularization in Libya, and the ascendency of a monarch, Idris I, whose only claim to legitimacy lay in his leadership of the Sanusiya sect, protected entrenched religion (Khadduri 1963; Deeb and Deeb 1982:96f; Anderson 1991). Even when the government tried to abolish the *shari^{c}a* courts in 1954, as was done in other Middle Eastern countries after independence, popular pressure forced their reinstatement four years later. When government programs produced a spread of secular educational institutions, religious institutions expanded Islamic education at the primary, secondary, and university levels explicitly to counter the dangers of moral laxity and leftist radicalism that secular education might bring.

Islam, the State Religion

The next stage did not wait until the first period of secularization was over to begin. The effort to rediscover Islam was a prolongation of the different uses that the Maghribi nationalist movements made of religious symbolism in order to oppose the Westerners. The difference was that efforts at state building forced the new elites again to bring in religion for two reasons: because religion was part of the nationalist strategy and, outside the elites, nationalism was indistinguishable from Islam; and because the construction of a centralized nation-state required an effort of mobilization and would end up in a search for unanimity (*wahda*) conceived only within an Islamic epistemology.

Between the beginning of the 1960s and the end of the 1970s, however, there was a gradual evolution in the way of defining the place of religion in the construction of the state. At first accepted as an element of ascriptive identity inherent in the region that had few effects on internal affairs, Islam went through multiple rereadings to become a basic element of the political practice, a source of legitimacy for those in authority and of delegitimization against the opposition. This effort of reinterpretation, though, was possible only after a neutralization of the historical guardians of the exegetic function, the ulama, by elimination, marginalization, or integration.

The Islam of the Commander of the Faithful

Upon his succession to the throne in 1961, King Hassan II of Morocco began the change from formal head of both the state and the religious community to a total command of the religious arena, clothed in a rewritten religious legitimacy woven with *makhzen*ian skill out of hagiographic, juridical, and theological strands (Tozy 1981). This process was focused in two directions, political (weakening the religious authorities and encouraging religious pluralism) and doctrinal (monopolizing religious interpretation and personal sacralization of the "grandson of the prophet").

The secular orientation of the government of Prime Minister Abdellah Ibrahim in 1959 was taken up by the king in 1963. By that time the electoral victory of the Front for the Defense of the Constitutional Institutions (FDIC), dominated by the liberal faction of Guedira, enabled the king to clear the political arena of the traditional ulama, who had been discredited by a campaign of criticism for their weak nationalism. This dilution of religious authority was carried out in two steps: the "nationalization" of the ulama through their massive enrollment in the civil service, and the political neutralization of the main religious leaders. Indeed, after the creation of the League of the Ulama of Morocco, offers of high positions around the palace were used to induce the main religious figures to break their ties with the political parties. With few exceptions, such as Allal al-Fassi and Abu Bakr Kadiri of the Istiqlal and Habib al-Forgani and Moulay Larbi al-Alaoui of the National/Socialist Union of Popular Forces (UNFP/USFP), most (including Mekki Naciri, Abdellah Guenoun, Mokhtar al-Soussi, and Ahmed Bensouda) were sent into early political retirement, ending their illustrious careers.

Encouragement of pluralism has been one of the favorite means of political action of the referee-monarch. In contrast to the Istiqlal party, which attacked any religious tendencies that did not follow the orthodox norms of the Salafiya, the king politically expressed the highest respect for the different expressions of popular Islam yet kept careful control over the development of the Zawiya. Even a brotherhood such as the Kettaniya, which officially supported the exile of Mohammed V in 1953, was given a second chance through a subtle dissociation between the Fez branch (forbidden) and that of Sale (still active today). There is, however, a difference in the king's relationship to the "popular" Islam of the brotherhoods and that of the marabouts. If the brotherhoods were not attacked, they were not all supported. In reality, several brotherhoods died by themselves or were neutralized through subtle matrimonial alliances (Sherqawiya, Wezzaniya). In contrast, the monarch led a maraboutic policy consistent with the *makhzen*ian tradition, including renewal of the *dahir*s (decrees) on *tawqir* (veneration) of the saints' descendants (Tozy 1988a:155, 182), homage paid every year with gifts (*hiba*) to the main marabouts (Moulay Idris of Fez and Moulay Abdessalem Ben Machich, Sidi Hmad ou Moussa, and the Regraga of Zerhoun) and dispatch of important delegations of ministers for the celebration of yearly festivals for the saints (*moussem*) (Pascon et al. 1984:141, 222).

Doctrinally, the revival of the *beyf a* (contract of allegiance) and its introduction as a constitutional element helped reduce the role of positive law and turn a historically sacred legitimacy into a mere institutional framework (Vedel et al. 1986:56f; Zartman 1962). Therefore, as said the young monarch, newly enthroned, "The constitution that I built with my hands and that will be published through out the territory of the kingdom and will be submitted for approval within a period of 20 days is above all the renewal of the sacred pact that has always united the people and the King" (Hassan II 1965:198). Sacredness is not to be confused with an object of worship. It means much more than that: a place in the hierarchy of norms and political actors, a capacity for a transhistorical symbolism, a standard by which laws are made or undone. It is supremacy as well as veneration and is rich in consequence: The shape of the regime has the same unquestionable status as that of religion; the royal person is sacred and unviolable (constitution of 1979) and can neither be criticized nor mocked (Article 41 of the *dahir* of November 15, 1958, modified by Article 41 of the *dahir* law of April 10, 1973); the decisions of the king are nonjusticiable (arrêt A. Ronda, Supreme Court 1960), superior to all other legal norms produced by the state. Hassan II told members of Parliament on October 13, 1978, that

> the exercised control by the one that God has made responsible for succeeding the Prophet is necessary, not only over the executive but also over the legislative power. . . . The Holy Book indicates that all whom God has charged with a legis-

lative or executive responsibility have to obey his control: a control from God first of all, a control from the one that God has charged with the responsibility of the Muslim community, and last of all a control by the voters. (*Le Matin du Sahara*, October 16, 1978)

The sacrality thrice justified by the *fiqh* (jurisprudence), the hagiography, and the constitution makes submission and obedience a triple obligation: civic through positive law, canonic through religious law (*shariʿa*), and charismatic as a source of blessing through the king and descendant of the Prophet (*sharif*).

The Islamic Coloring of Algerian Socialism

The virulent denunciation of Boumedienne's socialism by Shayk Abdellatif Soltani (who was to become an Islamic hero of the 1980s for his criticism of the regime) in an article published in Morocco and entitled "Mazdaqism Is the Source of Socialism" testifies to the difficulties of trying to reconcile Islam and socialism—even a socialism in which references to both class struggle and condemnation of private property were banished (Burgat 1988b:95). One of the first problems that Boumedienne's regime faced was brought on by an agrarian reform policy that dealt with the lands belonging to religious brotherhoods (notably in the region of Oulad Sidi Cheikh). The difficulties could no longer be brushed aside with a simple negative reference to religion, as in the Algiers Charter (Sanson 1983:64), nor even with a sarcastic exegesis, as used by Boumedienne on certain occasions, such as during the Islamic conference at Lahore: "I do not wish to philosophize on Islam. . . . Many of the most eminent scholars have done that already. . . . I think that if there is a spiritual link between all of us, that link should be made concrete and should be given material content. . . . A people that is hungry does not need to listen to verses, with all the respect that I pay to the Qoran that I learned when I was ten" (Leca and Vatin 1975:414).

Henceforth, an ideological undertaking became necessary, and it was carried out in two directions: elimination of the competing clerics and reinterpretation of Islam. Inaugurated with a witch-hunt as an extension of the liberation war, the drive to eliminate competing religious authorities aimed at the most popular embodiments of Islam: the brotherhoods and marabouts (Sanson 1983:106). It was sometimes led by religious groups close to the political authorities, such as the al-Qiyam (Values) association before the group was banned in 1966 and then dissolved in 1970. The objective was to assure that the state had the monopoly over the organization of the religious sources of reference and their interpretation. Two far-reaching reforms ensured the state of a relative and temporary success. One was a policy of widespread Arabization that first touched the members of the political elite before extending to the whole education system, and the second was the formation of an administrative body responsible for controlling and reflecting on religion.

Created by decree on February 13, 1966, the Higher Islamic Council was to issue *fetwa*s to inform the government of breaches and falsifications of Islamic law and to control the activities of groups that claimed a religious purpose. In addition, the state organized an annual seminar on Islamic thought, a sort of international forum for theologians and students of Islam whose debates were published in the journal *al-Assala* (Steadfastness). The role of the seminar was threefold: it served as an education circle, a locus of reflection on the ideologico-religious concerns of the state authorities, and a proof of the Islamicism of the party and of the modernity of Islam.

After a decade of institutionalized pragmatism in government, the national charter of 1976 came to formalize relations between socialism and Islam. The authors of the supraconstitutional basic text strove to show the absence of contradictions and even the complementarity between these two sources of legitimacy. The document offers a theoretical framework and a rereading of history that present the possible symbiosis between religious and socialist values. According to the charter, Islam "is one of the most powerful protections against the enterprises of de-personalisation," and an Islamicism that has its place alongside socialism can be approached through a particular reinterpretation that would break, for the most part, with clerical conceptions and would institute a state monopoly over the interpretation of dogma.

> In order to regenerate itself, the Islamic world has only one possibility: to go beyond reformism and strike out on the path of social revolution. . . . The revolution fits well into the historic perspective of Islam. Islam, in a proper understanding of its spirit, is not related to any particular interest [or] to any religious figure. . . . In order to be credible, the reconstruction of the Muslim thought must rest on a much wider undertaking: the total restructuring of the society. (Sanson 1981:101)

The reactivation of the FLN during the extraordinary congress of June 1980 in Algiers permitted an updating of the ideological concerns of the authorities. There it was said that "the FLN takes the responsibility for building socialism within the framework of the national and Islamic values" (FLN Statutes 1980: Art. 7). Islam was henceforth "a religion and an ideology" (*al-Moudjahid* [The holy warrior], July 31, 1981). This search for ideological consistence, however, belongs to another objective, that of outbidding the Islamicist competition.

Tunisian Islam in the Service of Modernity

The first article of the Tunisian constitution that stipulates that "the religion of Tunisia is Islam" refers more to identity than to political practice. In much the same way as he manipulated socialism, the supreme *mujahid* (combatant), Bourguiba, demanded of Islam an effort of interpretation that was facilitated by the forced resignation of the traditional clerics and above all by the hegemonic nature of the Salafi framework of "decoding" that legitimized *ijtihad* (interpretation) by the political authorities. There are, though, two limitations to the scope of this reinterpretation of religion in a modernist perspective: the fear of communism that always motivated the authorities and the pressure of public opinion expressed through social movements of a religious nature (such as the Kairouan riots of 1961).

To Bourguiba, "the progress of Islam and its evolution necessarily suppose an effort of constant research and free thinking in order to overhaul everything that can seem rigid and outmoded in legislation, everything that is no longer consistent with the requirements of a life under continuous renewal and that is no longer in tune with objective facts in constant evolution" (1961 speech at Kairouan, cited in Debbasch 1962:147ff). At no time was Islam to be explicitly called into question; even the operations considered by the observers (Ben Achour 1981:65) to be frontal attacks on Islam can be seen as a reinterpretation. With regard to the fast during the month of Ramadan, Bourguiba launched into a veritable *ta^{c}wil* (formal explication) to justify the fast for economic reasons. "I invite the Tunisian people with their ulama and sheikhs to try to think about the goal set for fasting and the reasons for dispensation. Every one has to be familiar with the problems of a healthy interpretation of the divine law. If God has given human kind an intelligence, it is in order to distinguish between good and evil" (Bourguiba, speech of February 5, 1960). However demagogic the demonstration could be, it was carried out within the Islamic system of values. By assimilation and *qiyas* (analogy), development became a sort of *jihad* that justified a dispensation.

> At a time when we are struggling against poverty, setting up programs and drawing plans to escape from underdevelopment, demanding an accounting from those who do not produce enough and who limit freedom of enterprise, at the time when our life and death are at stake, at a time when the recovery of this Muslim nation depends on our tenacious work, I enjoin you to take advantage of a dispensation clearly defined by a healthy conception of the religious laws. (1961 speech at Kairouan, cited in Debbasch 1962:148)

Libyan Islam in the Service of the Sects

No less than its secularist neighbors, the Libyan state crowned by a pious Sufi shaykh moved soon after independence to put competing Muslim institutions into a position subordinate to his own structures, in this case the Sanusiya sect. The Sanusi network operated as a direct extension of the royal household and outside the institutionalized religious structures, thus wielding significant power in a polity based on palace intrigue, whereas the ulama became civil servants under state control. Even the grand mufti became part of the government bureaucracy.

When the monarchy was overthrown in 1969 and until the middle of the next decade, the revolution of Muʿammar Qadhafi sought to present itself as more Muslim than the king, with the symbols of Islam rolled into those of revolution, anticolonialism, nationalism, and anticapitalism. "His first version of Islam (1969–1972) was naturally fundamentalist" (Bleuchot 1975:70). But the new government also moved to oust the Sanisiya and replace it with a similar structure that has been called the "Qadhafiya," staffed by family members and other close allies and reaching out from Qadhafi's headquarters throughout the country. The special privileges of the Sanusiya and then the Zawiya were abolished, Islam was used to legitimize its replacement, the state was used to redefine acceptable religious practice (often in very heterodox ways), and the religious establishment was further subordinated to state control. *Waqf* (*habous*) properties were eventually nationalized, along with all other private property, and the ulama were denigrated as standing between God and the believer. More than any other North African leader, Qadhafi moved to become his own Islamicist, calling for a return to the fundaments of Islam—but as he interpreted them. This evolution began a new phase between 1973, when the five principles of the cultural revolution were announced, and 1976, when the Green Book was issued.

Maghribi Islamicism

The Iranian revolution certainly helped accelerate the Islamicist movement, whose birth dates back to the early 1970s (Tozy 1984). But a study of events might suggest that the rise of Islamicism was part of the policies of the North African states after independence. The political counterbalancing undertaken in the 1960s in order to neutralize the Communist parties and the student movements of the left led the governments to undertake some very dangerous manipulations of religion, as in the case of the Moroccan Islamic Youth (Al-Shabiba al-Islamiya) in 1973 or the Tunisian Society for the Defense of the Quran in 1976.

There is no need to debate once again the proper choice of names for the movement (integrism, fundamentalism, Islamicism, radicalism, etc.) nor to try to explain its causes either as an aspect of postmodernity or as a reaction to the exhaustion of development ideologies and a disenchantment with growth policies. But it is useful to lay down a few facts in order to counteract any overenthusiasm with theory:

- Islamicism is not a single organized movement. At most, it is a sensitivity shared by different Muslim movements that distinguish themselves from ordinary Muslims. This rising tide (*madd*), as underscored by the

actors themselves, is part of an effort to reread religion with the double purpose of delegitimizing the "blasphemous" authorities and denouncing social inequalities and immorality, and of asserting a religious claim on modernity by harmonizing the reality of experience and the system of values.
- Islamicism is different from the political program of the Salafiya. The latter was the consequence of a fascination with the West by Muslims who sought an answer to the need for catching up with the West in a return to Islamic values, whereas Islamicism is the result of a disenchantment that rejects the Western model as an archetype.
- The organizers of the Islamicist movement are for the most part graduates of the modern public schools (Tozy 1988b). Maghribi Islamicism has both a Pan-Islamic and a national vocation. The first element accounts for the sensitivity of each religious actor to the doctrinal and phenomenological variations of the Muslim world, but the second provides the particular political form and practice that in the end depends on the margin of maneuver left by the state.

The Pan-Islamic vocation is conducted through two channels. On an ideological and doctrinal basis, all Islamicist movements draw on the same authorities: Sayyi Qutb, al-Mawdudi, Ibn Taymiya (Carré 1984). On a territorial level, because Islamicist activity was under surveillance in the countries of North Africa, the Maghribi component was nurtured in Europe within the framework of the transplanted Islamic movements (Keppel 1987:168–205). Jama ͨat al-Tabligh wa al-Da ͨwa, a Pan-Islamic group with Pakistani origins, found the conditions in France and Belgium propitious for the creation of an Islamicist elite. Most of the authorities of the Tunisian branch of the Islamicist movement and of the Algerian Bouyali group, a clandestine militant band, went through the study circles of the mosques of Belleville in Paris or of rue Pasteur in Marseilles. The pilgrimage to Mecca was also an occasion for inter-Islamicist exchanges. Moreover, the attack against the al-Haram mosque in Mecca involved the participation of several Maghribi militants, including Abdelkrim Moti ͨ, emir of the Moroccan Islamicist association Al-Shabiba al-Islamiya.

The Maghribi Islamicist movement developed unevenly in the three countries. In Tunisia Islamicism is more transparent and takes the form of a movement with a well-elaborated doctrine in the process of besieging the political system. In Algeria it appears as an opaque movement that revealed itself through coups or lawsuits until the polls opened to it and it faced responsibilities for government. In Morocco it surfaced in two waves: as several well-organized factions that arose through official indifference and even complicity and then, after the riots of 1984, as a clandestine group of elites abroad and a cultural current at home. In brief, an adherent of the Tunisian movement expresses a political awareness, the Algerian is a zealot, and the Moroccan is an evangelist (comparable to a Jehovah's Witness).

Moroccan Ulama and Study Groups

A distinction exists between the associative and individual modes of Islamicist expression. The first constitutes a reinterpretation of religious action within an institutionalized system, whereas the second is consistent with the tradition of the *alim* as "public prosecutor," and its development coincides with the reinforcement of state control. Out of a score of organizations, two are illustrative of associative Islam (Etienne and Tozy 1981:246): Jamaᶜat al-Tabligh wa al-Daᶜwa was introduced into Morocco at the beginning of the 1970s (Tozy 1984:307–345). It focuses on moralizing and promotes the mosque as the social center. Without any defined political program, it loses its most zealous members to other, more politicized groups. Before they move on, however, they learn the basic principles of religion very well and become familiar with the rules of proselytism. In a way, the group constitutes a necessary way station in the Islamicist itinerary.

The Islamic Youth association was created in 1973 by a group of teachers and pupils in order to fight the aggressive leftist movements of the late 1960s. Its first emir was Abdelkrim Motiᶜ, inspector in the national education system and former member of the UNFP. After the assassination of the socialist leader Omar Benjelloun in 1975 and the exile of its president, the movement underwent several splits (Tozy 1984:352–396), and its members scattered to become either independent entrepreneurs directing several Islamicist magazines or participants in the circles organized by Abdessalem Yacine. The Islamicist youth association works on the model of the Egyptian Jamaᶜat al-Takfir wa al-Hijra, seeking the overthrow of the blasphemous regime through the spiritual and physical training of so-called soldiers of God (Keppel 1982, vol. 1:117, 599). Each member who joins the association is taken in by a group of seven persons who chose their own emir, submission to whom is a religious obligation. There are militants who could not travel or marry without the agreement of their emir (Bouali 1988:91, 95). *Fi al-dhilal* (In the shadow [of the Quran]) and *Maᶜalim fi al-tariq* (Signs of the trail) by Sayyid Qutb are the official books that are memorized and interpreted. The training is spartan during the organized trips over weekends and summer vacations. Besides learning the Quran and the books of Qutb, the followers undergo political and paramilitary training.

The "Free-lance" Islamicists

> My letter is different from the ones you have received so far. It obliges you to answer, and even your silence will be eloquent. Whatever your answer, my dear nephew of the Prophet, you won't be able to stop the words of truth and justice

that I proclaim. Whoever will be the man to stand up before me, the king or his authority, or the faithful slave of God who accepts the advice, know that God the Glorious cannot fail. The duty to advise you is imposed on the ulama by God. (Yacine 1973; Tozy 1987)

Abdessalem Yacine, the author of this letter addressed to the king at the beginning of the 1970s, is looked upon by the observers as the spiritual leader of the Islamicist movement, and yet this former inspector of education in French does not direct any Islamicist group. The use of language typified by his letter is no longer likely, as the state has considerably restricted free speech. Since 1984, however, there has been a renewal of religious elite whose profiles mirror Yacine's. Although numerous, the traditional ulama no longer assume roles as "commanders of the good." New clerics now fill the position, almost all graduates of the modern universities, between the ages of thirty-five and forty-five, bilingual, and familiar with the academic technicalities of writing and analysis. They prefer cultural rather than political activism, they claim a desire to break with the traditional *fiqh* derived from a hierarchy of sources based only on chronology, and they defend the principles of direct access to the Quran and free interpretation of the *shari'a*. Magazines, lectures, and tapes are their preferred media (Tozy 1988b:20).

Algerian Rebels and Parties

In 1978, study groups appeared in the mosques of Oran, Laqhouat, and Sidi Bel Abbes and started to challenge the imams designated by the administration. After the Iranian revolution, these groups moved on to the university campuses, the first confrontation occurring between Marxist and Islamicist students in November 1982. The attack on a police station by the Bouyali group was the most impressive act of violence that drew the attention of the international press to Algerian Islamicism.

In reality, until the elections of 1990, little was known about the Algerian movement. An Islamicist tint was given by former president Ben Bella to his exiled Movement for Democracy in Algeria through press statements and his magazine, *al-Badil* (The change). The only known group inside Algeria was the Algerian Islamicist Movement, the result of a merger of several small groups, including the Group for the Defense of the Illicit and former members of the seminars on Islamic thought organized by the state. The best-known person in the Algerian movement was Mustapha Bouyali, shot during a confrontation with the police in 1987 after several years of clandestine activity. Contrary to the Tunisian and Moroccan experience, although the doctrinal production of the Algerian movement is insignificant, the riots of October 1988 showed its capacity for popular organization, even if not mobilization, in the field left open by inadequate social development (Keppel 1987:345; Etienne 1984; Burgat 1988b:164, 170).

Islamicists' ability to capitalize on popular disenchantment with the ruling National Liberation Front was shown in March 1989, when constitutional amendments permitted the organization of additional parties. Despite a prohibition against religious parties, the Islamic Salvation Front was recognized. The party's vague positions did not prevent it from sweeping the communal and provincial elections of June 1990 and immediately demanding the end of the "impious regime" of Chadli Benjedid. However, as the general elections of June 1991 approached and preelection indications showed a loss of support for the increasing militantism of the party, its aggressiveness only rose, and the party was banned as the army took over. When the rescheduled elections in December produced a victory for the FIS, the second round of elections was cancelled, the party banned again, and a secularist regime installed.

Tunisian Parties and Militants

The choice of legality by the Tunisian Islamicist movement, even during the worst times of the Bourguibist repression, allows us to understand the process of its formation and its passage from a fundamentalist tendency in the Salafi tradition to an Islamicist movement. It has the particular distinction of being a movement that from the beginning chose to situate itself in the political sphere without claiming to be an exclusive alternative to the social programs of the other political forces (Hermassi 1984; Ghannouchi 1981; Magnuson 1991). As in the Moroccan case, the Tunisian Islamicist movement developed in the shadow of the government in the early 1970s, centered on the magazine *al-Maʿrifa* (The knowledge), edited by all the future leaders of the movement (Ahmida Ennifer, Rashid Ghannouchi, Abdelfatah Mourou).

After 1972, three activities were developed before the Islamicists became a political force organized as the Movement of the Islamic Way: the reappropriation of the mosque and the reactivation of the sermon as an effective means of social action; the penetration of university campuses as a prelude to the harsh confrontations of 1979–1980; and the adoption of a distinctive appearance (beard, cowl, rigorous behavior at work, etc.) to mark a break with an "impure" environment and, by troubling the surrounding environment, to force the simple Muslim to define himself in relation to a behavior that is difficult to criticize in terms of the official religion. In June 1981, as much by deliberate initiative as because the police had just seized some documents related to its international organization, the MTI published its constitution. Since then, its history has been marked by cycles of repression and rapprochement—and even negotiations.

In terms of ideology, the MTI claims its own path, different from eastern Islamicism. Moreover, rather than an Iranian-type revolution or a break with political or even civil society like the Egyptian group al-Takfir, it prefers a gradualist approach combining political compromise and in-depth penetration of society. The absence of a clear agenda and a coherent political vision, however, led to a split in 1982. As a result, an intellectual movement broke off to form the magazine *15/21* (named for the coming century in the Muslim and Christian calendars), whose main editors are Ennifer and Salaheddine Jourchi.

The kinship between the Renaissance party of the MTI and *15/21* is obvious, even if the former remains a mass movement and the latter an organ of doctrinal innovation. Ideologically, both tendencies develop a firm but moderate language that promotes Tunisian Islamicism as an essential component of the political game. There were great expectations for such developments when the departure of Bourguiba revealed the advanced state of erosion of the credit of the traditional political elite and of its ability to encourage Tunisians' hopes before a chronic shortfall of resources (Burgat and Tozy 1988:13–14). The new political system established by Zine al-Abidine Ben Ali gave the *15/21* groups hope for dialogue and the MTI hope for political participation as a recognized party. When Hizb al-Nahda (the Renaissance party) was refused authorization for either the 1989 national election or the 1990 local elections, relations with the state turned sour again, and the movement returned to its clandestine, violent conflict with the authorities, especially in the realm of student politics (in which it represents a dominant faction): When it provoked campus confrontations, urban bombings, and a military plot in the first half of 1991, it again was subject to heavy arrests and underwent a second split, with Mourou considering the creation of a legalized party and Ghannouchi in exile speaking for the embattled militants.

Libyan Protests on the Fringes

The unusual ideological nature of the Libyan regime offended orthodox Muslims and undercut Islamicists, leaving little room for the currents of religious protest that marked the neighboring countries. Two types of religious opposition arose on the margins of state control, one the orthodox revivalist preachers who sought to appeal to youth in religious terms and the other the clandestine militant opposition (Joffe 1988). Qadhafi's new version of Islam issued during the cultural revolution of the mid-1970s aroused critical sermons in the mosques from such popular imams as Shaykh al-Bishti in Tripoli; like secular opponents of the increasingly authoritarian regime, al-Bishti was the subject of state control and disappeared in 1980. Some criticism of the regime surface in Friday sermons after the liberalization measures of 1989 and thereafter.

Austerity and repression fed opposition and drove it underground, and Qadhafi frequently inveighed against Communists, Baathists, Muslim Brothers, and Hizb al-Tahrir al-Islami (the Islamic Liberation party). Members of these groups and others were arrested periodically after 1973. The Islamic Liberation party was allegedly involved in a plot within the army in 1983 and among the students in 1984, and other alleged conspirators from al-Jihad al-Islami (Muslim Holy War) and Hizb Allah (the Party of God) were executed in 1986 and 1987. The Islamic content of these groups is secondary to their political intent, and (unlike the MTI in Tunisia) they have been unable to capitalize on any popular opposition to the national leader to draw a mass following. The liberalization of 1988–1992 produced student protests at the universities, followed by arrests and accusations against the Muslim Brotherhood. Whether in its repressive or its liberalized mode, the regime has kept Islamicist activity on the margins of society.

State Islamicism

The Maghribi states reacted to the Islamicist challenge by rising to the defense of respect for the places of worship and appropriating the production and diffusion of religious discourse. At no time did they issue a firm refusal to Islamicist demands by adopting a secular position, nor were they prepared to take the responsibility of declaring Islam to be the religion of the state rather than the state religion (Sanson 1983). But they all adopted about the same responses: acceleration of the state-run religious education for religious personnel, control of the mosques, and repression.

State Takeover of the Mosque in Morocco

Historically, relations between the state and the Islamicist movement in Morocco have been marked by ambiguity, and actors on the political stage develop specific strategies that best answer to their own particular interests (Leveau 1981b). The king, whose legitimacy is essentially religious, cannot, because of his status of *emir al-muninin* (commander of the faithful), accept an explicit recognition of the movement as he would then either have to become its chief—and in that case himself become an Islamicist—or recognize the existence of a schism within the *umma*—and in response give up his own monopolistic role.

The government's mission, different from that of the king, is to control the society in order to prevent any malfunction. The riots in Casablanca in 1981, in Nador and Marrakesh in 1984, and in Rabat and Tangier in 1990 provided an explicit and official recognition of an Islamicist danger. Even if the thesis of foreign interference was advanced, the state reacted with strict control of movements that had previously been tolerated (such as Jama'at al-Tabligh) and the development of a security policy based essentially on administrative divisions (breaking up the urban areas of Casablanca and Rabat) and the control of the cities.

Political parties have a particularly difficult time in maintaining a clear position toward religion. The Istiqlal, the only party that could have challenged the king on his religious legitimacy, instead reverted to its Salafi perception of religion during its years in power (1976–1983) and thus accelerated the marginalization of the ulama by creating new channels of education for religious clerics within the faculties of letters. Nevertheless, in preparation for its return to the opposition, it changed its language so as to remain close to the Islamicist groups. Beyond these tactical variations, however, there appears to be a common desire among the parties to reshape the entire institutional space where politico-religious competition takes place. A sort of complicity has arisen between the different actors in order to promote the *raison d'état* and to assure control of the civil society. This policy appears at three levels: reproduction of the religious personnel, control of the mosque, and institutionalization of the clerics.

The *alim* is no longer the sole depositary of the religious knowledge; indeed, he is even a minority. The end of the 1970s witnessed an impressive increase in the number of students in the subjects related to Islam and in the diversification of the educational programs and sensitivities that underlie them. Although the Qarawiyin system is maintained, it is overwhelmed by the number of graduates from the faculties of letters (around 10,000, compared to 1,000 from the Qarawiyin). They prepare for a four-year program in Islamic studies and as a consequence qualify for admission to the master's degree program in religious studies. In addition, the Ministry of the Habous trains its own personnel of worship (Imams, muezzins, etc.).

Second, since the mid-1970s, the state has used indirect means to control the use and proliferation of mosques. These interventions are carried out either through urban-planning programs and the establishment of strict zoning measures or through preliminary review of the construction of places of worship by the Ministry of the Habous to access need. A *dahir* (1-84-150) of October 2, 1984, regulates the building and use of the mosques, requiring a construction permit by the governor of the prefecture or province. The same text also stipulates that "the management and functioning [of the places of worship] are assured by the Ministry of the Habous and of Muslim Affairs. The *khatib* [preacher] and the imam are appointed by the minister after consultation with the governor."

Between 1979 and 1984 the sermon saw such a revival that it became one of the most impressive Islamicist means of action. The model of the Egyptian preacher Abdulhamid Kishk produced imitators who proliferate throughout most of the mosques of Casablanca, Tangier, Nador, Ksar el-Kebir, and Rabat. The reaction of the state was first procedural, through suspension of ulama categorized as free-lance preachers; it then became substantive, through the distribution of a standard sermon that the *khatib* is supposed simply to read. National celebrations are also used as themes: On November 4, 1988, a memorial service was held for the Green March into the Western Sahara in 1974, and as the country's independence day approaches each March, the theme becomes the monarchy and its fight for independence.

For more than twenty years, the authorities have been dealing with a body of ulama whose only organization was the League of the Ulama of Morocco, sort of a syndicate that defends the moral interests of members and during annual meetings allows them to remind the authorities of their existence by means of recommendations, often censored by the newspapers. Around the end of the 1970s, the authorities had to face contradictory needs: On the one hand, the Islamicist challenge imposed on them the need to prepare realistic answers in religious terms, even to pursue the ideological escalation by making themselves the champions of rigorist Islam and therefore to sustain and support the only actors capable of playing the role. On the other hand, because of their historical function, the very ulama the state had to rely upon turned out to be the virtual animators of a religious contest and above all the logical beneficiaries of a desecularization of the state, all the more so because they were familiar with the themes developed by the Islamicists.

Political urgency has forced the authorities to reconcile the need to institutionalize the function of the *alim* by changing it into a strictly delimited profession and to organize a body credible enough to serve as a counterweight to Islamicism. The institutionalization of the clerics (*dahir* 1-80-270 of May 6, 1981) was accomplished through a pyramidal structure comprising all the ulama, who are divided into different districts supervised by regional councils whose presidents are appointed by the king and headed by a national council directed by him. The *alim* can no longer operate outside this framework, and he is often reminded that his role is precisely defined in the service of the state and not of morality. "Be careful, be careful!" warned the king, "Do not intervene in what does not concern you, like a rise in the price of gasoline or cigarettes." (*Daʿwat al-hal* 224, September 1982).

The Renunciation of Algerian Socialism

The constitutional amendments submitted to the Algerians on February 23, 1989, put a definitive end to explicit reference to socialism and at the same time reconfirm the Islamic character of the state. The national charter is no longer the highest authority, and the Islamic Council is constitutionally recognized. It is difficult to explain this change by a reference to the Islamicist movement alone, but it is just as difficult not to take it into account.

In fact, a long process since 1982 led the state to Islamize itself and to renounce progressively the options of revolutionary Algeria. In 1984, when the funeral of the Shaykh Soltani drew more than 20,000 followers and Islamicist militants, the government tried to anticipate the Islamicst demands. The eighteenth Congress of Islamic Thought on July 10, 1989, was devoted to the revival of Islam, and a month later, the Emir Abdelkader University of Islamic Sciences was created under the presidency of Mohammed Ghazali, a prolific ideologue of the Muslim Brotherhood of Egypt. The same year the head of the state ostentatiously made his pilgrimage to Mecca.

These proofs of Islamity were accompanied by an institutional reform aimed on one hand at defining the ideological prerogatives of the Ministry of Religious Affairs (decrees 80/30 and 80/31 organizing the ministry) and on the other hand organizing the management and use of the mosques and the training of the officials for worship service (decree of August 6, 1983, related to the organization of the National School of Meflah for the education of the staff of the worship service and the interministerial decree establishing the procedures for recruiting imams). The first article of the decree setting forth the attributions of the Ministry of Religious Affairs defines the components of a national religious policy and reveals the extent of the regime's concerns: "The Ministry . . . has the task of controlling the harmonious development of religious action . . . and of implementing the appropriate means for meeting the objectives of religious education in its ideological and moral perspectives." In addition, Article 4 provides for "the necessary steps for the continuation of efforts in quranic education and for making the mosque a place of prayer and a center for the propagation of education and Islamic civilization," in a sense taking over one of the strongholds of the Islamicists (Souriau 1981:348f).

Compromising Tunisia

The Tunisian regime was in its last days until November 1987 and in its honeymoon period for some time thereafter; in discussing its policies, we must be wary of introducing a semblance of coherence where there was none. The atmosphere of struggles for succession and then consolidation explains the many contradictions: the alternation of a period of organized repression (in July 1986 the Direction of Worship Service was moved from the Prime Ministry to the Interior Ministry) with one of rapprochement (on November 15, 1987, Prime Minister Mzali raised the possibility of a recognition of the MTI as a political party), and back again (the presidential office of Ben Ali conducted negotiations with the MTI in 1987 and included its representative on the committee for the national pact in September 1988, but Renaissance party leaders were arrested in late 1990, and a major crackdown came in the first half of 1991).

The moderate character of the MTI and Nahda, their ability to set up mass organizations such as the General Tunisian Union of Students (UGTE) to rival the official General Union of Tunisian Students (UGET) and to penetrate associations such as the Tunisian League of Human Rights (LTDH), and above all the guilt feelings that the elites developed in order to cover their neglect of religious duties (as in Algeria as well) all led the administration to perceive a policy of Islamization as a solution to the crisis of legitimacy—or at least to give up the more offensive measures that could have crystallized conflicts with the religious groups. Throughout the 1980s, a number of initiatives were undertaken that would have been difficult to carry out in previous years: a directive of the prime minister on the dress of civil servants approving the cowl as feminine apparel, a decision to close the law school cafeteria during the entire period of Ramadan, and the withdrawal of a similar directive extending the principle of closure to all public restaurants only after the intervention of the president of the republic.

The extraordinary (eleventh) congress of the Socialist Destourian party in 1981 provided an opportunity to raise the Islamic appearances of the regime and assume a better position in regard to the Islamicists. The congress recalled that "in terms of ideology, reality, and civilization, Tunisia is a Muslim country, and its people, who historically have rejected schisms and sects, have always been attached to its great religion. . . . The congress reconfirmed its attachment to the principles indicated . . . by our religion, which are essentially those of tolerance, discussion [*shura*], and interpretation [*ijtihad*]." On April 22, 1987, to further state control of the mosque, a Higher Islamic Council was created. Composed of a mufti of the republic, the dean of Zeitouna Theology University, the director of religious affairs, and seven specialists (including members of the MTI), the council was essentially responsible for defining a state religious policy. The same day a decree regarding the officials in charge of the mosques and prayer rooms was promulgated to strengthen control over these places and raise obstacles for the Islamicists.

Once at the helm, President Ben Ali began by relaxing the political environment. The liberation of Ghannouchi in 1988, even though part of a policy of general amnesty, takes on its real importance as a counterpart to the participation of the MTI in the debate on the national pact. For a while, the contradiction between the authorities and the Islamicists seemed to weaken. Ghannouchi even stated that the personal-status code, stumbling-block of all religious opposition, "is not an insoluble problem and that the Islamicists can adapt to it" (*al-Sabah* [Morning], August 10, 1988). The restrictions on confessionalism that the law on multipartism forsees did not seem to trouble the Nahda. It even seemed that the distinction between secularism and Islamicism was no longer relevant and that religion would play a more and more important role in political life in Tunisia. At least that is what can be understood in a manifest published by a group of independent intellectuals led by Hisham Djait in December 1988, in which they asked that Islam be revalued and integrated into politics.

By the beginning of 1990, however, the economic problems of the new regime only worsened, the restriction on confessionalism was reiterated as an obstacle to recognition of the Nahda party just before the April 1990 municipal election, and the militantism of the movement increased, pushing the government toward greater confrontation and repression in the 1990s.

The Neo-Islamicism of Qadhafi

Although the pattern of state relations with Islam in Libya has in many ways been similar to that of other North African countries, the major difference has come from the co-optation of both traditional Sufi and contemporary protest forms of Islam by the state under Qadhafi. Like its neighbors, the Libyan government established a Society of the Islamic Call (Jama'at al-Da'wa al-Islamiya) to spread the Islamic message soon after the revolution. Finding simple control of state apparatus inadequate to his revolutionary calling, Qadhafi took over the religion as well and put it at his service to reorient people's minds. The Quran was to be the sole religious source, untrammeled by interpreters (imams and ulama) and interpretations (*sunna* and *hadith*) but modernized by Qadhafi's own pronouncements (Anderson 1983, Davis 1987). The Green Book is taught in schools and universities and preached in mosques, bridging the secular and religious spheres.

6

Demographic Pressures and Agrarian Dynamics

Hamid Ait Amara

After more than three decades of independence, agricultural structures and production in the countries of the Maghrib are still largely determined by the strong demographic pressure on the land. The agricultural population has visibly increased despite a marked exodus toward the cities, which has not slowed since the 1960s. The jobs that were created have proven insufficient to absorb even a fraction of the agricultural population, creating a situation in which agriculture must employ and nourish more families today than ever before.

The structural reforms that were part of the nationalist parties' programs during their struggles for independence were limited to the recovery of colonial lands. As the number of landless peasants grew, there was a constant tendency to break up farmland into little pieces. Agricultural intensification was no more than a poorly pursued attempt to find an alternative to the lack of arable land. Agricultural development policies favored the irrigated sector and fruit and vegetable cultivation for local and export markets to the detriment of the rain-fed subsistence sector that supported the majority of the population. In general, production grew at a rate only slightly higher than that of the agricultural population. Under these conditions, the advancement of worker productivity does not constitute the principal source of improvement of the quality of life in the countryside. More and more, peasants have had to count on supplemental wage income from outside the agricultural sphere. One may thus question whether the beginnings of this grave agrarian crisis were not

---

Statistics in this chapter come from published and unpublished data from the respective countries' Ministries of Agriculture, unless otherwise credited.

part of a broader economic crisis that deprived agriculture of the support of a general dynamic of development.

Pressure on the Land

Since before World War II, the essential characteristic of the agrarian situation of the four North African countries has been the demographic pressure on the arable land. Contrary to the situation in Europe in the nineteenth century and China in the 1980s, the agricultural population in the Maghrib has continued to grow in size even if its weight relative to the total population has registered a major decrease. In the beginning of the 1960s, the active agrarian population represented on average 60 percent of the total active population. At the end of the 1980s, it did not total more than 39 percent in Morocco, 32 percent in Tunisia, 25 percent in Algeria, and 15 percent in Libya.

Although there was a measurable drop in fecundity in the late 1980s, the demographic explosion of the 1960s and 1970s and even the early 1980s meant that the population of the Maghrib countries increased by 2.5 times since independence to 24 million in Morocco, 23 million in Algeria, 7.7 million in Tunisia, and 4. 5 million in Libya. In Algeria, for example, the growth rate rose from 2.6 percent in the 1950s to 3.4 percent in the 1960s and 1970s, and fell only slightly to 3 percent in the 1980s. Despite rapid urbanization of 5 percent or more on average, the countryside has registered growth on the order of approximately 1 percent to 1.5 percent per year. Except in Libya, with 32 percent, rural dwellers still account for half or more of the total population: 56 percent in Morocco, 50.3 percent in Algeria, and 49.7 percent in Tunisia.

In Morocco the rural population included 8.2 million people in 1960 (70 percent), 9.9 million in 1971 (66 percent), and 10.3 million in 1984 (55.7 percent), an increase of over 2 million people (20.8 percent). In Algeria the rural population grew from 8.3 million (1966) to 10.3 million (1977) to 11.6 million (1987) for an increase of 3.3 million people from 1966 to 1987 (39 percent). Finally, in Tunisia the rural population practically stagnated: In 1961 it totaled 5 million, in 1985 it totaled no more than 4.9 million. In Libya the rural population rose from 1. 26 million in 1965 to 1.34 million in 1988, although the proportion that population represented dropped from 74 to 32 percent of the total. Although the statistical definition of *rural* differs a bit from country to country, one can observe that the rural exodus to the cities has been irregular. Tunisia transferred all of its demographic growth for a generation (1961–1985), and Morocco and Algeria had to consign a relatively significant portion of their demographic growth to the countryside—a little less than 1 percent per year in Morocco and 1.5 percent in Algeria.

If the country thus penetrated the city, the city has in turn modified the structure of activity in the rural areas through the expansion of nonagricultu-

TABLE 6.1 Evolution of the Population Employed in Agriculture in Tunisia

	Population Employed in Agriculture	Percentage of Total Active Labor Force	Women Employed in Agriculture	Percentage of Women
1966	448,000	42	8,000	1.8
1975	509,000	39	70,000	13.7
1980	552,000	37	113,000	20.4
1986–1987	554,000	30	107,600	19.4

Source: *Employment Survey 1986–1987* (Tunis: National Statistical Institute, 1988).

ral employment. In Algeria in particular, the policies of investment in economic and social infrastructure and of industrialization provided alternative employment for a fraction of the agrarian population. As a result, the active population counted as "farming" is less than 50 percent of the total rural population; in other words, only every other rural dweller is involved in farming. This development policy has allowed for the settlement of a maximum population and the limitation of the rural exodus. In Morocco the impact of the new employment possibilities is no less striking. In 1986–1987 there were 1.1 million nonagricultural jobs out of an actively employed population of 5.3 million rural dwellers, women representing 20 percent of this total. Industry, essentially artisanal, makes up 8.5 percent of rural employment sector, women occupying 77.3 percent of the jobs.

The rural exodus has above all involved landless peasants, agricultural wage earners, and in some measure family help. Movement toward the cities has not reduced the number of farms or of people who live on farms; as a result, the actual number of active agricultural workers in the three countries has grown by 1 percent to 1.5 percent a year since 1970. As shown in Table 6.1, the gross number of agricultural workers in Tunisia rose to 554,000 in 1986, according to the results of the population census—which are much lower than those obtained in agricultural surveys. Census figures indicate that agricultural workers have increased in number from 1966 to 1985 at a rate of approximately 1 percent per year. As evident in Table 6.1, however, since 1975 the growth of the agricultural labor force has essentially come about because of the growing participation of women in farming. Male participation, in contrast, remained remarkably constant during this period: 440,000 (1966) to 440,000 (1975) to 439,000 (1980) to 446,000 (1986).

Morocco shows a larger increase in the numbers of its population involved in agriculture concurrent with an even greater rise in the employment of women. In 1986, 1.97 million women declared themselves employed (including 1.74 million family helpers, 46,455 wage earners, and 183,311 independents, of whom 144,864 were in pastoral work); the number of men in the labor force rose from 1.67 million in 1960 to 1.74 million in 1977 and to 1.97 million in 1986. In other words, the population involved in agriculture more than doubled over a quarter century if one counts the male and female labor force together but increased just 15 percent if one considers only the employment of males.

This evolution is evident to the same extent in Algeria, although the employment of women does not appear in the census. If one counts only the number of men in the work force in order to establish a comparison between the three countries, the total rises from 784,000 in 1960 (during the war of liberation) to 852,300 in 1966 to 692,000 in 1977 to 890,000 in 1986 (a 12.7 percent increase). One would tend to conclude that for the Maghribi countries as a whole (Libya excepted for lack of data) there is a relative stagnation of male employment complemented by an increasing feminization of agriculture in Tunisia and Morocco. (Any conclusion needs to be qualified to take into account variations in women's employment due to survey differences and seasonal variations.) When related to the cultivated areas in each country, however, the evolution of the agrarian population shows a deterioration according to the principal indicators of land utilization.

In each country, the cultivated agricultural areas have remained practically unchanged in twenty-five years, for they reached their limit decades ago. Set against statistics from the early 1960s, the figures for the cultivated areas in 1986–1987 for the three countries show no significant changes: 7.8 million compared to 8.1 million hectares (19.3 million to 20.0 million acres) for Morocco, 4.8 million compared to 4.9 million hectares (11.8 million to 12.1 million acres) for Tunisia, 6.8 million compared to 7.2 million hectares (16.8 million to 17.8 million acres) for Algeria, and 2.4 million hectares (5.9 million acres) in Libya in 1960. The countries of the Maghrib are poorly endowed with arable land, and the obligatory dry-fallow practice below a certain rain level reduces further the cultivated area and constrains the extensive farming systems on a large portion of the territory. (Fallow land is 15.3 percent of the arable land in Tunisia, 20.5 percent in Morocco, and 28 percent in Algeria.)

The development of irrigation is an important means for making up for weaknesses in the land; one irrigated hectare is equal to four or five nonirrigated ones. But irrigation is dependent on the availability of water and the cost of moving it. Morocco irrigates 800,000 hectares (1.9 million acres), a bit more than 10 percent of its arable land, whereas Algeria and Tunisia irrigate only 4 percent to 5 percent, or 300,000 and 200,000 hectares (741,000 and 494,000 acres), respectively.

The availability of land per habitant and per active agricultural worker has decreased. Per habitant in Algeria and Morocco, the figure went from 0.65 hectares (1.6 acres) in 1960 to 0.33 hectares (0.8 acres) in 1987, and in Tunisia from 1.2 to 0.7 hectares (3 to 1.75 acres). Per agricultural worker, the availability of land went from 4.7 to 3.47 hectares (11.6 to 8.6 acres) in Morocco, from 8.6 to 8.0 hectares (21.5 to 19.7 acres) in Algeria, and from 10.7 to 8.8 hectares (26.4 to 21.7 acres) in Tunisia for the same period (1960–

1987), showing a far greater labor intensity for agricultural production in Morocco than in the other two countries.

The result of this strong demographic pressure on the land is the extension of the system of "minifundia" (extreme smallholdings), which blocks improvement in production and agricultural productivity and is a consequence of the inability of the economy to eliminate unviable farms. Statistics on landownership in general are completely lacking for the Maghrib. The data deal solely with farming activity, are rarely exhaustive, and date back to the beginning of the 1970s; since then, land censuses have been replaced by partial surveys.

In Morocco three-quarters of the privately owned farms average less than 2 hectares (5 acres), about the same proportion in 1981 as in 1974, when they totaled 997,370 farms, 73.7 percent of the total landed farm area of 1.8 million hectares (4.4 million acres) or 24.5 percent of the arable. In 1981–1982 their number was almost the same, at 963,500 farms and 23.5 percent of the usable agricultural area. To these figures should be added the tenant farms, which numbered 450,240, that is, roughly one out of four.

In Tunisia half of the landed private farms average 2.25 hectares (5.56 acres). Their number has risen from 133,000 in 1960 to 149,000 in 1980, an increase of 7 percent. In Algeria 74 percent of the privately owned farms are less than 5 hectares (12.5 acres) and on average are 1.64 hectares (4.1 acres). Throughout the Maghrib, if the category of private farms is raised to 10 hectares or less, it includes a very high percentage of all farms but less than half the land: 87 percent of the farms in Algeria with 46.9 percent of the arable land, 88.5 percent in Morocco with 45 percent of the arable land, and 63 percent in Tunisia with 18.2 percent of the arable land. All of these farms are obviously too small to support and provide work for households, who are then obliged to supplement their incomes to a large extent from nonagricultural activities.

If minifundism is extensive, privately owned farms of 20 hectares (50 acres) or more, which could be considered to be viable agricultural exploitations, occupy different proportions of the arable land in the three countries. The highest index of the concentration of farmland can be observed in Tunisia. Farms larger than 20 hectares amount to 60.5 percent of the arable compared to only 32 percent in Algeria and Morocco. Farms larger than 50 hectares (123 acres) (4.9 percent of all Tunisian farms) represent 33.1 percent of Tunisian arable, compared with 15.2 percent for the same category in Morocco and 12 percent in Algeria. In all categories of farms there has been a general decrease in size. Those farms between 10 and 50 hectares (25 to 125 acres) are the only ones to effectively maintain their proportion of the useful agricultural area. In Tunisia, for example, the farms of 100 hectares (247 acres) or more have diminished in number by 13.7 percent and have lost 31 percent of the area they had between 1961 and 1980. Those between 50 and 100 hectares (123 to 247 acres) have grown in number by 26.5 percent but only gained 20.3 percent in area, implying a decrease in the average size per farm. In the middle-sized class of farms of 10 to 50 hectares, the percentage of the total useful agricultural area rose from 45.4 percent in 1961 to 48.1 percent in 1980, but the average farm size diminished by 1 hectare from 20.59 hectares in 1961 to 19.59 (50.9 to 48.4 acres) in 1980.

With such a landownership structure, the agriculture of the Maghrib suffers from a major handicap that blocks the agricultural intensification process. Modernization will involve only a limited number of farms having a critical size, amounting to 15 percent to 20 percent of all farms and covering about half the total useful agricultural land. This situation comes about because the smaller, economically nonviable farms manage to survive and division creates a tendency to maintain or increase the number of small farms. Apparently, the number of farms varied little in the 1970s and 1980s in Tunisia and in Morocco. In Tunisia, they grew from 325,800 farms in 1961 to 355,000 in 1980, an increase of only 7 percent in twenty years. These data conform to those regarding the agricultural population, which has grown roughly in the same proportions. For Morocco, the agricultural census of 1973–1974 found 1,517,010 self-worked farms and 450,240 tenant farms for a total of 1,967,250 (Pascon 1986:115–141). The agricultural survey of 1981–1982 provided the figure of 1.4 million arable farms, and the survey of 1984 found 1.5 million arable and 400,000 nonarable farms. This would indicate a stable or very slightly declining number of farms from 1974 to 1984.

Though the surveys seriously underestimate the number of small farms, there seems to be a rough stability in the number of farms in both Morocco and Tunisia. This stability, however, is quite surprising considering the inheritance practices of the Maghrib, which lead to a decrease in the size of a property with each generation. The consequence is that a number of small-property owners are obliged either to rent or sell their land when it becomes unviable for farming. The progressive division of property is likely to be accompanied by a reverse trend of consolidating properties by rent or sale to reconstitute middle-sized and large farms.

If Tunisia and Morocco seem to present relatively stable land-related characteristics, the data on Algeria to the contrary show an accentuated process of fragmentation. The number of farms rose from 543,000 in 1960 to 630,000 in 1966 to 701,243 in 1973 to 902,726 in 1981. The agrarian reform of 1971 thus favored the breakup of the large farm. In order to avoid expropriation measures of large properties above a certain size (variable according to land type and use), some farms were divided among heirs. In Algeria a major portion of the minifundia maintain themselves through the extension of wage-earning nonfarm labor to the countryside.

The growth of the agricultural population and thus of the number of heirs of farm leads to the dismemberment of family property. In all Maghribi countries, inheritance law is based on the rule of equal division among all male heirs, contrary to Europe, where priority succession mechanisms were generally applied in order to safeguard the unity of the farm. Underlying the Western practice is a fundamental cultural difference that has accorded prime importance to the unity of property at the expense of hereditary equality among kin. But the division of inheritance raises the question of viable farm size, as the average size of a farm becomes smaller with each generation. The minimum size for a farm to feed an average peasant family without generating a surplus is approximately 10 to 15 hectares (25 to 37 acres) for rain-fed land. It is clear that the great majority of farms fall below this limit.

Despite general awareness of the gravity of the situation, no solution to the problem of the breakup of property has been found—with one exception. In Morocco it has been proposed that the coheirs could select one among them to take charge of the farm, and agricultural credit could be used to indemnify the others. This solution would imply that the rights of inheritance would be adapted to the economic conditions of the farm in order to create a new system of farming. The proposal implies a dual reform, both economic, as it would be necessary to find work for those who could not stay on the farm, and cultural, as the plan would also necessitate a reform of Muslim law.

Agrarian Individualism

The state has not attempted to influence either the allotment of land or the size of the farm in any significant way. Nevertheless, in the 1960s the need for agrarian reform was not questioned, and it figured prominently in the programs of all the nationalist parties. Their demands, however, focused on colonial rather than nationals' lands. Although the colonization of lands varied from country to country—1 million hectares (2.5 million acres) in Morocco, 2.3 million (5.7 million) in Algeria, 570,000 (1.4 million), in Tunisia and 310,000 (766,000) in Libya—it seemed to constitute a pool large enough to implement land distribution programs. Algeria launched an agrarian reform in the beginning of the 1970s in order to restrict nationals' ownership of private property. Reforms in Morocco and Tunisia, in contrast, were limited to land the state recovered from colonial holdings or from nonprivate holdings such as collective (tribal or religious) land.

Of the four Maghribi countries, Morocco has most favored the maintenance of colonial property intact in large farms. It is estimated that 45 percent of the colonial lands of 500,000 hectares (1.2 million acres) have been transferred to large Moroccan landowners. For the rest, 30 percent was distributed to the peasants within the framework of agrarian reform programs and the remaining 25 percent was given over to state farms; 380,195 hectares (939,000 acres) (5 percent of the usable agricultural area) was distributed to 23,260 beneficiaries in 704 cooperatives. In all, 500,000 hectares were distributed by rent, with option to buy, to close to 60,000 farmers between 1966 and 1978, out of approximately 700,000 male adults without land in 1971. "The agrarian reform was thus able to absorb a bit fewer than 10 percent of the peasants without land. It was therefore not a successful social operation. Nor could it have a decisive economic effect. It was a political operation (Pascon 1986: 46). The administration, continues Pascon, sought to create a balance to the new class of capitalist landowners by generating a class of privileged small farmers beholden to the state, a buffer class between the large farmers and the mass of unemployed rural labor.

Out of the 750,000 hectares (1.85 million acres) entrusted to the Office of State Lands in Tunisia, 135,000 hectares (333,000 acres) were ceded to small farmers between 1970 and 1974 after the dissolution of the cooperative movement. The remaining 615,000 hectares (1.51 million acres) were used, as in Algeria, to construct 221 cooperative units administered directly by the state and incorporating the salaried workers from the colonial lands (233,000 hectares, or 575,000 acres), the major agroindustries, and pilot farms (216,000 hectares, or 533,000 acres), the rest of the land going to various state enterprises. Essentially, the state thus managed to maintain colonial lands under a system of state ownership.

The 2.3 million hectares (5.7 million acres) of colonial land nationalized at independence in Algeria were the object of coadministration by the state and the farmers until 1987. The regime of collective farms varied over this period from an administration shared with the workers (especially during the first decade) to an administration run by the state as an absentee landlord. The state held all management rights and made all decisions concerning production, finances, and salaries but did not directly manage the units of production. Everyday management was the duty of a delegated workers' group that continued to be called the "management committee" in reference to its initial function of self-management during the early years (Clegg 1971, Blair 1970, Chaulet 1971).

The reform law of December 8, 1987, constituted an important turning point in the privatization of public lands. Although the state remains formal owner of the land, the law creates a right to farm separate from ownership, which can be held by individuals and can be ceded and transmitted. This right carries many consequences, including confiscation by creditors, which was not possible under the public regime.

The law provides that the right to farm must be exercised collectively, however. It has thus divided former colonial latifundia into new production units averaging 80 hectares (197 acres) farmed by seven to eight workers each, creating 20,975 farms in the place of 3,000 latifundia. The state also gave 3,022 farms in full ownership to individuals. In total there are 164,100 farmers—mostly state wage earners in the category of permanent laborers on former state farms—who have benefited from this reform, amounting to about 16 percent of the employed agrarian population. All of this seems to indicate a step toward the individualization of farming and the creation of a true land market fed by the pool of public lands. Since the end of the 1980s, there has been a reduction of collective farms and unofficial renting of plots and buildings by entrepreneurs who usually come from the urban sector.

The extension of agrarian reform to private property is limited in Morocco as in Tunisia to the promulgation of laws governing irrigated projects created by the state, about 100,000 hectares (247,000 acres) in Tunisia and 580,000 (1.4 million) in Morocco. The laws require a contribution by landowners to the costs of the irrigation infrastructure, which can be paid either in cash or in land. In Morocco the payments to the cost of equipment provided by landowners of 5 hectares or more has only very rarely been collected (El Khyari 1989). Payments by land have been replaced by direct payment of 1,500 dirhams ($250) per hectare plus a fee for the irrigating water itself. In Tunisia these measures serve more to establish minimum and maximum surfaces for each perimeter and to recover in land the surplus value created by irrigation. Not only are these maximum levels too high (at 50 to 60 hectares, or 123 to 148 acres, for most projects), but these measures are also applied extremely slowly by the local commissions. Finally, recourse to expropriation provided for by Article 10 of the law of 1963, which permits rapid application of agrarian reform, has rarely been used. Within the oldest irrigation projects—those of 1958 in the Mejerda Valley—the state has managed to recover only 4,800 hectares (11,900 acres) so far (Ben Achour 1988).

Measures of some effectiveness have been carried out in Algeria only since the agrarian reform law of 1971. This law brought to bear two essential principles. The first is to limit the ownership of private land according to a ceiling based on annual revenue, and the second, more important, is to restrict access to land to peasants who actually farm it. This implies the nationalization of absentee-owned property and the interdiction of farming by salaried workers. It was, therefore, a reform that favored the peasants. The lands incorporated into the land pool of 1971–1979 were small indeed. They included 450,000 hectares (1.1 million acres) taken from private property and approximately 600,000 (1.5 million) that the state added from collective (communal) holdings. In all, a little more than 1 million hectares (2.5 million acres)—much of it poor-quality land—was distributed to the benefit of 100,000 landless peasants. The state required the recipients to form groups of ten in order to constitute agricultural collectives, farming approximately 100 hectares (247 acres) each. In theory, these units of production were cooperatives benefiting from a type of management different from those run by the state, but because of poor land and bad equipment, the cooperatives quickly ran into financial difficulties, forcing the state to tighten administrative control over them and incorporate them into the state-run system.

Beginning in the early 1980s, however, the liberalizing reforms of the Benjedid government included agriculture as well as other activities, and agrarian reform was brought into question. Agrarian reform officially ended in 1982, and some discreet restitution of nationalized lands was begun. The cooperative sector dissolved, one part being converted to state farms and the other being distributed among the individual cooperative farmers. The timidity of the land redistribution programs reflects the government's indecision over agricultural policy choices concerning the social forms of production.

It is well known that in the eighteenth century northern Europe, notably Denmark, opted for "the peasant model" (Suvolin 1989), which favored the direct producer: The land to those who work it. This option contains measures that progressively lift the constraints blocking the growth of the family farm. A system of long-term credit was created to help the peasants become property owners and to establish a beneficial level of interest, and share-cropping was replaced by rental. On the fundamental question of the status of farm workers and their relation to the land, the European model opted for independent workers who are also owners of the land they farm. Even though the winds of liberalism that have been shaking up the economies of the Maghribi countries since the early 1980s favor private farming and private property as opposed to collective and state farms, they do not point to a clear choice in favor of peasant agriculture or peasant ownership of the land.

In Tunisia as well as Morocco, although the liberal option has been confirmed, the state directly or indirectly administers the farming of the relatively large agricultural areas. In Tunisia the cooperative units of production, agroindustries, and pilot farms occupied some 450,000 hectares (1.1 million acres) at the end of the 1980s. In Morocco two state-run offices, the Agency for the Administration of Agricultural Lands (SOGETA) and the Agency for Agricultural Development (SODEA), administer respectively 100,000 and 62,000 hectares (247,000 and 153,000 acres) each. In Algeria the breaking up of the public-sector farms as a result of the reforms of 1987 substituted a type of private management for state-run farms, but the new production units created seem more akin to enterprises where the workers are shareholders than to family farming.

The ambiguity of structural policies—ones that bear on the status of labor and property ownership—also rests on the support that the state gives to the development of either artisanal or capitalist entrepreneurial farms that require salaried farmers. In Morocco agrarian capitalism is strongly implanted in all of the irrigated as well as extensive agricultural areas. It continues to attract a significant amount of state agricultural assistance and plays an important role in the development of agroalimentary industries. In Tunisia the state favors the recovery of state lands by banking agencies as well as by agencies of farm management and development. Large agricultural enterprises (sometimes as large as 4,000 hectares, or 9,900 acres) are created to take over the administration of lands that had previously been given to cooperative production units.

In addition, the rise in agricultural prices since the late 1980s favors the penetration of urban capital into agriculture and into the means of production by entrepreneurs who do not belong to the rural or peasant class. In this way, with regard to the accession to landownership, the new policy measures in essence ignored the principles claimed by the nationalist parties in the beginning of the 1960s: The land to those who work it.

It is no longer necessary to be a peasant or to live in the countryside to become a landowner. The peasants have to face competition from civil servants, agricultural school technicians, and entrepreneurs and merchants who wish to invest their capital in agriculture and to whom the state offers favorable investment conditions. This policy also serves as an effort to resolve the new problem of educated unemployment, notably among agricultural school graduates, by giving them access to landownership.

The Algerian state, which seeks to attract capital for agricultural development, particularly in regions of new irrigation, no longer poses conditions of class membership for access to landownership. Concessions are made to merchants, civil servants, industrialists, and peasants alike. In the poor regions of light rainfall in the south alone, the state handed over 253,354 hectares (626,000 acres), including 94,900 (235,000) for farming, to 59,900 individuals. The majority of the peasantry finds itself excluded from the agricultural modernization process in a more general way. Technical improvements apply for the most part to the medium-sized and large farms that are also favored by material supplies and credits.

In its assistance programs, the state gives priority to what it considers to be "viable farms," that is, those capable of producing for local markets or for export. The failures of the cooperative experiments are a pretext for refusing a democratic organizational structure to small farmers that would permit them access to modern means of production and to their productive development. The dismantling of the cooperative sector in Tunisia as in Algeria brought an end to any policy of support for cooperatives.

The Evolution of Revenues

Despite—or as a result of—the demographic pressure on the land, its productivity has improved little outside the irrigated areas. In the rain-fed sectors, there has been no substantial increase in productivity. In total, agricultural production over two decades has grown on average 1.5 percent per year, a level slightly higher than the growth of the agrarian population. In fact, the observed improvement in revenues has been more the result of the rise in agricultural prices and related resources than by the increase in worker productivity.

The Maghribi countries have sought rapid growth in production by the extension of irrigation rather than by the improvement of productivity and rain-fed production. The irrigated sectors have attracted the most important part of public and private agricultural investment, on average close to 40 percent of total investment. Because of its export production policy, Morocco has accentuated its irrigation efforts the most. Over two decades, irrigated land rose from 134,000 hectares (331,000 acres) in 1967 to 416,008 (1 million) in 1980 and to 587,440 (1.45 million) in 1986, thus multiplying by six the irrigated area of the country. In the final decade, irrigation absorbed 80 percent of the state resources devoted to agriculture, whereas the rain-fed sector (which composes 92 percent of cultivated land) received only 20 percent (Pascon 1986). Hydraulic investment was much slower and less important in Tunisia and Algeria, where the harnessed water resources are much smaller: 3.5 million cubic meters (924 million gallons) in Algeria and 1.8 million (445 million) in Tunisia compared with 6 million (1.6 billion) in Morocco. In total, public and private irrigated farms make up some 800,000 hectares (nearly 2 million acres) in Morocco, 250,000 (617,000) in Algeria, and 210,000 (520,000) in Tunisia. They employ from 15 to 20 percent of the agrarian population and produce 60 percent of the productive value in Morocco, 32 percent in Tunisia, and 20 percent in Algeria. Water resources are primarily used by fruit growers and market farmers for local markets or export, notably in Morocco, and secondarily for industrial farming, oil production, and growing sugar beets.

The cultivation of cereal—wheat and barley, the basis of local food consumption—has improved little. Wheat production from 1950 to 1990, for example, rose 3 quintals per hectare (662 lbs per acre) in Morocco, 4 (882) in Tunisia, and were practically stagnant in Algeria; as a result, dependence on foreign sources are reinforced. Cereal cultivation associated with fallow land took up 83 percent of the arable land in Morocco (1986), 74.6 percent in Algeria (1987), and 54 percent in Tunisia (1985). Nevertheless, Maghribi countries have progressively become the largest importers of cereals in the region and face a deeper and deeper food deficit each year.

In 1986 the four countries had to import nearly 8 million metric tons of wheat: 3.2 in Algeria, 1.8 in Morocco, 1.8 in Libya and 1 in Tunisia, for a total of 50 percent of their consumption. Morocco's agricultural balance for 1986 registered a slight surplus as a result of the excellent cereal crops of the previous few years. In Tunisia and especially Algeria, which are less able to cover consumption with production, imports constitute a heavy, if not crushing, burden. In 1986, considered to be a good year, Tunisia imported 314 million dinars ($345 million) worth of alimentary products and exported 126 million dinars ($145 million) worth, for a deficit of 188 million dinars ($200 million). In 1987 and in 1988, the agroalimentary deficit grew to an average of 92 million Tunisian dinars ($100 million). Algeria annually paid the equivalent of $1.5 million to $2 million for its agroalimentary purchases in the late 1980s.

Given the annual demographic growth rates of 2.6 percent in Tunisia, 2.7 percent in Morocco, 3 percent in Algeria, and 4 percent in Libya, and the agricultural production growth rate of 1.5 percent in all countries, the gap between production and consumption is getting wider. In the 1970s and 1980s the annual rate of production growth in Tunisia was 1.2 percent, in Algeria less than 1 percent; in Morocco it was 1.5 percent during the 1970s and only 0.5 percent between 1980 and 1985, the years of a terrible drought. In the second half of the 1980s, the harvest was excellent in Morocco, but these recorded results were still too dependent on variations in rainfall to be considered steady progress. The case of Tunisia is striking in this regard: Compared to a normal production of 10 to 12 million quintals (2.2 to 2.6 billion lbs), the harvest of 1988 was only 3 million quintals (662 million lbs) and that of 1989 was 4 million quintals (882 million lbs). Algeria recorded the same production discrepancy, varying from 30 to 8 million quintals (6.6 to 1.8 billion lbs).

The famous fodder (grazing) revolution that played such an important role in the agricultural progress of Europe in the nineteenth century is not yet part of the general agroeconomic picture of the Maghrib. Legumes and fodder still take up only a small part of the land, from 8 percent to 10 percent of the usable agricultural area, depending on the country. More generally, the structure of production has not undergone any important modifications in the rain-fed areas exclusively given over to the extensive cultivation of cereals associated with livestock. Only Morocco, because of its larger irrigated area, was able to diversify its cultivation—most notably its industrial crops—to include sugarcane, sugar beets, sunflowers, and peanuts.

The absence of significant progress in rain-fed agricultural production is strongly accentuated by the disparity in revenues between the different cultivated areas. Morocco presents the strongest contrast between rain-fed and irrigated areas: The latter, with only 10 percent of the arable land, make up 60 percent of the total agricultural added value; rain-fed agriculture is largely dominated by the extensive subsistence cultivation of cereals, with low productivity.

Price policy in the 1970s greatly contributed to the widening of this gap in favor of irrigated production; prices of irrigated crops have tended to increase whereas those of rain-fed products (most notably wheat and barley) were held down by the state. Beginning in the early 1980s, a price policy clearly more favorable to the producers was implemented in order to stimulate the growth of the agricultural sector and its revenues. The policy included a progressive price liberalization for principal products such as fruits and vegetables, meats, dairy products, and others. Similarly, those prices fixed by the state and provided with commercial guarantees rose progressively. Thus, in order to encourage the cultivation of cereals, the prices of durum wheat were multiplied

TABLE 6.2 Evolution of Wheat Prices, 1980–1989 (in local currency)

	1980		1985		1989	
	Hard Wheat	Soft Wheat	Hard Wheat	Soft Wheat	Hard Wheat	Soft Wheat
Algeria (dinars)	125	110	200	190	400	360
Tunisia (dinars)	8.6	7.7	9.5	14.5	22.5	19.9
Morocco (dirhams)	125	125	150	150	180	200

by three in Algeria between 1980 and 1989, by 2.6 in Tunisia, and by 1.4 in Morocco (see Table 6.2).

In Algeria a rapid growth in agricultural prices forced households to devote a larger part of their budgets to food costs—50 percent in Algeria compared to 48.6 percent in Morocco and 41.7 percent in Tunisia in 1980. More generally, however, the rise in agricultural prices made it necessary to maintain consumer subsidies for key products such as cereals, vegetables, and dairy goods. In Tunisia as in Morocco, hunger riots in the early and mid-1980s underscored the need to accompany an agricultural policy based on higher farm prices with an urban policy of subsidies for basic foodstuffs in order to maintain a minimum standard of living for low-income social classes. In both countries, consumer subsidies, aimed at the city rather than the countryside, absorbed an average of 8 to 10 percent of ordinary state expenditure.

There are no data on the evolution and distribution of agricultural revenues for different groups of farmers, but household spending supplemented by consumer subsidies is a good indication of the standard of living of the rural population. Total expenditure per inhabitant per year rose in real terms by 4 percent on average during the 1960s and 1970s, a little more in Algeria (5 percent) than in Tunisia (4.2 percent) and Morocco (4 percent in 1959–1970 but only 1.1 percent in 1970–1985). The early 1980s were marked by an acute slowing down of household expenditures, and in 1985–1989 there was even a reduction. The change in the portion of the budget devoted to foodstuffs points to the improvement in the quality of life in urban and rural areas alike. In Morocco this portion decreased from 70.2 percent in 1959–1960 to 54 percent in 1970 to 48.6 percent in 1984–1985; in Tunisia it went from 50.3 percent in 1966 to 41.7 percent in 1980 to 39 percent in 1985. In Algeria, however, for an equivalent alimentary ration (2,500 to 2,600 calories), households in 1980 had to devote a larger part of their budget: 57.7 percent. In a bit more than two decades, the consumption of foodstuffs improved both quantitatively and qualitatively, mostly with regard to meat, fresh fruits and vegetables, and dairy products.

But is important to note that the quantity of cereals consumed (mainly wheat, which furnishes more than 60 percent of the total daily ration of calories) continues to grow at the rural level. In Tunisia, for example, the consumption of cereals in urban areas stagnated at 170 kilos (375 lbs) per person in 1980, whereas a notable rise took place in the countryside—203 kilos (440 lbs) per person in 1975, 204 (441) in 1980, 247 (543) in 1985. In Morocco it was also quite high, at 245 (540) kilos in 1970 and 242 (532) kilos in 1985.

A reduction in the gap between urban and rural consumption can be considered an indication of the evolution of the redistribution of revenues among social classes. In the Maghrib the ratio of the average expenditure per person between the urban and rural sectors went from 1.6 in 1960 to 2.1 in 1970 to 1.9 in 1985. In Morocco the annual growth in rural expenditures in constant dirhams fell from 2.4 percent between 1959 and 1970 to 0.92 percent from 1970 to 1985. Since 1970, however, the average annual growth was only 0.4 percent in the urban sector. In Tunisia an equally important gap appears between the expenditures of urban and rural households: 318 dinars ($350) in the city in 1980 against 149 ($160) in the country. Since 1980 the food situation in the country has deteriorated with regard to numerous commodities—dairy products, meats, and fruits and vegetables; this decline has been accompanied by a strong rise (20 percent) in the consumption of cereals.

But more than an evolution in the quality of life, the most important changes in the last two decades concern the activity and origin of incomes in rural households. On the one hand, an increasingly significant fraction of family help that was once, for the most part, employed on the farm as salaried farmers is now engaged in activities besides agriculture. On the other hand, the pluralization of employment has extended to the heads of farms themselves, especially small farmers and young heads of households. Only half of all farmers live by agriculture alone.

In Tunisia the situation is similar to that in Morocco and Algeria. Of the 355,000 farmers surveyed, 142,000 (40 percent) have a second job outside of farming, and 52 percent devote less than two months per year to farming, 23 percent less than three months, 12.5 percent less than five months, and 13.6 percent spend only six months or more working the farm. Therefore, 49 percent of the total active agricultural population—12 percent of the farmers, 28 percent of the family help, and 9 percent of the salaried workers—combine work inside and outside of the agricultural sector. A diminishing proportion of the resources of agricultural households is furnished by income from farming (Zghidi 1985).

Conclusion

If the economic expansion of the 1960s and 1970s was able to assure the transfer of additional agrarian populations toward other activities and furnish supplemental resources to the majority of those who kept farming, the debt crisis of the 1980s led to a reactivation of the process of rural impoverishment in the Maghrib. The reduction of investment brought about a significant decrease in employment opportunities (and thus a rapid rise of unemployment) for a quarter of the active population. If the four countries are to avoid further problems, agricultural policy will need to keep pace with the growing population and will therefore have to delay any rapid structural modernization.

The search for solutions has become stuck in the application of the prescriptions of agrarian individualism (liberalism) and the external adjustment to the capitalist system, all focused on the growth of production as the desired result. Agricultural policies thus tend to favor the penetration of speculative capital in agriculture and the marginalization of the bulk of the peasants. In an unfavorable demographic context, the inadequacy of these policies, which are based on those of the industrialized countries, simply aggravates an already serious agrarian crisis. North Africa will again face—in a much more acute form—the problems of land distribution and structural reform—problems it thought it had left behind.

7

Economic Crisis and Policy Reform in the 1980s

Rhys Payne

A Convergence of Development Strategies

Comparative analyses of the Maghrib generally stress the distinctions between the political regimes of Morocco, Algeria, Tunisia, and Libya. Yet the concept of the Greater Maghrib is increasingly gaining currency as these diverse regimes have moved toward a convergence of development strategy in the 1990s. Why have such different states adopted such similar economic policies, and are the prospects of the reforms the same across the Maghrib?

The end of colonialism in the 1950s and 1960s ushered in an era of markedly dissimilar governmental institutions in North Africa, and subsequent comparative analyses stressed the distinctions between the political orders of the Maghrib, with forecasts regarding development largely based upon these differences (Moore 1970; Hermassi 1972; Entelis 1980). But each of the countries experienced remarkably similar political and economic crises during the 1980s, belying the institutional and ideological differences that figured so prominently in analyses of the region during the 1960s and 1970s. Across the Maghrib, the 1980s was a decade marked by chronic governmental financial crises, severe shortfalls in food security, and violent civil unrest. As the diverse nation-states of the Maghrib entered the 1990s, it was equally notable that the four regimes pursued quite similar structural adjustment programs.

The government of the Maghrib have all been engaged in an unsteady balancing act involving economic accountability to foreign creditors and political accountability to domestic populations. Falling world market prices for key exports, inefficiency in vast parastatal enterprises, and heavy debt-repayment obligations contributed to severe financial crises during the 1980s. The response of each of the Maghribi rulers to the shortfalls in current accounts has been surprisingly uniform: to embark on a program of structural adjustment based on economic decentralization and increased integration into the world economy. The economic policy reforms each regime enacted during the 1980s may be characterized as promoting a process of slow and gradual decentralization, encouraging export growth, enhancing incentives for agricultural production, and imposing austerity measures aimed at trimming government budget deficits.

These structural adjustment programs represent a particularly bitter medicine in the context of contemporary North African society. Violent episodes of civil dissent afflicted Morocco, Algeria, and Tunisia during the 1980s into the early 1990s in response to government reforms that undermined the standard of living, with higher food prices threatening popular entitlement to basic goods. The present development strategies of structural adjustment do not promise immediate relief but a further tightening of the belt in the short run. The austerity measures will continue to strain the standard of living in each country by increasing unemployment and inflation as public spending is slashed, inefficient parastatals are reorganized, and consumer subsidies on basic goods are reduced.

In this comparative study I address three basic questions regarding the political economy of the Maghrib. What is the specific nature of the economic reforms being undertaken in each of the four countries? Why have such diverse political regimes adopted such similar economic policies? What is the relationship between structural adjustment and political legitimacy?

The Economic Rationale of Structural Adjustment

The economic rationale underlying structural adjustment policies in the Maghrib is compelling and is itself sufficient to explain why regimes of such diverse ideological persuasions have embraced common ground. Excessive debt-servicing burdens, current account deficits, government budgetary constraints, and adverse market conditions have all contributed to a radical reconsideration of government intervention into the economy. The growing gap between government revenues and expenditures cannot be met from domestic sources alone, and external financing is needed to support the development plans formulated in the late 1980s. In order to resolve recurring financial crises, the Maghribi states have undertaken reforms that liberalize their influence over market forces.

Despite the differing national ideologies fashioned during the struggles for independence, a common legacy of the colonial period was heavy state intervention in the economy, with state planning in the 1960s and early 1970s seen as the key to development. In Morocco, Algeria, Tunisia, and Libya, the principal sectors of the economy have been dominated by parastatal enterprises, prices for essential goods have been strictly regulated, and national currency has been overvalued. The essence of the structural adjustment programs in all these countries is a gradual economic decentralization and greater exposure to world market forces. Further increases in public spending are being curtailed as the state can no longer afford to play as socially benevolent a role, and the government in each country has moved to divest itself of nonessential parastatal operations. The new credo is economic accountability and austerity. The reduction of public investment and spending is being complemented by measures designed to enhance incentives for foreign and private investment. But as private investment in the short term has been less forthcoming than hoped and as domestic demand remains sluggish, the new economic reorientation will continue to rely on substantial infusions of external capital.

The imposition of austerity measures and the heavy reliance upon borrowing from abroad do not mean that the ruling elites have forsaken the priority of national concerns. Without abandoning their commitment to social improvement, the leaders of the Maghribi states have made common cause with foreign creditors in the search for development. Social pressures are such that economic growth is essential to regime survival; the states therefore continue to pursue their developmental goals just as avidly as before, but through a new strategy that makes more room for private initiative and international market forces. Such structural adjustment would not be possible without continued access to transnational sources of finance, and the conditions attached to further loans and credits reinforce the orientation of the reforms. Given these constraints, governments throughout the Maghrib have taken care to ensure good relations with the international financial community, especially the World Bank and the IMF, along with consortia of private banks and the Paris Club (a grouping of creditor governments who cooperate in negotiating rescheduling accords with individual debtor countries).

A principal consequence of the economic reforms introduced in the late 1980s is that the Maghribi economies will become increasingly integrated with transnational capitalism. The prospects for sustained economic growth are mixed, with higher levels of support from external partners of critical importance yet domestic demand and private investment remaining limited. In the political realm, the likelihood of more stable state-society relations will depend upon the ability of the respective regimes to balance external pressures against domestic demands.

Structural Adjustment and Political Legitimacy

The structural adjustment programs are not solely the result of conditionality and pressure from abroad, for a growing number of the North African ruling elite have also embraced the principles behind the reforms. A younger and more technocratic segment of the ruling elite has been growing in strength at the same time the reach of the patrimonial networks nourished by state control over the economy is increasingly being challenged from below. Given the inability of patrimonialism to accommodate the demands of rapidly growing populations, government leaders in the Maghrib have discovered that they share with foreign financiers a mutuality of interests in externally sponsored development.

The similarities of both the structural adjustment programs and the political challenges to these policies in Morocco, Algeria, and Tunisia imply that the regimes are in part relying upon externally driven economic development to remain politically accountable to the subordinate classes that constitute the bulk of the population. (The case of Libya differs significantly from the other three, as explained in the subsequent section on Libya.) The legitimacy of the Maghribi states hinges upon the ability of their governments to manage both increased integration into the world economy and increasingly mobilized social groups. The ruling elites thus play crucial intermediary roles. In order to maintain national solvency, they must adhere to the conditions attached to critically needed external revenues. But in order to sustain the reform programs, they also must respond to the strident demands of their own populations.

Since independence, political legitimacy in each of the Maghribi states has relied heavily upon the ideology of nationalism and upon abundant government coffers to support clientelistic networks. But the glow of national unity is fading in the wake of mounting social differentiation and conflict, and the combination of modest economic growth with a population explosion has challenged the capacity of established patrimonial networks to fulfill their pivotal role. The food riots of the 1980s made it clear that the legitimacy of the contemporary North African political order is tied to narrowing the gap between population growth and the spread of economic opportunity (Payne 1986). Given the new development strategy, hope is now more than ever pinned on greater integration with global capitalism, and if this course is to succeed it will have to provide material security to a rapidly expanding number of Maghribi.

Food security stands as one of the most sensitive political issues in North Africa, as in most agrarian societies (Chabal 1986). The ability of national governments to assure popular food entitlements has in a sense become an acid test of regime legitimacy in North Africa. As such, the food issue crystallizes the political challenge of transnational capitalist development. Prior to the civil disturbances of the 1980s, the Maghribi states did not base their development strategies on the attainment of food self-sufficiency. Instead, the best agricultural resources were directed toward cash cropping for export, whereas the production of cereals, the principal foodstuffs, was subject to numerous producer disincentives (Swearingen 1987). During the 1960s, Maghribi governments did not expect chronic food deficits to become a serious problem, for they believed foreign exchange would be available to finance any needed imports. Society's vulnerability to food shortfalls, however, has intensified because of rapid population growth, the dwindling of foreign exchange reserves, and the greater use of marginal lands for cereal and livestock farming in a context of recurrent drought. Once known as the granary of Rome, the Maghribi countries are now obliged to import increasingly large amounts of food in order to meet basic needs, even during years of abundant precipitation (Swearingen 1985). The political importance of food security in North Africa has been heightened by years of massive food subsidies by the state, which has led to the perception that food is the responsibility of the government. These huge subsidies will no longer be available to regimes that have had to turn to international agencies to help them through their financial crises. The governments of North Africa cannot afford to continue providing artificially cheap food to urban consumers as they lack the resources and foreign exchange needed to subsidize ever higher imports of food. Yet food shortages severely endanger political legitimacy and must be minimized if the increasingly external orientation of the Maghribi economies is to persist. International and transnational food aid has thus assumed a critical political role by supporting the legitimacy of the state.

The structural adjustment programs under way in each Maghribi country represent significant alterations in the relationship between state and society. The appeal of nationalist ideology to younger generations is diminishing as economic opportunity continues to lag behind demographic growth despite the attainment of independence more than thirty years ago. The ruling elite in each of the Maghribi states have been obliged to turn to the market to supplement their control over the government in an attempt to maintain power and privilege. Yet if the liberalizing economic reforms are to persist and succeed, domestic demands for political accountability will also have to be met. In the Maghrib reform programs have similar origins, but their prospects vary according to the nature of the political regime.

Tunisia

Tunisia's commitment to structural adjustment is particularly striking because the reforms survived numerous governmental reshufflings during the 1980s as well as the country's first presidential succession since independence. The removal of Bourguiba from the presidency in November 1987 signaled a key transition in Tunisian politics, but not the abandonment of structural adjustment. As under Bourguiba, the new government of President Ben Ali is also relying upon transnational financial support to see through a program of economic liberalization.

Tunisia was heralded as a model of political development during the 1960s because of the grassroots formation of its ruling political party and because of the country's high degree of national unity, which was facilitated by

Bourguiba's charisma. But by the 1980s, the principal supporters of the Bourguiba regime had been rewarded with control over the parastatal corporations that dominated the Tunisian economy or with the disbursement of public spending in its various forms. Problems emerged as demographic changes altered the basis of political legitimacy. Bourguiba's regime had for too long leaned heavily upon a combination of charismatic appeal, nationalist ideology, and patrimonialism to maintain its legitimacy. In the 1980s a younger and larger population meant that the appeal of the political order was determined less by ideology and more by performance. As the economic payoffs of consistent government control over the economy began to decline and Bourguiba's personal charisma began to degenerate, the legitimacy of the state was increasingly called into question by violent outbursts of civil unrest, most notably in 1978 and 1984. During 1986 and 1987, the government and foreign observers alike viewed the growing militancy of Islamic fundamentalists with increasing apprehension, as the political situation showed signs of rapid deterioration.

Bourguiba's enduring presence at the apex of the Tunisian political system partially obscured subtle yet far-reaching changes that affected the ruling elite. Two major factors may be identified as having caused a significant realignment of the social underpinnings of the state since the uprising of 1984: The financial crisis that the government faced in 1985 obliged Tunisia for the first time to turn to the IMF for a standby loan and to the World Bank for structural adjustment supports. Increasing political mobilization in opposition to the government—particularly among youth—threatened to engulf the general public. International financial agencies called for reform of the government's management of the economy, whereas domestic opposition demanded more participation in the political process that Bourguiba and his loyalists had hitherto so tightly controlled.

The political realignment resulting from these two forces of change led to the ascendance of a more technocratic segment of the ruling elite within the inner circles of government. A prime indicator of the change was the 1986 replacement of Mohammed Mzali (the designated heir of Bourguiba's patrimonial network) as prime minister of Raschid Sfar who—along with Ismail Khelil—had been serving as a principal intermediary with international finance. Bourguiba's subsequent replacement of Sfar by Ben Ali as prime minister was followed by the latter's seizure of the presidency from Bourguiba himself, marking the advent of what is qualified as the "New Era." One of Ben Ali's first moves was to make sweeping reforms in the top management personnel of the parastatals, replacing established party retainers with younger technocrats whose training, ideology, and personal interests were compatible with greater economic integration with transnational capitalism.

The reorientation of development strategy that emerged during the 1980s reflected changes in Tunisian politics. A new fusion of elites took place, leading to a coalition substantially founded on policy preferences. The new ruling elite was united not as much by its institutional basis as by a common allegiance to the reform policies. A surprising consensus among the country's elite allowed Ben Ali to commit himself to both economic and political liberalization at a time when many analysts were forecasting economic disaster and a decline into military authoritarianism. General Ben Ali's accession to the presidency did not lead to an abandonment of the ongoing structural adjustment program but in fact to its intensification.

There are, of course, other reasons why the reorientation of the state's development strategy remained so remarkably intact during the prolonged period of significant changes in top governmental personnel that occurred during the late 1980s. Severe economic pressures have also contributed to the resilience of the structural adjustment program, most notably the large external deficits regularly run by the country. The problems with Tunisia's current account are largely due to a structural trade deficit, which is only somewhat offset by a positive service and transfer balance from tourism and by remittances from emigrant workers. Tunisia's current account deficit went from $354 million in 1980 to $770 million in 1984 (IMF 1988:504), foreshadowing a turn toward external sources of capital as international reserves fell to dangerously low levels.

Prime Minister Mzali took action in January 1984 to reduce the budget deficit but was warded off by violent popular opposition to the sharp reductions in food subsidies. Before initiating further austerity measures, the government invited a team from the World Bank to suggest how to ameliorate the country's structural economic problems, and in January 1985 further high-level missions from the both the World Bank and the IMF visited Tunis. The recommendations of these agencies were consistent with one another and included a devaluation of the dinar, cuts in customs duties, and further attempts to reduce the budget deficit. The government initially resisted many of these measures because of their political sensitivity and because of the government's overly optimistic economic forecasts. But economic pressures worsened as foreign exchange reserves fell to a record low in summer 1985, and the high budget deficit for 1985 of 485 million dinars ($581 million) made it clear that Tunisia would be forced to turn to international financial markets in 1986.

The Tunisian government's determination to follow the advice of the IMF and World Bank by engaging in structural reform was signaled by Mzali's austerity budget of 1986. This was Tunisia's first budget in which investment was less than debt servicing, public investment being slashed by 18 percent and debt servicing rising by 26 percent. A disastrous economic performance followed in 1986: Gross domestic product dropped by 1.6 percent as drought ravaged the agricultural sector, oil prices fell, and tourism suffered because of regional tensions. In mid-1986 Mzali's successor, Sfar, implemented more extensive economic reforms that involved further cuts in state spending, a 10 percent devaluation of the dinar, and the liberalization of import restrictions on raw materials, spare parts, and semifinished goods. The government also submitted an application to the General Agreement on Tariffs and Trade (GATT) during autumn 1986. In October 1986 Tunisia was rewarded for its willing ingestion of the IMF prescription by receiving $250 million in credits from that agency along with a record $150 million loan from the World Bank to support structural reform in the agricultural sector. These actions by the international financial agencies were of special importance in restoring Tunisia's credit rating, which had been battered by the tense political climate, allowing for a rewarding return to commercial capital markets. The country's Western allies also helped support the reform program with additional loans. This infusion of foreign capital came as the country's debt-service payments reached 29 percent of exported goods and services.

The 1987 budget held firm to the government's program, with a 4 percent decline in real public spending. Payments to the Caisse Générale de Compensation (CGC), the agency responsible for food subsidies, were slashed by half. Throughout 1987, Sfar's government continued to announce further measures envisaged in the reform program, such as the liberalization of trade through tariff reductions on some imports and the deregulation of prices for many manufactured goods, especially in construction and textiles. Incentives for private investment were enhanced through a new industrial investment code, and a more flexible interest rate system was introduced. The 1987–1991 Five-Year Plan also clearly reflected the priorities of the new development strategy; the plan was directed toward the three primary objectives of creating employment, developing the rural sector, and stabilizing the balance of payments while meeting debt obligations.

Despite its adherence to the IMF-sanctioned targets, Tunisia's credit rating in 1987 suffered from a lack of confidence in the country's political stability, leading Ben Ali to seize the presidency by having Bourguiba declared senile through constitutional procedures. Ben Ali has since consolidated his own power base among the governmental elite and, more importantly, began his rule by taking steps to reverse the state's trend toward authoritarianism under Bourguiba by promising some democratizing reforms. These pledges of political liberalization brought Ben Ali popularity early in his rule, but he subsequently reversed himself as the state tightened the reins after 1989.

Ben Ali's decisive action to stabilize Tunisia's political situation met with considerable success during the late 1980s. The situation on the street calmed noticeably, and even initially skeptical opposition figures expressed more favorable impressions of the former interior minister once known as the ruthless enforcer of Bourguiba's hard-line tactics. Press censorship was relaxed, opposition parties were accorded more official recognition, political exiles were allowed to return, and a good number of political prisoners were amnestied. Yet the growing strength of the Islamic movement known as Nahda was to lead the government to crush the hopes it had raised for political liberalization as it embarked on a vigorous campaign to eradicate the much-touted fundamentalist menace. The turning point was the June 1989 elections, which Nahda officially boycotted because of accusations that they were not allowed fair participation. Nevertheless, many of the Islamicist candidates ran as independents, and their apparent appeal to a growing segment of the population sent shock waves through the presidential palace in Carthage. The Islamicists, who were dismayed at the state's refusal to accord them free participation in the elections, began to turn to more violent tactics. After the government announced its discovery of a coup plot engineered by the Islamicists in spring 1991, Ben Ali began to crack down in earnest. The Tunisian state has since pursued a policy of repression that has been severely condemned by Amnesty International and other human rights observers. The political costs of structural adjustment apparently have been higher than Ben Ali had initially foreseen.

Given Ben Ali's apparent concern with political stabilization, it is noteworthy that throughout the period of political turbulence experienced in the late 1980s, the government did not shy away from the structural adjustment program initiated under Mzali. The state's clear commitment to holding steady to this development strategy was facilitated by both the political honeymoon that followed Ben Ali's accession to the presidency and by favorable economic performances in 1987 and 1988, despite continued structural weaknesses. The 1988 budget held real spending constant at 1987 levels yet gave priority to debt obligations, the largest increase in public spending being a 10 percent rise in debt repayments. Further signs of the government's commitment to reform followed in 1988 as the government liberalized financial regulations, loosening exchange regulations in an attempt to ease the inflow of foreign exchange and permitting nationals to open hard-currency bank accounts provided they are exporters or receive foreign exchange from abroad.

The 1989 state budget closed out the decade on a similar note. Debt servicing increased by 16 percent over 1988 to 297 million dinars ($312.6 million), with repayment of the debt principal rising sharply by 21.1 percent over the previous year. Public investment was also up substantially (by 29.2 percent), reflecting the government's confidence in its ability to attract external financing, a key aspect of the regime's new development strategy. Recurrent spending was essentially held in line with inflation, except for the effects of a general pay raise to public employees—which along with the increase in debt repayments drove current expenditures up by 13.7 percent. Another notable feature of the 1989 budget was a dramatic 29.8 percent decline in state subsidies to public enterprises. Ben Ali also specifically targeted consumer subsidies for sharp reductions during the 1990s, despite their political sensitivity.

The Tunisian state indeed appears intent on carrying through with its program of structural adjustment, and the IMF has joined the World Bank in giving Tunisia the stamp of approval by citing the country as an example of good management (EIU 1988:26). This endorsement should have helped the government raise the $7 billion it expected from international sources during the 1987–1991 Five-Year Plan. Indeed, the external support for Tunisia's economic reforms is more assured than is a sufficiently quiescent domestic atmosphere, for the social costs of structural adjustment in the short term are likely to be measurable: Unemployment will rise as the vast parastatal enterprises are trimmed and privatized; the standard of living for most will decline as government subsidies on basic goods are reduced and public wages and salaries held in check. Ever higher levels of public spending will no longer provide a panacea for underdevelopment, especially given the demographic bulge coming of age.

The benefits of the structural adjustment program are available primarily to an elite. Attractive incentives are offered to those Tunisians with investment capital for export industries and for those in a position to establish joint ventures with foreign concerns; similarly, the relaxation of import regulations and foreign exchange controls mainly benefits the relatively few Tunisians who might claim the title of private entrepreneur. The Tunisian state certainly has the will to pursue structural adjustment as per the IMF, but whether it has the capacity to do so remains to be seen.

To political analysts, the economic reforms being pursued in Tunisia have worrisome implications. The gap between the rulers and the ruled will intensify as the state is increasingly supported by foreign interests. The Tunisian regime clearly was undermined by a crisis in political legitimacy during the 1980s that was in part related to inadequate economic growth and opportunity. As the nation entered the 1990s, the government was abandoning its tentative moves toward political decentralization while still pinning its hopes for development on economic liberalization. A rejuvenated ruling elite had bought time with promises of democratization, but the prospects for the 1990s are far from certain. The success of both the economic and political reforms will in large part depend on the impact structural adjustments have upon growth, but the Tunisian regime has encountered difficulties in accommodating external demands for financial solvency with domestic demands for political accountability.

Morocco

The structural adjustment program being carried out in the kingdom of Morocco is in many respects similar to that of Tunisia. During the 1980s, the Moroccan government engaged in a series of economic reforms aimed at decentralizing the state's management of the economy and redressing structural problems with the external account. These reforms encompass the enhancement of incentives for export production, the privatization of nonessential parastatal corporations, and sharp cuts in public spending coupled with increased priority on meeting external financial obligations. Morocco's structural adjustment program has largely come in response to external financial pressures, but as in Tunisia, the strength of the internal political coalition supporting this developing strategy will also be of critical importance in determining the prospects of the economic reforms.

The pressures for change in Morocco, too, have been both political and economic. The Moroccan monarch, Hassan II, is at the center of a patrimonial network of elites that exercises considerable control over economic resources and opportunity through substantial government intervention into the economy. However, as the proportion of the population lacking access to the clientelistic distribution networks has risen, periodic outbursts of violent opposition to the regime have occurred, most recently in 1981, 1984, and 1990–1991. As a result of a crisis in political legitimacy, the state faces political pressures from below to amend its development strategy.

The economic pressures for reform are primarily external in origin. As in Tunisia, the government in Morocco has been going through a period of chronic financial deficits that has obliged it to rely on conditional assistance from the international financial agencies and allies. In addition, Morocco has already been forced to reschedule its foreign debt and will most likely have to again in the early 1990s. As a result of these pressures, Moroccan economic policy in the 1980s departed from the all-encompassing state planning and high public investment of the 1970s to embrace a new and pronounced orientation toward austerity budgets and a decentralization of the government intervention in the economy.

The economic structures of Morocco were little affected by the transition to independence. Large state enterprises continued to dominate the economy, especially with regard to mining (mostly phosphates), transportation, and agriculture. Despite the gradual replacement of French nationals by Moroccans in ownership and management positions, the economy has retained a fundamentally externalist orientation. A reliance upon the export of phosphates (of which Morocco is the world's largest exporter and third largest producer) to assure a steady stream of foreign exchange is paralleled by the use of state-sponsored irrigation to encourage the growth of export crops in agriculture. As in the colonial period, the government continues to offer incentives to attract private capital investment in export production.

National unity is more elusive in Morocco than in Tunisia, with profound splits among the Moroccan ruling elite. The urban bourgeoisie is divided between a conservative segment with an interest in maintaining the status quo and a reformist, educated segment that tends more toward state planning and agrarian reform. The rural notables make up yet another stratum of the dominant class. These rural elites owe their continued political power in the countryside to their intermediary role between the state and peasantry, which continues to form the bulk of the population. The notables are known for their collusion with the monarch in resisting fundamental agrarian reform. The monarchy, of course, remains at the center of the Moroccan ruling class, and the king's manipulation of the political elite helps sustain the schisms within the upper social stratum. National unity has been further undermined by the sharp and growing differentiation between the dominant and subordinate classes. The legitimacy of the political order in Morocco was historically sustained by the monarch's spiritual attributes as defender of the faith, but this religious status has been undermined by King Hassan's close association with foreign powers, fundamentalist ideology providing an alternative vision for the faithful.

Two distinctive sets of intermediary elites have been particularly important in determining government policy in monarchical Morocco. Mediating between the state and the vast rural population, the rural notables exercise localized authoritarianism with the support of the coercive capabilities of the national government. Operating as representatives of the state in the world economy, a younger, technocratic elite has emerged that manages Morocco's interactions with transnational finance. Although the monarch remains closely allied with the rural notables, the policy shifts of the 1980s indicate that their influence is beginning to give way to that of the technocratic elite. In particular, a crisis in government finances along with outbreaks of violent unrest spurred by shortfalls in food security have made it clear that the maintenance of political order is more dependent upon access to transnational capital than upon the declining ability of the rural notables to stem the rural exodus. The intermediary rural elites continue to provide a key support for the monarch in the countryside, but their distribution of opportunity has not been able to keep pace with population growth.

Mounting budgetary and current account problems during the 1970s preceded the shift in Morocco's development strategy. Government revenues from phosphates exports were undercut by a fall in prices after 1975 and by a decline in demand due to the downturn in the world economy. Premised upon overly optimistic forecasts, the 1973–1977 Five-Year Plan envisaged an ambitious 39.8 billion dirhams ($8.7 billion) in investment, led by a substantial increase in public spending. As phosphate exports fell in both volume and value, the costs of imports rose higher than expected because of rises in world petroleum prices and growing food deficits that became increasingly severe from the latter half of the 1970s through the 1980s. The 1973–1977 period was thus marked by structural deficiencies in Morocco's external account and runaway budgetary deficits as the government continued to pursue a strategy of inordinately high public spending. By 1976 the Moroccan state was forced to turn to international capital markets to an unprecedented degree, a solution that was to have significant repercussions the following decade. The percentage of exports needed to service these credits began to soar, as the country's debt-service ratio went from 8.7 percent in 1970 to 36.5 percent in 1980.

The collapse of the external account and the high spending of the 1973–1977 plan were not the only causes of Morocco's surge in indebtedness during the late 1970s. Another major factor in the accumulation of debt and the regime's turn toward structural adjustment was the ongoing war in the Western Sahara against the Algerian-backed Polisario movement, which began in 1975. Drawing upon popular support for the historical claims of a greater Morocco, this international venture was acclaimed by virtually all internal political factions and served as an important aid in sustaining the legitimacy of the state. The war effort has since lost some of its glamor as it contributed to the escalation of the external public debt to the point at the end of the decade where it came to dominate government economic policy.

In 1978 these combined pressures encouraged the Moroccan government to undertake a significant shift in government policy. The 1978–1982 Five-Year Plan was scrapped before it came into effect, and the alternate 1978–1980 transitional Three-Year Plan represented a marked shift in development strategy, with structural adjustment and austerity the new watchwords. Public spending was sharply cut, except for expenditures on social welfare and agriculture, both of which reflected the priority placed on maintaining order. The monarch's concern with political stability was augmented by events elsewhere, when Tunisia experienced bloody rioting in 1978 and as Iran began its revolutionary convulsions.

The 1981–1985 Five-Year Plan, however, revealed a lingering reluctance on the part of the government to redress its structural problems. Public investment under the new plan was to rise sharply from the previous three years, reaching record levels. The plan predicted a rosy 6.5 percent annual GDP growth rate, but prolonged drought led to a 1.3 percent reduction of the GDP in 1981, as cereal yields were half those of the previous harvest. Although 1982 saw a 6.8 percent increase in the GDP, the government's heavy reliance on external financing began to take its toll. By 1983 Morocco's public external debt exceeded $10 billion, up from $712 million in 1970, with a debt-service ratio of over 45 percent. Unable to meet its financial obligations, the government began to abandon its investment targets and was forced to seek a rescheduling of its debt. The negotiations over rescheduling involved the IMF, World Bank, commercial creditors, and foreign governments in the Paris Club.

The Moroccan government succeeded in rescheduling over $1 billion of the debt and in obtaining further credits, but stringent conditions on these new loans circumscribed the state's selection of economic policy. Most major development projects were cut as public investment again plummeted. Stringent austerity measures were implemented to hold the budget deficit in check, with the politically sensitive government subsidies on basic consumer goods targeted for substantial reductions. The dirham was devalued, both foreign trade and investment regimes were liberalized, and the vast public sector began a gradual process of privatization. Priority was to be given to meeting Morocco's growing external obligations.

Countrywide food riots in January 1984 forced a slowdown of the austerity measures and the government announced a greater commitment to rainfed agriculture, which still supports over half of the Moroccan population. Taxes on agricultural production were annulled until the year 2000, and pricing policies were relaxed, enhancing incentives for rural producers. But despite the clear social pressures, Morocco could not afford to deviate much from its structural adjustment program, as imports shot up by 34.6 percent in 1984 as a result of the structural food and energy deficits, both of which had been exacerbated by currency devaluation. In 1984 the government introduced legislation designed to liberalize trade, including significant reductions in both export and import controls.

Negotiations over debt rescheduling were not finalized until October 1985, with the 1986–1988 Three-Year Plan articulating the priorities of the structural adjustment program as negotiated with the IMF and World Bank. The new plan was more in line with the reform program than the last, reducing public investment to 16.7 percent of GDP. Budget deficits were to be kept in check, and a modest annual growth rate of 2.9 percent was forecast in calculations of government revenues for the period covered by the plan.

Having successfully rescheduled its debt, however, the Moroccan government backed away from its reform program in December 1985. The 1986 budget reflected this latest shift in orientation, with a dramatic 67 percent rise in investment. Morocco also defaulted on an $85 million commercial debt repayment that was part of the rescheduling agreement. Although Morocco paid up in January 1986 and the rescheduling agreement was reinstated by the banks, both the default and the 1986 budget cast considerable doubt on Morocco's willingness to meet the conditions upon which further transnational credits were premised. That such financing would indeed be needed was indicated by predicted increases in both Morocco's debt repayments and its current account deficits.

In June 1986 the IMF cancelled the standby credit arrangement it had reached in 1985, expressing a lack of faith in the Moroccan government's willingness to meet its structural adjustment targets. The IMF was particularly worried about the 1985–1986 budgetary deficits and Moroccan hesitancy to move ahead with the austerity measures as scheduled. Commercial banks also indicated serious concern over Morocco's political will to stick to the reform program as rescheduling negotiations for the 1985–1986 repayments were prolonged.

King Hassan attempted to placate foreign anxieties during August and September 1986. The prime minister was replaced in a cabinet reshuffle that suggested forthcoming changes in political priorities. King Hassan made it clear in a speech to Parliament that the new government headed by Prime Minister Ahmed Laraki would follow policies more in line with IMF recommendations and that public-sector management would come under increasing scrutiny by an investigative commission. Hassan also abrogated Morocco's 1984 treaty with Libya. Although Libya expressed sharp displeasure with Morocco's dissolution of their union, Hassan was anxious to mend relations with the United States before seeking credits for the acquisition of new military equipment and to increase the prospects for restoring higher levels of economic aid.

The IMF responded to these political moves and to preliminary figures showing Morocco's balance of payments to be improving by agreeing to a new $280 million standby loan in December 1986. The commercial banks of the London Club, whose own rescheduling negotiations were coordinated with the IMF position, agreed to reschedule $1.8 billion of medium- and long-term debt and indicated that they were further prepared to provide the $400 million that Morocco needed to cover its 1986 financing gap. The World Bank also indicated that it was favorably considering a further $200 million in loans for the energy and transport sectors in 1987. The conditions of the new aid package as negotiated with the IMF included reduction of the budget deficit to 4.3 percent of GDP in 1987, more rapid privatization of the public sector, and a renewed priority on balancing Morocco's current account. The 1987 budget also cut consumer subsidies by 12.5 percent and subsidies to parastatal enterprises by 20 percent. New guarantee funds were introduced to enhance incentives for exports, and import taxes were reduced.

By 1987 it appeared that Morocco had convinced its foreign creditors that the political will to carry out a sustained program of structural adjustment did indeed exist. In March of that year, the World Bank's consultative group—composed of seventeen financial institutions and fourteen donor nations representing key sources of potential future financing—gave Morocco's economic reform program its stamp of approval. Although Morocco's debt was mounting at an alarming rate—to over $14.6 billion in 1986—it was clear that the state's strategy was to finance future development by even more borrowing, so the endorsement by the consultative group was critical.

Access to transnational sources of capital has become increasingly important to the Moroccan state, and with it, the influence of a younger, well-educated, and more technocratic segment of the elite has also begun to mount. The state's approach toward structural adjustment went from vacillation in the mind-1980s to sustained commitment over the latter part of the decade. Statistics at the end of 1987 showed that Morocco was meeting IMF targets regarding both the current account and the budget deficits. As the political will to implement the structural adjustment program has grown, so has the availability of external financing. The World Bank continued to endorse the government's program and provide further loans at the end of the 1980s, and in September 1987 the London Club agreed to reschedule another $2.4 billion in debt obligations, covering repayments due from 1985 to 1988. International allies such as the United States, France, and Spain also increased their aid packages.

The 1988–1992 Five-Year Plan optimistically forecast a GDP growth rate of 4 percent per year with 205 billion dirhams ($24.5 billion) in investments expected over the duration of the plan. In the meantime, liberalizing reforms have proceeded apace, with the privatization of sugar refineries and bus companies leading the way and with an easing of restrictions on capital transfers, a move intended to step up international investment. The 1988 budget was in line with the structural adjustment program with the deficit down by close to 10 percent, and subsidies for parastatal corporations fell to 2 billion dirhams ($239 million) in 1988, from 3.8 billion dirhams ($378 million) in 1986 and 3 billion dirhams ($330 million) in 1987. Investments were reduced by 19.4 percent. The 1989 budget cut investment by yet another 13 percent to 13.93 billion dirhams ($1.7 billion), although recurrent expenditure rose by 14.7 percent, reflecting a confidence that fiscal reforms would lead to significantly higher state revenues. The 1989 budget deficit was to be even 21 percent less than in 1988, down to 6.97 billion dirhams ($849 million).

The regime's commitment to structural adjustment clearly gained in strength as Morocco based its new development strategy on continued access to transnational capital. In 1988 Morocco became one of the world's top borrowers from both the World Bank and the African Development Bank. In August 1988 the IMF approved another standby credit for $287 million over sixteen months in support of the government's economic policies. Morocco's total external debt exceeded $22 billion as the country entered the 1990s, and an estimated $3.71 billion of debt servicing in 1989 have led to yet more discussions about rescheduling. Although there were repeated rollovers of Morocco's external debt, the regime demonstrated sufficient political will in support of the structural adjustment program to ensure that a steady flow of foreign capital would remain forthcoming.

Yet despite the king's endorsement and the support of transnational capital, the prospects for Morocco's structural adjustment program are far from certain. Further incidents of violent protests against the austerity measures in particular or the political order in general could jeopardize Hassan's willingness to further back the strategy. The structural adjustment program carries with it significant social costs, as prices on basic goods steadily rise while wage increases are capped. Both the 1988 and 1989 budgets were bitterly criticized by the opposition, who expressed resentment toward the "antisocial" elements of the government policies, particularly the austerity measures. The political situation remains strained as the king's advisers continue to resist demands for political liberalization and as the authorities use harsh measures against overt dissent. The country's penitentiaries, where many political prisoners still remain in the wake of the 1984 riots, have become cauldrons of dissent, hunger strikes becoming widespread and jailhouse riots breaking out in Kenitra in 1987. Increasing evidence of torture and deprivation has led to condemnations of Morocco's human rights abuses by the European Parliament and Amnesty International. A group of prominent Moroccan intellectuals formed a human rights organization autonomous of the government in order to campaign for an independent judiciary, but the government banned the group's meetings. Most political prisoners were released and abuses curtailed, however, in a widespread human rights reform in 1991.

Labor unrest also rose, making the continued imposition of austerity even less palatable to the regime. A strike by miners at the Jerada coalfields in northeast Morocco set off a wave of protests in 1989. The mine was temporarily shut down after being seized by 400 strikers for four days, but this was shortly followed by strikes in the flour-milling and petroleum-refining industries. Banking employees also went on strike in support of higher pay. The regime responded to the wave of walkouts by announcing pay increases for state employees—which, when actually implemented, benefited primarily the higher civil servants. Subsidies on basic goods were left untouched in 1989 despite the further reductions that had been recommended by the IMF and World Bank, reflecting the government's sensitivity to the social impact of the austerity measures. The fragility of the political order was again demonstrated by rioting in Fez in 1990.

The prospects for structural adjustment in Morocco are constrained by the nature of the political order. The parameters set by the monarchical system mean that the partial disengagement of the government from the economy will be hindered by the need of the state to retain its patrimonial distributive mechanisms. The transnationally oriented managerial elite favors the decentralizing reforms, but their rise to power has thus far not been accompanied by the political liberalization needed to firmly overcome the monarch's patrimonial domination over the economy. Popular demands on the regime are bound to increase as the social impacts of structural adjustment become more acutely felt. Conflict between the dominant and subordinate classes is likely to simmer as the legitimacy of the political order deteriorates further and as a lack of consensus among the ruling elite persists.

Algeria

On February 23, 1989, a referendum of the Algerian people approved a new constitution. One of the most striking features of the document is that it omits explicit reference to socialism, unlike the previous constitutions, in which the socialist ideology of the state was affirmed in Article 1. The Algerian state is now officially described as a "democratic and popular republic," a semantic alteration that reflects profound changes in the relationship between state and society in Algeria.

Two features of the 1980s challenged the regime's hold on power. First, the collapse of oil prices derailed the government's development strategy by forcing a curtailment of the high levels of capital investment that had been planned and by undermining the debt-repayment schedule that had been forecast. Second, political legitimacy during the 1980s was strained in part by chronic food deficits in the context of a rapid demographic growth of 3.1 percent. The food deficit arose as a result of a development strategy that until recently had concentrated on heavy industry to the neglect of agriculture, despite the population boom. The state had not foreseen that the threat of food shortages would endanger its legitimacy, for in the era of abundant hydrocarbon revenues, it was assumed that any needed imports during times of drought could be financed from domestic sources. Moreover, the majority of the population did not experience the liberation struggle and was consequently less and less susceptible to the state's revolutionary symbolism, with many turning to Islamic fundamentalism as an alternative. The uprisings of 1986 served notice that Algerian political order could no longer be taken for granted.

The financial crisis that resulted from the collapse of export revenues during the 1980s obliged the Algerian state to embark on a vast decentralization program built around the restructuring and privatization of state enterprises. The restructuring process has involved the breakup of huge centralized state corporations into more regional and specialized enterprises with a high degree of operational autonomy. Since 1980, the number of parastatals has risen from 61 to over 400 as the decentralization program moved ahead (Rummel 1989).

Algeria's financial difficulties were in part a result of the development strategy pursued during the previous decade. Heavy borrowing in the 1970s followed by the decline of world petroleum prices left Algeria with the most severe debt burden of the Maghribi nations. President Chadli Benjedid signaled a change in this strategy as early as 1980, putting a limit of 50 million dinars ($13 million) on annual borrowing in the country's first five-year plan (previous Algerian development plans had covered four-year spans). Nevertheless, Algeria's total external debt reached $24.9 billion by 1988. Considerable short-term debt came due as the country entered the 1990s, making it difficult for Algeria to meet its obligations without a rescheduling. By 1988 the debt-service ratio was 77 percent, and by 1989 debt repayments were estimated at close to 60 percent of the export of goods and services.

Algeria scrupulously honored its repayment obligations during the 1980s rather than reschedule its debt, despite many predictions to the contrary. The government's adamant resistance to any rescheduling perhaps reflects the spirit of sacrifice born among the senior members of the ruling elite during the war of national liberation. In contrast to Morocco, the state embarked upon its structural adjustment program not because of conditions imposed as a result of a rescheduling but in order to avoid such an eventuality. Even with an overwhelming debt burden, Algeria nevertheless maintained a sound credit rating throughout most of the decade because of its clear demonstration of the political will needed to meet its external obligations. The riots of 1988 led to speculation that the government might be forced to stray from its course, but the state responded to the unrest through political reform, still avoiding a rescheduling or any fundamental alteration to its structural adjustment program.

Algeria's structural adjustment program is, however, contingent upon the sustained imposition of austerity measures that carry significant social costs. Dwindling export revenues in relation to external obligations have forced the government to cut back on subsidies to consumers and to the public sector, which must increasingly fall in line with the standards of economic efficiency. Benjedid's success in so consistently carrying out these reforms during the 1980s demands closer inspection, for the Algerian regime has been known for elite fragmentation that makes consensus difficult to achieve. The economic reforms are thus best understood from a perspective that encompasses both financial pressures and changes among the ruling elite.

Houari Boumedienne's presidency was associated with the state's commitment to government planning, national autonomy, agrarian reform, and public order. Its development program was founded on high public investment and spending and financed by hydrocarbon exports. Heavy state spending helped ensure political stability through massive public works and employment, in part masking growing problems. Boumedienne's sudden death in December 1978 led to the presidency of Benjedid, ushering in the contemporary era of structural adjustment.

The Five-Year Plan of 1980–1984 was the first plan the Benjedid government produced. This document did not radically break from past development strategy, essentially adhering to the orthodox policies of investing in heavy industry. However, early signs of departure from the strategy of the 1970s were evident in that the 1980–1984 plan was a scaled-down version of previous plans, reflecting the increasing financial pressures on the regime. Close to half of the investment during this period was designated for completing ongoing projects, with few new ones initiated. (As it was, actual investment during this period fell far short of the plan's targets.)

Benjedid cautiously began introducing liberalizing economic policies soon after taking office, at the same time solidifying his support among the ruling elite. As is often the case, the Algerian elite were factionalized when the FLN chose Benjedid, the senior active colonel of the armed forces, as the new presidential candidate, to be confirmed by national plebiscite in 1979. Benjedid moved with dispatch to consolidate his leading position through personnel changes in the government and in the parastatal sector (Zartman 1984, 1988a). As Benjedid presided over this partial circulation of the ruling elite, the state became increasingly committed to structural adjustment. The privatization and restructuration of the vast parastatal sector was given higher priority after 1980, even though the attempt to make the public sector more economically efficient was generally unpopular because of its negative impact upon employment and wages. Constrained by the heavy debt obligations incurred during the previous decade, the regime was forced to include a strong dose of austerity as part of its structural adjustment program. Political pressures began to mount as opposition to the regime was expressed from the left, from Berber dissidents in the Kabylia, and from Islamic fundamentalists.

Two events in the mid-1980s led to an accelerated implementation of the structural adjustment program. During 1985 a series of public debates were held on the revision of the country's national charter, and a new draft was written that expressed approval of the economic reforms yet reaffirmed the nation's commitment to social justice and Algerian nationalism. This new national charter was overwhelmingly approved in January 1986, solidifying Benjedid's claim to a mandate for his liberalizing policies. The second event that served to reinforce the regime's predisposition toward structural adjustment was the oil price crash of 1985–1986. In 1986, hydrocarbon exports represented 97.6 percent of export revenues, and the price collapse signaled the onset of severe current account difficulties. In resisting a debt rescheduling, the state was forced to turn to international sources of capital to finance its budgetary shortfalls.

Algeria's credit rating remained good in spite of the financial crisis because of the government's well-established commitment to structural adjustment and a stamp of approval from the World Bank. But concern still mounted over the government's ability to stick to its promise of no rescheduling. A standby loan from the IMF would have involved foreign intervention in the management of Algeria's economy, which the government feared would be politically unacceptable to the populace. The regime was anxious to preserve political stability, as Algeria was considered to be the most stable of the Maghribi countries at this time, a reputation that enhanced its credit rating.

Political pressures, though, were being fueled by the social impacts of the austerity measures. There were some isolated incidents of violent protest during the early months of Benjedid's presidency, but the political order was maintained until spring and summer 1985. The first sign of trouble occurred with the outbreak of violent protests in the Algiers Casbah and in Ghardaia. A few months later, militant fundamentalists raided a police academy outside of Algiers, killing a policeman. In November 1985 a riot broke out in the Kabylia city of Tizi-Ouzou; a public strike followed in response to the arrests that were part of the government's crackdown. The two-day uprising was a protest against the detention of political prisoners.

The country's political order was even more severely rocked the following year, when widespread disruptions upset numerous cities. The worst rioting occurred in Constantine, where students angered over poor living conditions and changes in their curriculum took to the streets in bloody clashes with authorities. The youth then represented a majority of the population who had not experienced the revolutionary struggle and were consequently less imbued with the spirit of national sacrifice than their elders. Furthermore, the sharp reductions in public spending meant that the creation of new jobs was to fall even further behind the demand for meaningful employment, limiting the economic opportunities available to the increasing numbers entering the job market.

The moratorium that Benjedid had placed on additional external borrowing in the early 1980s gave way when the economy's external situation was further aggravated by the collapse of oil prices in 1985–1986. Steadfast in its determination not to reschedule, the regime borrowed heavily from Euromarkets and Japanese banks. In 1986, a year in which the debt-service ratio shot up to 57 percent from 37 percent the previous year, the country borrowed over $2 billion. The World Bank praised the regime's structural adjustment measures in 1986, although the increasing debt burden was singled out for concern.

The 1985–1989 Five-Year Plan underlined the government's commitment to reform by sharply breaking with the priorities of the preceding plans. Agriculture and water resources replaced heavy industry as the centerpiece of national planning, the state grappling with the political implications of its growing food deficits; housing and manufacturing were also slated for greater levels of investment. The unveiling of this plan was closely followed by the presentation of the 1986 budget, which further reflected the financial pressures. Originally calling for an 18.5 percent rise in public spending, this figure was abandoned in the wake of the oil price collapse, and the revised budget actually saw spending reduced to slightly less than in 1985. The bulk of the cuts occurred in the capital budget, with sharp reductions in public investment, though a trimmed recurrent budget also marked a renewed wave of austerity measures. Prices of gasoline and cigarettes were raised, tighter limits were placed on imports, and foreign currency allocations for Algerians traveling abroad were reduced.

The political disturbances of 1986 that came in the wake of this belt-tightening made the government reluctant to cut recurrent spending through further austerity measures, and the 1987 budget showed a 5.9 percent increase over the revised 1986 budget. The regime continued to restrict investment, however, which was cut by around 5 percent from 1986 levels. Taxes were raised on company profits, luxury imports, and ostentatious buildings, affecting mostly the wealthy. In early 1987 Benjedid's government further sought to defuse the political situation by relaxing security measures and by taking steps to distinguish radical from moderate opposition. New legislation permitting associations outside the FLN was passed with the vague provision that any such associations "not act against the interests of the revolution." Several human rights leagues were recognized, and Amnesty International was permitted to open an Algiers office. State security, however, remained tight; the pace of political liberalization could at best be described as gradual.

Throughout this period, President Benjedid continued to reinforce his control over the government by reshuffling top governmental personnel, building a team solidly committed to his reform policies. Featuring a relatively high turnout, the elections of February 1987 returned a legislature that was considerably younger, better educated, and more receptive to Benjedid's strategies of economic liberalization and privatization than many of the more established members of the elite that had dominated the Assemblée Populaire Nationale (APN) in the past. In October 1987 the president submitted a new set of decentralizing economic reforms to the APN for ratification, and they were duly approved in December. In the agricultural sector, prices were to be brought more in line with market forces (except for cereals and other basic food products considered to be of strategic importance to the state), and over 3,000 agricultural collectives were to be broken up into smaller autonomous units, involving close to 3 million hectares (1.3 million acres) of farmland. The subdivision of the massive state conglomerates was to continue, with decisions regarding salaries and personnel to give ever greater priority to economic efficiency. The government also embarked on a campaign to encourage joint ventures with foreign companies. The reforms moved ahead at a more rapid pace than before, despite opposition from ideological conservatives, vested interests, left-wing radicals, and Muslim fundamentalists.

External indebtedness continued to climb in 1987 as the government was steadfast in refusing any politically risky rescheduling and as banks remained willing to lend in substantial amounts. The World Bank provided several large development loans, and Japanese banks began to play an increasingly prominent role as European financial consortia were constrained by concern over Algeria's heavy debt repayment burden. This trend persisted through 1988, as Algeria emerged as the heaviest Maghribi borrower from the World Bank, having gone from no credits in 1986 to $464 million in 1987 and $648 million in 1988. The Japanese government offered up to $339 million in new credits and guarantees in 1988, and substantial credits from Japanese banks allowed Algeria to obtain more than $900 million in medium-term commercial borrowing in 1988. Other significant credits were also obtained from the African Development Bank, the Islamic Development Bank, the European Community, and the International Fund for Agricultural Development.

With a more supportive APN and a handpicked cabinet and after numerous personnel changes in both the FLN and army, the president began pushing his reform program more aggressively in 1988, reaffirming yet again the regime's commitment to structural adjustment and to avoiding a debt rescheduling. The fiscally prudent approach of preceding years carried through to 1988, with the budget giving priority to avoiding a balance-of-payments crisis. Recurrent spending continued to be held in check, with less than a 4 percent increase, but investment spending in the capital budget rose by 5.6 percent to 47.5 billion dinars ($9.8 billion) after being reduced the year before. Optimistic forecasts regarding the price of oil along with continued access to international capital markets helped contribute to a decision to increase investment, although the trend toward austerity remained.

Benjedid's reform program was again seriously challenged in October 1988, when demonstrations by disaffected youths in Algiers sparked off the worst episode of civil unrest since the revolution. The cities of Algiers, Blida, Annaba, Oran, and numerous villages in the north were brought to a standstill as authorities responded with unprecedented ferocity, leaving at least 600 dead and many more wounded. The rioting, which had been sparked off by rising prices on basic goods and disputes over national salaries, was principally directed against institutions and symbols of the government and ruling party. A drought during the 1987–1988 crop year had also contributed to food and water shortages, which were largely blamed on government authorities.

Benjedid's response to the events of October 1988 was a bold repudiation of his opponents among the Algerian elite. In a public address that effectively brought to a close this period of disturbances, the president interpreted the rioting as a popular demand for more political participation rather than as a rejection of the government's economic policies. Benjedid proposed a series of reforms to liberalize the political system, including the revision of the constitution and the weakening of the FLN's hold over national politics. He again reaffirmed the state's commitment to the structural adjustment program, coupling the liberalization of both the economic and political systems. The October 1988 political crisis thus provided Benjedid with the opportunity to further weaken those factions of the elite opposed to his policies while drawing popular attention away from his economic reforms to the political arena. The president called for a popular referendum on his proposals and leadership the next month, which the public approved by an overwhelming margin, although the turnout was much lower than in past Algerian elections. Benjedid's astute and successful handling of this crisis did much to defuse foreign concerns over the government's ability to pursue its development program, and the political reforms promised to weaken opposition to the policies among the elite even further.

The passage of the 1989 budget by the National Assembly in December 1988 illustrated the muted effects of the political developments upon Algeria's structural adjustment program, with the essence of the economic reforms remaining intact. Although the National Assembly approved the budget, it did so only after considerable and atypical debate, with concern voiced over the social impact of austerity and the persistence of widespread unemployment. The anxiety over public order was reflected in a 9.8 percent increase in recurrent spending, which financed public-sector pay raises in 1989, including a 34 percent increase in the minimum wage. Spending on public investment remained capped at a modest 4.2 percent above the previous year, the government forecasting a significant decrease in the budget deficit.

Algeria's development strategy during the late 1980s relied heavily upon the ready availability of concessionary credits. Yet the political disorders of 1988 intensified doubts about the regime's capacity to avoid a rescheduling of the debt, which had risen to $24.9 million by 1988 (World Bank 1990a). The government's sustained adherence to its structural adjustment program was no longer in itself sufficient to keep the flow of external capital coming at the high levels required by the country's financial gaps.

The Algerian government was forced to take drastic action in 1989, which it did by reaching an unprecedented agreement with the IMF for over $600 million in standby credits. The regime in the past had gone to great lengths to avoid such a move because of the strong nationalist resistance to foreign intervention into the economy. Yet coordinating national development strategy with the IMF had become a prerequisite for obtaining high levels of credits from the World Bank, commercial capital markets, and Western governments. The conditionality of the IMF agreement did not signal an abrupt departure from government policy except for demanding a sharp devaluation of the Algerian dinar. Collaboration with the IMF on economic policy is unpopular, but it will allow the state to put off any rescheduling of the national debt even longer.

As in Tunisia, economic decentralization in Algeria has been linked to promises of political liberalization. The FLN remains resistant to a more liberal political system that might challenge its hegemony, but popular pressures for participation outside the FLN are growing, as reflected in the challenge to the regime posed by the Islamicists during the early 1990s. The success of the FIS in the municipal elections of 1990 and its expected victory in the second round of the legislative elections of 1992 led the military to bring Benjedid's program of political liberalization to an abrupt halt, deposing Benjedid in the process. The Algerian state's flexibility in the economic domain has thus not been matched in the political sphere, and the 1990s promise to be a troubled time, especially given the limited hydrocarbon revenues. The government will have to impose unpopular economic reforms on a largely recalcitrant population.

Libya

A more generous ratio of population to natural resources differentiates Libya from its Maghribi neighbors. This sparsely populated nation enjoys immense oil riches, which allowed the state to embark on the most ambitious development strategy of the African continent during the 1970s. Revenues from Libya's high-quality oil funded some of the most remarkable advances in the Third World in health, education, and other social services, and the country has gone from one of the world's poorest to one whose per capita GDP far exceeds that of the other North African countries. It is the only Maghribi economy with a critical shortage of labor power.

The character of Libya's national leadership also distinguishes it from the other states of the Maghrib. The transformation of Libyan politics under the rule of Qadhafi has left a fragmented political elite that lacks cohesion and identity other than allegiance to the visions of the leader. Unlike the other cases considered in this study, the postnationalist generation of political elites has not yet clearly consolidated its power in the great *jamahiriya*. There is no room in Tripoli for even a loyal opposition; dissidents are exiled or persecuted. After several reports of coup attempts in the mid-1980s, Qadhafi has kept a close eye on the military, trying to retain its allegiance in part through high defense expenditures.

Financial pressures during the 1980s led the Libyan state to make substantial adjustments to its development strategy, as in the rest of the Maghrib. In particular, the downward fluctuation in oil prices during the decade led to chronic deficits in the current account, forcing the government to sharply scale back on public spending and investment. Yet unlike the other Maghribi states, the Libyan regime could shift the burden of the ensuing austerity measures upon the substantial numbers of foreign workers through layoffs, mass expulsions from the country, and limits on wage repatriation. Libya has thus been able to enjoy the privilege of easing up on restrictions on consumerism when growing signs of discontent became apparent. The government did indeed pay homage to popular pressures toward the end of the decade by relaxing restrictions on imports of consumer goods into the country and loosening controls on travel and capital flight. Although they acted as a political sedative, the combined effect of these measures led to a rapid drain on foreign reserves in the late 1980s, raising questions as to the long-term prospects of this strategy.

The mercurial colonel has shown a remarkable ability to adapt state policies to changing world markets, a skill that served Qadhafi well in the shifting sands of the 1980s. Even though Qadhafi based his ambitious development strategy on the high oil prices of the 1970s, his government was able to adapt to the declining oil revenues of the 1980s by cutting public expenditure without incurring widespread unrest. Libya also succeeded in coping with its adjustment without accruing the huge debt obligations characteristic of the other Maghribi experiences.

The 1981–1985 development plan set the tone for the decade with its wariness regarding dependency upon oil revenues, seeking to enhance economic diversity by allocating 17 percent of investment to agriculture and 22 percent to industry. The decision to move away from reliance on oil, however, came too late to save the plan, which had to be abandoned as revenues were less than forecast. Consequences of the price slippage were already evident in 1982, when Libya began to experience cash flow problems and spending on development projects was scaled back. The development plan was virtually suspended and restrictions were placed on imported goods. A slight reduction in budgetary expenditures foreshadowed the austerity years that were to follow.

Libya attempted to shore up its revenues in 1982 through an increase in oil production in defiance of OPEC recommendations, allowing the government to persist with many large development projects. Debt began to rise even though Libya was gaining a reputation for being late in repaying its trade debts. By the end of 1983, total external debt was estimated at $2.8 billion, most of that in nonbank trade obligations. The current account remained in heavy deficit for the second year running as it became clear that the boom years of the 1970s were over.

The 1983 state budget reflected government recognition of the new constraints, with spending down by 9 percent and forecasts of GDP growth scaled back to 5.5 percent from the 10.8 percent envisaged in the 1981–1985 plan. The GDP was actually in decline, as it would remain for the duration of the decade. The budget was slimmed yet again in 1984 as revenues fell by another 10 percent and further restrictions were placed on imports.

Challenges to Qadhafi's rule surfaced as the financial difficulties intensified. An attempted coup in May 1984 combined with opposition to Qadhafi in the General People's Congress in March of that year led the Libyan leader to seek to defer some of the social impacts of the budgetary cutbacks. Restrictions were imposed on external remittances by foreign workers, trade debt repayments were allowed to lapse, and barter deals were resorted to in response to the prolonged shortage of hard currency.

The sharp collapse of oil prices in 1985 made it apparent that Libya's economic woes would not be solved by short-term measures but would require a more far-reaching structural adjustment program. Rumors of another coup in April 1985 encouraged Qadhafi to place the burden of the needed austerity on the emigrant workers, and in August the colonel summarily expelled some 30,000 Tunisian migrant workers from Libya. The 1986 budget showed no increase in the capital budget and only a slight increase in the recurrent budget. This was to be followed by steadily more austere budgets for the rest of the decade.

The Libyan regime faced two significant challenges as the end of the 1980s drew near. The attempts to repress dissent had led to a backlash of growing popular anger at the abuses committed by the colonel's overly zealous "revolutionary committees," and the persistent current account deficits and drain on foreign reserves made it clear that the state would have to reduce its intervention into the economy even further. Qadhafi met these political and economic challenges in early 1988 by following the examples set by the other Maghribi states and announcing a program of political and economic liberalization.

Qadhafi's "green *perestroika*" illustrated the Libyan leader's keen ability to make pragmatic economic decisions politically acceptable. A forthcoming liberalization of the economy was to be accompanied by an increased emphasis on human rights and political reform. The merging of these twin decentralizing programs served to cloak the austerity measures within a popular package that included curbing the power of the revolutionary committees, granting an amnesty to political prisoners, and adopting a more tolerant position toward the many exiles who constitute the bulk of the organized opposition groups to the Tripoli regime. Restrictions on foreign travel were also to be relaxed. In addition to austerity, the economic aspects of the green *perestroika* were to include the legalization of private ownership of shops, medical practices, small businesses, and farms, and the enhancement of private retail trade incentives.

Qadhafi's approval ratings soared, once again confirming his leadership as he grabbed the initiative in imposing the reforms. Although limited in comparison to the rest of the Maghrib, the Libyan liberalizing measures have been distinguished by their popularity. The revival of private retail trade was accompanied by Qadhafi's public praise for the black market, officially condoning and encouraging what already existed. The most popular reforms were the opening of the border with Tunisia and the relaxation of foreign currency restrictions (both allowing for a renewed wave of consumerism).

The substantial increase in the importation of consumer goods resulting from these liberalizing measures put added strains on Libya's foreign reserves, which fell to $5.8 billion at the end of 1988, threatening modification of the program. The 1989 budget continued the trend toward austerity, slashing the capital budget by one-third and reducing the recurrent budget by 5.5 percent. A sharp increase in oil prices during 1989 raised prospects that Libya would be able to ease up slightly on its structural adjustment program, but even under favorable economic conditions it is not likely that the regime will reverse its gradual trend toward liberalization given the experiences of the 1980s.

Libya's structural adjustment experience offers unique lessons despite apparent similarities with the other Maghribi cases. All of the countries discussed above engaged in liberalizing reforms during the 1980s in response to financial pressures related to fluctuations in international market prices for key exports. Yet Libya's case stands apart from the others in that the political pressures for reform were significantly less than those in the rest of North Africa. Libya was the only Maghribi country to avoid crippling debt obligations, giving the regime more flexibility in dealing with its foreign creditors and trade partners. Moreover, the social impact of the austerity measures in Libya was buffered by the large proportion of foreigners in the work force and by the lack of a substantially volatile urban underclass, although a huge food deficit still led to outcries of dissatisfaction when shortages occurred.

Libya's case is instructive because its economic liberalization was not simply a reaction to overwhelming debt obligations but rather to a recognition of the limits of growth by a pragmatic state. Qadhafi's green *perestroika* was not popularly seen as a sellout to the forces of imperialism but as a move to restore the state's credibility and accountability on the domestic scene. Viewed from a comparative perspective, the Libyan example clearly indicates that the negative impact of structural adjustment upon political legitimacy is heightened when the austerity measures are commonly perceived as due to foreign influence. The Libyan case suggests that a reduction of state intervention in the economy will not in itself necessarily lead to discontent, although popular entitlement to basic goods remains essential to political stability.

Conclusion: Transnational Capitalism in the Postnationalist Age

The 1990s are a decade of profound changes in the relationship between state and society in the Maghrib. In contemporary North Africa, a conjuncture of crises in the governments' finances and the legitimacy of the state led to a political realignment that enhanced the relative power of the managerial segments of the ruling elite. The development strategies of four very different regimes have begun to converge as external accounts have been given increased priority and as a circulation of political elites ushers in a new era.

Structural balance-of-payments deficits and heavy debt obligations require the Maghribi states to undertake significant alterations in their development strategies. All four states have turned to transnational finance in their quest for national development, enhancing the position of the managerial segment of the elite. This rising young managerial fraction does not claim its cohesion from any role in the national liberation struggles, as does the first generation of elites, but from an adherence to a particular policy platform. Elites have coalesced around an externally oriented development strategy that relies upon the young technocrats as intermediaries (cf. Sklar 1976).

The managerial segment of the ruling elite in all four countries derives much of its power from an intermediary role between the nation and transational capitalism. The ascending influence of this managerial sector has brought with it a trend toward economic liberalization. This elite generally lacks populist appeal but commands access to the external resources needed for regime survival. The conditions for this access include a decentralization of the national economies and increased exposure to the world market. The policy changes associated with structural adjustment in the Maghrib are thus closely linked to the circulation of elites.

The generation of elites that took power during the struggle for independence is giving way with the passage of time to both domestic and external demands for greater efficiency, and to the new visions of a rising class of managers. But will a rejuvenated ruling elite be able to maintain national political legitimacy, also a requisite for successful structural adjustment? Access to international capital may help in this regard, but it will not in itself be enough. The Maghribi states have all bowed to the pressures of transnational capitalism by adopting structural adjustment programs, but their ability to stick to this new path in large part depends upon the response to popular demands for greater participation. As the 1990s began to unfold, both the Tunisian and Algerian regimes took steps to reverse their nascent efforts at democratization.

The political orders of three of the four countries were called into question during the 1980s by violent uprisings. The traditional touchstones of legitimacy were undermined by the disparity between the spread of economic opportunity and population growth. The peoples of the North African countries are holding their states accountable for their basic needs at the same time that the governments' external financial obligations dictate a reduction of the state's role in the economy.

The economic liberalization programs of North Africa reflect the influence of transnational capitalism. But the forecast for the resilience of these programs in the Maghrib will primarily revolve around the government's accountability to its domestic constituency rather than to its external patrons. The political will to carry out these programs must be coupled with the political capacity to do so if they are to succeed. Given the high degree of patrimonialism evident in all four states since independence, political liberalization appears to be a critical adjunct to the structural adjustment programs. In the end, it may be the issue of political accountability that will determine the fate of decentralizing efforts in North Africa.

8

Local Societies

Nicholas S. Hopkins

Local society and politics in the Maghrib from the 1970s into the 1990s must be situated in relation to state and national societies and a context of development. In North Africa, as elsewhere, people live in local communities and seek first of all satisfaction at that level. Their willingness to subscribe to the ideals and projects of the national system depends in large part on their satisfaction with the degree of political participation available to them in the local system, access to resources such as land or education, and a sense of shared progress and improvement. Thus two main considerations are (1) to understand something of the workings of local political systems, in the broadest expression of that phrase, and (2) to grasp the ways in which these local systems are linked with one another and with the national system of which they are, in some sense, a part.

The Maghrib—which includes Morocco, Algeria, Tunisia, and Libya—stretches 3,000 km (nearly 2,000 miles) from Tangier to Kufra. What is meant by "local" society in this region? The referent of this word varies considerably and can be used to refer to anything from communities of a few hundred in Kabylia (Lacoste-Dujardin 1976) or the Atlas (Hammoudi 1988) to amorphous collections of 8,000 in the Gharb plain of Morocco (S. Davis 1983) or to structured settlements of several thousand, as in the Sahel zone of Tunisia (Abu-Zahra 1982; Brown 1981; Boukraa 1976, 1980) or Morocco (Eickelman 1976) or to largely new towns such as Ajdabiya in Libya (J. Davis 1987). But even such a typology does not conclude the issue. In many areas of the Maghrib the population lives in scattered homesteads, where *neighborhood* might be a better term for the local group than *village*. Both clustered and scattered habitats are sometimes said to be occupied by "tribes," that most problematic of words in the Maghrib (Berque 1974; Eickelman 1981:87–90). For some people, "belonging" to a "tribe" (taken as a group of variable size defined in principle by kinship) is an important form of identity. This chapter is concerned with "local" societies in the rural areas and in the towns and small cities. These local societies are thus seen in silhouette against a background of the major cities of the Maghrib, the states that are centered in them, and the international order.

The nature of local societies and their relations to wider ones has been changing in the past generation, with increasing national independence and international dependence. We must look closely at the way in which economic and social development affect the relations of local communities in the larger system. In a more specific sense, we must consider the impact of particular development projects—state control of agriculture ("socialism"), resettlement on agricultural schemes, roads, telephones, television, potable water projects, family planning, and so on—on the structure and integrity of local societies. Such a point of view leads us to note, in addition to "older" forms, the presence of many new forms of community: new settlements on irrigation schemes in Tunisia (Zghal 1967; Ferchiou 1985) and Morocco (Popp 1983; Pascon 1977; Seddon 1987), "socialist villages" in Algeria (Burgat and Nancy 1984; Sutton 1984), crossroads towns that spring up around new transportation nodes (Troin 1979; Combs-Schilling 1985), new factory or mining towns, administrative centers, and so on. So it is not just a matter of the impact of development on existing communities but of the way in which development projects on a wider scale create new local societies.

The main trend in the development of local societies has been toward increasing monetization of social relations (hired labor replaces family labor, producers produce for market sale, land sales develop, etc.). Such a trend is partly the outcome of deliberate state choices, partly the result of the general pattern of social forces in the area. The change in the mode of production has implications for local-center linkages in the context of national societies, and for the form of integration into the world economy. Although personal links always remain important, categories such as class are useful. Through class we can better understand the general pattern of differentiation in local societies and the ways in which they are assembled into a larger whole. Giving a cultural or ideological dimension to class refines and extends the concept.

What is the evidence for these processes at the local level, keeping in mind that whatever is true at the national level has local expressions as well? Is there a link between the changing role of the state and the emergence of a different kind of society—one marked more by a national division of labor, by increased "rationalization" in the sense of centrally organized discipline, and therefore by different options open to individuals and in turn a larger role for "class"?

Responses to Development

The first set of cases below includes an extended example from each of the four Maghribi countries. They represent a base line, all the more for including substantial evidence of change in response to development.

Hababsa, Tunisia

Hababsa is a rural zone (*secteur*) in the southern part of Siliana governorate, Tunisia. This rural area appears relatively isolated from the main currents that have transformed local societies elsewhere in the Maghrib—it has no colonial or capitalistic farming, no major development projects, no notorious involvement in national political movements. Yet even here there are changes.

In 1977 Hababsa had a population of around 5,000 divided almost exclusively into farming households (Zghidi 1978), devoted to cereals and animal husbandry. Most farmers used family labor and their own seed. Tractors were introduced into the area in 1972 and were still scarce in 1978. A majority of households kept sheep, cattle, and goats, which were tended by children. Cash income came from the sale of animals or tree crops (such as olives or almonds) and from migration outside the area, which was usually for relatively brief periods (one to two months) and involved members of around one-third of households in any year. Thus the area appears to be devoted to subsistence agriculture (Zghidi 1978).

The entire area was *habous* (religious endowment) until the Tunisian government abolished the system in 1957 and the land was formally distributed among the inhabitants, who probably already had informal claims to their land. The social organization reflects the "tribal" structure that dominates the area. Most of the inhabitants are the descendants of a saint (Nasr Ben Abderrahman Bel Habbes) and have been assimilated to the Ouled Ayar confederation; others are immigrants from other branches of the Ouled Ayar and other tribes. Although dwellings are scattered, close relatives live near one another. By national standards, this is an area of small and medium-sized landowners.

The dominant form of social organization in the area is kinship, perceptible in the patterns of exchange among households. The area is lightly administered, with party branches the most evident feature (cf. Zamiti 1977:327). The nature of the wider society is reflected in growing monetization of the economy, undercutting the significance of kinship, as people now expect wages for their help. There is some market in land, 14 percent of Zghidi's respondents having bought their land. Thus a process of differentiation has begun. Further, the peasant in trouble now no longer looks to kin for help but to the state: Only the state can change the situation (Zghidi 1978). Thus the relative isolation of Hababsa is only apparent, and in fact the sector is progressively being integrated into the national structures, through migration and state penetration. Since 1978 the road network into Hababsa and the water supply have been improved, both as a result of state investment. In the 1980s there was also a small private development project (Save the Children Foundation) in one corner of the area that was bringing irrigation and potable water as well as income-generating activities for women and trying to empower the small Hababsa community of Magrouna.

Ait Zouaou, Algeria

In Algerian Kabylia, in the range of mountains overlooking the Mediterranean, some 2,470 people known as the Ait Zouaou form one-third of the commune of Iflissen (Lacoste-Dujardin 1976). They live in nine villages that had between 77 and 842 in 1971. In precolonial days, the main village was known as a center for armorers specializing in side arms (Lacoste-Dujardin 1976:38). When that was broken up during the colonial period, some of the smiths scattered to other parts of Kabylia. Other early migration included that to the colonial farms in the Mitidja. Later there was migration to France, helped by the school that functioned until the war of independence began. Women and children did not migrate generally until after 1962. About 20 percent of the group live in three "saintly" or "holy" villages. These villages have a history of quranic schools and a higher level of education that has allowed a different kind of integration into Algerian national society; they also follow Islamic law in allowing women to inherit (Lacoste-Dujardin 1976:31).

The Ait Zouaou were gravely affected by the independence war. A village of 842 people in 1971 lost around 50 war dead between 1954 and 1962. Of eighty-six males born between 1921 and 1936, thirty-six (41 percent) were killed in the war. Several of the villages were declared off limits by the French army and largely destroyed (Lacoste-Dujardin 1976:21, 81).

Since the war, migration has been the main source of income, and many men and some women and children are absent in France. Some families are in their second generation of migration: when the father returns home to retire, the son goes to France. The strategy is usually a family decision, the migrant sending money to support the family, which remains together, perhaps under the authority of a brother or another relative.

Agriculture is declining in this marginal area as activities such as services and migration become more attractive. Local production suffers, in part because there are simply not enough people to make it work. As farming declines, there is a less clear role for women in the sexual division of labor. But some women are taking over running small grocery stores, which also serve as a meeting place for women (Lacoste-Dujardin 1976:74). Many women receive pensions as the survivors of war dead. Men are more involved in services and working for the government, especially local government. But, "the transition from peasant work to salaried work produces a considerable uncertainty in the concept of work itself" (Lacoste-Dujardin 1976:56, 80), and hence the emergence of the new concept of unemployment.

The local economy and the household structure depend on money from the outside, whether the wages from France or war pensions. Drawing on the savings from migration works as long as local needs remain at the low level of the subsistence economy. People compensate for the breakup of families through war and migration by grouping together in extended families. This spreads the risk by diversifying resources and allows for more efficient consumption and care of the elderly and widows. The men contribute the most income to the households but are absent. Women are more dependent, as production takes place elsewhere. The older men who act as surrogates for absent heads of these households have had their power strengthened, thus reinforcing patriarchal authority. A few households are able to accumulate wealth locally, and most local politicians are from these larger, more successful households.

Thus the Ait Zouaou have moved from a situation based on a regional division of labor (smithies to supplement agriculture, religious specialists) to one in which they are involved in an international division of labor yet at the same time participate in the national movement and political system of Algeria. Local resistance reflected and supported the national war of independence, but the war had the effect of breaking down whatever local ecological balance may have existed. The peasant society has given way to a form of rural proletariat. In the short run this has reinforced patriarchal authority in the household and produced a local leadership based on wealth.

The Sous Valley of Morocco

In the Sous Valley is the settlement of Ouled Filali (Dwyer 1982). The ninety-five households of 725 people work around 500 hectares (1,250 acres) mostly in dry farming of cereals but with considerable investment in irrigated cultivation of vegetables. The village was founded by immigrants, one-third of the people descended from people who arrived after 1900. About the same number of people have moved on. The villagers nonetheless all recognize membership in a local "tribe." Formal local government consists of a shaykh and three *moqaddem*s for an area of 10,000 people, under a *qaid* in Ouled Teima (Dwyer 1982:31).

The villagers imagine that in the past they were able to maintain subsistence agriculture, producing cereals, vegetables, and animals for meat and milk (Dwyer 1982:131). However true that may have been, they are at present part of a very different economic system involving mechanized irrigation, labor migration, considerable local wage labor, and the sale of their produce. Nearly two-thirds of the men of working age work for wages or trade in the market, although only six households receive no income from the land. Part of the outcome is a substantial difference between the top few, who control one-third of the wealth, and the poorest half, who hold only 6 percent of the wealth (Dwyer 1982:7–13). Ecological and economic changes led farmers to introduce pumps to irrigate former cereal land and to try to grow cereals on former pastureland. Nearby mechanized farms (an "imported" model) recruited wage labor; other men tried their luck in Europe. The new farms provided the model that others tried to imitate but with less success, as they could not compete on the market and did not have the connections. The modern farms also pump water effectively, and the water table is dropping.

Like the Kabyle mountaineers, the Soussis live in an increasingly monetized economy, and their economic and political activities are encapsulated in wider frameworks. The village notables link to the lowest echelon of Moroccan officials (shaykhs and *moqaddem*s) but also to religious figures, townspeople, and others from the wider society. Travel is common. Like the Kabyles, the Soussis have essentially retained independent households—probably more so, as they did not suffer from a devastating war and are less involved in migration. They control enough of their economic base (farmland) to uphold, for the moment, a degree of self-sufficient independence.

The Zuwaya of Libya

The Zuwaya are a "tribal" group of about 18,000 traders spread from Ajdabiya in the north to Kufra in the south of Libya (J. Davis 1987). They make up significant parts of the towns of Ajdabiya (32,000 people) and Kufra (10,000 people). Thus the Zuwaya are involved in both tribal and local sociopolitical systems; through their trading they also symbolize the penetration of the world economy. The Zuwaya tend to act as a group in opposition to other similarly formed groups ("tribes"); when there is no opposition, they split in segmentary fashion. All such political involvement takes place in the context of national politics informed by Qadhafi's ideas of participatory democracy and revolution.

John Davis argues that there are parallels and convergences between the "tribal" values of the Zuwaya and the Libyan government under Qadhafi. These parallels include the absence of government, the preference for "no government," and the concern for certain kinds of participation and discourse in politics. One of the major political functions is the resolution of local disputes though mediation (J. Davis 1987:223). People act according to social relations as well as ideology—there are limits on how they carry out the revolution because unlike those living in faceless cities, they know those with whom they interact (J. Davis 1987:92, 127, 136).

Elections (as in Ajdabiya in 1978) turn into competitions among the large lineages or tribal alliances. A problem emerges because people are not allowed to campaign for election, though that does not stop political goal seeking (J. Davis 1987:94–107). Elections are thus a "contest between voters" rather than "one between candidates" (J. Davis 1985:372). In Ajdabiya the conflict was between Zuwaya and Majabr, in Kufra between two branches of the Zuwaya. The segmentarism is not the outcome of a formal segmentation. Davis argues that "egalitarian emphasis on nonrepresentative government entails—in Ajdabiya and settlements like it—segmentary action" (J. Davis 1985: 376) because it denies or plays down the existence of any "government. " Yet one must note that in prerevolutionary, oasis Libya, elections also turned on clan and tribal affiliations (Dalton 1973); in Sawknah it was considered more important to hold the tribe together than to join a winning coalition.

There is also a nascent and somewhat bureaucratic political system affecting local societies in Libya, despite the hostility to government. The Ajdabiya district has about 232 committee and popular congress members, in a total population of 45,000 (including 18,000 Libyan adults). There are popular committees for schools, health, water, development, taxation and finance, municipal affairs, and so on, with members chosen by subdistrict. There is also a popular congress of some forty members charged with supervising the popular committees. An annual general assembly reviews the work of committees and discusses the agenda for the National People's Congress. The idea is that there should be no delegation of personal sovereignty and so no representation. In fact, however, all these elected committee members are representatives.

The case of the Libyan Zuwaya illustrates a high level of mutual involvement between the local community and the state. In the guise of reinforcing traditional patterns, the regime in Libya is in fact introducing considerable change. At the same time, there is uncertainty between the individualization implied by the new institutions—people simply come together to vote—and the collectivities, such as tribe, rooted in the past. In contrast to the cases considered in the next section, where the state intervenes to develop, here the state is present but development is not the issue.

The Impact of Development Projects

In the four cases presented in the sections above, we can already see the impact of the wider system—through economics, politics, or ideology—on local society. A second set of cases shows how development, in the shape of capitalist agriculture, state-sponsored directed change and central planning, or more specific development projects, has had a formative impact on local society. The result is the transformation of the nature of local society (or the creation of a new one altogether) and its linkage to the wider society in new ways. Conditions in Morocco, Algeria, and Tunisia are similar enough to warrant discussing the cases together.

Irrigation and Local Society

The landscape in the agricultural heartland of Morocco, the Gharb, is dominated by large estates and state farms, although there is also some smallholding agriculture. The state controls 27 percent of the land (Mernissi 1982:18) and compels farmers to meet quotas in such crops as sugar beets in order to benefit from the state-run irrigation system (cf. Popp 1983).

The Gharb village of Beggara (949 inhabitants) has a primary school (minus the final grade level) as well as a number of shops and services strung out along its paved road. But there is no electricity, no potable water within homes, and no regular public transportation.

Most smallholder households rely on wage labor for all or part of their livelihood; for many, female wage labor plays an important part. Although the large farms and government projects in the area hire men as regular employees, they rarely hire women except as day labor. The household remains patriarchal, but the extended family pattern has deteriorated into individualism, thus leaving the wife more vulnerable to divorce, for example, as it has become more difficult to count on a father or brother to counterbalance the husband. It is hard for women to play independent roles because they often lack identity papers, and the scarcity of public transportation hampers movement (Mernissi 1982:29). Yet both men and women understand the value of a large household. As one young man living in a large extended family put it, "A small family can't survive given the insecurity of salaried work, floods and drought. You have to belong to a large group to survive" (Mernissi 1982:38).

Also in the Gharb is an agricultural town of 8,000 people. This town has electricity and an elementary school but lacks running water and sewage and has no government offices. Most of the population works for wages in the large farms in the irrigated plain (S. Davis 1983:55). Many of the workers are women and girls who are paid 75 to 80 percent of men's wages. This is low-status work, and women who do this work have to accept the stigma. Many of the men work in a nearby market town, most notably in an oil refinery that pays good salaries.

The political structure of the town is amorphous. The major kin groups (such as the descendants of the saint whose shrine is in the town) have been swamped by migrants looking for work, and no alternative political structure has emerged. The town is politically subordinated to the adjacent market town.

Behavior in the town is regulated through gossip and concepts of honor, and a kind of respectability ranking serves as an organizing principle. Information circulates somewhat erratically, and control of that information is power (S. Davis 1983:99–100, 137). Men often do not share information with their wives, or vice versa, so that some political conflict takes the form of rivalry between men and women, a form of social control. The social structure of this area reflects more heavily the integration into the world economy. Wage labor and individualism are clearly present, and there appears to be a kind of political anomie that has appeared where once there was a communal life. Connections to the outside world run through the communities' employers and somewhat distant government offices. This is what the women interviewed by Mernissi sensed when they suggested that the state might intervene on their behalf, as their partners in life (Mernissi 1982:24).

In the state-developed irrigation perimeters of Sidi bou Zid in central Tunisia, the application of a production-centered development policy has led to the marginalization of women (Ferchiou 1985). In precolonial times people in this area practiced a combination of animal husbandry and agriculture, women and men each having a role. Since independence this area has seen a tremendous expansion of irrigated agriculture, both official schemes and individual well-digging for private farms. By offering credit to farmers in part as a function of the labor they provide, the agricultural policy has encouraged them to assign women and girls to agricultural work, thus contributing to a decline in literacy among school-age girls. Women predominate in field tasks and in animal husbandry and weaving, whereas men handle the linkages with the wider world: marketing, administration, migration for wage labor. Men have become the privileged intermediaries between the state and their households; women have been marginalized. The male bias of the development schemes reinforces the male bias of rural Tunisian culture. Thus the continuing integration of these households into a technologically different and market-oriented agriculture also has an effect on their internal organization.

If development has led to growing inequality between men and women, it has also resulted in the inequality of chances among men. An irrigation project in Morocco serves as an example. The erstwhile impoverished area around Zaio, the Sebra plain irrigation area in the lower Moulouya Valley, was transformed by the introduction of irrigated agriculture in the 1970s (Seddon 1987; see also Popp 1983:149–165). The people of this area first moved into the cash economy via labor migration to Moroccan towns and to Europe. The early return migrants invested their money in housing in the towns and, to some extent, in agriculture. Then in the 1970s land in the new irrigated areas was distributed and cooperatives were formed. Some of the holders were linked to the state through a contract of tenancy, others were private, but all were affected by state policy on agriculture. Agricultural incomes and wages have risen (Seddon 1987:241). The most successful areas are those where outside owners have worked through sharecroppers and disregarded the rules (Popp 1983:165).

The irrigated zones are tied to state policies through a production quota system, especially for sugar beets. The state has thus become a major player in agriculture. At the same time, the new social organization of production has created new classes—owners, renters and sharecroppers, workers—whose interests are to some extent opposed. During the 1960s, local politics was fairly personalized, even though most politically active men belonged in some sense to the local elite (Seddon 1981:282–289; 1987:233). The effect of migration and irrigation on local politics is not yet clear.

Agrarian Reform and Cooperatives

Rural Algeria has been particularly buffeted by the politics of the colonial and postcolonial periods. Algeria seems to have "lost its 'traditional' coherence without having achieved a more modern equilibrium" (Côte 1979:7). The result has been the creation of a large rural proletariat together with marginalized small farmers (Côte 1977). Both, however, have been successful in following their own design for living rather than the one proposed by the state (Chaulet 1987:6). One can only speculate what the long-term disruption of rural Algeria means for Algerian society.

In the high plains around Constantine and Setif, the colonial system found tribally organized societies with collective land tenure and was able to acquire substantial amounts of land. Colonial farmers still held considerable land at independence. This land became the core of the socialist sector (the *autogestion,* or self-management, sector), which eventually covered 20 percent of the land in the high plains and 25 percent in all Algeria (Côte 1979: 28). The labor force was provided by the former workers on the colonial farms, who had been proletarianized and integrated into the wider system a generation or two earlier. Later the agrarian revolution sector was created by transforming some Algerian-owned farmland into cooperatives. This covered 23 percent of the land in the high plains and 22 percent in all Algeria, leaving 57 percent of the land in private hands (53 percent in all Algeria), but with considerable variety, ranging from marginal hillside land to intensively irrigated gardens. During this period, mechanization through tractors and irrigation proceeded apace. By the late 1970s the private sector employed 90 percent of the workers, the remainder being divided between the socialist sector (3 percent) and the agrarian revolution sector (7 percent). Thus the most advanced institutional farms employed only a small minority of the workers.

In the first phase of the 1970 agrarian reform in the commune of Caid-Belarbi (governorate of Bel Abbes, western Algeria) common land was turned into six cooperatives (Marouf 1981:393–396). Around 5,000 people had farmed the common land, but it was decided that there was room for only 3,600 in the cooperatives that were formed. The remainder (around 30 percent) were excluded. Along with the organization into cooperatives, a new central village was supposed to be constructed using local labor, but by April 1974 it had not been started. The cooperative members gave several reasons for the lack of progress: First, their work did not leave them enough time; they believed the houses they already had were as good as any they might build and in fact did not need; third, their houses were scattered, and each had a stable that would be hard to retain in a village. The people traditionally relied on animal husbandry for much of their income, and the shift from renting common land to a cooperative already impeded the practice. Moreover, people were assigned to particular cooperatives before new housing was built. Because they continued to live in their old houses, some had to travel quite a distance to their new farmland. The program of the state and the program of the people had reached a standoff. It is thus not surprising that rural Algerians rejected agrarian reform (Zghal 1985).

In general, the state attempts to impose structures whereas the people try to follow their own goals (Marouf 1981). The local elites, both agricultural and administrative, tend to dominate political structures, including the local party branch, so that majority rule does not apply. National plans are reinterpreted locally in a variety of ways—sometimes they are misconceived and people manage to save something from them; sometimes they are subverted or captured by local elites; sometimes they are simply blocked by these elites. Some of the elites' power goes back to judicial disputes over land, some to a policy of marriages with powerful people elsewhere in the system. The position of the local elites is shaky, however, given the disruption before, during, and after the war.

Moreover, the state itself is not coherent: There are conflicts between ministries (Marouf 1981:426) and between central and local authorities. Even many agents are not convinced of the correctness of the policies they are to carry out (Marouf 1981:418). The party represents the local elite and tries to dominate the administration. In addition, there are differences among the people reflecting various experiences during the war of independence and with life in Morocco or France. All this has accentuated an individualism that was always present (Marouf 1981:236–241).

The Tunisian parallel to the Algerian *autogestion* farm is the cooperative production unit. Like the *autogestion* farms, they were formed from colonial farms and drew on the farm workers for their labor force. At the height of the movement in Tunisia in 1968, there were 348 such units on 378,000 hectares (945,000 acres) with 30,000 members (Troin 1985:197). The cooperative movement collapsed in 1969; by 1982 there were 212 units with 6,786 workers and 26.4 hectares (66 acres) of usable land per worker (Cherif 1986), that is, 180,000 hectares (450,000 acres). Overall the wage workers, in theory seasonal but in fact permanent, do around 30 percent of the labor. Around 10 percent of the 1977 workers, mostly younger ones, have since left, moving to the cities. As a group, they are semiurbanized, as 33 percent live in nearby towns and 20 percent in nearby villages whereas 47 percent live on or near the farms (Cherif 1986). Thus they do not always share a common residence.

One such cooperative farm is the Ghanima unit located in the rich valley near Testour (Hopkins 1988). The land was originally endowed for the Testour mosque, was made into a colonial farm, then became government land rented to the cooperative. In 1973 it had seventy members and hired another twenty-three regularly. The original membership of the cooperative was drawn from salaried workers on the colonial farms; many came from families originating outside the area. However, about half lived in Testour town, as a result of a government policy encouraging residence in clustered settlements.

The cooperative was run by a president elected by his fellow members and a director appointed by the government. In 1973 the president had been in office for ten years, the director for two. The president organized the allocation of labor in the cooperative, whereas the director managed technical advice and assistance and was responsible for relations with the various government agencies that aspire to control the cooperative. Fifteen years later, the cooperative existed with approximately the same structure.

The cooperative's freedom of action was circumscribed in that almost all decisions, such as those on wages and bonuses, were made at the regional or national level to which the director and president had little or no access. The cooperative was nonetheless resourceful in initiating lucrative activities such as livestock and dairy programs and at developing new skills such as those involved in irrigation and truck gardening.

About two-thirds of the members worked on the cooperative simply as laborers, and the others in specified jobs such as mechanics, irrigation chiefs, or beekeepers. They were paid for days worked plus a share of any profits. Workers who were not members received at least the official minimum wage. Members also received some benefits in kind from the harvest; there was also free medical care and a retirement pension. With all this, the cooperative members considered themselves relatively well-off.

Members felt that the cooperative owed its success to the mutual trust of the workers and to the sense of commitment and responsibility. Many members also valued the working conditions, which gave them a fairly high degree of independence: No one stood over them, as in private agriculture.

The cooperative is linked to the national system through the administrative hierarchy, specifically that of the Ministry of Agriculture. As the cooperative is not a residential community, its members are also involved in Testour politics and issues or in the affairs of the rural areas where they live. The efforts of the UGTT to incorporate cooperative members in the 1970s provoked an ambiguous response: How, people asked, could they join a labor union when they were not workers?

Pressure and Response

Some Tunisian scholars have commented caustically on the impact of government development projects on local communities. Some projects were aimed to benefit local communities; in other cases a local community had to pay the price of a development project whose benefits went elsewhere. In the cases described by Khalil Zamiti and Brahim Bouzaiane, development projects undercut community and encouraged individualism. Mouldi Lahmar analyzes the contemporary political response of two communities to government price policy in terms of the differential impact of colonial policy. New forms of community and local society may emerge from such policies, but they will be more closely linked to national structures and will rely more on money and wages than before.

In 1984 Zamiti investigated the situation of the people displaced by the construction of the Sidi Salem barrage near Testour. He argues that the dam was built by the state as a consequence of class interests (Zamiti 1985:155). Thus the ordinary people displaced by the dam were not the beneficiaries. The flooded area of 8,000 hectares (20,000 acres) was inhabited by 6,700 people, including landowners and landless. The area included state farms as well as private land. A few of the largest farmers received new farms as a trade, but the small farmers often felt very strongly that their way of life had been destroyed. Many of the small farmers and landless (about 40 percent of those displaced) were relocated in a new community but had a hard time financially. Wages were hard to come by, and the new houses needed improvements. In their new situation, the people were forced into a more intimate relationship with the state, especially with the party branch, which helped them find jobs. But though the men were absorbed into this system, the women remained unmollified and outspoken.

In Tunisia the state finances rural development, including projects authorized by each governor to meet particular local needs. Bouzaiane (1985:41) argued that the programs proposed represent an urban model of rural development, which sees rural society as an empty box into which one may put whatever one wants, as "nothing" is there (Bouzaiane 1985:41). In fact, of course, rural social structure exists and shapes responses. Rural people, often uncertain about these projects, may either reject them or try to modify them to fit their own needs. Adaptation mostly implies transforming the programs from something collective to something individual, as the greatest perceived goal is the improvement of family and household strategies within the present system (Bouzaiane 1985:61). This individualism is expressed as jealousy—that is, others regard the beneficiaries with envy—the only way they know to handle a situation in which some are (inevitably) favored (Bouzaiane 1985:67). Those who have dealt with the state in the past are likely to continue to play such a role and to be chosen by the population for it (Bouzaiane 1985:63). As for responses to the cadres, they are often slanted and biased by the desire to capture the project for local goals. People use state assistance and ask for more, but they use it in their own way (Bouzaiane 1985:67–68). Even if the goal is to support communities, then, the outcome is to help individuals and thus to increase individualism. This misdirection might be changed if rural communities were more often brought into the debate about policy.

Lahmar (1985) compares two communities in the region of Sfax. In one, the 1984 price rise for food provoked a demonstration; in the other, it did not. In La Hencha, north of Sfax, the movement started with the young women working in a small textile factory. Their public demonstration drew along young men; when the police suppressed the demonstration, three persons were killed. In Bir Ali Ben Khalifa, west of Sfax, the local notables worked with the administration to stifle any attempt at a demonstration, perceived in any case as an attack by a local tribe on the weekly market. In tracing out the social history of these two areas, Lahmar shows that the rural population in La Hencha had been expropriated during the colonial period whereas that in Bir Ali had not. Thus at Bir Ali the traditional local leadership persisted in the same family, which since independence dominated the local party branch. This oligarchy controlled the political situation and prevented an outbreak of violence. At La Hencha, the traditional local leadership was destroyed or marginalized, and the party branch was controlled initially by people who had participated in the national struggle. However, one remaining family of notables tried to take over the party branch around 1980, with the result that the party branch split in two, neither side having much influence among the young students, workers, and unemployed who joined the demonstration.

In other words, in La Hencha the population has become progressively proletarianized, and this proletarianization has acquired a political expression. In Bir Ali, in contrast, a hierarchical structure remains and dominates local politics. In La Hencha the capitalist relations of production in agriculture are not softened or disguised by kinship, as they are in Bir Ali. Lahmar's implication is that the state prefers to rely on a local hierarchy, which is sometimes challenged by new forces at the local level. Zamiti, Bouzaiane, and Lahmar all show how the state used the party branch and the bureaucracy to penetrate and control the rural populations.

Class and Small Towns

Larger communities are more complex, with long-standing patterns of stratification. The contrasting cases of Sefrou and Testour illustrate this complexity and help bring out the issue of class, a factor missing from actor-centered interpretations of politics. A model that stresses the individual actor and neglects the changing circumstances within which that actor moves is inadequate. It is true that those circumstances are in part created by the individual's acts, but they are also the outcome of other actors—some of them distant from the local scene.

The population of Sefrou, a town 40 km (25 miles) south of Fez in central Morocco, doubled from 20,624 in 1960 to well over 40,000 in the early 1980s (Rosen 1984:14). Over this period, the town evolved from essentially a trade and craft center into a "city of salaried workers" (Rosen 1984:16). In 1960, 64 percent of the employed were in the bazaar sector and 16 percent were salaried (Geertz 1979:144). In 1971, 45 percent of all employed persons were salaried, 27 percent in the private sector and 18 percent in the public sector (Rosen 1984:16, from Benhalima 1977:79). About 20 to 25 percent were unemployed. The discrepancy between the rich and the poor widened between the mid-1960s and the late 1970s (Rosen 1984:16).

In the 1960s, the market seemed like a suitable metaphor for local society. The Sefrou market included a permanent market of traders and craftspeople, a lively weekly market that served the surrounding countryside, and a small modern business sector focusing on trade and services rather than manufacture. Market people relate to each other as individuals, using ethnic origin and occupation as a guide, but such considerations do not give rise to classes or even categories, because people do not form corporate groups and have no "effective reality as collective social actors" (Geertz 1979:145). These relationships of role and origin do not become dependency relations, even when they become regular (as when people are each other's clients); instead, they are merely "repetitive exchange between acquainted partners" (Geertz 1979:218). The exchange may involve labor or the products of labor, but normal employment is rare (see, however, Geertz 1979:179, 191, 247). Although some individuals in the market are richer than others, their importance may be transitory (Geertz 1979:232).

The model based on individual relationships extends from the market to politics. Rosen (1979) notes that the formal administrative hierarchy is a poor guide to politics because people work around it to achieve their goals. Political parties are weak in the area because people are more interested in constructing networks of potentially useful relations than in sharing in the fate of a group (Rosen 1984:115). Rather, the Sefrou and national political systems are of the same nature, only of a different scale (Rosen 1979:52), and the links within and between them involve personal relations between particular individuals. "Throughout, the individual, as a freely contracting party arranging ties in accordance with acknowledged standards for interpreting the meaning and import of another's actions, has remained central to the Moroccan style of social organization" (Rosen 1984:17). Hence elections are matters of building personal networks rather than confrontations of ideologies or conflicting interests (Rosen 1984:99–117).

Yet the reluctance of Geertz and Rosen to consider the class implications of the social structure of Sefrou—they prefer to analyze the town in terms of "origins," basically a permutation on the distinctions between Arab, Berber, and Jew—means that they overlook the changes that occurred between 1960 and 1971 and may have continued since then. If it makes analytic sense to deemphasize class distinctions among market people, in a way the whole category stands as a class against at least the two other main categories recognized in Sefrou—the farmers and the employees (Geertz 1979:183). The 1960s saw a major shift in the occupational structure of the town away from the market and toward salaried employment. Combined with increasing economic differentiation, this may have produced a society that is linked into the national system in very different ways, that is no longer based on intricate interpersonal ties. The changes in Sefrou may mean that the town is integrated into the nation through its participation in the class structure of contemporary Morocco; categorical relations may be replacing personalistic ones in everyday practice.

In the early 1970s, the inhabitants of the Tunisian town of Testour lived primarily from agriculture and related activities such as the marketing of agricultural crops and the supply of consumer goods to farmers. The market in the town has a long tradition of acting as a link between the farmers of the surrounding rural areas and the trades and crafts of Tunis. Although there were some salaried government workers in town, they did not by themselves form a dominant group. However, wages were the primary form of mobilization of labor in agriculture. The market folk mostly worked alone or in pairs; the scale was small and the operations complex (Hopkins 1977).

Thus it was possible to see local politics in terms of a clash between different classes as defined by their position within this mode of production (Hopkins 1986). The basic tone was set by the opposition between the large farmers and their workers. The market people, although economically not much better off than the farm workers, were socially distinguished from them and were tied into a social system dominated by the life-style of the local rich farmers. In practice, town politics was run by a coalition of the big farmers and the civil servants of local origin (often from market families), with the support of the traders and artisans; the agricultural workers mostly lived in a separate part of town and were largely excluded from local politics. Since the 1970s, the major visible change has been the creation of several factories on the edge of town and the expansion of the local educational system. The logical outcome of these changes is the reinforcement of the categorical nature of local politics.

Class is a useful interpretive device in Testour, but that does not mean that corporate groups systematically confront one another. Instead, a certain self-consciousness of economic interests, modified by cultural and symbolic factors pushing people to identify with some protagonists more than others, guides political choices. Whether looking ahead or looking back, we will no doubt find class more helpful in interpretation than the assertion that we are only dealing with manipulative individuals (as of course we are) operating in a context in which no groups or other kinds of regularities emerge.

The uneasiness of Testour people in participating in the national political system suggests that all those in the town occupied a subordinate position in the national class system. Of course there were personal links between local leaders and figures at the regional or national level, but these seemed less important than the operations of a political system at the local level according to ground rules provided by the state. Generally, factions at the national level, whether based on palace intrigue or conflicting interests, did not seek alliances with local factions, so that the local political process remained relatively autonomous. There were moments when the struggle at the national level led contestants to seek local support: the Youssefist movement in the 1950s (Testour had supporters of both Bourguiba and Ben Youssef) and, in the mid-1970s, the effort of the Tunisian labor union to mobilize support at the local level. Neither had a lasting effect. The local and national systems are characterizedc by both interpersonal alliances and coalitions, but the interests and goals are dissimilar.

Conclusion

Some trends and themes stand out in the evolution of local societies in North Africa since independence. The various national governments have all been, in their ways, interventionist and have directed change according to a central plan (so, of course, did the colonial ones, with different goals). This pressure has been neither continuous nor consistent, but it has had considerable influence on the formation of local societies. In Libya the ideological component (Qadhafi's image of the ideal society) stands out. In Tunisia and Algeria, the state has attempted to build on the economic circumstances of the colonial period through the creation of cooperatives, new settlement forms, and an intensification of local government. In Morocco the state is also heavily involved through the creation of irrigated zones. In addition to the interventionism of the state, world market forces have an influence through the option of migration to Europe, the availability of new technologies for local development, and the multiplication of consumer options.

According to the conventional definitions of *farmer* and *peasant*, nowhere in North Africa is there a peasantry—in the sense of communities of farmers, practicing an agriculture that is essentially oriented toward their own subsistence, subordinated to a state and a wider culture. Instead, we observe market-oriented farmers, tied into the international division of labor through the sale of their agricultural products but also often through the sale of their labor. Thus there are entire zones, and many smaller communities, that are "proletarianized" in the sense that the primary source of income is wage labor, either at home or away. Even where farmers operate their own enterprises, they are often integrated into the market, purchasing inputs and selling a substantial part of their crop. Only in a few, probably marginal, areas do we find substantial remnants of a subsistence orientation. Everywhere there are people who aim to earn a living by trading, transporting, small-scale workshops, and so on and who are perforce tied into the market economy. There is some difference in the impact of this change on men and women: The greater involvement of men in the wider system puts more burden on the women but at the same time often deprives women of some of their status.

Many studies of North Africa have noted a trend toward individualism, meaning in part that people are no longer responsive to the old ideals (if they ever were). To the extent that we can accept such an analysis, it should be noted that such individualism makes way for people to recognize common economic interests, free from concern for the ideology of older forms of solidarity. In fact, older forms of solidarity ("tribalism," religion) remain as options. Thus individuals act within a system of understandings that gives meaning to their acts. One persistent motivation is to seek the well-being of oneself and one's family. Change affects the material options available and the value given to those options, implying also a different pattern of choice. In seeking their goals, people live with one another in local societies. They may find satisfaction at that level and may associate themselves with others to advance their interests; in so doing, new local societies come into being. These local societies are the outcome of the interventionism of the state, the impact of world market forces, and the culturally formulated purposes of the individuals. One can no longer fully analyze local society in isolation from these broader forms of integration.

What the future holds for local societies in North Africa is, of course, uncertain. One outcome might be the gradual destruction of local life, leading to a concentration of the uprooted in the cities where, as in Iran, they become the allies of revolutionary forces (Hooglund 1982). Or the various categories present in local societies (proletarians, small farmers, market folk, local elites) may, through individual relations, ally themselves with other classes (urban elites, intellectuals, etc.) to create new conditions in the countryside (Zghal 1985), using ideologies drawn from Islam, socialism, or capitalism. Or the state may remain dominant and use its powers to impose a certain model of development on local societies, despite the reluctance of many individuals (Chaulet 1987). To the extent that the state is successful at imposing a unitary development model on local societies, it creates a single division of labor and so also it incites resistance from those subordinated. Perhaps the very process of development—technological progress, spread of education, better public health, changing gender roles—may alter local societies, including their elites, to the point where the state no longer dominates.

PART THREE

Foreign Relations

9

The Arab Maghribi Union and the Prospects for North African Unity

Mary-Jane Deeb

On February 17, 1989, in Marrakesh, the heads of state of Morocco, Algeria, Tunisia, Libya, and Mauritania announced the formation of a union of the Greater Arab Maghrib. This was not a surprise declaration but a well-prepared and well-publicized plan that had been developed over the past year. Three major documents were signed at the summit: a communiqué marking the official birth of the union, a treaty setting up the principal provisions and political structures of the union, and a resolution drawing up an action program to be implemented by the structures created by the treaty.

In this chapter I put the Arab Maghribi Union (UMA) into a historical context and analyze the conditions under which it was created, comparing it with previous attempts at integration in the region. I explore some of the reasons behind the formation of the union as well as the benefits each state will derive from it. Finally, I examine the political and economic implications of this new attempt at integration within the wider regional and international context.

Models of Integration

In his article on the foreign relations of North Africa, I. William Zartman discusses three models of intra-Maghribi relations: the integrative, the pluralist, and the hegemonic (Zartman 1987a). Integrative attempts, that is, attempts at unity, were made at different times during the past three decades but were not very successful (Damis 1983a). The pluralist mode of interacting as sovereign states has been the longest lasting of the three models. The major states (Algeria and Morocco) have vied for power (Damis 1983b), and the smaller states have allied themselves in such a way as to keep a balance of power that would ensure their territorial sovereignty and independence. The hegemonic model, in which one of the major powers dominates the others, never actually materialized. It was, however, the threat of hegemonic domination that was at the root of the complex relationship among the Maghribi states.

The first attempt at integration took place in April 1958, at the Conference of Unity in Tangier, when the leaders of the Moroccan Istiqlal party, the Tunisian Neo-Destour party, and the Algerian National Liberation Front adopted a resolution to establish a federal union among the states of the Maghrib. This union was announced two months after similar unions had been set up between Egypt and Syria and between Iraq and Jordan (Jabri 1985). The attempt was unsuccessful because Algeria was still in the throes of its war of decolonization and, upon attaining independence, became embroiled in a border war with Morocco.

In October 1964 there was another move toward integrating. In Tunis at a conference of the economic ministers of Algeria, Morocco, Tunisia, and Libya, the Permanent Consultative Committee of the Maghrib was created and given provisional executive powers to study and then set up the gradual economic integration of the Maghrib (Slim 1980). Despite Libya's withdrawal in 1970, the committee continued to function for more than a decade. The beginning of the Algerian-Moroccan conflict over the Western Sahara, however, sounded its death knell.

From 1969 to 1970 political rapprochement among the states of North Africa led to further discussion about setting up a united Maghrib. At Ifrane in January 1969, Algeria and Morocco signed a treaty of solidarity and cooperation, and the two countries reached an agreement on border demarcations in Tlemcen in May 1970. At the Islamic summit in Rabat in September 1969, Morocco finally recognized Mauritania and signed a treaty of fraternity, friendship, and good neighborliness with that country in June 1970. This rapprochement, however, also came to naught (Deeb 1989).

Inter-Maghribi relations during the subsequent eighteen years followed Zartman's pluralist model. In a classical balance-of-power pattern, the states of the Maghrib created blocs and counterblocs to ensure that neither Algeria nor Morocco would gain ascendancy and become a hegemonic regional power. The Hassi Mas'ud treaty of December 1975 set up a very important alliance between Libya and Algeria that perpetuated the conflict in the Western Sahara in an attempt to weaken and isolate Morocco. The treaty of brotherhood and concord of March 1983 between Algeria and Tunisia, which was joined by Mauritania in December 1983, isolated both Morocco and Libya. The latter two states then formed their own Arab-African Federation in August 1984, in part at least to counterbalance the 1983 treaty among the three other states (Deeb 1989).

Conditions for the Integrationist Model

In another study (Deeb 1989) I have argued that the Maghrib has closed ranks and opted for an integrationist model of relations rather than a pluralist one when it has perceived itself, as a region, threatened by external powers, whether from the east or from the west. In Tangier in 1958 the threat came from both directions. Jean and Simone Lacouture have argued that the Tangier declaration was prompted by the formation of the union between Egypt and Syria and that between Jordan and Iraq in February 1958. The Maghribi leaders wished to placate their populations, which were demanding a union of their own (Lacouture and Lacouture 1958). In fact Gamal Abdel Nasser of Egypt, after having successfully confronted the Western powers over the Suez Canal in 1956, was extending Egypt's influence beyond its borders. His call for Arab unity was falling on receptive ears, especially among the youth in the Arab world, and was beginning to materialize in the form of a union between Egypt and Syria—a union that was sure to be dominated by Egypt.

The Maghribi leaders felt threatened by Nasser, who was already having a divisive influence in the region. As early as 1955 he was supporting Salah Ben Youssef, Bourguiba's challenger in Tunisia, who had begun advocating Nasserism for North Africa (Grimaud 1984). Nasser was also attempting to extend his influence over the National Liberation Front and rally all the Maghribi states in a confrontation with France under his leadership (Grimaud 1984). Thus the show of unity at Tangier in 1958 strengthened the leaders via-à-vis Egypt and at the same time satisfied the unionist demands within their respective countries.

From the west came the threat of France. Although both Morocco and Tunisia had achieved their independence two years earlier, in 1956, French troops still occupied both countries. Furthermore, Algeria was fighting for its independence, and both Morocco and Tunisia were supporting it—and paying a high price for doing so. (In February 1958 the village of Sakiet Sidi Youssef in Tunisia was bombed by the French army in retaliation for Tunisian support for the Algerians.) The external political and military threat from the west was obvious.

The Tangier agreement did bring about an improvement in the security of the region. It convinced the French government to withdraw its troops from Tunisia and Morocco (Grimaud 1984). The declarations made at the conference also helped in bridging the divisions within the Maghribi leaderships, especially in Algeria, as the FLN was recognized as the only representative of "l'Algérie combattante (embattled Algeria)" (Grimaud 1984).

The second attempt at integration, in 1964 among Morocco, Algeria, Tunisia, and Libya, was an experiment in regional economic cooperation. The creation of the Permanent Consultative Committee of the Maghrib was in part a response to bloc formations in the Mashriq. In March and April 1963, Egypt, Syria, and Iraq began serious negotiations to set up a union (Kerr 1971). An agreement was signed on April 17, 1963, but the union never materialized because of a breakdown in the negotiations between Nasser and the Syrian Baath party. The Syrians then turned toward Iraq, and a bilateral union became imminent by November 1963; it, too, failed.

Thus the months preceding the creation of the Permanent Consultative Committee saw a flurry of unionist activities in the Mashriq. Furthermore, Egypt was not only encouraging such activities but also extending its influence in the Maghrib and supporting Algeria against Morocco in their border conflict. Thus one of the principal reasons for the creation of the committee was to ward off Egypt's growing influence in the region by presenting a united political front. It was also designed to create economic bridges between the states to overcome the political divisions that made the region vulnerable to external interference (Kerr 1971).

The rapprochement among states of the Maghrib that occurred during 1969–1970 can be understood, in part at least, as a reaction to the developments that were taking place on the eastern borders of the region. The Egyptian-dominated bloc that emerged in late 1969 after two pro-Nasser military coups in Sudan and in Libya that year was perceived as a serious threat to the security of the Maghribi states west of Libya. It changed the balance of power in North Africa and threatened to dominate the region politically if not militarily as well. Although each Maghribi state may have perceived the danger differently, the closing of ranks strengthened all of them against the external challenge (Deeb 1984).

Thus whereas the pluralist or balance-of-power model of inter-Maghribi relations maintains a kind of stability within the North African subsystem of states, the integrationist model maintains a balance within the larger framework of the Arab and the Mediterranean regions.

Conditions for the Creation of the UMA

The UMA was born in the rapidly changing political, social, and economic environment of the late 1980s. The economic situation was deteriorating markedly in all five states of the region. The fall in the price of oil on the world market starting in the mid-1980s hit hard the economies of Algeria, Libya, and Tunisia, all three major exporters of oil. Drought conditions as well as a plague of locusts ravaged the agricultural sectors in Morocco, Tunisia, and Mauritania. The financial situation was equally grim: The major regional powers were strapped with mounting debts. Algeria's foreign debt had reached $22 billion in the late 1980s, with an annual servicing charge of $5.8 billion, which absorbed a significant part of its revenues (*LeMonde*, December 23, 1988). Morocco and Tunisia faced similar problems, and the U.S. economic boycotts of Libya further weakened that country's economy.

But it was the enlargement of the European Community (EC) to include Spain and Portugal in 1986 that worried the Maghribi countries most. Both European countries competed with the Maghrib to sell their agricultural products to Western Europe. With their inclusion in the EC, their products would benefit from a number of economic advantages over those coming from North Africa. Furthermore, Maghribi exports to the EC could be drastically reduced after 1992, when the twelve members of the Community removed all custom duties between their countries yet retained them with their external trade partners (Valmont 1988). The significance of this factor cannot be underestimated, as the value of Maghribi exports to the EC constituted more than two-thirds (or 65.6 percent in 1986) of the value of its total world exports (IMF 1987).

The regional political environment was changing as well. Since Hosni Mubarak's rise to power in 1981, Egypt had begun gradually moving back toward the Arab fold. The main thrust of Mubarak's foreign policy was to restore Egypt's power in the Arab world, as well as in the Islamic and African worlds (Dessouki 1984). His efforts were marked with success first when Egypt was reinstated in the Islamic Conference Organization in 1986 and then after the Arab summit in Amman in November 1987, when Arab states agreed to bilateral relations with Egypt. Within a few months, almost all Arab states (except for Libya, Syria, and Lebanon) had renewed their diplomatic ties with Cairo. Thus by the end of 1987, Egyptian influence in the Middle East was being felt again, stronger than ever. This process culminated in February 1989 with the creation of the Arab Cooperation Council made up of Egypt, Iraq, Jordan, and the Yemen Arab Republic.

The cease-fire between Iraq and Iran began changing the balance of power in the Middle East to a somewhat lesser degree. Iraq emerged as the dominant military power in the Arab world and consequently won increased political influence in the region. The Iraqi and Egyptian return to the forefront of inter-Arab politics undermined Syria's power in the region, and by the same token that of Syria's allies, namely, Algeria and Libya.

The changes taking place on the domestic, regional, and international levels in the second half of the 1980s, then, did not favor the states of the Maghrib. Their economic and political powers were being eroded. A union agreement that could strengthen all of the states of North Africa and allow them to face the new challenges was therefore in order.

Structure of the Arab Maghribi Union

The UMA is the first alliance of its kind that has included the five nations of the Maghrib. It was presented as the culmination of efforts to unite the Maghrib dating back to the Tangier conference. The heads of state signed three documents to officially set up the UMA. The first was a brief communiqué described by Algerian foreign minister Boualem Bessaieh as "a certificate for the political birth of the Maghreb" (FBIS-NES February 21, 1989:5). This document gave a historical background to the treaty and spoke of the "unity of religion, language and history" among the peoples of the five states. It also put the treaty into the context of the changing international environment: "In view of the transformations and the ties and integrations under way at the international level as well as the challenges facing our peoples and our countries in the political, economic, cultural, and social fields in general, we are required to achieve more inter-solidarity" (FBIS-NES February 21, 1989:5). The document was probably referring to the European Community when it mentioned integrations at the international level but may also have meant the creation of the Arab Cooperation Council that was announced in Baghdad a day before that of the UMA. Finally, the document described the union as "a fundamental phase on the path toward Arab unity," thus not breaking with the tradition of viewing all alliances in the Arab world from the perspective of greater Arab unity.

The second document was the treaty itself, described by the Algerian foreign minister as "a certificate for the legal birth of this Maghreb" (FBIS-NES, February 21, 1989:5). It outlined the institutional framework of the UMA. The union was to be headed by a presidential council composed of the political leaders of the five countries, who would meet every six months to review the affairs of the union. Its first chairman, King Hassan II of Morocco (who hosted the summit), was to preside for six months, until the next session was to be convened. All decisions by the council were to be taken by consensus, and emergency sessions could be held at any time.

The treaty set up other structures as well: a ministerial council of foreign ministers as an advisory body to the presidential council; a general secretariat composed of representatives of all member states; a consultative instance made up of ten representatives from each state's legislative institutions; and, finally, a legal body that would be formed by ten judges, two from each country. This body was to be a kind of high court that would adjudicate conflicts arising from differing interpretations of the UMA treaty or of any other agreement entered into by the five states of the Maghrib (*Le Renouveau*, March 2, 1989: 11).

Another significant clause of the treaty was the commitment of all five states of the union to ban from their respective territories any activity that would threaten the security of the other states. This presumably referred to the activities of opposition groups against the Maghribi regimes in power—opposition groups had always sought and received safe haven, protection, and financial support from competing regimes in the region (FBIS-NES, February 21, 1989). Part of that clause also stipulated that no member state could join an alliance or a military coalition that could threaten the territorial integrity or political independence of the other member states of the union.

Finally, the third document the Maghribi heads of state signed in Marrakesh was presented in the form of a resolution that approved the work done by a number of sectoral committees since summer 1988 to facilitate the implementation of the UMA's policies in various domains. The Algerian foreign minister called the resolution "a certificate of economic, cultural and social birth" (FBIS-NES, February 21, 1989:5).

The Maghribi Common Market

The UMA is meant to be an economic integration on the model of the European Community. The countries of the Maghrib are to turn inward and create a market for their products and their labor that will make up for the one they fear they may be losing in Europe after 1992. The shared economic projects have already begun to see light.

As early as April 1988 the Maghribi states were reaching many bilateral economic agreements that remain binding and are still part of the general activities of the UMA. Tunisia and Libya agreed to cooperate on a number of agricultural, industrial, and infrastructural projects. Industrial projects included the assembly of agricultural equipment and trucks, the production of fittings for electric lines and high-voltage cables, and the manufacture of white cement, steel structures, diesel engines, as well as passenger and desert vehicles. They also agreed to share geological and hydrological information that would help both states make better use of their water for agriculture and undertook to cooperate on projects to fight against desertification, plant diseases, and insect infestation. Tunisia and Libya finalized agreements on infrastructural projects, including reactivating a joint company for maritime transport, completing an underground axial cable between the two countries, and constructing a major road between Ras Jadir in Libya and Mednine in Tunisia (FBIS-NES, April 7, 1988:10).

In June 1988 Algeria and Libya signed certain agreements to facilitate economic exchanges between the two countries. Those agreements included freedom of movement across each other's borders as well as the removal of trade barriers on goods produced by the two states, the setting up of a joint bank to be called the Arab Maghribi Bank for Investment and Trade, and the establishment of a joint petrochemical company (FBIS-NES, June 30, 1988: 10–11). Furthermore, the two delegations appointed boards of directors for eight joint companies that had already been created for the exploration and production of oil, geophysics, buses and light transportation, desert vehicles, diesel engines, gearboxes, digging of water wells, and construction.

Perhaps the most ostentatious project was the one undertaken by Algeria and Morocco to construct a pipeline for natural gas that would start in Algeria and end in Europe (*Al-Hurriyu*, February 15, 1985). The pipeline is to go through Morocco at Oujda, Fez, Meknes, and Tangier and then across the Straits of Gibraltar; it should become operational by 1995 (Soudan 1989b).

These are just examples of the type of cooperative effort being made in the region to create joint ventures to link the Maghribi economies to one another and make the UMA a viable economic unit. The idea of a central bank and a single currency system that would facilitate economic transactions in the region has also been discussed but may take some time to materialize.

Despite talk of replacing the lost trade with the countries of the European Community with intra-Maghribi trade, many in the region see the UMA as an economic bloc that can cooperate rather than compete with Western Europe. As a bloc it may have more leverage than individual states in negotiating for preferential treatment of its products on the European market. As a potential consumer market of 60 million people it may offer greater opportunities for European companies interested in doing business in the region. The hope is to attract foreign capital from Arab and European nations alike to be invested in large-scale projects that would serve the whole region (Soudan 1989b).

In fact, talks are under way between some states of the EC and the UMA. In June 1990 a conference was held in Marseilles to discuss the future of French-Maghribi cooperation. French businesspeople seemed interested in investing in the industrial development of North African states if they could be assured of a regional Maghribi market (*Jeune Afrique Economique*, July 1990). French and other EC members at the conference discussed limiting North African migration to Europe by creating industrial jobs in the Maghrib. French officials from the Ministry of the Economy proposed lending money to the private sector rather than to individual states in the Maghrib to encourage the development of indigenous, large-scale private enterprises.

Thus significant economic cooperation between the northern and southern regions of the Mediterranean is possible but will depend on the ability of the Maghribi leaders to sustain the effort at integration and to create the conditions necessary to attract substantial capital from Europe. These conditions may have to include not only the liberalization of the economies of Maghribi states but also the liberalization of their political systems. Setting up a common market in the region implies a certain degree of economic decentralization and consequently a diminution of the role of the state. It also implies a recognition of competitive market forces and the need to allow the private sector the freedom to compete in that market. This in turn suggests the transference of economic power from the state to the private sector, which could then be in a position to demand a greater say in the affairs of the nation.

King Hassan II of Morocco was well aware of such implications and in his news conference after the declaration of the formation of the union referred to Algeria's response to the imperative to change:

> Algeria, its president and its people, understood perfectly well that integration in the Maghreb, the taking in hand of their future by the Algerians, required an internal opening—a system in which more than one party could exist, a taking on of responsibility in the area of management of affairs, whether they be muncipal or national. In the economic field, Algeria had to tune in to the wavelength of the time. (FBIS, February 22, 1989:3)

Political Implications

When the Tunisian head of state, Zine al-Abidine Ben Ali, addressed the Maghribi summit in Rabat on February 17, 1989, he made the following statement concerning the declaration of the creation of the UMA: "This declaration in itself represents a core political choice whose features became clear in the agreement that defines the legal and institutional framework for unified Maghreb action" (FBIS-NES, February 21, 1989:4). Ben Ali's remark made it clear that the UMA had been created not only as an economic alliance but also as a political one to serve the interests of each state in the union.

For Morocco, it was an alternative to confrontation with Algeria over the Western Sahara. It provided the institutional framework within which negotiation and discussion could proceed unhampered by matters of precedence, protocol, or appearance.

For Algeria, the union provided additional benefits: It allowed the state to introduce major economic reforms and explain them to its population in terms of the requirements of Maghribi integration rather than in terms of the failure of the system. Although the initial reforms were a response to the October 1988 riots in Algeria, the state did not wish to be seen as making too many concessions that could be perceived as a sign of weakness. The UMA had another political function in Algeria: to mobilize public support for the Algerian government at a time of serious domestic crises.

For Tunisia, the UMA provided greater freedom of action and more security. It removed the threat of Algerian hegemony over the countries bound by the 1983 treaty of brotherhood and concord and allowed for unfettered cooperation with Morocco. Libyan subversive interference was less likely because of the clauses of the treaty, and Libyan economic pressure became less effective. Rather than being dependent on the whims of the Libyan leadership, Tunisian-Libyan economic relations were regulated by the demands of a much larger market. Within the framework of the UMA, Algeria and Morocco were the guarantors, ensuring that all member nations abide by the rules of the treaty (interview with Oussama Romdhani, Washington, 1989).

Mauritania's interests were similarly served by the union. In fact, the 1983 treaty became redundant with the new UMA declaration (Soudan 1989b).

From Libya's viewpoint, its inclusion in the Arab Maghribi Union brought it out of the regional isolation it had been in since 1986, when Morocco dissolved the Arab-African Federation that bound the two countries in an alliance. Furthermore, Qadhafi's acceptance as an equal partner in the union enhanced and strengthened his position domestically. From the perspective of the rest of the Maghribi countries, Libya's inclusion was important for other reasons. If Qadhafi had been kept out of the union, he would undoubtedly have turned against it and attempted to disrupt it by whatever means at his disposal (*Washington Post,* February 25, 1989). More significnatly, he might have tried to improve his relations with Egypt in a balance-of-power game that would have brought the threat of Egyptian influence to the doorstep of the Maghrib, a situation reminiscent of the 1969–1970 period (FBIS-NES, May 3, 1988; *Al-Sharq al-Awsut,* October 27, 1988).

In terms of the regional and international environments, the Arab Maghribi Union provided all the states with a number of political advantages. The provision in the treaty that stipulated that no member state could adhere to a military coalition or to any pact that would threaten the territorial integrity or political independence of any other state within the union ensured that no alliance could be entered into by any member state without the permission of all the others (FBIS-NES, February 21, 1989). The most likely state to want to enter other coalitions, Libya, is thus restrained from pursuing alliances (with Egypt, for instance) that would weaken the Maghrib (*New York Times,* Feburary 17, 1989).

The Arab Maghribi Union became one of three major political blocs in the Arab world. As a bloc it was more powerful than any of its constituent states could ever have been. Its strength lay in a number of factors—demographic, strategic, economic, and military: It represented almost one-third of the total population of the Arab world; it occupied the whole Mediterranean coast south of Europe (Egypt and the Levant are primarily located south and southeast of the Turkish coast); although perhaps the poorest of three Arab blocs, it still constituted a very important market, with significant natural resources in oil, natural gas, and phosphates; and its combined armed forces of an estimated 400,000 were almost as large as Egypt's forces of a little over 450,000 (Heller 1984). In regional terms, then, the UMA altered significantly the balance of power in North Africa and to a somewhat lesser extent in the Arab world as a whole. For Egypt, that meant a reduction of its sphere of influence in the Maghrib and perhaps even on the Arab-African political scene.

The creation of the Arab Cooperation Council, which in 1989 included Egypt, Jordan, Iraq, and the Yemen Arab Republic, can therefore be explained, in part at least, as the setting up of a counterbloc to the UMA in the Mashriq. That it was a reaction is demonstrated by the choice of timing for the announcement of the creation of the Arab Cooperation Council: It took place twenty-four hours before the official creation of the Arab Maghribi Union, on February 16, 1989, thus taking the wind out of the sails of the UMA declaration and to some extent reducing its regional impact.

Although Egypt never mentioned the Arab Maghribi Union in its pronouncements regarding the formation of the Arab Cooperation Council, the inherent rivalry between the two blocs surfaced in a statement made by Tariq Aziz, the Iraqi deputy prime minister and foreign minister: "One of the provisions of the ... [Arab Cooperation Council] plan says that the grouping is not closed or based purely on geographical or political considerations like the 'Arab Maghreb Union,' which is impossible for Sudan or Iraq, for example, to join" (*Al-Ra'y*, February 15, 1989).

The formation of those regional blocs throughout 1989 and the first half of 1990 appeared to have introduced a new element into the pluralist or balance-of-power model discussed above. Rather than the occurrence of a balance of power among the major states in the Arab world, as had been the case in the last three decades (Taylor 1982), the political game seemed to be played among blocs of nations. Until summer 1990, almost every Arab state was part of a regional alliance: the UMA, the Arab Cooperation Council, or the Gulf Cooperation Council (formed in 1981). By 1991, however, the Arab Cooperation Council had collapsed as a direct consequence of the Gulf crisis.

The Changing Regional and International Environments

Since the formation of the UMA, the international and regional events that have taken place have changed the context in which the UMA operated and the variables to be considered when analyzing regional integration in North Africa.

With the collapse of communism in the Soviet Union and Eastern Europe in 1989, Libya and Algeria found themselves deprived of a major ally and supporter on the international scene. By August 1990 the USSR had stopped all arms shipments to Libya, demanding it repay its $3 billion debt first and even refusing to send Libya spare parts for existing materiel (FBIS-NES, August 10, 1990:19). The political implication of those changes was the narrowing of the ideological differences dividing the pro-Western nations of the UMA, such as Morocco and Tunisia, and the pro-Soviet states, like Algeria and Libya. The process of political liberalization of Algeria was hastened by developments on the international scene.

The economic changes were even more significant. Because the model of state-controlled economies in the Soviet Union and Eastern Europe failed, there was no longer any justification for maintaining state controls in North Africa. In fact, Algeria's economy underwent very rapid transformation after

1989, and the direction was unequivocally toward a free-market economy. Libya trailed behind but introduced limited changes in the domestic market. Thus the difference in economic systems among the nations of the UMA is being reduced as well.

Europe is also experiencing a migratory wave of skilled and semiskilled workers from Eastern Europe as a result of the collapse of the Communist economies. This means that Western Europe will no longer need cheap labor from the Maghrib. All EC countries have indeed been tightening their immigration policies, and a number of them have been repatriating non-European workers. A major source of revenue—as well as an outlet for the rising number of unemployed in the region—will therefore become unavailable to the Maghrib in the near future. The pressure is on to create the conditions necessary to attract foreign investment in the region to help create new businesses and new industries to provide jobs for the growing ranks of the unemployed. That may also have an integrative effect on the region as a whole.

The Gulf crisis that erupted in August 1990 with the invasion of Kuwait by Iraq may, in contrast, have a divisive effect on the UMA as it has had on the Arab world. On August 3, the day after the invasion, the Arab League ministerial council issued a statement in Cairo condemning the Iraqi aggression against Kuwait. Two of the six resolutions included in the statement were the immediate and unconditional withdrawal of Iraq from Kuwait and the rejection of any foreign intevention in the region. Fourteen countries endorsed this statement whereas six either abstained from voting or rejected it. The latter included Yemen (made up of North and South, united in May 1990), Jordan, Iraq (all three members of the Arab Cooperation Council), as well as the PLO, Sudan, and Mauritania. Libya did not attend the meeting, and the minister of foreign affairs of Tunisia condemned the invasion and expressed the opinion that the Arab League was the best framework for resolving the crisis (FBIS-NES, August 6, 1990).

This was the beginning of the split in the Arab world. The bone of contention appeared to be not so much the cause of the crisis, the Iraqi invasion, as the consequence of the invasion, namely, the Western military intervention in the Gulf. The UMA did not take a unified stand on the crisis; instead, as in the pluralist model, each state took an independent position that reflected its own interests and domestic concerns.

Mauritania took the most radical stand vis-à-vis the crisis, supporting Iraq's position and offering to send troops to fight with Iraqi forces in Kuwait. Iraq was reported to have payed $1,500 for every volunteer and promised a salary of $1,000 a month for Mauritanian volunteers in its so-called popular army. The determining factor behind Mauritania's stand may have been its weak economy and high rate of unemployment. Iraq was seen as the state that would give Mauritania economic aid in exchange for political support.

Libya did not participate in the original Arab League council meeting in Cairo and consequently did not take an official stand on its resolutions. Its position was that "all parties . . . adhere to the Arab League Charter, which stipulates the resolution of all problems between Arab states through dialogue, understanding and the nonuse of force. This latter is unacceptable between brothers" (FBIS-NES, August 3, 1990:12). Qadhafi was highly critical of the Western military intervention in the Gulf linking it to the desecration of religious sites, but fell short of condoning the Iraqi invasion of Kuwait or sending Libyan volunteers to Iraq, as Mauritania did. Instead, he tried to find an Arab formula to resolve the crisis.

Algeria condemned the invasion on the very day it occurred and demanded the immediate withdrawal of Iraqi forces. A week later, however, Foreign Minister Sid Ahmed Ghozali stated in an interview that "Algeria's official position was not to take one side or the other, as they [Kuwait and Iraq] are two brother countries" (FBIS-NES, August 9, 1990). He condemned foreign intervention and called for an Arab solution to the crisis. Algeria thus positioned itself as a potential negotiator in the crisis, but to no avail.

Tunisia's position was not very different from that of Algeria. Soon after the event, it also condemned the Iraqi invasion and called for the withdrawal of Iraqi forces. President Ben Ali was in the difficult position of having to criticize foreign intervention even though Tunisia had called for foreign assistance at the time of the Gafsa attack by Libyan-supported Tunisian troops in 1980. Domestic concerns with the Muslim fundamentalists forced the Tunisian government to take a critical stand vis-à-vis Western forces in Saudi Arabia because of their proximity to the holy cities of Mecca and Medina.

Morocco condemned the Iraqi invasion in no uncertain terms, stating that it violated the basic principles of international law as well as the charters of the United Nations and the Arab League. Morocco was also one of only three Arab states (with Egypt and Syria) that sent 1,200 troops to Saudi Arabia (*New York Times*, August 25, 1990). In retaliation, Iraq forced Moroccan diplomats in Kuwait to leave their embassy compounds and go to Baghdad, where they were held hostage for a short period.

Members of the Arab Maghribi Union expressed different views on the Gulf crisis but, at least publicly, did not take a critical view of their fellow members' positions. Within this context, Mauritania's expanded political independence as part of the UMA was especially noteworthy: It no longer had to toe the line behind either Algeria or Morocco, as it was protected by the union rather than by the individual states.

Conclusion: The UMA's Problems

The Arab Maghribi Union faces some daunting problems in a number of spheres. In the economic field it has to overcome several hurdles. Intra-Maghribi trade as a percentage of each state's total international trade is extremely low. In 1986 it constituted 8.7 percent of Tunisia's trade, 2 percent of Algeria's trade, and 0.4 percent of Morocco's trade (World Bank 1987). Yet over 65 percent of those states' total world trade was with the nations of the European Community. This pattern of trading may be very difficult to change even over a long period of time because there is very limited economic complementarity in the region.

In terms of labor, the UMA offers little that could seriously turn the tide of the soaring unemployment rate in the three core Maghribi states. In Algeria the unemployment rate has reached 25 percent (*New York Times*, October 16, 1988); in Tunisia the official figure is 15 percent but could be much higher (*Jeune Afrique*, February 15, 1989); and in Morocco it may already have reached 40 percent (*Jeune Afrique*, February 15, 1989). Except for Libya, therefore, none of those states can import labor from any other, and Libya's labor market can probably absorb only a section of Tunisia's unemployed. Although the UMA is planning to set up a number of new projects that would create many new jobs, it remains to be seen how many jobs, at what rate, with what resources, and whether they keep up with the population growth.

The third problem concerns the different economic systems of the members of the UMA. Despite liberalizing measures instituted recently in Algeria and Libya, the gaps between the economies of the five countries is still very wide.

The UMA also faces the unresolved intra-Maghribi political problems of the past decade, the most important being the Western Sahara conflict. King Hassan referred to it as "the banana peel" and the "grain of sand which is preventing the engine from operating" (FBIS-NES, February 21, 1989), thus acknowledging that it could derail the whole process of integration.

The issue of borders remains one of the main stumbling blocks in the region. In the 1980s Algeria moved toward consolidating its borders with all the states around it, including Niger, Mali, and Mauritania. In fact, one of the major sources of tension in Algerian-Libyan relations has been Libya's refusal to give up the Ghat region, which Algeria claims should fall under its territorial jurisdiction. The principal impediment in Libyan-Tunisian relations in early 1988 concerned the problem of the Continental Shelf, which (though technically resolved by the International Court of the Hague) has continued to cause friction between the two states.

Within the UMA there may be a replay of the Algerian-Moroccan rivalry over leadership in the region. When major decisions are taken, who will be the final arbiter? Will there be bloc formations within the UMA, some of the small states siding with Morocco and others with Algeria? Will we see a return of the pluralist model of interaction in the Maghrib but within an integrative framework this time?

The political crises Algeria and Libya faced in the first quarter of 1992 had an impact on the relations of the states of the UMA. The aborted legislative elections in Algeria and the resignation of Benjedid, one of the founding leaders of the union, destabilized the region as a whole. Islamic fundamentalism is now perceived as the primary threat to all the regimes in power in the Maghrib, and the leaders have closed ranks to face the mounting confrontation with Islamicists. On another level, Islamic leaders have also coordinated their activities in the Maghrib in an attempt to challenge the governments in power.

The April 1992 UN sanctions against Libya, in contrast, created greater solidarity among the people of the Maghrib in support of Libya. But they embarrassed Maghribi governments, who found themselves obliged to turn away Libyan planes attempting to cross their borders, in direct contravention to the UMA agreements of free passage for people and goods between member countries.

Intra-Maghribi relations have always been complex, and the UMA has been an attempt to institutionalize the ties that bind those countries economically, culturally, politically, and geographically. Although this organization may not offer solutions to the region's problems, it remains a forum for the peaceful negotiation of differences and the facilitation of communication among North African states.

10

The Maghribi States and the European Community

William Mark Habeeb

The economic relationship between the Maghribi states and the European Community is one of extreme asymmetry. It is an interdependency between two economically unequal partners. In practical terms, this means that (1) policies of the EC and economic developments in Europe have a greater determining impact on the relationship than do policies of and economic developments in the Maghribi states; (2) production structures of the Maghribi states are oriented toward Europe and not vice versa; and (3) the ability of the EC to determine the outcome of interaction is greater than that of the Maghribi states (that is, there is an imbalance of power in the relationship).

The nature of this asymmetry is vividly revealed by statistical evidence. These data show a tremendous disparity in the relative importance of EC-Maghribi trade to each side's total trade. During the 1980s, nearly two-thirds of the Maghribi states' total trade was with the EC, whereas less than 2 percent of the EC's total trade was with the Maghrib (see Tables 10.1 and 10.2).

The structure of Maghribi trade is typical of developing countries' trade with developed countries: There is a high percentage of primary commodity exports, especially for Morocco and Algeria; a low percentage of manufactured exports, with the exception of textiles, a typical low-technology, developing country export; and a high percentage of manufactured goods imports (see Table 10.3).

Trade data for 1990 reveal large trade deficits with the EC for Morocco (−$868 million), Tunisia (−$758 million), and Mauritania (−$6.2 million), and surpluses for Algeria ($1.3 billion) and Libya ($4.0 billion), although the surpluses of the latter two have declined dramatically from the peak years of the 1970s (European Economic Community 1990).

TABLE 10.1 Maghribi States' Trade with the EC (as a percentage of the value of their total world trade)

	Exports	Imports
1980	42.1	60
1981	49.1	59.1
1982	69.1[a]	58
1983[b]	63	58
1984[c]	69	58.1
1985[c]	73.4	60
1986[c]	72.1	62.1
1987[c]	74	60
1988[c]	67	56
1989[d]	69	60.2
Average	65	59.2

[a] Does not comprise Libya's share, as data is unavailable.
[b] Figures do not comprise Libya's share, as data is unavailable.
[c] Figures do not comprise Mauritania's share, as data is unavailable.
[d] Figures only for Morocco and Tunisia.

Source: International Monetary Fund, Direction of Trade Statistics Yearbook, 1989 (Washington: IMF, 1991).

TABLE 10.2 EC States' Trade with the Maghrib (as a percentage of the value of EC total world trade)

	Exports	Imports
1980	5.4	4.7
1981	6.6	5.2
1982	5.1	6.4
1983	5	6.1
1984	4.5	6
1985	4	6.1
1986	3.7	4.4
1987	3.1	4.2
1988	3.1	4
1989	3.3	3.9
1990	3.5	4.4
Average	4.3	5.1

Source: European Economic Community, Eurostat External Trade Statistics Yearbook, 1990 (Brussels: European Community, 1991).

The Impact of Asymmetry

The asymmetry with the EC has several deleterious effects for the countries of the Maghrib:

1. The production structures of their economies are oriented toward exporting to and importing from the EC, creating a structural asymmetry that has discouraged greater inter-Maghribi trade and thus hindered greater Ma-

TABLE 10.3   Structure of Maghribi States' Trade (as a percentage of total trade), 1990

	Algeria	Morocco	Tunisia
Exports			
Fuels, minerals, metals	96	23	19
Other primary commodities	0	30	12
Manufactures	4	66	104
(of which textiles)	(2)	(20)	(35)
Imports			
Food	27	12	10
Fuels	2	15	9
Other primary commodities	8	12	9
Manufactures	63	61	71

Source: World Bank, World Development Report, 1992 (Washington, D.C., World Bank, 1992).

TABLE 10.4   Maghribi Trade with Eastern Europe and the Former Soviet Union (as a percentage of the value of Maghribi total world trade)

	Exports	Imports
1980	3.4	4.2
1981	3.4	4.1
1982	2.1	5.1
1983	1.1	5.0
1984	1.2	3.2
1985[a]	2.0	1.2
1986[a]	1.2	1.2
1987[a]	1.0	1.4
1988[a]	1.1	1.3
1989[b]	1.0	3.4
Average	2.5	3.0

[a]No data for 1985 to 1989 is available for Mauritania.
[b]Data for 1989 comprises only figures for Morocco and Tunisia. Data for other countries is unavailable.

Source: International Monetary Fund, Direction of Trade Statistics Yearbook, 1989 (Washington: IMF, 1991).

ghribi integration. The issue of integration will be addressed in greater detail later (see also Chapter 9 of this volume), but for now it is sufficient to note that trade among the Maghribi states has been surprisingly insignificant.

2. Because Maghribi exports are targeted to the European market, very little trade has developed between the Maghrib and North America, the former Eastern bloc (see Table 10.4), or other developing regions. This fact has reduced alternatives for the states of the Maghrib and has made them dependent on Europe for both export markets and many imports. It has thus tended to reinforce the asymmetry and render it self-sustaining.

3. The structural nature of Maghribi-EC trade—which sees the Maghribi states exporting products with only a small degree of net value added yet im-

porting products with a high degree of net value added—has discouraged greater industrial and technological development in the Maghribi states and led to a deterioration in their terms of trade.

4. Because of the asymmetry, economic production in the Maghrib has been determined more by external demand than by internal demand and, more specifically, by European economic trends, business cycles, and policies. This situation has reduced the economic sovereignty of the North African states and has minimized the effectiveness and relevance of their own economic policies.

Applicability of the Dependency Model

It is reasonable to ask whether the economic dependency model applies to the Maghribi-EC relationship (the relative merits of dependency theory will not be analyzed here, merely its applicability). At first glance, the dependency model seems relevant, particularly the concepts of center-periphery and metropole-satellite put forward by Raul Prebisch and André Gunder-Frank (for an extensive discussion of the dependency model, see Chilcote 1984). Theontonio dos Santos, building on Prebisch's center-periphery approach, described dependency in a way that would appear to apply to the Maghribi-EC relationship: "The relation of interdependence between two or more economies . . . assumes the form of dependence when some countries [the dominant ones] can expand and can be self-sustaining, while other countries [the dependent ones] can do this only as a reflection of that expansion" (Dos Santos 1970:231).

On closer look, however, the dependency model does not seem to apply. Classic dependency theory generally includes domination by center capital investment in periphery economies; collusion between elites in the dependent state and foreign capital; and penetration of the dependent state by multinational corporations based in the center. None of these aspects of classic dependency theory characterizes the Maghribi-EC relationship.

Thus, instead of conceptualizing this relationship in terms of dependency theory, it would be more useful simply to look at it as one of extreme asymmetrical interdependence. Interdependence implies that both sides would incur costs if the relationship were broken—but it does not imply that each side would incur equal costs, that is, it does not suggest that each side is equally dependent upon the other. Rather, asymmetrical interdependence means that one side (in this case, the Maghribi states) would incur far greater costs if the relationship ended. The weaker side in an asymmetrical interdependency generally has fewer alternatives to the relationship and less control over outcomes than does the stronger side. In short, it has less power in the relationship (for an expanded discussion of asymmetrical negotiation, see Habeeb 1988).

By defining this relationship as one of asymmetrical interdependence, we can also perhaps point to some steps that the Maghribi states can take to lessen the impact and even the degree of the asymmetry. Dependency theory, of course, similarly prescribes steps to achieve dependency reversal, but as will be seen, the options for reducing asymmetrical interdependence are considerably more realistic and do not require the radical structural changes usually called for by dependency theorists. Moreover, the prescriptions of dependency theorists have more often than not resulted in economic stagnation and inefficiency.

Past Efforts at Institutionalization

There have been a number of efforts to institutionalize the Maghribi-EC relationship via negotiated agreements. It would be useful to look briefly at what the Maghribi states have attained from these agreements, how the asymmetry has affected the negotiations and the outcomes, and whether the agreements have helped to reduce the asymmetry or have only served to perpetuate it.

In 1963 Morocco and Tunisia requested negotiations with the EC (then made up of six member countries) on establishing association agreements with the Community. The agreements, reached in 1969, had as a goal the establishment of a free trade area between the EC countries and their former colonies by gradually eliminating tariffs and quotas. The agreements gave Morocco and Tunisia free access to the EC market for virtually all of their industrial products (which were then quite few) and preferential treatment for certain agricultural products (see European Economic Community 1982).

Algeria got off to a slower start. Algeria had separate agreements with France, which granted duty-free access to Algerian goods, and agreements with Germany and the Benelux countries, which granted tariff reductions. Negotiations between Algeria and the EC did not begin until 1972 (see European Economic Community 1982). Libya never signed an association agreement with the EC, although it, too, pursued separate arrangements with individual European states (Zartman 1971).

In 1972 the EC adopted a so-called global Mediterranean policy, whereby it attempted to develop a comprehensive policy toward the Mediterranean countries. As part of this process, parallel negotiations were begun with Algeria, Morocco, and Tunisia on the conclusion of full cooperation agreements. New agreements were reached in 1976 and went into force in 1978 (see Renier 1988). Again, Libya, now under the rule of the radical Qadhafi regime, did not sign a cooperation agreement.

The cooperation agreements were wide-ranging: They covered not only trade but also technological and financial cooperation. The financial provisions included concessionary loans, market-rate European Investment Bank

(EIB) loans, and grants. The technological protocols offered EC cooperation in the development of production and economic infrastructure in the Maghrib and in encouraging private-sector European investment (Pomfret 1987).

The specific trade aspects of the agreements included free access to the EC market for raw materials and industrial products from the Maghrib (though, as discussed just below, there were certain exceptions for "sensitive" industrial products). Maghribi agricultural products were to be given preferential access in comparison to that offered to other third countries. However, there were some initial quotas (and some added later) to "protect the legitimate interests of Community producers" (European Economic Community 1982).

In fact, the benefits the Maghribi countries have derived from these agreements have eroded since 1978. As one observer noted, "the contrast was glaring between what was rhetorically promised with the launching of the 'global Mediterranean policy' and what was initially delivered" (Sutton 1989:29). First came "revolutionary" self-restraint agreements that the EC essentially forced upon Morocco and Tunisia to limit their exports of "sensitive" industrial products, specifically, textiles and footwear (Table 10.3 shows that textiles alone account for a significant portion of both Morocco's and Tunisia's manufactured exports to the EC). These "voluntary" constraints would seem to contradict the cooperation agreements, which in principle allowed free access for Maghribi industrial goods. The EC justified the constraints by pointing to the "economic crisis which hit the Community," and especially "the crisis in the textile industry in the Community" (Renier 1988:53). In fact, these limits were merely penalizing the Maghribi states for their comparative advantage, as it was principally the rising unit labor costs that hurt European textile manufacturers.

The second erosion has occurred in the area of agriculture, where the EC has attempted to impose "reference prices" as well as quotas on "sensitive" agricultural products, such as wine, tomatoes, and tinned fish (Duchene 1985). When combined with the EC's indirect protectionism, such as its Common Agricultural Program (CAP), which grants subsidies to its own producers, the result has been to restrain exports of agricultural products from the Maghrib. Furthermore, the CAP also offers subsidy aid to European processors of agricultural goods, such as olive oil and tomato concentrate manufacturers; this has discouraged investment in agricultural modernization in the Maghrib. Subsidies to Italian tomato paste manufacturers were largely responsible for the closure in 1979 of a large Heinz tomato concentrate factory in Morocco (Sutton 1989).

The failure of the EC to fully abide by the 1976 agreements is a function of and simultaneously reinforces the Maghribi-EC asymmetry. The Maghrib's relative economic unimportance to the EC, combined with its extreme economic dependency on the EC and lack of alternative markets, deprives the North African countries of bargaining power and renders retaliation futile.

The Maghribi states have nevertheless become increasingly outspoken about the EC's lack of compliance with the 1976 pact. In 1985 Tunisian foreign minister Beji Caid Essebsi, speaking before a European audience, said that the 1976 agreements "have not been implemented either in letter or in spirit" (FBIS-NES, February 28, 1985:Q2). Indeed, even some official EC studies have commented on the problems and inadequacies of the agreements. As one EC analysis concludes, the "Maghreb countries deserve better treatment at the hands of the Community" (Subhan 1985:50). Faced with these complaints from the Maghribi states, the EC has attempted to replace commercial advantages with development assistance and greater financial compensation in the form of grants and EIB loans. These actions have so far not been acceptable to the Maghribi states.

The critical question raised above is whether these agreements have served to lessen structural asymmetry by encouraging structural change in the Maghrib or have only strengthened the existing asymmetry. The answer is clear: The agreements, at least as they have been carried out in practice, have essentially maintained the economic status quo and thus served to perpetuate the asymmetry:

- The protectionist limitations placed on manufactured exports have discouraged structural change in the Maghrib and have discouraged investment in industrialization, particularly in those areas—such as textiles, footwear, and food processing—in which the Maghribi states have the greatest economic potential.
- The quotas and price setting on agricultural products have also discouraged investment and weakened economic confidence in the agricultural sectors of the Maghribi economies.
- Since 1972, the only area in which the states of the Maghrib have significantly increased their exports to the EC is that of nonagricultural raw materials, the most "typical" Third World export sector.

To conclude this brief overview of past agreements, we can say that the asymmetrical nature of the Maghribi-EC relationship, by leaving the Maghribi states with few alternatives and little control over outcomes, has limited their power (defined as their capability to affect outcomes). The needs and desires of the EC have tended to dictate the terms of the negotiations, and the Maghribi states have only been able to protest in futility when the EC has changed or modified the terms or the spirit of existing agreements. Indeed, the EC has appeared to pursue a traditional self-interested policy: When the going gets tough, beggar thy neighbor. At the same time, the agreements themselves have served to perpetuate the asymmetry by maintaining traditional trade patterns.

Future Shocks

As if the current situation is not bad enough, there are on the horizon several future shocks—developments that have the potential to compound the asymmetry to the future detriment of the Maghribi states. These are (1) the full accession of Spain abnd Portugal into the EC, (2) the integration of the EC as a truly common market beginning in 1992, (3) the EC's increasing focus on developing closer links with Eastern Europe, and (4) the Maghribi states' own demographic and economic trends.

EC Enlargement

Spain and Portugal will become fully integrated into the EC in 1993 (for industrial products) and 1996 (for agricultural products). Their full integration will accelerate the trend toward self-sufficiency in the EC. The problem this poses for the Maghrib derives from similarity in agricultural produce. Morocco appears to face the greatest threat because its principal agricultural exports to the EC (citrus fruits and tomatoes) are also among Spain's major agricultural products. Tunisia, with its large olive oil exports, also faces new competition from Spain. With the full accession of Spain, the EC will have year-round surplus in tomatoes, wine, and olive oil (in fact, the EC's surplus of olive oil is projected to be four times Tunisia's current olive oil exports to the EC) (Taylor 1980:10). In addition, Spain and Portugal will add to the EC's production capacity in textiles and footwear, products already noted as the target of "voluntary" Maghrib restraints. Finally, after accession, Spain and Portugal will have equal voices in Brussels. Because they have weaker economies than the rest of the EC, their voices are more likely to be ones of protectionism, particularly in areas such as textiles and footwear.

In an attempt to ease the concerns of the Maghribi states, the EC in June 1985 adopted a statement that confirmed the importance of preferential relations between the EC and the countries of the Mediterranean and pledged to "maintain traditional exports" (Renier 1988:54–55). This announcement did little, however, to alleviate the Maghribi states' apprehension, particularly because they hope to expand *beyond* "traditional" exports.

The Single European Market

The second potential future shock is the impending full economic integration of Europe, a process commonly referred to as "1992," the year in which its implementation was scheduled to begin. Under the program the EC is to become the world's largest industrialized market, in which there is completely free circulation of persons, goods, services, and capital among the twelve member states. Although many elements of the program (such as elimination of border controls) may take years to put into effect, the prospect of complete integration has raised fears of a "fortress Europe" enjoying newfound self-sufficiency behind protectionist walls. These fears have been fueled by a latent neomercantilist sentiment in Europe, evidenced by a desire to achieve balance-of-payments surpluses yet protect domestic industries from competing imports, and a concern about protecting domestic industry from "cheap foreign labor" (for more on this issue, see David 1986). EC officials vigorously deny that protectionism will accompany 1992, but business, labor, and political forces in individual EC member states often feel otherwise, especially in Spain, Portugal, Italy, France, and Greece (see "Europe," 1988).

The EC's Cecchini Report, an assessment of the effects of the integration program on the developing world, downplays the negative consequences of European integration, calling it "a shot in the arm for other markets and economies in less buoyant shape" (Cecchini 1988:xix). The Cecchini Report argues that the greater economic activity in Europe generated by integration will lead to increased imports from the developing world.

Yet an important economic analysis by London's Overseas Development Institute (ODI) is more pessimistic. It argues that "the rising tide of economic activity in the EC will not carry the developing countries far up the beach," largely because economic integration will foster improved productivity throughout Europe (Davenport and Page 1991:7). The ODI study claims that trade creation (the increase in demand for developing world imports by the EC) will be offset by trade diversion (the reduction in demand for developing world imports by the EC). Moreover, the study estimates that in manufacturing sectors, trade diversion will actually exceed trade creation.

Another aspect of integration that may affect the Maghribi-EC relationship is the result of the Single European Act. This act, passed by the European Parliament in July 1987, extends the range of decisions that the EC's Council of Ministers may take by qualified majority in cooperation with the European Parliament rather than by unanimous agreement. This is the latest step in a trend toward the centralization of EC decisionmaking, a trend that will see less influence for individual member states such as France (which has traditionally defended the interests of the Maghribi states in the EC).

Developments in Eastern Europe

The dramatic political and economic changes that have occurred in Eastern Europe since 1989 have stimulated greater interest among EC states in developing closer economic links with these recovering socialist economies. There is a very real possibility that closer ties between the EC and Eastern Europe will come at the expense of developing countries, such as those of the Maghrib. For one, the countries of Eastern Europe will attempt to penetrate the EC market with labor-intensive manufactured goods. In addition, Maghribi economies will face new competition for EC investment. Finally, and perhaps most importantly, the EC is likely to focus more attention on its Eastern European neighbors, with whom it shares greater cultural affinity.

It is only natural that the EC will attempt to forge links with Eastern Europe and that this trend will accelerate as political and economic reforms in the Eastern European countries proceed. By June 1990, the EC had already negotiated a series of trade and cooperation agreements with the countries of Eastern Europe. These agreements include progressive liberalization of trade, leading ultimately to free trade and the free movement of persons, services, and capital; technical assistance; and joint ventures, especially in infrastructure projects (Andriessen 1990; Commission of the European Communities 1990). Although the EC denies that these agreements should be seen as forerunners to automatic accession, EC Commission president Jacques Delors has claimed "that option is being left open" (Andriessen 1990:4). The former territory of East Germany already gained EC membership upon its unification with West Germany in October 1990.

A closer bond between the economies of the EC states and those of Eastern Europe poses a number of problems for the Maghribi states: First, the lure of Eastern Europe is likely to attract significant amounts of EC private investment that might otherwise be directed to the Maghrib. The creation of the European Bank for Reconstruction and Development has also led to increased official bilateral investment and financial assistance. Second, the improved trade regime that will accompany the new association agreements will lead to a substantial growth in Eastern European manufactured exports to the EC. In certain sectors (such as textiles, footwear, and light manufactures) this increase may come at the expense of exports from the Maghrib. Third, stepped-up immigration to the EC from Eastern Europe may intensify the already growing efforts in EC countries to limit immigration from the Maghrib; such immigration has traditionally served as a safety valve for the struggling Maghribi economies. Finally, the greater political attention being directed toward Eastern Europe may divert attention and bureaucratic energy away from the Maghrib, and indeed the entire developing world.

Maghribi Demographic Trends

The final future shock that may worsen the asymmetry derives from the economic, demographic, and social trends in the Maghrib (these trends and their implications are discussed in greater detail in Chapters 4 and 12 in this volume). The Maghribi states are witnessing rapid population growth. According to the United Nations, the current population of around 60 million will rise to over 80 million by the year 2000 (United Nations Development

Programme [UNDP] 1990). The urban population is also expanding: In 1988 Morocco and Algeria were almost 50 percent urban, Tunisia was over 50 percent urban, and Libya was nearly 70 percent urban (UNDP 1990).

Unemployment and underemployment throughout the Maghrib is high, as is annual growth in the labor force. The implications of these trends are obvious: There will be more mouths to feed, greater need for structural change in the economies so as to provide employment for the expanding urban population, and an increased need to import advanced technology.

Options for Reducing Asymmetry

When the impact of these future shocks is combined, one can only conclude that the next decade will see greater tensions in the Maghribi-EC relationship and an increase in the degree of asymmetry—*unless* steps are taken to reduce the symmetry.

The Maghribi states might pursue a range of policy options as a means of reversing the asymmetry in their relationship with the EC, or at least of lessening the negative effects of this asymmetry. Some of these options are strategic, meaning they would bring about a permanent or structural change in the states' economies or in their external relations. Others are essentially tactical, meaning the Maghribi states might pursue them during specific encounters with the EC (such as during trade negotiations) in order to achieve more of their preferred outcomes. Most of these options, however, contain both strategic and tactical aspects.

Import Substitution Industrialization

The Maghribi states could undertake national economic policies of import substitution industrialization behind high protectionist walls. This is the solution that many dependency theorists, such as Prebisch, have prescribed. Moreover, it is a policy that worked well in the postwar period for many of the young economies of Asia. The Asian cases, however, are unique, in part because those states benefited from immense U.S. economic aid and preferential trade agreements, and in part because the Asian nations were able to develop economies of scale and to proceed fairly rapidly to policies of export-led growth. There are so many more examples of unsuccessful import substitution policies, such as in Nasser's Egypt, that they have been widely discredited.

In the Maghrib, as in most other regions, import substitution industrialization would probably lead to resource misallocation, increased imports of raw materials, declining relative income in the agricultural sector, and economic inefficiency due to diversion away from sectors in which there is a comparative advantage (for a concise survey of the arguments for and against the import substitution policy, see Meier 1976:648–654).

Trade Diversification

Another strategic option the Maghribi states could pursue would be to increase their trade with other regions of the world, such as other developing states, North America, or Eastern Europe. The objective of such a strategy would be to reduce the proportion of EC trade in the Maghribi states' total trade, thus increasing alternatives and reducing dependence on the EC.

Unfortunately, this does not appear to be a realistic option in the short or medium term, in large part because the current level of Maghribi trade with regions other than the EC is so insignificant that they would be starting at a very small base. The Maghribi states' trade with other developing states amounts to less than 20 percent of their total trade. It is hard to imagine how this figure could grow by a substantial amount (at least in the short or medium term) or where the increase would come from. African economies are stagnant and in any event would be weak markets for the types of manufactured goods the countries of the Maghrib would like to export. The trade infrastructure between the Maghrib and Latin America and Asia is not sufficiently developed to render an increase in trade practical in the short term.

Maghribi trade with Eastern Europe and the former Soviet Union is also minimal, averaging less than 3 percent of total trade in the 1980s. These levels are not likely to increase dramatically any time soon for a host of reasons, such as the former COMECON countries' largely nonconvertible currencies and lack of suitable products to barter.

Nevertheless, the ongoing economic changes in Eastern Europe could eventually benefit the Maghrib. As Eastern European countries move toward freely convertible currencies, their trade with the rest of the world will be greatly facilitated. In addition, rising incomes in Eastern Europe, combined with a greater emphasis on meeting consumer needs, will afford new opportunities for Maghribi exports, especially fruits, vegetables, and processed food. It would thus behoove the Maghribi states to pursue such opportunities aggressively as they arise.

In short, although it is always beneficial to try to diversify markets, such a strategy does not promise significant near-term benefits. Moreover, the Maghribi states' production structures are oriented toward trade with the EC, which is, after all, geographically the closest market for exports and imports.

The Military/Strategic Card

In the past, the Maghrib could have tried to gain leverage in its relationship with the EC by playing the military/strategic card—for example, by offering, or threatening to offer, military facilities to the Soviet Union. This would have been both a strategic and a tactical option (in particular, the *threat* to play this card would have been a tactical option) in the bipolar context.

In the post–cold war era, however, this option has ceased to exist. Even before its disintegration, the Soviet Union faced economic problems that led

Moscow to disengage from the Third World, especially from areas of peripheral importance, such as the Maghrib. The Maghribi states are not alone among Third World states in no longer being able to play (or threaten to play) the superpowers against each other. Until and if the Maghribi states ever acquire renewed strategic importance to the West, the military/strategic card will not be a viable option.

Coalition Building with Arab Oil-producing States

The Maghribi states could attempt a coalition with the Organization of Arab Petroleum Exporting Countries (OAPEC), using the Gulf's oil as leverage in negotiations with the EC. This would be a tactical option if used as a source of negotiation power, though if it became an enduring coalition or alliance it would also take on strategic characteristics. This option seems to have little chance of success, however. It would require an unprecedented and unlikely degree of unity in the Arab world. The Maghribi states have not even been able to negotiate as a bloc with the EC using Algerian and Libyan petroleum resources as leverage. Furthermore, even if the political will and unity existed, for this option to work there would have to be a considerably tighter oil market than currently exists; it would probably require an oil crisis. Moreover, this tactic could backfire if it weakened Europe economically or led to economic retaliation.

Tactical Maneuvers

The next option is really a set of options, that is, various tactical steps the Maghribi states could take, either individually or jointly, in any future negotiations with the EC. Most of these have been tried in one form or another.

- *Demanding membership in the EC.* Morocco applied for membership in the EC in 1987 and was rejected (Article 237 of the Treaty of Rome, which established the EC, specifies that only European states can join). On the surface, this seems to be a strategic option, and if it worked, it certainly would be. But in fact, it is more tactical, in that by forcing the issue of EC membership, the Maghribi states would be forcing the EC to reject them; the countries of the Maghrib, following unwritten bargaining norms, could then ask for compensation. This was probably King Hassan's objective in 1987.
- *Building allies within the EC.* The Maghribi states might try to build allies among domestic special interest groups in the EC to help fight for their cause, whether those be industry groups who want access to raw materials from the Maghrib, consumer groups who want cheaper agricultural products, or entire countries (such as France) that have traditionally been more attentive to the Maghribi states' interests in the EC.

There has not been much success with this strategy so far, although Algeria used it profitably in the gas negotiations of the early 1980s by reaching agreements with several of the smaller EC states and then using these agreements as precedents in negotiations with the larger states (Zartman and Bassani 1987).

- *Arguing from weakness.* Arguing from weakness is a negotiation tactic in which the weaker side admits its inability to "win" but raises awareness of the repercussions of its defeat. One target of this tactic would be European constituencies that are especially concerned about and sensitive to the problems of the developing world (such as some left-wing political parties in EC member states and those with a humanitarian interest in the fate of the developing world). But there is also an element of leverage to this tactic: By pointing to their growing populations and economic problems, the countries of the Maghrib can tap into European fears of immigration, sending the message: "You can either help us employ our people at home, or you can employ them yourselves." Some observers have suggested that the demographic and immigration issue may be the most important factor in stimulating greater interest among European states in the Maghrib's economic well-being (Romdhani 1989). In 1991 Tunisian president Ben Ali referred to European concerns over immigration when he proposed the establishment of a special EC fund to finance labor-intensive projects in the Maghrib. The threat of immigration may thus replace the former threat of flirting with the Soviets as the principal bargaining chip in the Maghribi states' relationship with Europe. "Arguing from weakness" should thus not be underestimated as a psychological tactic. Moreover, some have maintained that because of Europe's declining working-age population, European states may actually welcome new immigrants and imported labor (Harris 1988–1989). Nevertheless, growing opposition in Europe to greater immigration from the Maghrib—characterized by the growing political successes of Jean Le Pen's National Front in France and similar anti-immigrant movements in Germany and Italy—means that pursuit of this tactic will, at a minimum, be difficult. Confronted with the option of economic concessions versus increased immigration, the EC states would likely make a cost-benefit calculation, comparing the economic costs of trade concessions with the economic and political costs of allowing freer immigration.

Maghribi Economic Integration or Unity

The option of Maghribi economic integration or unity can be conceived of strategically (in the case of full-fledged unity or economic integration) as well as tactically (in the case of negotiating as a bloc, with or without full political or economic unity). As a strategy, this option would have clear benefits for the Maghrib's relations with the EC. It would help the Maghribi states diversify their production structures, develop their domestic markets, and reduce their dependence on trade with the EC.

On the surface, it would appear that economic integration is at least a viable option: The Maghrib is a fairly large market that will have potentially 75 to 100 million people by the year 2000; the Maghribi economies are relatively well-off compared to other developing countries; and the Maghrib enjoys a considerable degree of potential economic complementarity: Algeria and Libya have energy resources, Morocco and Tunisia agricultural products, and all have the capability to explore joint industrial projects.

The record on Maghribi unity has been less than encouraging (see Chapter 9 for more on this issue). In sum, even in light of recent efforts, economic integration is an issue for the future, for intra-Maghribi trade is currently so small that it would take many years to expand to the levels required to achieve even a minimal degree of economic union.

The tactical aspect of the integration option involves simply negotiating as a bloc with the EC. All of the Maghribi-EC negotiations so far have been bilateral. Creating a common negotiating front, even without economic integration or political unity, could reduce the asymmetry by combining negotiation resources, enhancing each state's commitment by adding to it the commitment of its neighbors and preventing the EC from consecutively playing off one Maghribi state against the others.

Going It Alone

The final option of going it alone is of course the polar opposite of unity and in fact describes the history of Maghribi-EC negotiations up to now. Going it alone has some potential advantages in that it may be easier psychologically for the EC to grant concessions to individual states than to a unified Maghribi bloc. There is also the "leapfrogging" factor: Each state could demand to receive at least the benefits that its neighbors have received and maybe even push for more. Going it alone would be most effective if it were a "coordinated" going it alone, in which the states negotiated with the EC separately but with the objective of comparing notes and building on one another's gains. Such a tactic would in fact be a form of negotiating together.

Conclusion

None of the above options—conceived of either strategically or tactically—offers the Maghribi states a panacea for reversing the asymmetrical nature of their relationship with the EC. No other conclusion is possible, given the structural nature of the asymmetry.

Despite its extreme asymmetry, however, it is nevertheless a symbiotic relationship. The economic deterioration or marginalization of the Maghrib would benefit neither the Maghrib nor Europe. This fact is acknowledged in a recent internal EC report, which asks: "Can the EC—at a moment when it is reinforcing its own political cohesion and economic dynamics—allow the development of such a wide economic and social development gap with its southern neighbors?" (*Middle East International*, February 16, 1990:11).

This rhetorical question alludes to the very serious social and political consequences of continued, or growing, asymmetry between the Maghribi states and Europe. The Mediterranean Sea, much like the Rio Grande in North America, delineates one of the borders between the developed and developing worlds. The EC states are deceiving themselves if they believe that they would be shielded from the effects of political upheaval, religious extremism, and economic disintegration in the Maghrib. Such turbulence would lead not only to greater immigration but to the loss of export markets and possibly a threat to important sources of energy. Demographic trends will only intensify the pressure on Europe to address the effects of the asymmetry. A 1991 United Nations study estimated that by the year 2000, Europeans would represent only one-third of the population living near the Mediterranean, compared to one-half in 1980 and two-thirds in 1945 (*Washington Post*, February 1, 1992:A16).

The EC is increasingly cognizant of the potential dangers inherent in the Maghribi-EC asymmetry. In October 1990, representatives of Spain, Italy, France, and Portugal met with their Maghribi counterparts in Rome to discuss creation of a Conference on Security and Cooperation in the Mediterranean (CSCM), modeled on the Conference on Security and Cooperation in Europe (CSCE). The Italians and Spanish proposed that one-quarter of 1 percent of the combined gross national product (GNP) of the EC states be allocated to a development fund for the Maghrib. In return, the Maghribi states would agree to restrict immigration to the EC (Hitchens 1990).

Yet despite periodic expressions of concern, ultimately the EC, like most political entities, will be guided by short-term self-interest. There is no reason to believe that the EC will unilaterally take steps to alter an imbalance that is so clearly to its economic benefit. The North African states will thus have to adopt a less passive approach in addressing their asymmetrical relationship with the Community; they cannot simply wait for the EC to offer greater concessions and trade benefits.

Perhaps the most important step the Maghribi states could take is to pursue the long road to greater economic, if not political, integration. As one analyst warns, "the EEC has sufficient strength to marginalize the Maghreb if the Maghrebi states fail to agree on an appropriate form of horizontal interdependence" (Ware 1989). For the reasons outlined above, a greater degree of economic interdependence among the states would build up their collective self-sufficiency, thus reducing their asymmetry with and increasing their power vis-à-vis the EC. At a minimum, a coordinated or even unified negotiating posture might strengthen the Maghribi states' bargaining positions.

Individually, the states would benefit from domestic policies of export-led growth, focusing on well-identified sector niches for which markets exist in the EC states and elsewhere. As an EC official points out, "the elimination of customs barriers is not enough to boost exports on its own. It has to be accompanied by energetic measures in the country concerned to develop new exports" (Renier 1988). Greater Maghribi-EC trade should be seen as in the interests of all, for by raising the income level in the Maghrib, it will lead to an expansion of EC exports of both consumer goods and industrial inputs. Such a policy, of course, will offer no guarantee against EC protectionism. Thus, despite the difficulties already alluded to, the Maghribi states should seek other potential export markets.

Similarly, the countries should encourage greater direct foreign investment in their economies by means that protect their economic sovereignty yet offer enticing benefits to the investor. Japanese and other Asian companies, whose direct access to the EC market is more restricted than the Maghrib's, are especially promising candidates for investment in the Maghrib.

The Maghribi states will have to acknowledge that their relationship with the EC will remain one of asymmetry for the immediate future. Their success in adapting to this situation will derive directly from their ability to devise strategies and tactics that utilize their strengths in the relationship: their importance as export markets for certain EC sectors, the energy resources of Algeria and Libya, and the potentially traumatic consequences for Europe of economic and social collapse in the Maghrib.

11

The United States and North Africa

John Damis

American relations with the Maghrib are more notable, perhaps, for their early history than their present significance. In the course of the American Revolution, for example, so many American ships called at Tangier that the Continental Congress found it prudent to seek recognition from the emperor of Morocco, Sultan Mohammed III. Thus it was that in December 1777, Morocco earned the distinction of being the first country to recognize the fledgling American republic, even edging out France, which played such a vital role in aiding the revolution. During the following four decades, to ensure freedom of the seas for its commerce, the United States entered into negotiations with the various ruling authorities along the North African coast. One result of these negotiations was the 1786 Moroccan-American treaty of friendship, the longest unbroken treaty in U.S. history. The need to protect commerce also led to the famous encounters with the Barbary pirates. This military episode is etched in American lore by a refrain in the Marine Corps hymn: "to the shores of Tripoli." Beyond this stirring reference, one can find the beginnings of the U.S. Navy in these early nineteenth-century Mediterranean naval battles.

From the end of the Napoleonic Wars in 1815 until World War II, however, contacts between the United States and the Maghrib were few and far between and of little importance by any standard. This pattern changed dramatically in November 1942 with Operation Torch, the joint U.S.-British military campaign that drove the Axis armies out of North Africa within six months. Since this venture, the U.S. connection with North Africa has been unbroken but uneven in intensity.

What is the Maghrib's place in U.S. foreign relations in the present era? The official government position is that the region is of "key importance" to the United States. In congressional testimony in March 1989, a State Department official argued that because the Maghrib forms the southern shore of the western Mediterranean, it is "vital to the security of southern Europe and to U.S. communications in the Mediterranean."

Key importance and *vital security,* however, are relative terms. Most students of U.S. foreign relations would limit the "vital security" areas of the United States to Western Europe, Latin America, Japan, and perhaps the Persian Gulf. The Maghrib clearly does not belong in this category. It is also obvious that North Africa has considerably less importance for U.S. interests than the Middle East. Unlike the Middle East, the Maghrib—with the occasional exception of Libya—seldom commands front-page attention in the United States. At the same time, however, the Maghrib has greater strategic importance for the United States than west, central, east, or even southern Africa. This suggests that the Maghrib's proper place in U.S. foreign relations is at a third level of importance: behind the vital security areas and the Middle East but ahead of other areas of lesser importance.

In the early 1980s, the Maghrib was somewhat important as a source of U.S. energy needs. In 1981, for example, Libya and Algeria together provided 15 percent of U.S. crude oil imports. For reasons explained later in the chapter, however, neither country has exported crude oil to the United States since 1982 (though the supply of Algerian condensate, or natural gas, has continued). At the same time, the federal government rapidly built the strategic petroleum reserve to protect the country against a sudden cutoff of oil imports. Thus the potential threat by Arab oil producers—Maghribi as well as Middle Eastern—to use oil as a political weapon largely disappeared. U.S. capacity to withstand pressure on energy imported from the Maghrib was demonstrated by the refusal of the administrations of both Jimmy Carter and Ronald Reagan to authorize a renegotiation of a natural gas deal with Algeria that would have sharply raised prices.

Nevertheless, the 1990 Persian Gulf crisis showed that North African oil producers could drive up the price of oil. In August 1990 Libya and Algeria (along with Iran) led a militant group of oil producers that blocked an attempt by Saudi Arabia and Venezuela to convene an emergency meeting of the Organization of Petroleum Exporting Countries. In the absence of an OPEC meeting to stabilize prices, the price of oil increased by over 50 percent within a few weeks—from about $18 a barrel to over $30 a barrel.

Some general observations about U.S. relations with the Maghrib would include the following. First, strategic and political interests have been most important to Washington in its relations with the four countries of North Africa since their independence. This was especially true during the eight years of the Reagan administration, which gave a very high priority to the global-strategic competition between the United States and the Soviet Union. But it was also true, albeit to a lesser extent, with earlier administrations.

A second and related observation is that the United States has tended to view the countries of the Maghrib as either friends or foes and has sometimes taken sides in their regional squabbles. Accordingly, Washington has had a policy of close cooperation with Morocco and Tunisia because their governments have supported Western interests. Relations with Algeria have been correct but not close, despite important bilateral commercial relations; U.S.-Algerian relations have improved to the extent that the Algerians have distanced themselves from the Soviet Union and have played a positive and constructive role in the international arena. At the other end of the spectrum, since the early 1970s, the United States has had poor and sometimes hostile relations with Libya because of the Libyan regime's strident anti-Western orientation and its penchant for foreign and destabilizing interventions; for several years prior to 1982, these poor bilateral relations existed simultaneously with large-scale imports of Libyan crude oil.

Third, the importance of the Maghrib for U.S. interests has been enhanced somewhat in recent years by that area's influence on the Middle East. The focus of mainstream Palestinian decisionmaking is now in Tunisia, not Lebanon, Syria, or Jordan. With the Palestine Liberation Organization (PLO) headquarters in Tunis, the U.S.-PLO dialogue, begun in early 1989 and suspended in mid-1990, increased the importance of Tunisia for U.S. efforts to promote the Middle East peace process. In addition, Morocco is the frequent host for Arab League summits, and the leaders of Morocco and Algeria compose two-thirds of the Arab League Committee formed in May 1989 to resolve the Lebanese conflict.

Finally, the basic approach of U.S. diplomacy with the Maghrib has been to focus on bilateral relations with each of the four North African countries. There has been little effort to fashion a regional approach to the area—an approach that might allow the United States to step back from one-sided involvement in regional disputes. The structure of this chapter reflects the operation of U.S. diplomacy as I examine successively U.S. relations with Morocco, Algeria, Tunisia, and Libya.

Morocco

Though much has been made of Morocco's early recognition of America, of far greater importance are the close bilateral political relations that have developed since the late 1960s and the close military relations that date from the mid-1970s. U.S. interests in Morocco derive from two basic factors: its geographic location and its orientation in global politics.

Morocco is strategically located at the western end of the Mediterranean Sea. If Morocco were someday controlled by a regime hostile to Western interests, freedom of passage through the Straits of Gibraltar could be threatened in a crisis. This could make the U.S. Sixth Fleet a hostage in the Mediterranean and could seriously undermine the United States' ability to assist such allies as Spain, France, Italy, Greece, and Turkey. Because of Morocco's strategic position, Washington has a vested interest in keeping a friendly government in Rabat.

The two countries also tend to line up on the same side of a broad spectrum of international political issues. For example, Morocco consistently condemned the Soviet Union's 1979 invasion of, and subsequent military involvement in, Muslim Afghanistan. Washington and the moderate government of King Hassan II shared much the same assessment of the destabilizing potential in Africa of Cuba and the Soviet Union. Beyond its official pronouncements and votes in international forums, Rabat supplied training and weapons to the National Union for the Total Independence of Angola (UNITA), which resisted the control of the Cuban-backed Marxist government in Angola. And in both 1977 and 1978, King Hassan dispatched 1,500 Moroccan troops who proved effective in helping to repel invasions of Zaire's mineral-rich Shaba province by Angola-based rebels.

Washington values Rabat's pragmatic approach to Middle East issues and its commitment to a negotiated solution of the Arab-Israeli conflict. King Hassan helped arrange and initially supported the peace efforts of President Anwar Sadat of Egypt before falling in line with the general Arab condemnation of the 1979 Egyptian-Israeli peace treaty. In Washington's view, Hassan has worked constructively in his capacities as chairman of the Arab Summit, the Organization of the Islamic Conference (OIC), and, since 1979, the OIC's Higher Committee for the Liberation of al-Quds, the so-called Jerusalem Commmittee. In these capacities, the king has lobbied effectively for the reintegration of Egypt—an important friend of the United States—into the Arab world. In late 1987, following authorization by the Arab League, Rabat hastened to reestablish full relations with Cairo. More recently, in August 1990 in the wake of the Iraqi invasion of Kuwait, Morocco voted at the emergency Arab summit in Cairo in favor of an Arab deterrent force to defend Saudi Arabia against a possible Iraqi attack. At the same time, King Hassan sent a "limited symbolic contingent" of 1,200 troops to Saudi Arabia plus a force of comparable size to the United Arab Emirates, where Morocco has had a training detachment of 600 since 1988.

Almost alone in the Arab world, Morocco has taken concrete steps to improve relations with the Jewish community both within the country and abroad. In 1984 the Moroccan government received a high-level delegation of thirty-five Israelis, marking the first time since the founding of the Jewish state in 1948 that an Arab state other than Egypt had received an official delegation from Israel. In July 1986 Hassan went so far as to host a two-day visit by Prime Minister Shimon Peres. Though the visit did not produce a breakthrough in the Middle East peace process, the king's invitation to Peres marked the first public meeting between an Arab leader and an Israeli prime minister since 1981.

Bilateral relations between Morocco and the United States were strengthened in the course of visits to Washington by King Mohammed V in 1957 and by King Hassan on several occasions since 1963. During the Reagan administration, U.S.-Moroccan relations entered a period of exceptionally close cooperation evidenced by reciprocal high-level visits. Since 1987 this pattern has continued with visits by Secretary of Defense Frank Carlucci in 1988, Joint Chiefs of Staff Chairman Admiral William Crowe in 1989, and Secretary of Defense Dick Cheney in 1990.

The United States has tried to protect and promote its interests in Morocco through grants and loans of economic and military assistance. From the time of Morocco's independence from France in 1956 to 1991, U.S. assistance totaled over $2 billion, including over $1 billion in grants. As Table 11.1 shows, U.S. aid to Morocco ranged from $50 million to $152 million a year during the twelve-year period from 1980 to 1991. Though the totals have since declined from the peak levels of 1983–1985, it is important for Morocco that the percentage of grants has more than doubled from about 33 percent for the years 1980–1983 to 72 percent for fiscal year 1990.

U.S.-Moroccan military cooperation is extensive and includes an important military supply relationship. Since the mid-1970s, the United States has become, behind France, a major source of military weaponry for Morocco. Morocco has signed agreements to purchase about $1.2 billion worth of U.S. arms under the Foreign Military Sales (FMS) program, plus about $130 million worth of commercial arms. The FMS deliveries have included M-48 tanks, F-5 jet fighters, Bronco armed reconnaissance planes, Hughes helicopters, and Maverick air-to-ground missiles. In 1980–1981, the United States proposed to sell Morocco 108 M-60 tanks. In the end, this highly publicized deal never materialized because of budget constraints on the Moroccan side. Instead, Morocco agreed in 1987 to buy 100 M-48 tanks released by the California National Guard, and these reconditioned tanks were delivered in 1988. Since 1985 Rabat has been interested in buying two squadrons of F-16 jet fighters to replace its aging F-5s but thus far has been unable to obtain the outside financial assistance necessary for the $550 million package deal.

During the Carter administration, the arms supply relationship became strained over the issue of the Western Sahara, which Rabat considers to be part of Morocco. Because the United States did not recognize Moroccan sovereignty in the Western Sahara, the Carter administration took the position that Morocco could not use U.S.-supplied arms intended for internal security and legitimate self-defense in the disputed territory. In 1978 the United States imposed arms sales restrictions on Morocco. King Hassan made it clear to Washington at that time that continued U. S. military aid was the price of Moroccan friendship.

TABLE 11.1 U.S. Foreign Assistance to Morocco, Fiscal Years 1980–1991 (in millions of dollars)

	1980	1981	1982	1983	1984	1985	1986	1987	1988	1989	1990	1991 (requested)
Development assistance (grant)	9.1	12.1	11.7	11.2	19.4	23.3	20.3	17.8	12.5	12.5	11.5	12.5
Economic support funds (grant)	0.0	0.0	0.0	0.0	7.0	15.0	16.5	10.1	20.0	20.0	20.0	12.0
Public Law 480, Title 1 (loan)	5.8	25.0	35.0	27.5	45.0	55.0	40.0	56.0	36.0	44.0	35.0	35.0
Public Law 480, Title 2 (grant)	9.9	16.1	13.4	12.7	9.8	10.1	5.8	12.5	12.8	14.7	15.7	4.0
Foreign military sales (guaranteed loan)	25.0	33.4	30.0	75.0	38.8	8.0	0.9	12.0	12.0	0.0	0.0	0.0
Military assistance program (grant)	0.0	0.0	0.0	25.0	30.0	40.0	33.5	32.0	40.0	52.0	42.8	40.0
International Military Education and Training Program (IMET) (grant)	0.9	1.0	1.1	1.3	1.6	1.5	1.4	1.5	1.0	1.0	0.9	1.0
Total	50.7	87.6	91.2	152.7	151.6	152.9	118.4	141.9	134.3	144.2	125.9	104.5
Total grant	19.9	29.2	26.2	50.2	67.8	89.9	77.5	73.9	86.3	100.2	90.9	69.5
Percent grant	39	33	29	33	45	59	65	52	64	69	72	67

Source: U.S. Department of State, Bureau of Near Eastern and South Asian Affairs, Office of North African Affairs.

Tensions eased in 1979 when the Sahara war spilled over into southern Morocco. The Carter administration concluded that Morocco, a trusted and supported ally, faced a threat to its internal security, and it approved a $235 million arms package eagerly sought by Rabat. In defending this arms package in Congress in early 1980, the Carter administration identified the avoidance of a Moroccan military defeat in the Sahara as a major U.S. interest.

When it came to power in 1981, the Reagan administration identified Morocco as one of "America's traditional and historic friends" and declared that its policy was to support such allies. It then proceeded to remove the limitation on arms sales to Morocco and greatly expanded bilateral military and security cooperation. In late 1981, for example, Rabat requested additional U.S. military assistance to counter Soviet-made SA-6 missile systems introduced into battle by the guerrilla forces of the Polisario Front who were fighting for an independent Saharan state. The United States agreed to provide Morocco with such help as training in evasive flying tactics and electronic countermeasure equipment.

U.S.-Moroccan military and security cooperation reached a new level in 1982 with the establishment of a joint military commission in February and the signing of a facilities access agreement in May, following King Hassan's official state visit to Washington. The agreement involves transit rights that would allow U.S. military planes to land and refuel at two Moroccan air bases during emergencies in the Middle East and Africa. Rabat retains a veto over the transit of U.S. forces if they are to be used against an Arab country friendly to Morocco. Because of Moroccan sensitivity on the subject, the text of the agreement was not made public. The new level of military cooperation was accompanied by greater U.S. financial assistance (see Table 11.1).

Moroccan ports are generally open to visits by the Sixth Fleet, and Rabat has not raised questions about nuclear-powered or nuclear-armed ships. Morocco has allowed overflights of its territory by U.S. military aircraft. The U.S. Marines have conducted amphibious landing exercises, and U.S. and Moroccan forces have held extensive joint maneuvers on several occasions. To help Morocco in its war in the Western Sahara, the United States reportedly supplied satellite photographs of Polisario Front bases in the desert and offered the use of aircraft equipped with special radar to follow troop movements. Of benefit to the U.S. military, the Moroccans supplied intelligence on Soviet weapons captured in the Sahara (Parker 1984:143). Finally, Morocco has offered to serve as an alternate landing site for the space shuttle in case of emergency.

In contrast to the important bilateral military relationship, U.S.-Moroccan commercial relations have been—and remain—modest. During the 1970s, private U.S. investment in Morocco ranged from $40 million to $60 million, and by 1988 it had declined to $26 million. The United States accounts for only about 6 percent of Morocco's foreign trade. Because of the importance of the French language in Morocco's commercial life, the country's imports have long centered on French products. In addition, there is very little complementarity between the U.S. and Moroccan economies: Morocco's major export is agricultural produce, and the country is the world's largest exporter of phosphates, whereas the United States is the world's largest agricultural exporter and the largest producer of phosphates.

U.S. relations with Morocco were jolted in August 1984 when King Hassan suddenly signed an agreement with Libya establishing the Arab-African Federation for close economic, social, defense, and political cooperation. A specific concern in Washington was that Libya would thus have access to U.S. arms supplied to Morocco (Parker 1985; Damis 1985). Within a few months, the uproar in Washington over the treaty had largely blown over, however. The Reagan administration wisely chose to take a wait-and-see position; instead of lashing out against Morocco, it lowered its response to one of merely warning Rabat not to trust the Libyan government. An uneasy two-year period in U.S.-Moroccan relations ended abruptly in August 1986, when King Hassan abrogated the treaty of union.

The one prominent issue remaining in U.S.-Moroccan relations is Morocco's continuing war in the Western Sahara. Washington has tried to avoid any direct involvement in the conflict, which it views as a regional issue that requires a regional solution. Partially as a result of U.S. military assistance, Moroccan forces have gradually gained the upper hand on the battlefield. Although the United States has no interests in the Western Sahara, Washington is anxious to avoid a Moroccan defeat that could threaten the stability of King Hassan's regime or produce a new, radical regime on Morocco's southern border. As the level of fighting in the Sahara escalated during the 1980s, U.S. military involvement deepened to the point where the two countries now share military intelligence. The task of U.S. diplomacy is to stand by a friendly country in its time of need without being drawn into the Sahara conflict and without giving an impression to the rest of the world of full and open-ended U.S. support of Morocco's war. U.S. policy under George Bush welcomed diplomatic efforts led by UN secretaries general Javier Pérez de Cuéllar and Boutros Boutros Ghali to organize a referendum in 1992 to decide the future of the Western Sahara.

Algeria

U.S.-Algerian relations are just the reverse of those with Morocco: Priority is given to economic considerations rather than political and strategic ties. Because of its successful anticolonial revolution, Algeria is highly respected in the Third World and is, among North African countries, by far the most influential in the international arena. It has been a strong supporter of national liberation movements in general and the Polisario Front in particular. Its economic orientation has been socialist, at least until recent efforts to decentralize and restructure the economy, and it was an architect in 1974 of the New International Economic Order. From Algiers, the United States has been seen as the most powerful capitalist country in the world and the leader of the "haves" on North-South issues. Often, the United States and Algeria are diametrically opposed on international political and economic issues. Political relations between the two countries, therefore, are correct but not close.

Because Algerians do not mix politics and economics, however, large-scale commercial relations have developed between the two countries since the mid-1970s. In 1977 the United States replaced France as Algeria's principal trading partner and absorbed nearly half of Algeria's exports, including 56 percent of its crude oil and 28 percent of its liquefied natural gas. The value of Algerian imports to the United States reached a high of $6.6 billion in 1980 and oil imports peaked at 500,000 barrels a day in January 1981. In 1987, though no longer Algeria's leading trading partner, the United States remained Algeria's leading client, with purchases totaling $2.1 billion; and in 1988 the United States absorbed an estimated 29 percent of Algerian exports.

Algerian natural gas also has made important inroads into the U.S. market, although deliveries under a major contract were halted in 1980 because of a price disagreement. Algeria insisted that the price of its gas be tied to that of crude oil, which made Algerian gas considerably more expensive than gas imported from Canada. By 1986, faced with the harsh realities of the world market, the Algerians became more realistic and began to adopt a more flexible pricing policy. Outstanding disputes with two U.S. firms were finally resolved the next year. In late 1988 Cabot Corporation signed an agreement to import Algerian liquefied natural gas. And in early 1989 Algeria reentered the U.S. natural gas market with Washington's approval of the sale of Algerian natural gas to Boston's Distrigas, a subsidiary of Cabot. The Bush administration welcomed the sale as part of the goal of diversifying U.S. energy sources (see Zartman and Bassani 1987).

Completing this commercial relationship, since the mid-1970s, U.S. firms have signed contracts worth $6 billion with Algerian state-owned companies to provide technology and construction for Algeria's extensive development efforts. By the mid-1980s, however, the value of contracts was down to between $1 billion and $2 billion; a large part of this difference resulted from the suspension of liquefied natural gas contracts.

U.S.-Algerian relations improved after the more moderate regime of Chadli Benjedid took office in early 1979. These relations benefited from Algeria's displeasure with the massive Soviet intervention in Afghanistan. In 1980–1981 Algeria played an effective mediating role to help bring an end to the hostage crisis between the United States and Iran. The first U.S. naval visit to an Algerian port in seventeen years took place in 1980 and led to the first invitation to Algerian military officers to visit the United States.

Nonetheless, the improvement in U.S.-Algerian relations has been slow and uneven. At the time of the hostage crisis, Algerian leaders expressed their desire for better and closer relations with the United States. They were resentful, however, when the Reagan administration approved a major tank sale to Morocco as one of its first foreign policy moves. In the following years, the Reagan administration tried to be more responsive and sensitive to Algeria's continuing evolution from revolutionary policies to relative international maturity. Between 1981 and 1984, Washington allowed the sale to Algeria of a total of seventeen Lockheed C-130 Hercules military transport planes worth about $300 million. In addition, between 1981 and 1983, the Algerian military purchased 4,000 heavy-duty trucks from American Motors.

One impediment to improved relations was the lingering perception of Algeria as a radical state. This perception derives from the former strident tone of Algeria's anti-imperialist rhetoric, Algerian support for Saddam Hussein in Iraq, the frequently identical Algerian and Soviet positions on international issues, and Moscow's position as the supplier of about 90 percent of Algeria's military equipment. The image of Algeria as a Soviet client state, however, is a gross misrepresentation. Algeria is a fiercely independent country that categorically refuses to be beholden to any outside power; it has not permitted Soviet bases on its territory, although Soviet vessels are allowed to make port calls. Though Algiers abstained on the annual UN General Assembly resolutions that called for the withdrawal of foreign troops from Afghanistan, in 1984 it voted in favor of a resolution by the Organization of the Islamic Conference calling for the withdrawal of Soviet troops from Afghanistan and in subsequent years voted for similar resolutions adopted by the Arab League.

The improvement in U.S.-Algerian relations has been most noticeable since 1983, when Algeria was made eligible to purchase defense services—that is, training—from the United States. Also in 1983, Vice-President Bush became the highest-ranking U.S. official ever to visit Algiers. Despite the disagreement at that time over natural gas prices, Algiers wanted to expand economic contacts with the United States in other areas. Secretary of Agriculture John Block visited Algeria in 1984 to sign the first agricultural aid agreement between the two countries.

In the aftermath of Morocco's 1984 treaty of union with Libya, Algiers saw a new opportunity to improve relations with Washington. In April 1985 President Benjedid made the first official visit to the United States by an Algerian chief of state since the nation achieved independence in 1962. Just prior to this visit, President Reagan made Algeria eligible for the first time to purchase U.S. arms under the FMS program. During the six-day visit, the two leaders held wide-ranging discussions that added a new element of warmth to U.S.-Algerian relations. Two months later, Algeria agreed to purchase 1 million tons of U.S. wheat at subsidized prices. And that same month, Algeria earned U.S. gratitude for helping to negotiate the release of hostages aboard a hijacked TWA flight.

Since the 1985 Benjedid visit, U.S.-Algerian relations have continued on a fairly even keel, with both sides open to possibilities of gradual improvements. These prospects are explored through occasional high-level visits in both directions. Military sales and training programs thus far have been quite modest. The United States has expanded military cooperation with Algeria in small increments, with an eye to encouraging Algeria's goal of diversifying its sources of military equipment and supplies from the Soviet Union. Like their Moroccan neighbors, the Algerians would like to purchase advanced fighter aircraft but are partially constrained from doing so by budget deficits and by reluctance in both Congress and the executive branch to offend the Moroccans. In any event, a major U.S. arms transfer to Algeria is far in the future. For the present, both sides agree on a step-by-step approach to military relations.

In the wake of the bloody riots that shook Algeria in October 1988, the United States made clear its support of Benjedid and his efforts at economic reform and political liberalization. The executive branch accelerated and expanded technical assistance programs. These programs involved agricultural development projects, feed grain projects, and technical assistance in forestry. Most importantly, the Department of Agriculture provided $750 million in credit guarantees for Algerian purchases of U.S. wheat and other agricultural commodities. The United States welcomed Algeria's first open multiparty elections, held in June 1990. More recently, however, the Bush administration deplored the military takeover in January 1992 that forced Benjedid to resign, cancelled the second round of parliamentary elections, and declared illegal the first round held in December 1991.

Despite improvement in bilateral relations, the United States and Algeria continue to disagree on some international issues, such as relations with Libya and Iraq and a constructive approach to the search for peace in the Middle East. Nonetheless, U.S.-Algerian relations are considerably better than they were during the 1960s and 1970s.

Tunisia

If U.S.-Moroccan relations are important and close and U.S.-Algerian relations are important but not so close, U.S. relations with Tunisia are close but not so important. The United States and Tunisia have nearly always been friendly. A small country with modest resources surrounded by larger and more powerful neighbors, Tunisia necessarily seeks to avoid disputes. The country's pragmatic governments have looked to the United States (and France) for development assistance and occasional shows of force against neighboring Libya. Although Washington has no economic stake in Tunisia, it wants to assist the most moderate country in the Arab world. At the geostrategic level, a strong Tunisia helps to maintain stability along the coast of North Africa to protect the southern flank of the North Atlantic Treaty Organization (NATO).

Before 1980, the United States mainly provided Tunisia with economic assistance, as President Habib Bourguiba kept his country's military down to a very modest size. Total U.S. economic aid to Tunisia since independence in 1956 is over $1 billion; U.S. officials have often cited Tunisia as a model of successful aid-assisted economic development.

Bourguiba's sensible approach to internal development was overtaken by national security concerns in 1980 when Libya organized an armed attack against the Tunisian mining town of Gafsa to spark an uprising against the government. Tunisian leaders had been trying for several years to improve the defensive capabilities of their country's 28,000-man military force, and in 1980–1981 they turned to the United States for help. The Reagan administration responded with about $100 million in military aid annually from 1982 to 1984; these funds went toward the purchase of U.S.-made M-60 tanks, a squadron of F-5 jet fighters, ground-to-air missiles, a radar system, coastal patrol boats, helicopters, and armored personnel carriers. There were grounds for criticizing the nature of the arms acquired, which were poorly suited to deal with internal subversion, but the choice of weapon systems came from Tunis, not Washington.

Washington responded once again to Tunisia's appeal for help after nine days of violent bread riots swept the country at the end of 1983 and during the first week of 1984. The Reagan administration quickly pledged additional food assistance; Congress increased economic support funds for the country from $1.5 million in fiscal year 1984 to $20 million in fiscal year 1985. At the same time, the U.S. Agency for International Development (USAID) made a decision in mid-1984 to continue economic assistance to Tunisia. This reversed a decision in 1981 to phase out the USAID program in Tunisia over five years on the grounds that the country had reached a level of economic development—$1,400 annual per capita income—that no longer justified U.S. funding.

Military aid levels for Tunisia since 1985 have been reduced considerably from their peak during 1982–1984. At the same time, however, more of this assistance has been either grant aid or aid at concessional rates. And the total U.S. security and economic assistance for Tunisia during the twelve-year period from 1979 to 1990—over $1 billion—is sizable for a relatively small country of 8 million people. The United States' ongoing concern for Tunisia's national security was reflected in 1990, when Congress appropriated a grant for $30 million in foreign military funds to promote stability, enhance combined U.S.-Tunisian military exercises, and sustain existing military infrastructure.

The usually harmonious relations between the United States and Tunisia were temporarily strained in October 1985 following a devastating Israeli air raid on PLO headquarters near Tunis. When Washington initially backed Israel's right to respond to terrorism, President Bourguiba expressed his "profound regret and great astonishment" at the U.S. reaction and sponsored a UN Security Council resolution condemning the air attack. Bourguiba's sentiments, in fact, reflected an enormous outcry in Tunisia and throughout the Arab world against the U.S. position. The Reagan administration prudently abstained when the Security Council resolution came to a vote out of concern that a U.S. veto would set off riots in Tunisia by Libyan-backed leftists that would threaten Bourguiba's moderate, pro-Western regime. Bilateral relations were further complicated a few days later when Egypt accused Tunisia of colluding with the United States in the capture of four Palestinian gunmen who had hijacked the Italian cruise ship *Achille Lauro*.

Washington welcomed Prime Minister Ben Ali's smooth transition to power in 1987 and his moves to open up the political system and improve human rights. In particular, the U.S. government approved of Ben Ali's commitment to continue the comprehensive economic reform program initiated in late 1986 (a program analyzed in Chapter 7). The Reagan administration encouraged the economic reform program in 1988 by allowing Tunisia to refinance $196 million of its military debt.

Bilateral economic cooperation has proceeded in several areas since the Bush administration came into office in January 1989. A bilateral tax treaty was initiated, renegotiated, and amended in 1989. In May 1990 President Ben Ali traveled to Washington, the first North African head of state to visit the United States during the Bush administration. During Ben Ali's stay, the two countries signed a bilateral investment treaty. A few weeks earlier, Tunisia had acceded to the General Agreement on Tariffs and Trade. These developments reflected Tunisia's efforts to create a favorable environment for foreign investment; in addition, the U.S.-Tunisian Joint Commission on Trade and Investment was revived in 1989 after ten years of disuse and was active in helping Tunisia to solicit U.S. investment. In this area, Citibank opened a full operating branch in Tunis in 1989, and General Motors began assembly of Opels and Isuzus at its plant in Kairouan in spring 1991.

The United States and Tunisia have agreed to disagree about how to deal with Libya, but relations soured over how to deal with Iraq. Tunisia received a great financial boon after it resumed relations with Libya in December 1987. Libya allowed back some Tunisian workers, who send remittances home, and 1 million Libyan tourists visited Tunisia in 1988, contributing to the country's first current account surplus in many years. At the same time, Washington warned Tunisia against giving Libya opportunities to promote unrest.

The difference over Iraqi policy was more serious and led to a sharp reduction of U.S. aid to Tunisia in 1991. It is likely that the crisis will pass, however.

When Bourguiba was deposed after thirty-one years in power, there was concern in Washington that U.S.-Tunisian relations would suffer because of the removal of an old and reliable friend. Since taking over as head of state, Ben Ali has tried to raise the Arab and Islamic profile of Tunisia in recognition that Bourguiba's secular and Westernized orientation was somewhat at odds with basic Tunisian values. At the same time, however, Ben Ali has maintained his country's firm ties with the West. As a result, all aspects of U.S. relations with Tunisia—diplomatic, political, economic, military—are likely to stabilize.

Libya

U.S.-Libyan relations are poor. What is more, bilateral relations have been poor for at least fifteen years and, short of a change in government in Tripoli, are unlikely to improve much in the immediate future. The source of friction has little to do with what happens inside Libya, where U.S. business personnel and their families are treated very well. The problems stem, in Washington's eyes, from the destructive and destabilizing nature of Qadhafi's actions on the international scene.

Throughout the 1970s, successive U.S. administrations declined to improve relations with Libya for two reasons: the Qadhafi regime's support of international terrorist activities and its opposition to a negotiated solution of the Arab-Israeli conflict. The Nixon administration reduced diplomatic representation in Tripoli to the level of chargé in late 1972. For the next several years, Washington refused to approve delivery of eight C-130 military transport planes that Tripoli had purchased from Lockheed for $48 million. In December 1979 the Libyan government stood by when the U.S. embassy in Tripoli was attacked and badly damaged. Following this attack, the Carter administration withdrew all diplomatic personnel, closed the embassy, and reduced diplomatic relations to the lowest level. In May 1981 the Reagan administration ordered the Libyan diplomatic mission in Washington to leave the country because of Libya's involvement in acts of violence. Since 1981 Belgium has represented U.S. interests in Tripoli, whereas the United Arab Emirates has represented Libyan interests in Washington.

The Reagan administration raised opposition to Libya to the level of active confrontation. President Reagan called Qadhafi "the mad dog of the Middle East" and "the most dangerous man in the world." Secretary of State Alexander Haig singled out Libya for its interventionist activities, and Vice-President Bush labeled Qadhafi "the world's principal terrorist and trainer of terrorists."

In August 1981 the United States directly challenged Libya's claim to the entire Gulf of Sidra as Libyan territorial waters by holding well-publicized naval maneuvers within the gulf. A clash ensued when two U.S. F-14s from the U.S.S. *Nimitz* shot down two Soviet-made SU-22s piloted by Libyans after the Libyans opened fire. Tensions between the two countries increased further in autumn 1981, when the White House revealed reports that a Libyan hit squad planned to enter the country to assassinate President Reagan. In December Reagan asked all Americans to leave Libya as soon as possible, and the government soon announced that U.S. passports would no longer be valid for travel to Libya. Not all Americans living and working in Libya heeded this call, but in the two years that followed, their number fell from about 2,000 to an estimated 600.

Before 1982, poor U.S.-Libyan relations did not interfere with the flourishing trade between the two countries. In March 1982, however, the Reagan administration imposed a boycott on the importation of petroleum products from Libya and established a license requirement for most U.S. exports to that country. The boycott dramatically reduced the total value of Libyan products exported to the United States, from a high of $8.6 billion in 1980 to only $824,000 in 1983. Licensing caused U.S. exports to Libya to fall from a high of $813 million in 1981 to $200 million in 1984 (IMF 1988a). Still, there was continuing U.S. business involvement in two major construction projects in Libya, the "Great Manmade River"—a 2,800-km (1,300-mile) pipeline to bring subterranean water from the Sahara to the coastal area of Libya for irrigation and urban use—and an oil refinery at Ras Lanuf. In March 1984, however, Reagan announced that there would be no more U.S. exports for the Ras Lanuf project.

The opposition of the Reagan administration to the Libyan government derived from four main factors. The first is Qadhafi's support of international terrorism as pursued by the Irish Republican Army, Corsican and Basque separatists, and the Abu Nidal group. Tripoli established a series of camps where training in terrorist tactics has been given to foreign revolutionaries, and Libyan hit squads have assassinated a number of exiled opponents of the regime in several foreign countries.

Second has been Libya's implacable hostility to Israel and to a negotiated settlement of the Arab-Israeli conflict. In 1978 Qadhafi pushed for the creation of the radical Arab Steadfastness Front, which rejected Egypt's separate peace with Israel. In 1983 Libya actively joined Syria to promote a rebel faction within the PLO that challenged the moderate leadership of Chairman Yasir Arafat.

Third, Libya repeatedly attempted to undermine the stability of moderate African states. In February 1983 Qadhafi tried to organize a coup to overthrow the government of the Sudan. The prompt deployment of U.S. AWACS (airborne warning and control system) aircraft and Egyptian F-5s blocked the coup. Libya also blatantly intervened in Chad, Niger, Tunisia, and Somalia, either with direct military force or by supplying arms and money to insurgent groups, and provided generous assistance to radical regimes in Ethiopia, Benin, Uganda, and Ghana.

Finally, the Sandinista victory in Nicaragua and the guerrilla war in El Salvador encouraged an activist Libyan involvement in the United States' own backyard. Qadhafi (FBIS 1983) made clear his objective of undermining the U.S. position in Central America in a speech in September 1983: "When we ally ourselves with revolution in Latin America, and particularly Central America, we are defending ourselves. This satan [the United States] must be clipped and we must take war to the American borders just as America is taking threats to the Gulf of Sidra." During the 1980s, Libya provided large amounts of arms, money, and training to Nicaragua and the Farabundo Martí movement in El Salvador, and important economic aid to Cuba. The Reagan administration was especially annoyed with Libya's growing supply of arms to Nicaragua. Smaller amounts of Libyan assistance have gone to a variety of leftist groups elsewhere in Latin America (U.S. Department of State 1983, 1986, 1989).

During 1986, U.S.-Libyan relations deteriorated to their lowest level yet as the two countries engaged in armed hostilities. In January, citing "irrefutable evidence" of Libya's involvement in Palestinian guerrilla attacks at the Rome and Vienna airports ten days earlier, Reagan called Libya "a threat to the national security and foreign policy of the United States." In March, during maneuvers in the Gulf of Sidra, U.S. forces sunk three Libyan patrol boats and twice attacked a Libyan missile site. Then in April, accusing Libya of complicity in a bomb explosion that ravaged a West Berlin nightclub frequented by U.S. servicemen, the Reagan administration launched a coordinated air attack against selected Libyan military targets.

World reaction to the U.S. air raid, in which more than thirty civilians were killed, was generally critical. The Soviet Union cancelled a planned meeting between its foreign minister and Secretary of State George Shultz. Western European governments, which tend to value their commercial ties with Libya, criticized both the attack and the British for their involvement in it. By contrast, most Americans supported the raid and expressed disappointment and sometimes bitterness at the lack of support by key U.S. allies. At the same time, Arab countries gave only lip service to Libya's complaints.

The intent of the April 1986 air attack was to moderate Libyan activities abroad and spark an internal move against Qadhafi, but the effects of the raid fell short of these objectives. Dissident officers within Libya did not attempt to overthrow Qadhafi; on the contrary, Libyans of all political persuasions rallied around the flag in the wake of a foreign attack. There is some evidence that Qadhafi was emotionally shaken for a few months by the raid; the extent of the attack's impact on Qadhafi, however, remains questionable. By October 1986, it was revealed that the Reagan administration had leaked false information to persuade Qadhafi that another U.S. attack was imminent and to suggest that he was in grave danger of being overthrown by dissident elements within Libya. The Libyans still support a variety of international terrorist organizations.

Periodically during 1987 and 1988, Libya expressed interest in improving relations with the United States. Qadhafi has a tendency to personalize bilateral relations and thus was optimistic that the two countries would get along better after Reagan left office. This view overlooked the obvious record of U.S.-Libyan problems that long predated the Reagan administration. In any event, the administration showed no interest in a dialogue or deal with Libya. At the same time, U.S. support in 1987 for Chad in its war with Libya was tied, at least in part, to the belief that a Libyan military defeat would lead to Qadhafi's overthrow. In January 1988, asserting that the Qadhafi regime still backed various terrorist groups around the world, Washington extended again the 1986 economic sanctions against Libya. And during fall 1988, the Reagan administration conducted an escalating international press and diplomatic campaign against the construction and near completion of a large-scale Libyan chemical weapons complex near Rabta, about 80 km (50 miles) southwest of Tripoli.

The Reagan administration left office in January 1989 with Libya high on its foreign policy agenda. Yet another military encounter occurred early in the month when two F-14 warplanes from a U.S. carrier on routine patrol in the Mediterranean shot down two approaching Soviet-made Libyan MiG-23s. The incident took place in the highly charged atmosphere produced by the Rabta complex charges and countercharges. Finally, on his last full day in office, President Reagan authorized the five U.S. oil companies in Libya to resume their operations without U.S. personnel or equipment, transfer them to foreign subsidiaries, or sell their assets. The move was intended to head off the potential nationalization of the five companies' large investment—estimated at between $2 billion and $4 billion—and to end the "significant windfall profits" Libya had reaped since the 1986 sanctions. When the sanctions were imposed, the administration authorized the oil companies to negotiate "standstill" agreements. The final Reagan decision allowed the companies to avoid defaulting on their agreements before their expiration in mid-1989.

During the Bush administration, Qadhafi tried to emphasize an element of moderation. In June 1989 he embarked on a reconciliation with Egypt. Libyan willingness to drop its irredentist demands over the Palestinian issue and its opposition to Egypt's peace treaty with Israel made possible the restoration of good relations between Tripoli and Cairo. At the same time, Qadhafi extended negotiations with U.S. oil companies over oil concessions and called the Bush administration "reasonable and mature." Later, in summer 1989, the Libyan leader began to cut off or trim funding for some seventy different liberation and terrorist groups; this included reduced Libyan support for Palestinian extremist organizations, particularly the Abu Nidal group.

Despite the Libyan "charm offensive," the Bush administration saw little significant change in Libyan behavior. If the Bush administration did not feel the same level of anxiety over Libyan foreign policy as did the Reagan administration, differences in U.S. policy after January 1989 were more in tone than in substance. U.S. officials cited eleven examples of Libyan destabilization activities in Africa during the first half of 1989, plus unresolved questions about the Rabta chemical weapons complex (Wayne 1989). In January 1990 President Bush renewed the economic sanctions Reagan had imposed against Libya in 1986, including a ban on travel. In March Bush administration officials charged that the Libyan plant at Rabta had renewed production of small amounts of mustard gas and perhaps other chemical weapons in late 1989. It was subsequently proven that in late May Libya provided support to the Palestinian Liberation Front, led by Abul Abbas, for its aborted attack on an Israeli beach. In June 1990 the position of the Reagan and Bush administrations on the Rabta plant was vindicated when a West German court sent to prison a West German businessman responsible for secretly selling a chemical production plant to Libya for $150 million. In August 1990 Washington alleged that Libya was supplying chemical warfare equipment by air to Iraq. In November 1991 the United States indicted two Libyan intelligence agents for their role in the 1988 bombing of Pan Am Flight 103 over Lockerbie, Scotland, that caused 270 deaths. In January 1992 the United States cosponsored with Britain and France a UN Security Council resolution that asked Libya to turn over the suspects for trial. At the end of March, Washington led the push for the adoption of a more forceful UN resolution that responded to Qadhafi's refusal to turn over the suspects by imposing air, military, and diplomatic sanctions against Libya; these sanctions took effect in mid-April. There would be no change of U.S. policy until there was a genuine change of Libya's policy—and none was expected any time soon.

Conclusion

In what directions are U.S. relations with the Maghrib heading? The safest approach in forecasting future international relations is to suggest that the future will most resemble a continuation of the present. And with U.S.–North African relations, such a case can certainly be made.

The broad and deep community of interests that link the United States and Morocco, for example, are likely to ensure that Morocco will remain the most important North African country for the United States. If Algeria continues to liberalize both its economy and political system, relations with the United States hold promise of continuing improvement. The solid basis of close U.S.-

Tunisian relations will survive the short-term strains that may develop from specific problems in coming years.

Because conditions for improvement are unlikely to be met, poor U.S.-Libyan relations will continue, as will the annual renewal of the 1986 sanctions against Libya. U.S. efforts to rally European and African states to oppose and isolate the Qadhafi regime are also likely to persist. Students of Arab politics and U.S. foreign policy might well question the wisdom of an activist U.S. approach in dealing with a national leader like Qadhafi, who thrives on confrontation. A more effective way of handling the Libyan leader may be simply to ignore him while protecting his threatened victims. Qadhafi's enemies are legion, and at some future moment at least some of them will find a way to move against him. If Washington is not involved in Qadhafi's overthrow, the new Libyan leaders will have a freer hand in establishing good relations with the United States.

Some current issues in U.S.–North African relations cut across the national boundaries of the Maghrib. One is the phenomenon of Islamic fundamentalism, with its obvious political implications. U.S. policymakers find themselves wrestling with the seemingly incompatible goals of promoting greater political pluralism that could lead to fundamentalist, nondemocratic regimes. This problem assumed new proportions in June 1990, when the Algerian local and regional elections produced an absolute majority for the Islamic Salvation Front. The full dimensions of this problem became clearer in December 1991 when the same Islamic party emerged from the first round of Algerian parliamentary elections poised to win a commanding two-thirds majority in Parliament. Another issue is human rights. Washington has concerns about human rights in both Morocco and Tunisia. The State Department's 1992 human rights reports clearly suggest that the governments of both these traditional friends of the United States need to improve their record in this politically sensitive area. (The human rights situation is no better in Algeria or especially Libya, but these countries are not recipients of U.S. aid.)

As the North African countries (including Mauritania) create new arrangements for regional economic cooperation, should Washington respond with a regional policy for the area? The U.S. government welcomed the establishment of the Arab Maghribi Union in February 1989 and saw it as a positive development for the region (see Chapter 9). Washington supports efforts at regional cooperation—in this case the building of a North African common market—because such cooperation can enhance stability, foster cooperation in noneconomic spheres, and promote economic prosperity. There are already indications, for example, that the UMA has moved the problem of the Western Sahara closer to a solution. Beyond this general level of support, U.S. policymakers are hard-pressed to flesh out the substance of a regional policy. They would like to see, for example, if and to what extent the European Community will treat the Maghrib as a bloc.

With the end of the cold war and the disintegration of the Soviet Union, certain implications suggest themselves for U.S. relations with the Maghrib. In this new era of East-West interdependence, superpower cooperation at the regional level becomes increasingly possible (Afghanistan and Namibia come quickly to mind)—indeed, the two developments go hand in hand. For the Maghrib and the Mediterranean, strategic assets will become less important whereas the significance of economic factors will increase (Zartman 1991).

With the growing weight of economic factors in the 1990s, Algeria may loom more important for regional U.S. interests. Algeria's economic significance might require some readjustment of U.S. priorities in the Maghrib. Fortunately for U.S. policymakers, readjustment can take place during a period of regional rapprochement within North Africa. In particular, as the former rivalry between Morocco and Algeria dissolves, their rapprochement will facilitate U.S. relations with both countries. This strongly suggests that a readjustment can be accomplished without disrupting the substance of U.S.-Moroccan relations.

12

15/21: The Maghrib into the Future

I. William Zartman

Depending upon which side of the Mediterranean or of history one stands on, the Maghrib will look either very different or much the same as it enters the twenty-first century (Christian era) or the fifteenth century (Muslim era). In any case, it is likely that the "real" Maghrib will stand up and that the future North Africa will be more authentistic, more Arab and Arabic, more autonomous, and more integrated in its state-society relations—until, somewhere further down the road, it will again come into closer symbiosis with the external world on all these dimensions. That increasing "authenticism," to seize on a single summarizing term, will not be retrograde, atavistic, backward, or reactionary but will merely mark a rejection of external models (and presumed models) for handling the modern world and an adoption and invention of local models.

But not only will "neotradition" be a probable characteristic; there will also be ingredients in the area's future that the countries have never met before—extraordinary population size, massive conflicts between expectations and satisfactions, wide income spreads, and technology gaps. Rather than try to draw a single picture of life's content and quality in, say, 2025, then, it is more helpful to outline some major themes of change and continuity.

There have been few attempts to look at North Africa's future. For one, see Mahdi Elmandjra, "Maghreb 2000," *Futuribles* 58 (September 1982: 3–12). In this attempt, I am grateful for the comments of Jean Leca, Remy Leveau, Susan Waltz, Lisa Anderson, Mark Habeeb, Habib Slim, and Dale Eickelman.

Population

Any analysis of the future must begin with an attempt to comprehend the magnitude of the population problem. It is estimated that by 2025 Algeria's population will have increased by nearly five times its 1960 level, Morocco's by four times, Tunisia's by more than three times, and Libya's nearly tenfold. In totals, Tunisia and Libya will be about equal, at 13 million, and Algeria will have passed Morocco, at 50 versus 44 million. Average age is likely to be the late twenties in Algeria, Morocco, and Tunisia, and the late teens for Libya (World Bank 1990b:264ff). Well over half of that population—perhaps as much as 60 percent—will be in urban areas in Morocco and Algeria; this is already the case in Tunisia and Libya, and the percentages may increase to 70 percent and 80 percent, respectively. By contrast, although Algeria and Morocco will have turned into Egypts of the 1990s in terms of total population, their per capita arable land ratio will be three times that of Egypt, and even Libya's will be four times that of Egypt in 1990.

Population can be either a resource or a burden, depending on how it is used. As the current youth boom reaches productive age, the dependent (both young and old) population will be reduced and the productive labor force will be increased, providing large amounts of labor for industrial and service development. In Morocco, Algeria, and Tunisia, 68 percent of the population is estimated to be between fifteen and sixty-four years of age; in Libya the figure is 56 percent (World Bank 1990b: table 26). Agricultural and food productivity per capita has been growing significantly in all Maghribi countries except Algeria; Algeria could take part in this trend, too, if it ever develops an agricultural policy, and the whole region can continue to increase productivity for a while, even as population grows. Employment and productivity in the urban economy have not done as well. Only unemployment has shown a steadily increasing growth rate, and prospects for a turnaround are dim.

The general relation among the three countries' per capita gross national product—$900 in Morocco, $1,300 in Tunisia, and $2,500 in Algeria, in 1990—did not change during the 1980s and can be expected to hold into the near future at the modest (less than 1 percent) per capita growth rates of the previous decade. Libya's inflated figure of $5,000 has been dropping at a negative growth rate of 10 percent in the same period but will still remain out of sight of the other Maghribi countries. Thus the region spreads across the middle-income range of developing countries and has a solid possibility of staying there. But it will require some dramatic changes to take off into sustained development.

Along with population and productivity, education is also expanding. Algeria, Libya, and Tunisia have already achieved nearly universal primary education (Morocco was at about 75 percent at the turn of the decade)—in Tunisia even for girls. Algeria (and probably Libya) show about 55 percent enrollment in secondary school, the other two countries about 40 percent. Morocco, Algeria, and Libya have about 10 percent of college-age youth in higher education, and Tunisia has 6 percent (World Bank 1990b). Whatever the quality shortfalls that underlie these figures, they indicate an impressive growth since independence and a promise of further advances (although at a much slower rate than in the past, of course). The impact of the result is twofold: Productive skills are increased, but so are expectations and employment shortfalls.

Demographic and economic prospects, then, indicate a challenge to take off that can become a setting for stagnation and frustration if not fulfilled. The 1980s were a leveling-off period that pointed above all to its own continuation, to limits on growth that would run massively into the soaring expectations nurtured by the moment of independence and the quarter century thereafter. The countries at the start of the 1990s are in the hands of leaders who were in their twenties at the time of independence (except for Qadhafi), and national leadership will soon fall to those who grew up during the early years of independence, after colonial rule was gone. Life has been downhill since then in terms of meeting expectations, even though the actual figures show only a plateau. If there are policies, plans, programs, and answers, the moment can be turned into renewed national efforts at increasing productivity, expanding distribution, and aiming at new horizons for greater human resources.

Unfortunately, the 1980s saw mainly overturned policies, unfulfilled plans, failed programs, and inadequate answers, as the hollowness of the promise of socialism, the stringencies of the survival of the fittest, and the starkness of a clash with the West became apparent. As a result, Islamic fundamentalism and Arab nationalism suddenly became an attractive refuge to many, although to some their inherent inability to provide policies and answers to the basic economic questions was as rapidly evident as were all the preceding ideological shortfalls. Thus the growing population has become more of a demand than a supply factor, and its potential for political support lies more in solidarity making than in problem solving, causing leaders to harness rather than remove popular frustrations.

State Consolidation

The most striking political characteristic of the independence era has been the consolidation of the state. As both a symbol and a structure, the state is stronger than was either the colonial state or the new nationalist state in all four countries. It draws allegiance, regulates citizen activity, dominates the economy, is the largest employer, ties up and ties down local interactions into national networks, and has established itself as a corporate entity with its own interests that defy even the attempts of government (its nominal executive) to orient and reorient it. When, in a momentary attempt to curb its own excessive conflicts with its neighbors, it joins them in a regional integrative effort to supersede its autonomy, the state soon reasserts itself and domesticates its creation. The Maghribi state is here to stay.

The size of the state was established in the first twenty-five years of independence and is likely to remain at the same general levels. Expenditures for general government consumption stood at about 16 or 17 percent of GDP for the three countries in the latter half of the 1980s and thereafter, or about three times more per capita in Algeria than in Morocco and half again as much in Tunisia as in Morocco; figures in Libya rose from about one-fifth to over one-third of GNP in the first half of the 1980s (after which data were no longer available). Privatization will reduce these figures somewhat but not change the general order of magnitude. Some Maghribi countries are more efficient than the Third World average; statistics are not available for the most centrally planned—Algeria and Libya—which can be expected to be a good deal less efficient. A rough government efficiency index based on the ratio between expenditures for social services (education and health) plus economic programs (business and agriculture) and government operating costs (general public services) comes to 8:1 for Tunisia and 3:5:1 for Morocco. These figures (and the presumably lower ratio indicating less efficiency for the other two states) are unlikely to change much in the future and reinforce the notion that the state will survive (*African Economic and Financial Data* 1989).

The form of the state is a different matter. Although the Tunisian and Algerian party-state has both flexibility and a high capacity to absorb and convert other influences, the Moroccan and Libyan states are more specifically structured. The Moroccan *makhzen* system, of course, has shown a resilience born of centuries of experience in absorbing local structures and influences under the "great patron." But in case of "great patronicide," the central mechanism of resilience would be removed, and no replacement structures are evident. The army would probably take over, opening up a lengthy struggle with the established parties reminiscent in many ways of the various experiences in Egypt, Syria, and Nigeria. This is not to predict the fall of the monarchy by any means but simply to indicate the probable evolution if it fell. More likely is a continuation of the *makhzen* system under Mohammed VI and thereafter, absorbing, controlling, and relating to a kaleidoscope of forces involving the army and the parties. Libya is surer of change, as the personalized system of Qadhafi is unlikely to be perpetuated by his successor. Yet the new system will presumably be but a variant on the old because parties are not available to take over, opposition movements and the army are both weak, and the monarchy is, of course, gone.

The current response to the question of state futures is that democracy is the rising form of state structure, but it is safe to say that democracy will be

Maghribized as the Maghrib is being democratized. In other words, full, open, competitive pluralism with alternance among equivalent forces is an unlikely prospect, and a democratic evolution will instead be focused on a struggle by subordinate, fractionated, pluralist forces to keep dominant, centralized power from being monopolistic. Although the vote may be free for those parties admitted into the arena, loyalty will be the price of opposition in a restricted political system. Minority opposition parties will struggle for their own independence from the dominant party more than for power, always in danger of being co-opted, and if they should ever break out of their minority status, on the back of a sudden new issue that the majority party cannot handle, they will act to dominate the system like their predecessor.

Morocco has the oldest system of pluralistic competition, under the centralizing control of the monarchy, and it is the competition between pluralism and centralism, rather than the competition within pluralism, that provides the evolutionary dynamic of the political system. That evolution may have moved toward greater party power and responsibility by 2025, but it is unlikely to have changed in nature (barring great patronicide). The Tunisian multiparty system is built on a tradition of pluralism within centralism that has existed since before independence, with the dominant (formerly single) party continuing to overshadow the vain attempts of both religious and secular competitors to attract a solid clientele. A tripartite system corresponding to social currents involving a rural and urban elite party (like the RCD), a socialist labor party, and an urban fundamentalist party would be a stable and natural evolution, but the combined economic and fundamentalist issues of the 1990s may deflect those chances and with them the course of democratization (see Zartman 1991). Algeria's democratization occurs within monist tradition and may prove to be merely the transition from one party-state to another or from one military regime to preemption by another or from nationalized, secularized religion (as Tozy describes it in Chapter 5) to an open, pluralistic competition between secularism and atavism. The 1990s are certainly an interregnum into an uncertain future, but predominance by one party is an Algerian tradition. Libya, too, has had a centralized pluralist tradition dating from the multiple nonparty candidacies of individuals representing local factions under the monarchy and perpetuated in new institutions under the revolutionary system. The system has every promise of appropriating any type of democracy that would be introduced after Qadhafi, just as it permeated earlier regimes.

That the state will persist is further suggested by the limited effect of Maghribi unity efforts. Although continued attempts to coordinate, develop, and even integrate activities across North Africa may well be pursued, they are likely to remain on the sectoral and even private level and not to result in any supranational Maghribi institution. Maghribi states still need greater internal consolidation and expanded intra-Maghribi trade and transactions before they can be impelled into strong cooperation. Solemn and festive relaunchings of Maghribi unity will continue to succumb to gradual erosion as one country supports a neighbor's militant opposition movement, until some problem prompts Tunisia to rise and revive the call for unity and brotherhood as a limit on conflict. It is assumed here that by the mid-1990s, the dispute over the ownership of the Western Sahara will be ended in its current form by a referendum favorable to Morocco or that it will at least have petered out as a military and diplomatic issue. But it may well return in some other version, such as dissidence against Moroccanization and sedentarization, as the Tuareg have responded in Algeria. Competing efforts among Morocco, Algeria, Libya, and other Arab countries for predominance over Mauritania will be another source of conflict. These cyclical interferences and reconciliations that have marked pre-independent and independent North African history are unlikely to evaporate in the coming decades (as discussed in Chapters 10 and 11).

State-Society Relations

Yet for all the pervasiveness of the state in size and form, state-society relations appear to be entering a new phase. The uniform trend of state-parties since the mid-1970s has been a move away from civil society. Algeria's FLN and Tunisia's PSD became ossified and ingrown (see Entelis 1986; Camau 1987). Libya's party-parliamentary structures became a battleground between bureaucrats and vigilantes, and Morocco's renovated party system under Hassan II in the 1970s became marginalized in the 1980s as the people came to see clearly where responsibility lay (see Zartman 1987a). Although the state became stronger in all countries, then, it also became beleaguered and isolated from its populations. No longer was the state the nationalist movement in power, victory of *l'état réel* (the real state) over *l'état légal* (the legal state); by the last decade of the century it had again become the *makhzen* or a *kulughli* state, an ingrown, Weberian state of authoritarian bureaucracy distinct from its people, a lid on society. Thus throughout North Africa in the 1980s and the beginning of the 1990s, protest riots against the state were of an intensity not experienced since the nationalist violence of the 1940s and 1950s.

The most important manifestation of this trend was the rise of fundamentalist movements, each in a specific national form of the general wave sweeping the Islamic world. As in Egypt in the 1930s and 1940s, where the father of Islamicism, the Muslim Brethren, arose as a sociopolitical movement to fill the vacuum left by the bankruptcy of the political parties born of the nationalist movement and the palace, the Islamicist movements of North Africa started in the 1970s and burgeoned in the 1980s and beyond to give an ideological and organizational expression to the urban lower and middle classes left homeless by the ingrown political parties. On the way to consolidating their membership and buttressing their claim to be the voice of society, the movements seek to capture the state in the 1990s and to hold onto it in the subsequent decades.

Save the rule-proving exception, social movements of unity and orthodoxy always fall prey to division, as they contend over the proper nature of unity and orthodoxy. There is no single, united Islamic movement in any North African country, and as the movements take a more open and active role in politics, they will split further. The major split is already foreshadowed by the Tunisian and Algerian movements: The progressive Islamicists are moving into the fifteenth/twenty-first century (as the name of the Tunisian publication proclaims) away from the social Islamicists, in Magnuson's terms (Zartman 1991), and, more importantly, the social Islamicists are separating into a political wing and a subversive militant wing. Clandestinity turns fundamentalists into subversives and even terrorists but sets up splits in their movement. That is the dilemma of democracy. As the democratic West knew in facing Communist movements, the ultimate dilemma is whether to legalize undemocratic movements. Both Algeria's answer of hasty legalization and Tunisia's answer of stubborn refusal may be fatal to the development of democracy, as society takes over the state in one case and besieges it in the other. Fortunately, coming to power also brings out divisions in a movement, as the Algerian experience shows. In either case, society will be fractious and contestatory as it confronts the state.

When society completely takes over the state, it destroys state autonomy and the ability of the state to respond to society's needs. There needs to be a healthy medium between symbiosis and isolation. Like other states of the Third World, the North African states (or, more properly, politicians thinking and acting as the state) are searching for appropriate forms and institutions and will continue to do so in the early twenty-first century. In the late twentieth century, Qadhafi's experiment was the most innovative. But it failed to acknowledge that party and legislature perform different functions and so are not identical, nor could it overcome the contradictory challenge that revolutionary leaders must lead the people to want to transform themselves. In the other states, parliaments are coming back into vogue and will continue to do so into the next century, providing another potential link to society. This in turn poses the need and opportunity for better parties, to reflect salient demands and currents but also to present their own programs and leaders for handling the country's problems. By the turn of the century, the hollowness of purely Islamic programs will have become apparent, and governments and parties—Islamicist and secular—will have to face the need for real policies and answers. New mixtures of state and private roles that are neither stifling statism nor rapacious privatism will need to be devised, and that will doubtless become the focus of debate.

In the shorter run, however, a period of solidarity making and control may precede the era of problem solving. Rising population and declining economies, societal assaults on the beleaguered state, and the rise of movements of solidarity and identity are all elements in polity, economy, and society of the 1990s that call for sociopolitical control rather than favoring the open, freewheeling pluralism that democracy and free enterprise require. Control is necessary whether the besieging movement is inside or outside the state. The early 1990s should see secular state attempts to co-opt, resemble, repress, and discredit increasingly militant Islamicist movements, fueling and legitimizing their militancy. At the same time, the Islamicist states will attempt to enforce their rule and remain in power when politics have put them there. The model is found in many phases of the Sudanese experience throughout the 1980s. Thus it would not be surprising to see the Maghrib go through a time of troubles before it emerges into a much-needed and more creative pluralism.

Self-Reliance

These developments will take place under growing external pressures for self-reliance, in an increasingly Maghribi context, even if that context does not yet take on tighter institutional forms. Many aspects of the European dependency relation are closing, as Chapter 10 shows. Trade in prime Maghribi exports is subject to mounting competition from within the European Community as Europe expands its own Mediterranean membership; Maghribi emigrants constitute an important sociopolitical problem within European states and find increasing competition from other modernizing Muslim societies such as Egypt and Turkey. Eastern Europe will be North Africa's next expansion chamber for excess population, but without creating the ties that have been so important in regard to Western Europe. Yet massive attractions continue to exist toward Europe and the rest of the West. Family ties and remittances bind 5 to 6 million Maghribis in Europe to their homeland at the end of the century, and that figure is expected to triple to over 10 percent of the North African population by 2025. International ties in business and education for individuals as well as commercial and environmental exchanges for countries will further test and challenge the centripetal dynamics. For those who stay at home, European television captured through a forest of dish antennas shows fantasized life on the other side of the tracks.

The closing of Europe, the loss of strategic importance after the cold war and the Gulf War, and the rise of Islamic and Arab nationalism all point to a renewal of Maghribi ties to the east to compete with loosening ties to the north. Throughout North Africa, French is spoken less well and Arabic better than at the time of independence, a trend that will continue even as English begins to rise as a second or third language. The sharpened awareness of "us" and "them," with a broadened appreciation of "us" and a hostile reinterpretation of "them," reinforces the notion that models for the challenges of development and modernization will be sought and perhaps found in conjunction with the Mashriq (the Arab east), not with the Ruum (the Christian north). As the time of colonization slips further into the past, the Maghrib finds itself to be more a part of the contemporary Arab world and less a former French (or Italian) colonial area.

Rejected penetration, fascination and repulsion, and rediscovery of the self are all major facets of the Maghrib's entry into the new millennium. Economic growth, population absorption, political solutions, and cultural identity need to be found on home turf. North Africa's only significant area for trade expansion is itself, and trade expansion is its only way to absorb excess population. Economic structures and products are diverse enough to allow for trade creation rather than simply trade diversion among cooperating states. Algeria's vocation in heavy industry and energy, Morocco's in agriculture, and Tunisia's in light industry and agriculture can provide both for intra-Maghribi exchanges and for export to a diversified world market. Similarly, the turn of the millennium presents another moment in the cyclical dialect that seeks a satisfying synthesis between the thesis of authenticity and the antithesis of modernity. Such have always been the cross-pressures on the southern shore of the Mediterranean. They will continue in new forms as the real Maghrib tries to establish its own identity, its own path into the fifteenth/twenty-first century.

Appendix A: Political Parties in North Africa

TABLE A.1 Political Parties in North Africa

Present Name	Acronym	Date Founded	Founder	Date Legally Recognized
Algeria				
Front de Libération Nationale	FLN	1954	collective	1962
Parti de l'Avant-Garde Socialiste	PAGS	1936	collective (ex-PCF)	1989
Parti du Peuple Algérien	PPA	1936	Massali al-Hajj	refused
Front des Forces Socialistes	FFS	1963	Hocine Ait Ahmed	1989
Mouvement Démocratique pour le Renouveau Algérien	MDRA	1967	Krim Belkacem	1989
Parti Socialiste des Travailleurs	PST	1974	collective (Trotskyite)	1990
Organisation Socialiste des Travailleurs	OST	1980?	collective (Trotskyite)	1990
Parti Algérien du Peuple	PAP	1980	Miloud Nouari	1990
Mouvement pour la Démocratie en Algérie	MDA	1982	Ahmed Ben Bella	1990
Parti Social Démocrate	PSD	1988	Abderrahmane Adjerid	1989
Parti de l'Unité Populaire	PUP	1988	Djamel-Eddine Habibi	1989
Parti Algérien de l'Homme Capital	PAHC	1988	Malek Habouche	1990
Rassemblement pour la Culture et la Démocratie	RCD	1989	Saïd Saadi	1989
Front Islamique de Salut	FIS	1989	Abassi al-Madani	1989
Parti National Algérien	PNA	1989	Noureddine Houam	1989
Parti National pour la Solidarité et le Développement	PNSD	1989	Rabah Bencherif	1989
Parti du Renouveau Algérien	PRA	1989	Noureddine Boukrou	1989
Parti Social Libéral	PSL	1989	Ahmed Khelil	1990
Union des Forces Démocratiques	UFD	1989	Ahmed Mahsas	1990
Front National du Renouveau	FNR	1989	Mohammed Zine Charifi	1990
Union Nationale des Forces pour le Progrès	UNFP	1989	Bouabdallah Mentalechta	1990
Association Populaire pour l'Unité et l'Action	APUA	1989	Allalou El Mahdi Abbas	1990
Parti de l'Union Arabe Islamique Démocratique	PUAID	1989	Belhadj Khelil	1990
Umma party	Umma	1990	Benyoussef Benkhedda	1990
Parti Communist Algérien	PCA	1935	Kaddour Belkaim	1989
Morocco				
Istiqlal party	PI	1937	Allal al-Fassi	1955
Parti Démocratique Constitutionnel	PDC	1937	Hasan al-Ouezzani	1957
Mouvement Populaire	MP	1958	Mahjoubi Aherdan	1958
Union Nationale des Forces Populaires	UNFP	1959	Mehdi Ben Barka	1959
Union Socialiste des Forces Populaires	USFP	1972	Abderrahmane Bouabid	1975

(*continues*)

TABLE A.1 (continued)

Present Name	Acronym	Date Founded	Founder	Date Legally Recognized
Mouvement Populaire, Démocratique, et Constitutionnel	MPDC	1967	Abd al-Karim al-Khattabi	1967
Parti du Progrès et du Socialisme	PPS	1943	Ali Yata	1974
Parti de l'Action	PA	1974	Abdellah Sanhaji	1974
Parti Libéral et du Progrès	PLP	1974	Ahmed Oulhadj	1974
Rassemblement National des Indépendants	RNI	1978	Ahmed Osman	1978
Parti National Démocrate	PND	1982	Arsalane El Jadidi	1982
Union Contitutionnelle	UC	1983	Maati Bouabid	1983
Organisation d'Action Démocratique et Populaire	OADP	1970	Mohammed Bensaïd	1983
Tunisia				
Parti Communiste Tunisien	PCT	1921	Mohammed Harmel	1981
Rassemblement Constitutionnel Démocratique	RCD	1934	Zine Labidine Ben Ali	1988
Mouvement de l'Unité Populaire	MUP	1978	Ahmed Ben Salah	
Mouvement des Démocrates Socialistes	MDS	1978	Ahmed Mestiri	1983
Mouvement de la Tendance Islamiste (reconstituted as the Nahda)	MTI	1979	Rashid Ghannouchi	1988
Parti de l'Unité Populaire	PUP	1980	Mohammed Belhaj Amor	1983
Rassemblement Socialiste Progressiste	RSP	1980	Ahmed Néjib Chebbi	1988
Parti de Libération Islamique	PLI	1981?		
Hizb al Adala (Parti de la Justice)		1988	Sahbi Louhaïbi	
Mouvement du Baath		1988	Faouzi Snoussi	
Parti Ouvrier Communiste Tunisien	POCT	1988	Hamma Hammami	
Rassemblement du Maghreb Uni	RMU	1988	Chadly Zouiten	
Rassemblement Unioniste Démocratique	RUD	1988	Béchir Essid	
Parti Social du Progrès	PSP	1988	Mounir El Béji	1988
Union Démocratique Unioniste	UDU	1988	Abderrahmane Tlili	1988
Parti Socialiste Destourien	PSD	1934	Habib Bourguiba	1955

Sources: Abdelkader Djeghloul, "Le Multipartisme à l'algérienne," *Maghreb-Machrek* 127 (January- February 1990): 205–210; Mustapha Sehimi, *La Grande encyclopédie du Maroc: les institutions politiques* (Rabat: GEM, 1986), p. 107; *Réalités* (Tunis); *Middle East Economic Digest* (London).

Appendix B: Economic and Demographic Tables

TABLE B.1 Population Growth Rates, 1950–1990

	Algeria	Libya	Morocco	Tunisia
1950–1955	2.08	1.80	2.48	1.79
1960–1965	1.98	3.70	2.73	1.85
1970–1975	3.06	4.03	2.45	1.81
1980–1985	3.03	3.86	2.48	2.04
1985–1990	3.21	3.67	2.30	2.18

Source: World Population Prospects, Dept. of Economic and Social Affairs, 1986, pp. 181, 205, 211, 225.

TABLE B.2 Urban Percentage of Population by Decade, 1950–1985

	Algeria	Libya	Morocco	Tunisia
1950	22.3	18.6	26.2	31.2
1960	30.4	22.7	29.3	36.0
1970	45.6	34.3	34.6	43.5
1980	44.0	52.0	41.0	52.0
1985	43.0	60.0	44.0	56.0

Source: Demographic Indicators of Countries (New York: United Nations, 1982); World Development Report, 1982, 1987 (Washington, D.C.: World Bank, 1982, 1987).

TABLE B.3 Gross and Per Capita National Product by Decade, 1950–1987 (GNP in millions of dollars, at market prices)

	Algeria	Libya	Morocco	Tunisia
1960				
GNP	2,788.7	332.5	2,041.0	—
per capita	258	175	180	—
1970				
GNP	4,881.8	3,362.2	3,910.8	1,416.8
per capita	360	1,890	260	280
1980				
GNP	41,536.8	31,993.3	18,420.5	8,615.1
per capita	1,960	9,550	880	1,290
1989				
GNP	45,930.0	22,860.0	21,190.0	9,590.0
per capita	2,220	5,420	880	1,260

Sources: World Bank, World Development Report (Washington, D.C.: World Bank, 1984 and 1991).

TABLE B.4 Foreign Trade by Decade, 1950–1988 (in millions of dollars)

	1950	1960	1970	1980	1988
Algeria					
exports	333.1	558.0	1,008.8	13,660	8,216
imports	433.9	1,264.5	1,256.8	10,826	8,036
Libya					
exports	9.9	11.2	2,365.7	21,919	6,793
imports	19.4	169.0	554.4	6,777	6,225
Morocco					
exports	189.5	354.0	488.3	2,441.1	3,603.4
imports	328.1	397.2	684.3	4,255.3	4,772.6
Tunisia					
exports	113.7	119.6	180.8	2,231.4	2,394.7
imports	147.2	189.2	305.4	3,525.6	3,688.7

Sources: African Statistical Yearbook, 1975 (New York: UN, 1976), pp. 3-12, 4-12, 5-13; United Nations, UN Economic Commission for Africa Statistical Yearbook (New York: UN, 1970), pp. 2–3, 8–9; International Monetary Fund, Direction of Trade Statistics Yearbook (Washington, D.C.: IMF, 1984 and 1988).

TABLE B.5 Exports and Imports to Primary Trading Partner[a] by Decade, 1960–1988 (in millions of dollars)

	Algeria	Libya	Morocco	Tunisia
1960				
exports	318.7 (F)	3.6 (I)	142.4 (F)	62.5 (F)
imports	1,061.8 (F)	31.4 (I)	204.2 (F)	113.5 (F)
1970				
exports	540.2 (F)	613.73 (I)	178.70 (F)	44.545 (F)
imports	533.0 (F)	119.59 (I)	212.31 (F)	105.836 (F)
1980				
exports	6,256 (U)	7,779 (U)	611.7 (F)	353.1 (I)
imports	2,889 (F)	2,002 (I)	1,045.3 (F)	885.1 (F)
1988				
exports	1,793 (U)	2,316 (I)	891.3 (F)	616.0 (F)
imports	1,719 (F)	1,382 (I)	1,031.1 (F)	916.5 (F)

[a] F=France; I=Italy; U=United States.

Sources: African Statistical Yearbook, 1975 (New York: UN, 1976), pp. 3-12, 4-12, 5-13; United Nations, UN Economic Commission for Africa Statistical Yearbook (New York: UN, 1970), pp. 2–3, 8–9; International Monetary Fund, Direction of Trade Statistics Yearbook (Washington, D.C.: IMF, 1990).

TABLE B.6 Public and Private Long-term External Debt, 1970, 1985, 1990 (in millions of dollars, outstanding at end of year)

	1970	1985	1990
Algeria			
public[a]	945	13,664	24,316
private	0	0	0
Morocco			
public[a]	712	11,231	22,097
private	15	—	200
Tunisia			
public[a]	541	4,442	6,506
private	0	246	218

[a]Includes publicly guaranteed debt.
Sources: World Bank, *World Development Report* (Washington, D.C.: World Bank, 1987 and 1992).

References

Abu-Lughod, J., 1976. "Developments in North African Urbanism: The Process of Decolonization." In *Urbanization and Counter Urbanization*, B.J.L. Berry, ed. Beverly Hills: Sage.
Abu-Zahra, Nadia, 1982. *Sidi Ameur: A Tunisian Village*. London: Ithaca Press.
Achour, Habib, 1989. *Ma vie politique et syndicale*, vol. 1. Tunis: Alif.
Adda, Serge, 1989. "La Tunisie et le changement." *La Presse*, July 25.
Ahmed, Eqbal, 1967. "Politics and Labor in Tunisia." Ph.D. dissertation, Princeton University.
African Economic and Financial Data, 1989. Washington: IBRD.
Alarafi, Abdullah Belgasses, 1980. "Perceptions of Organizational Climate in the Elementary and Intermediate Schools in Libya." Ph.D. dissertation, University of Oklahoma.
Alawar, M., 1982. "Urbanization in Libya: Present, State and Future Prospects." In *Social and Economic Development of Libya*, E.G.H. Joffe and K. S. McLachlan. Cambridge: Middle East and North African Studies.
Algeria, Government of, 1988a. *L'Algérie en quelques chiffres*. Algiers: National Statistics Office.
———. 1988b. *Collections de statistiques*, no. 4, 3d trimes. 1988. Algiers: National Statistics Office.
Algerian Report to UNESCO Conference on Public Education 1966, 1968. New York: UNESCO.
Allioua, K., 1987. "Crise urbaine et crise financière." *Lamalif* 190 (July-August).
Allman, James, 1976. "Social Mobility After Independence." In *Change in Tunisia: Studies in the Social Sciences*, Russell A. Stone and John Simmons, eds. Albany: State University of New York Press.
Anderson, Lisa, 1983. "Qadhafi's Islam." In *Voices of Resurgent Islam*, John Esposito, ed. New York: Oxford University Press.
———. 1986. *The State and Social Transformation in Tunisia and Libya, 1830–1980*. Princeton: Princeton University Press.
———. 1991. "Tunisia and Libya: Responses to the Islamic Impulse." In *The Iranian Revolution: Its Global Impact*, John Esposito, ed. Miami: Florida International Press.
Andriessen, Frans, 1990. "Change in Central and Eastern Europe: The Role of the European Community," *NATO Review* (February), pp. 1–6.
Annales algériennes de géographie, 1967. No. 4 (July-December), pp. 119–124.

Ashford, Douglas E., 1961. *Political Change in Morocco*. Princeton: Princeton University Press.

———. 1963. "Second and Third Generation Elites in the Maghrib." Research study for the U.S. Department of State, Bureau of Intelligence and Research.

———. 1967. *National Development and Local Reform: Political Participation in Morocco, Tunisia and Pakistan*. Princeton: Princeton University Press.

Attir, Mustafa, 1983. "Libya's Pattern of Urbanization." *Ekistics* 50, 300, pp. 157–162.

Attir, Mustafa, and Robert Peterson, 1979. "Socio-economic Development Plans and Individual Satisfaction." Tripoli: Arab Development Institute, Research Group in Sociology, Working Papers Series, no. 4.

"La Banque algérienne développement et la restructuration," 1985. *Revolution Africaine* (March 1–7).

Belhassen, Souhayr, 1989. "Nous oeuvrons pour que l'Islam occupe sa place en Algérie." *Jeune Afrique* 1519 (February 12), pp. 52–55.

Ben Achour, Habib, 1989. *Ma vie politique et syndicale: Enthousiasme et déceptions*. Tunis: Alif.

Ben Achour, Yadh, 1988. "Preface." *L'Etat et l'agriculture en Tunisie*. Tunis: Impr. officielle de la Republique tunisienne.

Ben Achour, Yazd, 1979. "Islam perdu, Islam retrouvé." *Annuaire de l'Afrique du Nord, 1979*. Paris: CNRS.

Ben Ali, Zine el-Abidine, 1988a. Speech delivered at Congrès du Salut. *As-Sabah*, August 2.

———. 1988b. Letter addressed to Tunisian national organizations. *Le Renouveau*, August 5.

———. 1988c. Interview in *al-Huriva*, November 9.

Ben M'rad, Moncef, 1988. "Algérie: guerre de positions, guerre de mouvement?" *Réalités* 172 (August 25), p. 10.

Ben Salim, Lilia, 1969a. "Democratisation de l'enseignement en Tunisie." *Revue tunisienne de sciences sociales* 16, (March), pp. 81–135.

———. 1969b. "Origines géographiques et sociales des cadres de l'administration économique des offices et sociétés nationales en Tunisie." *Annuaire de l'Afrique du Nord, 1968*. Paris: CNRS.

———. 1976. "Développement et problème de cadres: le cas de la Tunisie—les cadres supérieurs de l'économie Tunisienne." *Cahiers de CERES*, Série Sociologique 3, pp. 1–234.

Benhalima, Hassan, 1977. "De la tradition du dir à l'intégration économique moderne." Doctoral dissertation, Université Paul Valéry-Montpellier III.

Benjedid, Chadli, 1981. *Revue de presse* (May). Algiers: Communications Ministry.

Bennoune, Mahfoud, 1988. *The Making of Contemporary Algeria, 1830–1987: Colonial Upheavals and Post-Independence Development*. Cambridge: Cambridge University Press.

Benzakour, S., 1978. *Essai sur la politique urbaine au Maroc: 1912–1975*. Casablanca: Editions Maghrébines.

Berque, Jacques, 1974. "Qu'est-ce qu'une 'tribu' nord-africaine?" In *Maghreb: histoire et sociétés*. Algiers: SNED.

Blair, Thomas, 1970. *The Land to Those Who Took It.* New York: Doubleday.
Blake, G. H., 1973. "Urbanization and Development Planning in Libya." In *Development of Urban Systems in Africa*, R. A. Abudho and S. el-Shakhs, eds. New York: Praeger.
Bleuchot, Hervé, 1975. "Les fondements de l'idéologie du Colonel Qadhafi." In *La Libye Nouvelle*, Maurice Flory, ed. Paris: CNRS.
Bouali, M., 1988. "Les Islamistes à Casablanca." Thesis, University of Mohammed V, Rabat.
Boukraa, Ridha, 1976. "La problématique de la communauté rurale au Maghreb: quelques observations sur le changement social dans la communauté villageoise de Hammamet." *Revue tunisienne des sciences sociales* 45, pp. 11–48.
———. 1980. "Notes critiques à propos de l'application du concept d'accumulation primitive au processus d'urbanisation à Hammamet." *Revue tunisienne des sciences sociales* 63, pp. 73–81.
Bourgi, Albert, 1989. "Etudiants: où menera de désespoir?" *Jeune Afrique* 1519 (February 12), pp. 38–42.
Bourguiba, Habib, 1961. "Building a New Tunisia." Speech of January 12. Tunis: Secretary of State for Cultural Affairs and Information.
———. 1963. "Dimensions of Underdevelopment." Speech of April 14. Tunis: Secretary of State for Cultural Affairs and Information.
———. 1965. "Education, Its Social Role." Speech of July 1. Tunis: Secretary of State for Cultural Affairs and Information.
Bouzaiane, Brahim, 1985. "Réaction des communautés rurales aux modèles proposés par le programme de développement rural 'P.D.R.'" *Revue tunisienne de sciences sociales* 82–83, pp. 29–74.
Brown, Kenneth, 1981. "The Campaign to Encourage Family Planning in Tunisia and Some Responses at the Village Level." *Middle Eastern Studies* 17, pp. 64–84.
Brown, Leon Carl, 1973. "Tunisia: Education, 'Cultural Unity,' and the Future." In *Man, State and Society in the Contemporary Maghreb*, I. William Zartman, ed. New York: Praeger.
Brown, L. Carl, 1974. *The Tunisia of Ahmad Bey, 1837–1855.* Princeton: Princeton University Press.
Bubtana, Abdallah Ramadan, 1976. "A Comparative Study of the Perceptions of Students, Faculty Members, Administrators and Government Authorities of the Role of the University System in the National Development of Libya." Ph.D. dissertation, George Washington University.
Burgat, François, 1988a. "L'Algérie: de la laïcité islamique à l'islamisme." *Maghreb-Machrek* 121 (July), pp. 43–59.
———. 1988b. *L'Islamisme au Maghreb: la voix du sud.* Paris: Karthala.
Burgat, François, and Michel Nancy, 1984. *Les Villages socialistes de la révolution agraire algérienne.* Paris: CNRS.
Burgat, François, and Mohammed Tozy, 1988. "Echanges sur l'islamisme maghrébin," *Lamalif* 195, pp. 12–14.
Camau, Michel, 1979. "Caractère et rôle du constitutionnalisme dans les états maghrébins." In *Développements politiques au Maghreb*, J. Leca et al., eds. Paris: CNRS.

Camau, Michel, ed., 1987. *La Tunisie au présent. Une modernité audessus de tout soupçon?* Paris: CNRS.

Camau, Michel, et al., 1981. *Contrôle politique et régulations électorales en Tunisie.* Aix-en-Provence: CRESM.

Carré, Olivier, 1984. *Lecture révolutionnaire du Coran par Sayyid Qutb.* Paris: Cerf.

Cecchini, Paolo, 1988. *The European Challenge, 1992.* Aldershot: Wildwood House, for the European Commission.

Chabal, Patrick, ed., 1986. *Political Domination in Africa: Reflections on the Limits of Power.* New York: Cambridge University Press.

Charlot, Jean, and Monica Charlot, 1985. "Les Groupes politiques." In *Traité de science politique*, M. Grawitz and J. Leca, eds. Paris: Presses Universitaires de France.

Chatelus, Michel, 1987. "Industry and Services." In *The Rentier State*, Hazem Beblawi and Giacomo Luciani, eds. London: Croom Helm.

Chaulet, Claudine, 1971. *La Mitidja autogérée.* Algiers: SNED.

———. 1987. *La Terre, les frères, et l'argent.* 3 vols. Algiers: Office des Publications Universitaires.

Cherif, Abdallah, 1986. "Secteur organisé et développement agricole: UCP et Fermes Domaniales du Haut Tell tunisien, étude de géographie économique." Doctoral dissertation, Université de Tunis.

Chilcote, Ronald H., 1984. *Theories of Development and Underdevelopment.* Boulder: Westview Press.

Claisse, Alain, 1987. "Makhzen Traditions and Administrative Channels." In *The Political Economy of Morocco*, I. William Zartman, ed. New York: Praeger.

Clegg, Ian, 1971. *Workers' Self Management in Algeria.* London: Penguin.

Clément, Jean-François, 1989. *Maroc: Les menaces et les composantes internes de la sécurité.* Paris: IFRI.

Combs-Schilling, M. Elaine, 1985. "Family and Friend in a Moroccan Boom Town: The Segmentary Debate Reconsidered." *American Ethnologist* 12, 4, pp. 659–675.

Commission of the European Communities, 1990. "The Development of the Community's Relations with the Countries of Central and Eastern Europe." Brussels: EEC.

Côte, Marc, 1977. "Révolution agraire et sociétés agraires: le cas de l'est algérien." In *Les Problèmes agraires au Maghreb.* Paris: CNRS.

———. 1979. *Mutations rurales en Algérie: le cas des hautes plaines de l'est.* Paris: CNRS.

———. 1983. "L'espace algérien. Les prémices d'un aménagement." Algiers: OPU.

Dalton, William G., 1973. "Economic Change and Political Continuity in a Saharan Oasis Community." *Man* 8, pp. 266–284.

Damis, John, 1983a. *Conflict in Northwest Africa: The Western Sahara Dispute.* Stanford: Hoover Institution Press.

———. 1983b. "Prospects for Unity/Disunity in North Africa." *American-Arab Affairs*, no. 6 (Fall), pp. 34–47.

———. 1985. "Morocco, Libya, and the Treaty of Union." *American-Arab Affairs*, no. 13 (Summer), pp. 44–56.

Daoud, Z., and M. Tozy, 1987. "Entretien avec A. Guenon." *Lamalif* 188 (May).

Davenport, M., and S. Page, eds., 1991. *1992 and the Developing World.* London: Overseas Development Institute.

David, Wilfred L., 1986. *Conflicting Paradigms in the Economics of Developing Nations.* New York: Praeger.
Davis, John, 1982. "Qadhafi's Theory and Practice of Non-representative Government." *Government and Opposition* 17, 1, pp. 61–79.
──────. 1987. *Libyan Politics: Tribe and Revolution.* Berkeley: University of California Press.
Davis, Susan S., 1983. *Patience and Power: Women's Lives in a Moroccan Village.* Cambridge: Schenkman.
Debbasch, Charles, 1962. *La république tunisienne.* Paris: CNRS.
Deeb, Marius, and Mary-Jane Deeb, 1982. *Libya Since the Revolution.* New York: Praeger.
Deeb, Mary-Jane, 1989. "Inter-Maghribi Relations Since 1969: A Study of the Modalities of Unions and Mergers." *Middle East Journal* 43, 1 (Winter), pp. 22–24.
Dessouki, Ali E. Hillal, 1984. "The Primacy of Economics: The Foreign Policy of Egypt." In *The Foreign Policies of Arab States,* Bahgat Korany and Ali E. Hillal Dessouki, eds. Boulder: Westview Press.
Digne, Paul, 1989. "Algérie: un navire à la dérive." *Jeune Afrique* 1519 (February 12), pp. 38–42.
Djait, Hichem, 1988. "La Deuxième heure." *Réalités* (September), pp. 11–17.
──────. 1989. Statement in *Monde diplomatique* (April), pp. 13–14.
Djeghloul, Abdelkader, 1989. "Fin du populisme en Algérie." *Monde diplomatique* (January), p. 14.
──────. 1990. "Le Multipartisme à l'algérienne." *Maghreb-Machrek* 127 (January-February), pp. 194–210.
Dos Santos, Theontonio, 1970. "The Structure of Dependence." *American Economic Review* 60 (May), p. 231.
Doumou, Abdelali, 1987. *Etat et capitalisme au Maroc.* Rabat: Edino.
"Du couscous sur toutes les tables au Maghreb," 1989. *Jeune Afrique* 1467 (February 15), pp. 6–11.
Duchene, Françoise, 1985. *The European Community and the Mediterranean.* Luxembourg: EEC.
Dufour, Dany, 1978. "L'Enseignement en Algérie." *Maghreb-Machrek* 80, pp. 33–53.
Dwyer, Kevin, 1982. *Moroccan Dialogues.* Baltimore: Johns Hopkins University Press.
Economist Intelligence Unit (EIU), 1988. *Tunisia/Malta Country Report No. 1.* London: Economist Intelligence Unit.
Ecrement, Marc, 1986. *Indépendance politique et libération economique: Un quart de siècle du développement de l'Algérie 1962–1985.* Algiers: ENAP, PUG.
Eickelman, Dale, 1976. *Moroccan Islam.* Austin: University of Texas Press.
──────. 1981. *The Middle East.* Englewood Cliffs, N.J.: Prentice-Hall.
──────. 1986. "Royal Authority and Religious Legitimacy: Morocco's Elections, 1960–1984." In *The Frailty of Authority,* Myron Aronoff, ed. New Brunswick: Transaction Books.
──────. 1987. "Religion in Polity and Society." In *The Political Economy of Morocco,* I. William Zartman, ed. New York: Praeger.
Entelis, John P., 1974. "Ideological Change and an Emerging Counter-culture in Tunisian Politics." *Journal of Modern African Studies* 12, pp. 543–568.

———. 1980. *Comparative Politics of North Africa: Algeria, Morocco, and Tunisia.* Syracuse: Syracuse University Press.
———. 1986. *Algeria: The Revolution Institutionalized.* Boulder: Westview Press.
———. 1988. "Algeria Under Chadli: Liberalization Without Democratization; or, Perestroika, Yes; Glasnost, No." *Middle East Insight* (Fall), pp. 47–64.
Escalier, R., 1981. *Citadins et espaces urbains au Maroc.* Tours: URBAMA, ERA 706, fasc. 8 and 9.
Etienne, Bruno, 1977. *L'Algérie, cultures et révolution.* Paris: Seuil.
———. 1980. *L'Islamisme radical.* Paris: Hachette.
Etienne, Bruno, and Mohammed Tozy, 1981. "Obligations islamiques et associations à Casablanca." *Annuaire de l'Afrique du Nord, 1979.* Paris: CNRS.
"Europe Without Borders: Answers to Some Questions," 1988. *Europe* (October), pp. 12–17.
European Economic Community, 1982. "Cooperation Agreements Between the EEC and the Maghreb Countries." Brussels: EEC.
El Fathaly, Omar, and Monte Palmer, 1980. *Political Development and Social Change in Libya.* Lexington, Mass.: D. C. Heath.
El Fathaly, Omar, Monte Palmer, and Richard Chackerian, 1977. *Political Development and Bureaucracy in Libya.* Lexington, Mass.: D. C. Heath.
Ferchiou, Sophie, 1985. *Les Femmes dans l'agriculture tunisienne.* Aix-en-Provence: Edisud.
Fleischer, Cornell, 1986. *Bureaucrat and Intellectual in the Ottoman Empire: the Historian Mustafa Ali (1541–1600).* Princeton: Princeton University Press.
Foreign Broadcast Information Service (FBIS), 1983. *Daily Report: Middle East and Africa,* September 2.
Gallagher, Charles F., 1963. *The United States and North Africa: Morocco, Algeria, and Tunisia.* Cambridge: Harvard University Press.
———. 1966. "Language and Identity." In *State and Society in Independent North Africa,* Leon Carl Brown, ed. Washington, D.C.: Middle East Institute.
Geertz, Clifford, 1979. "Suq: The Bazaar Economy in Sefrou." In *Meaning and Order in Moroccan Society,* C. Geertz, H. Geertz, and L. Rosen. Cambridge: Cambridge University Press.
———. 1989. Statement at Plenary Session. *Daedalus* (Winter), p. 238.
Gellner, Ernest, 1983. *Muslim Society.* London: Cambridge University Press.
Ghannouchi, Rachid, 1981. "Interview with Christiane Sourrau. " In *Annuaire de l'Afrique du Nord, 1979.* Paris: CNRS.
Gordon, David. 1962. *North Africa's French Legacy, 1954–62.* Cambridge: Harvard Middle East Monograph Series.
Grimaud, Nicole, 1984. *La politique extérieure de l'Algérie.* Paris: Karthala.
Guen, Moncef, 1988. *Les Défis de la Tunisie.* Paris: L'Harmattan.
Guenoun, Abdallah, 1987. "Interview with Zakia Daoud and Mohammed Tozy." *Lamalif* 188 (May).
Habeeb, William Mark, 1988. *Power and Tactics in International Negotiation.* Baltimore: Johns Hopkins University Press.
Hammoudi, Abdellah, 1988. *La victime et ses masques.* Paris: Seuil.
Hamrouche, Mouloud, 1989. Interview in *L'Express,* October 13.

Harris, Lillian Craig, 1988. "Europe and North Africa: Conflict and Opportunity." *Arab Affairs* no. 8 (Winter), pp. 78–103.
Hassan II, 1965. *Le Maroc en marche*. Rabat: Ministry of Information.
Hassani, Omar Abid, 1970. *Fiqh al-daʿwa*. Rabat: Al-Umma.
Heller, Mark, 1984. *The Middle East Military Balance 1984*. Tel Aviv: Jaffee Center for Strategic Studies, Tel Aviv University.
Hermassi, Elbaki, 1972. *Leadership and National Development in North Africa: A Comparative Study*. Los Angeles: University of California Press.
———. 1984. "La Société tunisienne au miroir islamiste." *Maghreb-Machrek* 103, pp. 39–56.
Hess, Andrew, 1978. *The Forgotten Frontier: A History of the Sixteenth-Century Ibero-American Frontier*. Chicago: University of Chicago Press.
Hinnebusch, Raymond, 1982. "Libya: Personalistic Leadership of a Populist Revolution." In *Political Elites in Arab North Africa*, I. William Zartman, ed. New York: Longman.
Hitchens, Theresa, 1990. "Italy, Spain Urge Mediterranean Alliance." *Defense News*, October 1, p. 1.
Hooglund, Eric J., 1982. *Land and Revolution in Iran: 1960–1980*. Austin: University of Texas Press.
Hopkins, Nicholas S., 1977. "The Emergence of Class in a Tunisian Town." *International Journal of Middle East Studies* 8, pp. 453–491.
———. 1986. "Class Consciousness and Political Action in Testour." *Dialectical Anthropology* 11, 1, pp. 73–91.
———. 1988. "Cooperatives and the Non-cooperative Sector in Tunisia and Egypt." In *Who Shares? Cooperatives and Rural Development*, D. W. Attwood and B. S. Baviskar, eds. Delhi: Oxford University Press.
Ibrahim, Youssef, 1990. "Militant Muslims Grow Stronger as Algeria's Economy Grows Weaker." *New York Times*, June 25.
International Monetary Fund (IMF), 1988. *International Financial Statistics*. Washington: IMF.
———. 1991. *Direction of Trade Statistics Yearbook, 1989*. Washington: IMF.
Jabri, Mohammed Abed, 1985. "Evolution of the Maghrib Concept: Facts and Perspectives." In *North Africa: Issues of Development and Integration*, Halim Barakat, ed. Washington, D.C.: Center for Contemporary Arab Studies.
Joffe, George, 1988. "Islamic Opposition in Libya," *Third World Quarterly* 10, 2 (April).
Kaïdi, Hamza, 1988. "Algérie: le FLN seul contre tous." *Jeune Afrique* 1452 (November 2).
Kapil, Arun, 1990. "Algeria's Elections Show Islamic Strength." *Middle East Report*, no. 166 (September-October), pp. 31–36.
Karoui, Naima, 1980. "Etude sociologique sur les ouvrières agricoles dans la région de Mateur." *Revue tunisienne des sciences sociales* 63, pp. 92–135.
El Kenz, Ali, 1987. *Le Complexe sidérurgique d'El Hadjar*. Paris: CNRS.
Keppel, Gilles, 1982. "Les Mouvements islamistes dans l'Egypte de Sadate." Dissertation, University of Paris.
———. 1987. *Les banlieux de l'Islam*. Paris: Seuil.

Kerr, Malcolm, 1966. *Islamic Reform: The Political and Legal Theories of Muhammad ʿAbduh and Rashid Rida*. Berkeley: University of California Press.

———. 1971. *The Arab Cold War: Gamal ʿAbd al-Nasir and His Rivals, 1958–1970*. London: Oxford University Press.

Kessab, A., and Sethoum, H., 1980. *Géographie de la Tunisie, le pays et les hommes*. Tunis: University of Tunis Press.

Kezeiri, S., and Lawless, R., 1987. "Economic Development and Spatial Planning in Libya." In *The Economic Development of Libya*, B. Khader and B. el-Wifati, eds. London: Croom Helm.

Khadduri, Majid, 1963. *Modern Libya*. Baltimore: Johns Hopkins University Press.

Khelil, Ismail, 1988. "Lettre de Ismail Khelil au président de la république." *Réalités* (September 16), pp. 12–14.

El Khyari, Thami, 1989. *Agriculture au Maroc*. Morocco: Editions Okad.

Lacoste-Dujardin, C., 1976. *Un village algérien: structures et évolution récente*. Algiers: SNED/CRAPE.

Lacouture, Jean, and Simone Lacouture. 1958. *Le Maroc à l'épreuve*. Paris: Seuil.

Lahmar, Mouldi, 1985. "La 'révolte du pain' dans la campagne tunisienne: notables, ouvriers et fellahs." *Esprit* (April), pp. 9–19.

Leca, J., and N. Grimaud, 1986. "Le Secteur privé en Algérie." *Maghreb-Machrek* 113 (July), pp. 102–119.

Leca, J., and J. C. Vatin, 1975. *L'Algérie politique*. Paris: Fondation Nationale des Sciences Politiques.

———. 1979. "Le Système politique algérien (1976–1978)." In *Développements politiques au Maghreb*, J. Leca et al., eds. Paris: CNRS.

Leveau, R., 1981a. "Islam et contrôle politique au Maroc." In *Islam et politique au Maghreb*, E. Gellner et al., eds. Paris: CNRS.

———. 1981b. "Islam officiel et renouveau islamique au Maroc." In *Annuaire de l'Afrique du Nord, 1979*. Paris: CNRS.

———. 1985. *Le Fellah marocain défenseur du trône*, 2nd ed. Paris: FNSP.

———. 1987. "Stabilité du pouvoir monarchique et financement de la dette." *Maghreb-Machrek* 118 (October), pp. 5–19.

———. 1991. "Maghrib: Immigration in Europe." *Annals*, AAPSS, 524 (November), pp. 170–180.

Lewis, John, 1964. *Quiet Crisis in India: Economic Development and American Policy*. New York: Doubleday.

Liauzu, Claude, 1987. "Etat, ville et mouvements sociaux au Maghreb et au Moyen Orient." *Maghreb-Machrek* 115, pp. 53–69.

Libyan Arab Republic, 1973. "The 1973 Population Census, Preliminary Results." Tripoli: Census Office.

McNeill, William, 1982. "The Care and Repair of the Public Myth." *Foreign Affairs* 61, 1 (Fall).

Magnuson, Douglas, 1991. "Islamic Reform in Contemporary Tunisia." In *Tunisia: The Political Economy of Reform*. I. William Zartman, ed. Boulder: Lynne Rienner Publishers.

Mahroug, Moncef, 1988. "Les Dessous de la chute de Messaâdia." *Réalités* (November 4), pp. 23–24.

Marais, Octave, 1965. "L'Election de la chambre des représentants au Maroc." In *Annuaire de l'Afrique du Nord, 1963*. Paris: CNRS.
Marouf, Nadir, 1981. *Terroirs et villages algériens*. Algiers: OPU.
Marquand, David, 1981. *The Unprincipled Society*. London: Jonathan Cape.
Mattson, James, 1971. "Development in the Arab World." In *A New Look at the Middle East: Proceedings of a Conference at the University of Wisconsin-Milwaukee*, Mark Tessler, ed. Milwaukee: Institute of World Affairs.
Meier, Gerald M., 1976. *Leading Issues in Economic Development*. New York: Oxford University Press.
Mernissi, Fatima, 1982. "Les Femmes dans une société rurale dépendante: les femmes et le quotidien dans le Gharb." *Maghreb-Machrek* 98 (October), pp. 4–45.
Metz, Helen Chapin, 1989. *Libya: A Country Study*. Washington, D.C.: U.S. Government Area Handbook Series.
Mezoughi, Abdelaziz, 1988. "les Enjeux du congrès du salut." *Maghreb*, no. 111, (July 29), pp. 4–8.
Micaud, Charles A., Leon Carl Brown, and Clement Henry Moore, 1964. *Tunisia: The Politics of Modernization*. New York: Praeger.
Miossec, J. M., 1985. "Urban Growth and Urban Policy in Tunisia." *URBAMA*, no. 365.
Moffett, George D., 1989. "North Africa's Disillusioned Youth." *Christian Science Monitor*, May 17.
Moore, Clement Henry, 1965. *Tunisia Since Independence*. Berkeley: University of California Press.
———. 1966. "Political Parties in Independent North Africa." In *State and Society in Independent North Africa*, Leon Carl Brown, ed. Washington, D. C.: Middle East Institute.
———. 1970. *Politics in North Africa*. Boston: Little, Brown.
———. 1986. "Money and Power: The Dilemma of the Egyptian Infitah." *Middle East Journal* 40, p. 637.
———. 1988. "La Tunisie après vingt ans de crise de succession." *Maghreb-Machrek* 120 (April), pp. 5–22.
Moore, Clement Henry, and Arlie A. Hochschild, 1968. "Student Unions in North African Politics." *Daedalus* (Winter), pp. 38–42.
Moroccan Report to UNESCO Conference on Public Education, 1966, 1968. New York: UNESCO, 1968.
Morocco, Government of, 1983. *Résultats des recensemenets de 1960, 1971 et 1982*. Rabat: Direction de la Statistique.
———. 1985. *Social and Economic Panorama*. Rabat: Ministry of Information.
Mutin, G., 1985. "Industrialisation et urbanisation en Algérie." *URBAMA*, no. 365.
Mzali, Mohamed, 1987. *Lettre ouverte à Habib Bourguiba*. Paris: Alain Moreau.
Nedelcovych, Mima, and Monte Palmer, 1980. "The Political Behavior of Moroccan Students: Democratic Indicators in a Quasi-Democratic Environment." Paper presented at the annual meeting of the Midwest Political Science Association.
Al-Nouri, Qais, 1975. "Modern Professionalism in Libya: Attitudes of University Students." *International Social Science Journal* 27, p. 691.

O'Fahey, Rex, 1990. *The Enigmatic Saint: Shaykh Idris al-Fasi*. Chicago: Northwestern University Press.
Panebianco, Angelo, 1988. *Political Parties: Organization and Power.* Cambridge: Cambridge University Press.
Parker, Richard B., 1984. *North Africa: Regional Tensions and Strategic Concerns.* New York: Praeger.
———. 1985. "Appointment in Oujda." *Foreign Affairs* 63, 5 (Summer), pp. 1095–1110.
Pascon, Paul, 1977. *Le Haouz de Marrakech*. Rabat.
———. 1986. *Trente ans de sociologie en Maroc*. Rabat: Bulletin Economique et Social du Maroc.
Pascon, Paul, and Mckki Bentahar, 1972. "Ce que disent 296 jeunes ruraux." In *Etudes sociologiques sur le Maroc*, Abdelkebir Khatibi, ed. Rabat: Bulletin Economique et Social du Maroc.
Pascon, Paul, Mohammed Tozy, A. Arrif, and H. van Wusten, 1984. "Le Grand Muggar d'août de Sidi Ahmed ou Moussa." In *La Maison d'Iligh*. Rabat: SMEA.
Paul, James, 1984. "States of Emergency: The Riots in Tunisia and Morocco." *MERIP Reports* 127 (October), pp. 3–6.
Payne, Rhys, 1986. "Food Deficits and Political Legitimacy: The Case of Morocco." In *Africa's Agrarian Crisis: The Roots of Famine*, Stephen Commins et al., eds. Boulder: Lynne Rienner Publishers.
Pomfret, Richard, 1987. "Morocco's International Economic Relations." In *The Political Economy of Morocco*, I. William Zartman, ed. New York: Praeger.
Popp, Herbert, 1983. *Moderne Bewässerungslandwirtschaft in Marokko: Staatliche und individuelle Entscheidungen in sozialgeographischer Sicht*. Special vol. 15. Erlangen: Erlanger Geographische Arbeiten.
———. 1986. "L'Agriculture irriguée dans la Vallée du Souss (Maroc)—formes et conflits d'utilisation de l'eau." *Méditerranée* 4, pp. 33–47.
"Pour une règle de jeu en méditerranée," 1990. *Jeune Afrique économie* 133 (July).
Qadhafi, Mu^{c}ammar, 1988. *Al-wathiqa al-khadra al-kubra al-huquq al-insan fi ^{c}asr al-jamahir* (The Great Green Charter in the era of the masses). Adopted by the General People's Congress at al-Bayda, Tripoli, June 12.
Qutb, Sayyid, 1964. *Ma^{c}alim fi al-Tariq*. Cairo: Maktabat Wahdah, 1964.
Renier, Y., 1988. "Europe and the Southern Mediterranean," *Courier*, no. 108 (March-April), pp. 53–57.
Roberts, Hugh, 1983. "The Algerian Bureaucracy." In *The Middle East*, R. Asad and R. Owens, eds. New York: Monthly Review Press.
———. 1984. "The Politics of Algerian Socialism." In *North Africa*, R. I. Lawless and A. M. Findlay, eds. London: Croom Helm.
Roemer, Michael, 1989. Statement on John Lewis's "Government and National Economic Development." *Daedalus* (Winter), p. 88.
Romdhani, Oussama, 1989. "The Arab Maghreb Union: Toward North African Integration," *American-Arab Affairs* (Spring), pp. 42–48.
Rosen, Lawrence, 1979. "Social Identity and Points of Attachment: Approaches to Social Organization." In *Meaning and Order in Moroccan Society*, C. Geertz, H. Geertz, and L. Rosen. Cambridge: Cambridge University Press.

———. 1984. *Bargaining for Reality: The Construction of Social Relations in a Muslim Community.* Chicago: University of Chicago Press.
Rousset, Michel, 1979. "Changements institutionnels." In *Développements politiques au Maghreb,* J. Leca et al., eds. Paris: CNRS.
Rudebeck, Lars, 1966. *Party and People: A Study of Political Change in Tunisia.* Stockholm: Almqvist and Wiksell.
Rummel, Lynette, 1989. "Privatization in Algeria: Implications for Development Theory." Ph.D. dissertation, University of California–Los Angeles.
Saaf, Abdallah, 1987. "Etat et classes moyennes au Maroc." In *L'Etat marocain dans la durée,* A. Doumou, ed. Rabat: Codresia, Edino, Publisud.
Sanson, Henri, 1981. "Statut de l'Islam en Algérie." In *Annuaire de l'Afrique du Nord, 1979.* Paris: CNRS.
———. 1983. *Laïcité islamique en Algérie.* Paris: CNRS.
Seddon, David, 1981. *Moroccan Peasants: A Century of Change in the Eastern Rif, 1870–1970.* Folkestone: Dawson.
———. 1987. "Zaio Transformed: Two Decades of Change in Northeast Morocco." In *The Middle Eastern Village: Changing Economic and Social Relations,* Richard Lawless, ed. London: Croom Helm.
Sehimi, Mustapha, 1985. "Les Elections legislatives au Maroc." *Maghreb-Machrek* 107, pp. 23–51.
———. 1986. *La Grande encyclopédie du Maroc: les institutions politiques.* Rabat: GEM.
Sklar, Richard L., 1976. "Postimperialism: A Class Analysis of Multinational Corporate Expansion." *Comparative Politics* 9, 1, pp. 75–92.
Slim, Habib, 1980. "Le Comité permanent consultatif du Maghreb entre le passé, le présent et l'avenir." *Revue tunisienne de droit* 12, pp. 241–252.
Soudan, François, 1988a. "Le Jour où Chadly a voulu démissionner." *Jeune Afrique* 1451 (October 26).
———. 1988b. "Point final ou point de départ en Algérie?" *Jeune Afrique* 1453 (November 9).
———. 1989a. "Algérie-Maroc: peut-on oublier le Sahara?" *Jeune Afrique* 1468 (February 22), pp. 28–30.
———. 1989b. "Grand Maghreb: une étape décisive." *Jeune Afrique* 1467 (February 15), pp. 13–14.
———. 1990. "Tunisie: Islamistes contre 'Albanais.'" *Jeune Afrique* 1519 (February 12), pp. 48–50.
Souriau, Christiane, 1981. "Quelques données comparatives sur les institutions Islamiques actuelles du Maghreb." In *Annuaire du l'Afrique du Nord, 1979.* Paris: CNRS, pp. 341–379.
"A Special Report on Tunisia," 1990. *North African News* 1, 1 (April), pp. 1–8.
Stone, Russell, 1973. "Anticipated Mobility to Elite Status Among Middle Eastern University Students." *International Review of History and Political Science* 5 (June), pp. 260–273.
———. 1982. "Tunisia: A Single Party System Holds Change in Abeyance." In *Political Elites in Arab North Africa,* I. William Zartman, ed. New York: Longman.

Subhan, Malcolm, 1985. *The EEC's Trade Relations with the Developing Countries.* Brussels: EEC.

Suleiman, Michael W., 1985. "Socialization to Politics in Morocco: Sex and Regional Factors." *International Journal of Middle East Studies* 17, pp. 313–327.

_____. 1987. "Attitudes, Values and the Political Process in Morocco." In *The Political Economy of Morocco,* I. William Zartman, ed. New York: Praeger.

Sutton, Keith, 1984. "Algeria's Socialist Villages—A Reassessment." *Journal of Modern African Studies* 22, 2, pp. 223–248.

Sutton, Michael, 1989. "Economic Aspects of Morocco's Relations with Europe." In *Morocco and Europe,* George Joffe, ed. London: Centre of Near and Middle Eastern Studies.

Suvolin, Claude, 1989. *L'agriculture moderne.* Paris: Edition du Seuil.

Swearingen, Will, 1985. "In Pursuit of the Granary of Rome: France's Wheat Policy in Morocco, 1915–1931." *International Journal of Middle East Studies* 17, 3, pp. 347–363.

_____. 1987. *Moroccan Mirages: Agrarian Dreams and Deceptions, 1912–1986.* Princeton: Princeton University Press.

Taylor, Alan, 1982. *The Arab Balance of Power.* Syracuse: Syracuse University Press.

Taylor, Robert, 1980. *Implications for the Southern Mediterranean Countries of the Second Enlargement of the European Community.* Brussels: European Economic Community.

Tessler, Mark, 1980. "Political Change and the Islamic Revival in Tunisia." *Maghreb Review* 5, pp. 8–19.

_____. 1982. "Morocco: Institutional Pluralism and Monarchical Dominance." In *Political Elites in Arab North Africa.* New York: Longman.

_____. 1986. "Explaining the 'Surprises' of King Hassan II: The Linkage Between Domestic and Foreign Policy in Morocco; Part I: Tension in North Africa in the Mid-1980's." *USFI Field Staff Reports,* Africa/Middle East, no. 39.

_____. 1988. "Libya in the Maghreb: The Union with Morocco and Related Developments." In *The Green and the Black: Qadhafi's Policies in Africa,* Rene Lemarchand, ed. Bloomington: Indiana University Press.

_____. 1991. "Anger and Governance in the Arab World: Lessons from the Maghrib and Implications for the West." *Jerusalem Journal of International Relations* 13 (Fall), pp. 7–33.

Tessler, Mark, and Patricia Freeman, 1981. "Regime Orientation and Participant Citizenship in Developing Countries: Hypotheses and a Test with Longitudinal Data from Tunisia." *Western Political Quarterly* 34, pp. 479–498.

Tessler, Mark, and Linda Hawkins, 1979. "Acculturation, Socioeconomic Status and Attitude Change in Tunisia: Implications for Modernization Theory." *Journal of Modern African Studies* 17, pp. 473–495.

Tessler, Mark, and Mary Keppel, 1976. "Political Generations." In *Change in Tunisia: Studies in the Social Sciences,* Russell A. Stone and John Simmons, eds. Albany: State University of New York Press.

Tessler, Mark, William O'Barr, and David Spain, 1973. *Tradition and Identity in Changing Africa.* New York: Harper and Row.

Toumi, Moshen, 1975. "La Scolarisation et le tissu social en Tunisie." *Revue française d'études politiques africaines* 10, 109, pp. 32–61.

Tozy, Mohammed, 1981. "Monopolisation de la production symbolique." In *Annuaire de l'Afrique du Nord, 1979.* Paris: CNRS.

———. 1984. "Champs et contre-champs politico-réligieux au Maroc." Dissertation, University of Aix-en-Provence.

———. 1987. "Du régicide à la munadhara." *Bulletin du CERI,* no. 3.

———. 1988a. "Quelques lieux de competition politique." *Bulletin économique et social du Maroc* 159–161, pp. 155–182.

———. 1988b. "Quelques modes d'acces à la maîtrise réligieuse en Islam marocain." In *Colloquium on New Intellectual Groups in the Modern Muslim World.* Paris: CERI.

Troin, J. F., 1979. "Les 'Agglomérations routières' du Maroc. Vers un nouveau mode de fixation des activités." *Méditerranée* 1–2, pp. 127–135.

———. 1985. "Le Maghreb—hommes et espaces." Paris: Armand Colin.

Troin, J. F., ed., 1982. *L'explosion urbaine au Maghreb. Maghreb-Machrek* 96.

Tunisia, Government of, 1972. *Tunisian Development: 1962–1971.* Tunis: Ministry of Cultural Affairs and Information.

———. 1981. *Structures des exploitations agricoles.* Tunis: Ministry of Agriculture.

———. 1988. *Employment Survey, 1986–1987.* Tunis: National Statistical Institute.

United Nations Development Programme, 1990. *Human Development Report, 1990.* New York: Oxford University Press.

U.S. Department of State, 1983. *The Libyan Problem,* Special Report no. 111. Washington, D.C.: Department of State, Bureau of Public Affairs.

———. 1986. *Libyan Activities in the Western Hemisphere.* Washington, D.C.: Department of State, Bureau of Public Affairs.

———. 1989. *Libya's Qadhafi Continues Support for Terrorisms.* Washington, D.C.: Office of the Secretary of State, Ambassador at Large for Counter-Terrorism.

———. 1992. *Country Reports on Human Rights Practices for 1991.* Washington, D.C.: Government Printing Office.

Valmont, André, 1988. "Le grand Maghreb: une communauté économique en devenir." *Les Cahiers de l'Orient,* 3d trimester, no. 11, pp. 190–191.

Vandewalle, Dirk, 1988a. "Autopsy of a Revolt: The October Riots in Algeria." Hanover, N.H.: Institute of Current World Affairs.

———. 1988b. "From the New State to the New Era: Toward a Second Republic in Tunisia." *Middle East Journal* 42, pp. 602–620.

———. 1989. "The Prospects for Algeria." *UFSI Field Staff Reports,* Africa/Middle East, no. 17.

———. 1990a. "The Libyan Revolution After Twenty Years; Part I—Evaluating the Jamahiriyah." *UFSI Field Staff Reports,* Africa/Middle East, no. 2.

———. 1990b. "Qadhafi's Unfinished Revolution." *Mediterranean Quarterly* (Winter), pp. 67–81.

Vedel, Georges, et al., 1986. *Edification d'un état moderne.* Paris: Albin Michel.

Waltz, Susan, 1986. "The Islamist Appeal in Tunisia." *Middle East Journal* 40 (Autumn), pp. 651–671.

Ware, Louis B., 1985. "The Role of the Tunisian Military in the Post-Bourguiba Era." *Middle East Journal* 39, 1, pp. 27–47.

———. 1989. "Toward a Euro-American Policy for the Arab Maghreb." *American-Arab Affairs* (Spring), pp. 49–59.

Waterbury, John, 1970. *The Commander of the Faithful: The Moroccan Political Elite—A Study of Segmented Politics.* New York: Columbia University Press.

Wayne, E. A., 1987. Report in the *Christian Science Monitor,* June 26, p. 7.

World Bank, 1982. *World Development Report.* Washington, D.C.: IBRD.

———. 1987. *World Development Report.* Washington, D.C.: IBRD.

———. 1988. *World Debt Tables.* Washington, D.C.: IBRD.

———. 1990a. *World Debt Tables.* Washington, D.C.: IBRD.

———. 1990b. *World Development Report.* Washington, D.C.: IBRD.

———. 1991. *World Development Report.* Washington, D.C.: IBRD.

———. 1992. *World Development Report.* Washington, D.C.: IBRD.

Yacine, Abdessalam, 1973. *Al-Islam aw al-tofan.* Rabat.

———. 1980. Press conference, June 27, reprinted in *Jamaʿa* 7, pp. 30–56.

Zaim, F., and Zakar, A., 1982. "Politiques régionales et locales du Maroc." Doctoral dissertation, Université des Sciences Sociales de Grenoble.

Zamiti, Khalil, 1977. "Exploitation du travail paysan en situation de dépendance et mutation d'un parti de masses en parti de cadres." *Les Temps modernes* 375 *bis* (October), pp. 312–333.

———. 1982. "Dialectique de la dissolution et du maintien des formes communautaires en Tunisie." *Peuples méditerranéens* 18, pp. 195–217.

———. 1985. "La Division du travail étatique: sociologie d'un barrage." *Revue tunisienne des sciences sociales* 82–83, pp. 139–191.

Zartman, I. William, 1962. "The King in Moroccan Constitutional Law." *Muslim World,* 59, 2, pp. 129–136, and 3, pp. 183–188.

———. 1971. *The Politics of Trade Negotiations Between Africa and the EEC.* Princeton: Princeton University Press.

———. 1984. "L'Elite Algérienne." *Maghreb-Machrek* 106 (October), pp. 37–53.

———. 1987a. "Foreign Relations of North Africa." *Annals, AAPSS,* no. 489 (January), pp. 13–27.

———. 1987b. "The Military in the Politics of Succession: Algeria." In *The Military in African Politics,* John W. Harbeson, ed. New York: Praeger.

———. 1988a. "The Opposition as a Support of the State." In *Beyond Coercion: The Durability of the Arab State,* A. Dawisha and I. William Zartman, eds. London: Croom Helm.

———. 1988b. "Political Succession as a Conceptual Event: The Algerian and Tunisian Cases." Paper presented at the Fourteenth World Congress of the International Political Science Association, Washington, D.C.

Zartman, I. William, ed., 1982. *Political Elites in North Africa.* New York: Longman.

———. 1991. *Tunisia: The Political Economy of Reform.* Boulder: Lynne Rienner.

Zartman, I. William, and Antonella Bassani, 1987. *The Algerian Gas Negotiations.* Washington, D.C.: Foreign Policy Institute.

Zghal, Abdelkader, 1967. *Modernisation de l'agriculture et populations semi-nomades.* The Hague: Mouton.

———. 1985. "Why Maghrebi Peasants Don't Like Land Reform." In *Arab Society: Social Science Perspectives,* Nicholas S. Hopkins and Saad Eddin Ibrahim, eds. Cairo: American University in Cairo Press.

Zghidi, Mohammed, 1978. "Monographie de Hababsa (Gouvernorat de Siliana)." Draft report. Tunis: Centre Nationale des Etudes Agricoles, Ministère du Plan.

Zussman, Mira, 1986. "Pendulum Swings in Land Laws and Rural Development Policies in Tunisia: History and Consequences." In *Social Legislation in the Contemporary Middle East,* L. Michalak and J. Salacuse, eds. Berkeley: Institute of International Studies.

About the Book

In the twenty-five years since the last comprehensive book on state and society in North Africa was published, the nations of the Maghrib have undergone profound social, political, and economic changes. The region has, for example, experienced one of the highest population growth rates in the world, accompanied by a dramatic increase in migration to urban areas, resulting in high unemployment and disaffection among youth. Economic challenges—how to compete in a rapidly changing international trade market and how to cope with the demands of the populace for educational opportunities and a higher standard of living—have put a noticeable strain on development efforts. Political turmoil has also come to the region. The long reign of Habib Bourguiba in Tunisia ended suddenly with a "constitutional coup" in 1987, and Tunisia has wrestled since then with the challenges of creating a true multiparty democracy. Algeria's one-party socialist regime was forced to reassess its economic policies and address demands for greater political participation. The resulting rise in power of the Islamic fundamentalist movement has left Algeria in a state of profound political distress. Even Libya's mercurial Mu'ammar Qadhafi has confronted muted political opposition as a result of failed foreign policy and the impact of depressed oil prices. In this book, the foremost U.S. specialists on the region and a number of prominent Maghribi scholars analyze the transformations in North Africa since independence and examine current trends that will shape the region in the future.

About the Editors and Contributors

Hamid Ait Amara is professor of economics at the University of Algiers.

John Damis is professor of political science at Portland State University.

Mary-Jane Deeb is director of the Omani Program at American University.

William Mark Habeeb, formerly director of programs and research at the Middle East Institute, is an international economic and political consultant based in Washington, D.C.

Elbaki Hermassi is professor of politics and law at the University of Tunis and Tunisian ambassador to UNESCO.

Nicholas S. Hopkins is professor of anthropology at the American University in Cairo.

Michel Le Gall is assistant professor of history at St. Olaf College.

Clement Henry Moore is professor of government at the University of Texas in Austin.

Mark Tessler is professor of political science at the University of Wisconsin-Milwaukee.

Mohammed Tozy is professor at the University Hassan II in Casablanca.

Rhys Payne is a Fulbright professor at the University of Tunis.

Dirk Vandewalle is assistant professor of political science at Dartmouth College.

I. William Zartman is director of African studies at The Johns Hopkins University School of Advanced International Studies.

Index

Agricultural sector, 27–28
  agrarian reform of, 129–133, 177–181
  cooperative farming in, 130–133, 169, 177–179
  employment and, 123, 125–126, 134, 137–138, 171, 175, 183–184
  farm size and ownership in, 65, 123, 126–129, 133
  irrigation and, 126, 131–132, 133–136, 169, 172–173, 174–176
  prices and, 135–136, 152
  production in, 134–136, 142–143, 151, 156, 170, 172, 242
Alawi dynasty, 8, 12, 16, 17, 36
Algeria
  colonialism in, 8–10, 12–13
  early history of, 4–7
  economic policies in, 25, 30–31, 63. *See also* Economic development
  economic reforms in, 24, 34, 65–66, 156–162
  education in, 78, 84. *See also* Education
  foreign affairs of. *See* Arab Maghribi Union; European Community; Soviet Union; United States
  independence movement in, 12–14, 17, 190
  Islam and the state in, 104, 108–109, 119–120. *See also* Islam
  Islamicist movement in, 112, 114–115
  political reforms in, 20, 32, 34–35, 63, 67, 155–162
  state building in, 21–22, 23, 26–27, 30–33, 36–41, 243–246
  See also Agricultural sector; Ben Bella, Ahmed; Benjedid, Chadli; Boumedienne, Houari; Elections, in Algeria; Political parties, in Algeria; Riots, in Algeria
ALN. *See* Armée de Liberation Nationale
Arab League, 200–201, 223, 224, 230
Arab Maghribi Union, 189, 194–195, 197–199, 199–203, 239
  Common Market of, 195–197, 217–218
  history leading up to, 189–193
Armée de Liberation Nationale (ALN), 30–31
Arms sales, 199, 225–228, 230–231, 232, 234
Austerity measures, 20, 24, 31, 141, 145, 151–152, 154, 157, 162, 164–165

Ben Ali, Abidine, 20, 23, 32–33, 36–37, 51–52, 60–61, 116, 120–121, 143–147, 197, 201, 217, 233–234
Ben Bella, Ahmed, 14, 17, 37, 104, 114
Benjedid, Chadli, 17, 25, 30–33, 61–63, 65, 115, 131, 156–162, 203, 229–231
Berbers, 4–5, 15
Boumedienne, Houari, 14, 17, 20, 23, 30, 40, 61, 108, 157
Bourguiba, Habib, 14, 17, 20, 21, 22, 30–31, 34, 36, 37, 41, 50, 52, 77, 104–105, 110, 115–116, 143–146, 232–234

Christians: history of rule in the Maghrib by, 3, 4, 5, 6
Class, 169, 181–184
  social mobility, 83–84, 87–91
  social stratification, 26, 38
  See also Elites
Clientelism. *See* Patronage

Colonialism, 3, 8–18
Communist Parti du Progrès et du
  Socialisme (PPS), 45–46
Coups and coup attempts
  in Algeria, 33, 39
  in Libya, 164
  in Morocco, 29
  in Tunisia, 51–52

Destourian Socialist Party (PSD), 14, 21, 30, 51–54, 59, 77, 121, 246
Dirigisme, 20, 22, 26, 27–28, 34

Economic development, 22, 24–25, 27–29, 166–167, 169, 207–208, 214, 232, 257(table). *See also* Austerity measures; Foreign investment; Privatization; Structural adjustment programs
Education, 10, 38, 75–79
  access to, 82, 89, 242–243
  employment and, 81–90
  primary and secondary, 76, 78–79, 81–82, 84–86, 88–89
  university, 76–77, 84, 87–90, 98–99
Egypt
  and Arab unity, 191–193, 198–199
  colonialism in, 12
  early history of, 5, 10
Elections, 32–33, 37, 245
  in Algeria, 56(table), 61–62, 64–65, 100–101, 115, 231
  effect of urbanization on, 53, 55, 57, 58(table), 59–60
  in Libya, 173–174
  in Morocco, 44, 45(table), 46–48, 56(table), 182
  in Tunisia, 51–55, 56(table), 57, 58(table), 59, 116
  voter turnout for, 46, 55, 56(table), 57, 58(table), 59, 62
Elites, 10, 12, 13, 26, 27, 40–41, 47, 50, 65, 71–73, 88–90, 92, 102, 141–142, 149–150, 156–158, 161, 166–167, 178
Emigration. *See* Migration
European Community, 49, 193, 194, 196, 200, 204, 207–208, 211–220, 248
  Maghribi agreements with the, 208–211, 218
  See also Trade, with the European Community

FIS. *See* Front Islamique du Salut
FLN. *See* Front de Libération Nationale
Foreign investment, 200
  in Algeria, 20, 65–66
  in Morocco, 26, 35, 154, 227
  in Tunisia, 233
France, 26, 191
  in Algeria, 8–10, 12–14, 31
  in Libya, 10, 16
  in Morocco, 12–13, 15–16
  in Tunisia, 9–10, 12–15
  See also European Community
Front de Libération Nationale (FLN), 14, 17, 21, 22, 30–33, 37, 38–39, 42, 61–67, 104, 109, 115, 157, 160–162, 190–191, 246
Front Islamique du Salut (FIS), 32–33, 64–66, 98, 100–101, 115

Great Britain, 11, 12, 16, 26. *See also* European Community
Great Green Charter of Human Rights, 20, 32

Hassan II (king), 17, 21, 23, 26, 33, 44, 47–49, 106, 149–150, 152–154, 194, 197, 202, 224–228, 246
Human rights, 239
  abuses of, 155
  recognition of, 20, 32, 51, 155, 160, 165

IMF. *See* International Monetary Fund
Inheritance laws. *See* Agricultural sector, farm size and ownership in
International Bank for Reconstruction and Development. *See* World Bank
International Monetary Fund (IMF), 24, 49, 141, 144–148, 151–154
Iran-Iraq war, 193
Islam
  in Maghrib during colonial period, 11, 18
  in Maghrib during early history, 3, 4–7

as official state religion, 102–110
political parties and, 33, 37–38, 41, 46, 49, 52, 55, 60–61, 63–65, 100–101, 115, 146–147. *See also* Front Islamic du Salut; Istiqlal party; Mouvement de la Tendance Islamique; Nahda party
Salafiya branch of, 12–13, 15, 16, 103, 104, 107, 110–112, 115
Sufi branch of, 5–7, 8, 9, 12, 13, 15, 122
See also Islamicist movement; Youth, Islamic movements by
Islamicist movement, 111–122, 203, 243, 246–248. *See also* Youth, Islamic movements by
Istiqlal party, 44–49, 103–104, 107, 118, 190
Italy, 6, 8, 9, 12–13, 16. *See also* European Community

Jihads, 5, 6, 9, 16

Libya
colonialism in, 8–11, 12–13
early history of, 6–7
economic policies in, 25–26. *See also* Economic development
economic reforms in, 20, 24, 163–166
education in, 79, 84–86, 89, 98–99. *See also* Education
foreign affairs of. *See* Arab Maghribi Union; European Community; Soviet Union; United States
independence movement in, 16, 18
Islam and the state in, 105, 110–111, 122. *See also* Islam
Islamicist movement in, 116–117
and oil, 26, 73, 84–85, 162–164
political reforms in, 20, 32, 163–166, 174
state building in, 21–23, 26, 32, 36–41, 243–246
See also Agricultural sector; Elections, in Libya; Political parties, in Libya; Qadhafi, Mu'ammar; Riots, in Libya
Literacy, 76, 78, 81–83

Mauritania, 190, 198, 200–201, 202, 246

MDS. *See* Mouvement des Démocrates Socialistes
Migration, 171–172, 176, 196, 200, 213, 217, 248. *See also* Remittances
Morocco
colonialism in, 8, 11, 12–13
early history of, 6–8
economic policies in, 26. *See also* Economic development
economic reforms in, 21, 24, 49, 66, 148–155
education in, 78, 81–82, 103. *See also* Education
foreign affairs of. *See* Arab Maghribi Union; European Community; Soviet Union; United States
independence movement in, 15–16, 17–18
Islam and the state in, 103–104, 106–108, 117–119. *See also* Islam
Islamicist movement in, 112–113
political reforms in, 21, 149–155
state building in, 21–23, 29, 32–33, 36–40, 43–44, 48–49, 107, 243–246
See also Agricultural sector; Elections, in Morocco; Hassan II; Political parties, in Morocco; Riots, in Morocco; Western Sahara
Mouvement de la Tendance Islamique (MTI), 33, 52, 115–116, 120–121
Mouvement des Démocrates Socialistes (MDS), 30, 51–52
Mouvement d'Unité Populaire (MUP), 30, 51
Mouvement Populaire, Démocratique, et Constitutionnel (MPDC), 45–46
MPDC. *See* Mouvement Populaire, Démocratique, et Constitutionnel
MTI. *See* Mouvement de la Tendance Islamique
MUP. *See* Mouvement d'Unité Populaire
Muslim Brotherhood, 99, 116–117, 120, 246

Nahda party, 52, 60, 96, 100, 120–121, 146–147
National Pact of 1988, 32–33

Neo-Destour party, 14–15, 30–31, 42, 190

OADP. *See* Organisation d'Action Démocratique et Populaire
Oil, 17, 18
  and development, 83–85
  effect on political system, 23, 26, 63, 73, 156, 158, 162–164, 216, 222
OPEC. *See* Organization of Petroleum Exporting Countries
Organisation d'Action Démocratique et Populaire (OADP), 45–47
Organization of Petroleum Exporting Countries (OPEC), 164, 222
Ottoman Empire, 3, 6–8, 10–12

Patronage, 93, 97
  family connections and, 86–87, 92
  political, 21, 28, 35, 43–44, 66: in Algeria, 31, 62–65; in Libya, 23; in Morocco, 44, 48–49, 149, 244; in Tunisia, 50, 60
Persian Gulf war, 101, 199–201, 222, 224, 248
Political parties, 42–43, 66–67, 245–246, 253–254(table)
  in Algeria, 30–33, 36, 37, 38–39, 61–66, 104, 109, 115
  in Libya, 31–32
  in Morocco, 33, 44, 45(table), 46–49, 106, 118, 182
  in Tunisia, 30–33, 36, 38–39, 50–55, 56(table), 57, 58(table), 59–61, 115–116, 120–122, 146–147
  See also Islam, political parties and
Popular Movement, 44–46
Population growth, 28, 74–75, 124–125, 213–214, 242–243, 257(table)
Portugal, 6–7. *See also* European Community
PPS. *See* Communist Parti du Progrès et du Socialisme
Private sector, 24–25, 27, 48, 60, 65, 196
Privatization, 20, 49, 65, 148, 152, 154, 158, 244
PSD. *See* Destourian Socialist Party

Qadhafi, Muᶜammar, 18, 23, 24, 26, 31–32, 36–37, 38, 73, 79, 89, 98–99, 111, 116, 122, 163–166, 173, 184, 198, 201, 234–239, 243, 244, 247

Rassemblement Constitutionnel Démocratique (RCD), 31–33, 36, 38–39, 42, 52–55, 57, 58(table), 59–61, 66, 245
Rassemblement National des Indépendants (RNI), 47–48
RCD. *See* Rassemblement Constitutionnel Démocratique
Remittances, 164, 233, 248
Riots, 41, 142, 246
  in Algeria, 30–32, 34, 39, 42, 61, 63, 66, 73–74, 97, 100, 114, 157–159, 161, 197, 231
  in Libya, 73
  in Morocco, 16, 35, 46, 71–73, 82, 93–94, 117, 136, 149, 152, 155
  in Tunisia, 72, 92, 105, 110, 136, 232
RNI. *See* Rassemblement National des Indépendants
Rural society. *See* Agricultural sector; Migration; Tribes

Socialist Union of Popular Forces (USFP), 44–49, 106
Soviet Union, 199, 206(table), 215–216, 236, 240
  and Algeria, 229–230
  and Morocco, 224, 227
Spain, 5–7, 11–12, 15. *See also* European Community
Structural adjustment programs, 139–143, 167
  in Algeria, 157–162
  in Libya, 164–166
  in Morocco, 148–155
  in Tunisia, 143–148

Trade, 206(table)
  diversification, 215
  intra-Maghribi, 195–197, 201–202, 205–206, 217–218, 245
  prior to independence, 5–7, 11

with the European Community, 193, 196, 202, 204, 205(table), 206–212, 216, 248
with the Soviet Union and Eastern Europe, 206(table), 215
with the United States, 227–228, 229–231, 235, 237
See also Arms sales
Tribes, 4, 15, 168, 170, 172–174, 177–179, 181, 185
Tunisia
   colonialism in, 8–10, 12
   early history of, 4–7, 9–10
   economic policies in, 25. *See also* Economic development
   economic reforms in, 66, 143–148
   education in, 75–78, 82–83. *See also* Education
   foreign affairs of. *See* Arab Maghribi Union; European Community; Soviet Union; United States
   independence movement in, 13, 14–15, 17
   Islam and the state in, 104–105, 109–110, 120–122. *See also* Islam
   Islamicist movement in, 112, 115–116
   political reforms in, 20–21, 24, 32–34, 34–35, 52, 144–148
   state building in, 21–23, 26–27, 29–32, 36–41, 50–51, 77, 243–246
   See also Agricultural sector; Ben Ali, Abidine; Bourguiba, Habib; Elections, in Tunisia; Political parties, in Tunisia; Riots, in Tunisia

UC. *See* Union Constitutionnelle
UGTT. *See* Union Générale Tunisienne du Travail

Unemployment, 81–83, 85–86, 97, 171, 181–182, 200, 202, 214, 242. *See also* Agricultural sector, employment and; Youth, employment for
Union Constitutionnelle (UC), 47–49
Union Générale Tunisienne du Travail (UGTT), 50, 66, 179
Unions, 21, 50, 77, 179
United Nations, 23, 203, 228
United States, 221–223, 238–240
   and Algeria, 228–231
   and Libya, 26, 234–238
   and Morocco, 153, 223–225, 226(table), 227–228
   and Tunisia, 231–234
Urbanization, 28, 137, 257(table). *See also* Elections, effect of urbanization on
USFP. *See* Socialist Union of Popular Forces

Western Sahara, 38, 119, 151, 190, 197, 202, 225, 228, 239, 246
Women, 89, 125–126, 171–172, 175–176, 180–181, 184–185
World Bank, 24, 49, 141, 144–148, 151, 153–154, 158–162

Yacine, Abdessalem, 113–114
Young Tunisians, 10, 14
Youth, 71
   alienation of, 86, 90–101
   demonstrations by, 38, 71–74, 88, 93, 97–99, 116, 144, 159, 161, 223
   employment for, 81–83, 86–90. *See also* Unemployment
   following independence, 74–75, 80–81, 83, 92–93
   Islamic movements by, 96–98, 100, 113, 120
   See also Education